International Library of Psychology
Philosophy and Scientific Method

Human Speech

International Library of Psychology Philosophy and Scientific Method

GENERAL EDITOR—C. K. OGDEN, M.A. (*Magdalene College, Cambridge*)

ANALYSIS OF PERCEPTION	J. R. SMYTHIES
ARISTOTLE'S THEORY OF CONTRARIETY	J. P. ANTON
BENTHAM'S THEORY OF FICTIONS	C. K. OGDEN
BERTRAND RUSSELL'S CONSTRUCTION OF EXTERNAL WORLD	C. A. FRITZ
CHARACTER AND THE UNCONSCIOUS	J. H. VAN DER HOOP
THE CHILD'S CONCEPTION OF GEOMETRY	JEAN PIAGET
THE CHILD'S CONCEPTION OF NUMBER	JEAN PIAGET
THE CHILD'S CONCEPTION OF SPACE	JEAN PIAGET
THE CHILD'S CONCEPTION OF THE WORLD	JEAN PIAGET
CRIME AND CUSTOM IN SAVAGE SOCIETY	B. MALINOWSKI
ETHICS AND THE HISTORY OF PHILOSOPHY	C. D. BROAD
FIVE TYPES OF ETHICAL THEORY	C. D. BROAD
THE FOUNDATIONS OF GEOMETRY	JEAN NICOD
THE FOUNDATIONS OF MATHEMATICS	F. P. RAMSEY
GESTALT THEORY	BRUND PETERMANN
THE GROWTH OF THE MIND	K. KOFFKA
A HISTORICAL INTRODUCTION TO MODERN PSYCHOLOGY	G. MURPHY
THE HISTORY OF MATERIALISM	F. A. LANGE
IDEOLOGY AND UTOPIA	KARL MANNHEIM
THE PRACTICE AND THEORY OF INDIVIDUAL PSYCHOLOGY	A. ADLER
JUDGMENT AND REASONING IN THE CHILD	JEAN PIAGET
THE LANGUAGE AND THOUGHT OF THE CHILD	JEAN PIAGET
THE LIMITS OF SCIENCE	LEON CHWISTEK
LOGICAL STUDIES	GEORGE HENRIK VON WRIGHT
LOGICAL SYNTAX OF LANGUAGE	R. CARNAP
THE MEANING OF MEANING	C. K. OGDEN AND I. A. RICHARDS
MENTAL DEVELOPMENT OF THE CHILD	KARL BUHLER
THE MENTALITY OF APES	W. KÖHLER
METAPHYSICAL FOUNDATIONS OF MODERN SCIENCE	E. A. BURTT
METHODS AND CRITERIA OF REASONING	R. CRAWSHAY-WILLIAMS
THE MIND AND ITS PLACE IN NATURE	C. D. BROAD
MORAL JUDGMENT OF THE CHILD	JEAN PIAGET
THE NATURE OF LAUGHTER	J. C. GREGORY
THE NATURE OF MATHEMATICS	MAX BLACK
ORIGIN OF INTELLIGENCE IN THE CHILD	JEAN PIAGET
OUTLINES OF THE HISTORY OF GREEK PHILOSOPHY	E. ZELLER
PHILOSOPHICAL STUDIES	G. E. MOORE
PHILOSOPHY OF "AS IF"	H. VAIHINGER
PHILOSOPHY OF PEIRCE	J. BUCKLER
PHILOSOPHY OF PLATO	R. C. LODGE
PHILOSOPHY OF THE UNCONSCIOUS	E. VON HARTMANN
PLATO AND PARMENIDES	F. M. CORNFORD
PLATO'S COSMOLOGY	F. M. CORNFORD
PLATO'S PHAEDO	R. S. BLUCK
PLATO'S THEORY OF ART	R. C. LODGE
PLATO'S THEORY OF KNOWLEDGE	F. M. CORNFORD
THE PRINCIPLES OF GESTALT PSYCHOLOGY	K. KOFFKA
THE PRINCIPLES OF LITERARY CRITICISM	I. A. RICHARDS
PSYCHE	E. RHODE
PSYCHOLOGICAL TYPES	C. G. JUNG
THE PSYCHOLOGY OF ANIMALS	F. ALVERDES
THE PSYCHOLOGY OF CHARACTER	A. A. ROBACK
THE PSYCHOLOGY OF CHILDREN'S DRAWINGS	HELGA ENG
THE PSYCHOLOGY OF CONSCIOUSNESS	C. DALY KING
THE PSYCHOLOGY OF INTELLIGENCE	JEAN PIAGET
REASONS AND FAITHS	NINIAN SMART
RELIGION PHILOSOPHY AND PSYCHICAL RESEARCH	C. D. BROAD
SCIENTIFIC THOUGHT	C. D. BROAD
SENSE-PERCEPTION AND MATTER	M. E. LEAN
SEX AND REPRESSION IN SAVAGE SOCIETY	B. MALINOWSKI
SPECULATIONS	T. E. HULME
SPIRIT OF LANGUAGE	K. VOSSLER
THE STRUCTURE OF METAPHYSICS	M. LAZEROWITZ
THEORETICAL BIOLOGY	J. VON UEXKÜLL
THOUGHT AND THE BRAIN	HENRI PIERON
TRACTATUS LOGICO-PHILOSOPHICUS	LUDWIG WITTGENSTEIN

Human Speech

Some Observations, Experiments, and Conclusions as to the Nature, Origin, Purpose and Possible Improvement of Human Speech

By

SIR RICHARD PAGET, Bart.

Late Fellow of the Physical Society of London.
Fellow of the Institute of Physics.

LONDON
ROUTLEDGE & KEGAN PAUL LTD

First Published 1930
Reprinted 1963
by Routledge & Kegan Paul Ltd
Broadway House, 68-74 Carter Lane
London, E.C.4
Printed in Great Britain
by Lowe & Brydone (Printers) Ltd
London

CONTENTS

		PAGE
PREFACE	. . . .	xiii

CHAP.
I.	INTRODUCTION	1
II.	PRELIMINARY OBSERVATIONS AS TO THE VOCAL ORGANS, AND THEIR FUNCTIONS IN SPEECH .	29
III.	OBSERVATIONS ON THE VOWEL RESONANCES . .	40
IV.	EXPERIMENTS WITH MODELS (VOWELS) . . .	53
V.	VOWEL SOUNDS—CONCLUDED—SINGLE OR DOUBLE RESONANCE?	77
VI.	OBSERVATIONS AND EXPERIMENTS ON THE CONSONANTS	99
VII.	THE ORIGIN AND DEVELOPMENT OF SPEECH . .	126
VIII.	VOWEL AND CONSONANT SYMBOLISM . . .	154
IX.	THE DEVELOPMENT OF DIFFERENT LANGUAGES .	176
X.	VOICE PRODUCTION	197
XI.	MOUTH RESONANCE IN RELATION TO LARYNGEAL PITCH	213
XII.	ARTIFICIAL SPEECH AND SONG	230
XIII.	THE ADVANCEMENT OF LANGUAGE AND ITS NOTATION	249

APPENDIX.
I.	A NOTE ON THE DOUBLE-RESONATOR THEORY OF VOWEL-SOUNDS. By W. E. Benton . .	275
II.	TABLE OF FREQUENCIES, i.e. NUMBER OF COMPLETE VIBRATIONS PER SECOND, CORRESPONDING TO THE EQUAL TEMPERAMENT SCALE	299
III.	AUDIOGRAM OF THE AUTHOR'S HEARING . .	300
IV.	RESONANCES OF VOWEL MODEL	302
V.	SOME EXPERIMENTS WITH TUBULAR VOWEL MODELS	303
VI.	CONSONANT RESONANCES	310
VII.	AMERICAN AND ENGLISH VOWELS	315
VIII.	POLYNESIAN LANGUAGE. By Dr. J. Rae . .	318

LIST OF ILLUSTRATIONS

FIG.		PAGE
1.	Middle C	2
2.	Bass G	4
3.	Soprano c'''	4
4.	Ocarina	7
5.	Ocarina, transverse section	7
6.	Kratzenstein's vowel-sounding pipes	12
7.	de Kempelen's talking pipe	13
8.	de Kempelen's first model	13
9.	Willis's adjustable vowel-sounding model	16
10.	Table. Willis's experimental results	17
11.	Wheatstone's talking machine	18
12.	Potter's vowel-sounding model	21
13.	Table. Lloyd's vowel resonances	23
14.	Table. Pitch-relation of resonances and phonation	25
15.	Aikin's Resonator Scale	26
16.	D. C. Miller's vowel-sounding pipes *between pages* 34 *and* 35	
17.	Lungs, windpipe, and larynx	29
18.	Vocal chords as in breathing . *between pp.* 34 *and* 35	
19.	Vocal cords phonating (closed) . *between pp.* 34 *and* 35	
20.	Vocal cords phonating (open) . *between pages* 34 *and* 35	
21.	Vocal organs and cavities	35
22.	Table. Range of voiced and unvoiced vowels	38
23.	Head note $\sharp g''$	41
24.	Chart. Author's English vowel resonances	42
25.	Resonance ranges	43
26.	Musical transcription of whispered sentence	46
27.	Table. Variation of upper resonance of **a** (calm) with laryngeal pitch	49
28.	Table. Variation of upper resonance of **ou** with laryngeal pitch	50
29.	Table. Harmonies of C	51
30.	Table. Vowel change by adding artificial " capacity "	52
31.	Original **ɞ** (earth) vowel-sounding model (without larynx)	53
32.	Squeaker made with a blade of grass	54
33.	Rubber strip artificial larynx	55

LIST OF ILLUSTRATIONS

FIG.		PAGE
34.	Vowel sounding model (ɐ) with larynx	56
35.	Diagram. Tuning by longitudinal tongue movement	57
36.	ɑ (calm) model	58
37.	Additional capacity	58
38.	u (who) made by adding capacity to ɐ model	58
39.	Egg-shaped resonator	59
40.	u model	59
41.	i (eat) model	60
42.	i (eat) model improved	60
43.	ei (baby) model	61
44.	Plasticine models on Lord Rayleigh's organ *between pp.* 34 *and* 35	
45.	ʌ (up) model	62
46.	ou (no) model	62
47.	ou (no) model (reversed)	62
48.	ɐ (earth) model	62
49.	ɑ (calm) model	62
50.	Table. Resonances of a cylinder	64
51.	Adjustable cylindrical resonator	65
52.	Cylindrical resonator with partial closure at one end	65
53.	Resonators in parallel—i (eat)	67
54.	Resonators in parallel—ʌ (up)	67
55.	Resonators in parallel—ɔ (all)	68
56.	Adjustable vowel model	70
57.	Adjustable vowel model, improved	70
58.	Spacing of tongue positions (front resonator)	72
59.	Spacing of tongue positions (back resonator)	72
60.	Organ reed and boot	73
61.	J. Q. Stewart's electrical Vowel-Sounding Circuit	74
62.	Dr. Eccles's electrical Vowel-Sounding Circuit	75
63.	Single resonator for D. C. Miller's resonance for ɔ (all)	77
64.	ɪ (it) model with removable bell mouth	81
65.	Chart. Author's English Vowel Resonances (revised)	86
65a.	Chart. Miss Somerville's English Vowel Resonances	87
66.	Chart. Crandal and Sacia's American Vowel Resonances	89
67.	Chart. Mdlle. Coustenoble's French Vowel Resonances	91
67a.	Table. Mdlle. Coustenoble's French Vowel Resonances	92
68.	Chart. Miss Mosolova's Russian Vowel Resonances *after page* 93	
69.	Table. Resonances of æ and æ̃ (American)	95
70.	Rubber tube vowel model	96
71.	Manipulation of ɐ (earth) model	101

LIST OF ILLUSTRATIONS

FIG.		PAGE
72.	Three resonators in parallel	104
73.	n, ð, k model	105
74.	t/d model	105
75.	n model	106
76.	Table, it, ʌt, ut resonances	107
77.	Table. Rubber tube resonances and consonant production	110
78.	Rubber tube vowel and consonant model	111
79.	Production of vɑ by rubber tube model	112
80.	Production of ʃ (sh) and ʒ (zh) by rubber tube model	114
81.	Table. Consonant sounds classified	115
82.	Cylindrical model with nasal cavity	116
83.	Windowed mouth-stopper	118
84.	Model with flexible pharynx	119
85.	Model producing whispered consonants	121
86.	Table. l resonances with different vowels	125
87. 88. 89.	} " Joseph " and Mrs. Wright	*facing* 128–9
90.	Siamang monkey's call	129
91.	Tongue postures—vowels	135
92.	Tongue postures—consonants	136
93.	Table. Synthetic words and confirmations	140–1
94.	Table. Further synthetic words and confirmations	142–3
95.	Table. Further synthetic words and confirmations	144–5
96.	Tongue gestures for shoots, plants, trees, etc.	147
97.	Tongue track of skɑd, skid	151–2
98.	Tongue track of stɑ	152
99.	Tongue track of stɑ (closure positions)	152
100.	Tongue track of stigh	152
101.	Musical transcription of Chinese " tones "	161
102.	Table. Cantonese " tones "	162
103.	Tongue track of gʻiäu	167
104.	Tongue track of tsiang	167
105.	Tongue track of daria	168
106.	Tongue track of kân	168
107.	Tongue track of tsʻün	168
108.	Tongue track of dxʻʌøn, dzʻüøn	169
109.	Tongue track of tsiang	169
110.	Tongue track of n′z′iäu	169
111.	Tongue track of t/d-a-k/g	177

B

x LIST OF ILLUSTRATIONS

FIG.   PAGE
112. Tongue track of t/d-a-k/g tip and back . . . 177
113. Tongue track of to turn 177
114. Tongue track of to pull or scoop out 177
115. Tongue track of to strike down and pull back . . 177
116. Tongue track of rounded 177
117. Table. Coincidences in Sumerian and archaic Chinese 178
118. Tongue track of kap 179
119. Musical rhythm of " eats " (itz) 184
120. Musical transcription of " Love whose month was ever May " 186–7
121. Vowel model with larynx between resonators . . 203
122. Tongue and vocal cords 205
123. Model of vocal cords (slit rubber tube) . . . 206
124. a (calm) model 210
125. a (calm) model with additional (pharyngeal) resonator 210
126. a (calm) model, triple resonator 210
127. Palatal arch 216
128. Palatal arch—during nasal intonation . . . 216
129. Palatal arch and tongue co-operating . . . 218
130. Tongue and palate forming ŋ (ng) 218
131. Baritone's mouth singing a (calm) 220
132. Baritone's mouth singing i (eat) 221
133. Diagram of tongue vowel posture, right and wrong . 222
134. Table. Variation of vowel sound with laryngeal frequency 223
135. Top note for u (who) 223
136. Abnormal phonation—tongue against throat . . 224
137. Tongue posture of s 225
138. Tongue posture of θ 225
139. Talking horn. (Away !) 232
140. German organ pipe, with pierced diaphragm . . 234
141. Coned gamba organ pipe 235
142. Adjustable, metal, vowel-sounding organ pipe . . 236
143. Adjustable, wooden, vowel-sounding organ pipe . 236
144. Vox humana pipe 237
145. Whistle actuated double resonator 238
146. Muted whistle mouthpiece 239
147. Wow-wow mute 240
148. Cheirophone 242
149. Cheirophone, hand positions 243
150. Miniature vowel-sounding models 248
151. Wilkins' lesser figures. (Vowels) 252
152. Wilkins' lesser figures. (Consonants) . . . 252

LIST OF ILLUSTRATIONS

FIG.		PAGE
153.	Melville Bell's visible speech	253
154.	Pictographic signs for mountain	263
155.	Hand gesture of 8	264
156.	Double resonator model (diagramatic)	276
157.	Double resonances (calculated)	280
158.	Double resonator (general form)	281
159.	Bottle-form resonator	291
160.	Relation of fundamental to first overtone	295
161.	Bottle-necked plasticine models	296
162.	Table of frequencies (Equal Temperament Scale)	299
163.	Audiogram of the Author's hearing	301
164.	Stops (orificed) for tubular models	303
165.	Tubular model	303
166.	ɑ model, 1084/683	304
167.	Cylindrical ɑ model	305
168.	Ditto, with reduced bore of back resonator	305
169.	Cylindrical u model	306
170.	Cylindrical e model	307
171.	Cylindrical i model	307
172.	Cylindrical ɔ model (intended)	307
173.	Plasticine ɔ model	308
174.	Cylindrical ɔ model (intended)	308
175.	Cylindrical ɔ model	309

PREFACE

THIS book is addressed to the general reader, with a preference for him or her that is interested in Speech from one or other of its practical aspects, namely, as a means for communicating and recording ideas, as the basis of the arts of literature, poetry and song, or as one of the principal accomplishments distinguishing man from the lower animals.

Some of the results arrived at may be of interest to linguists, to teachers of speech to the deaf, and to those musicians or scientists who are concerned in the practice or teaching of voice production and elocution, or in the improvement or "humanising" of the tone of organ pipes and other wind instruments.

Its aim is to give, in simple language, an account of some personal observations and experiments on the phenomenon of human speech, and some conclusions and suggestions as to its probable origin and future development.

It does not pretend to be a comprehensive treatise, or to describe the results of more than a very few of the large number of previous workers in various parts of the same field. It is fitting, therefore, to make, in advance, the necessary apologies for all those cases in which important work may have been overlooked, or in which my own observations, experiments or conclusions may have been anticipated by other workers.

In the course of the experiments I have been sometimes led to view human speech from a rather different standpoint from that usually taken by the philologist or the phonetician. In consequence, I have been driven to certain conclusions as to the directions in which improvement of our language is advisable; the substance of those conclusions is included in the last Chapter of this book.

Here also two apologies are necessary. In the first place to those persons interested in language, who believe that the origin of human speech is necessarily undiscoverable—such as the members of the illustrious Philological Society, quoted by Professor Max Müller in his *Science of Thought*, who passed a resolution never to admit a paper or allow a discussion on the Origin of Language ; in the second place to those persons interested in our English language who believe (quite wrongly as I think) that English is already perfect and incapable of improvement.

My thanks are due in the first place to my friends Sir William Bragg, F.R.S., and Professor Daniel Jones, of University College, London ; to Sir William Bragg for the encouragement which he has given to my work from its inception, and to Professor Daniel Jones for the same reason,and for the frequent help which he has given me in Phonetic matters, and especially in the revision of the MSS. of certain of my published papers.

I must also express my obligation to Mr. W. E. Benton, who has made a preliminary mathematical investigation of the resonances of the cavities formed in the human mouth during the articulation of vowel sounds, for allowing his results to appear as Appendix I to this Book.

Finally I must record my appreciation of the help which I have received, in turn, from my secretaries, Mr. C. T. Young, Miss G. M. Barker and Miss G. H. Glover, being well aware that without their personal interest in the work this book would probably not have been completed.

HUMAN SPEECH

Chapter I

INTRODUCTION

We are about to venture together in some by-ways of the field of acoustics, and, as it is hoped to enlist the company and sympathy of the general reader, I am venturing to preface this chapter with a brief account of the three fundamentals of our subject—the Sensation of Sound, the Nature of a Sound Wave, and the Nature of " Resonance ". To those who are already well acquainted with them I offer the alternatives of an apology from the author, or the right to skip.

Let the reader imagine that a fairy were to make herself small enough to creep into the passage of his (or her) outer ear, and were then to press her hand very gently against the delicate membrane which we call the " drum " of the ear. The reader might feel the pressure, but would hear no sound.

If the pressures were repeated at regular intervals, 5 or even 10 times a second, they might be felt as successive pressures but there would still be no sensation of Sound. If the fairy quickened her impulses up to about 16 to the second, the subject would begin to lose the sensation of separate pressures and receive in their place a new sensation of sound.

The sound heard would be what we should call a very low musical note—in fact the lowest note of a big organ. By the mere increase of frequency, the succession of silent pressures would have changed into an audible Sound.

At about 250 pulses per second our reader would hear the

note commonly called Middle C on the piano. At 6,000 to 7,000 pulses per second the note would have risen to a very shrill whistle—rather like the sound which we represent by the letter *s* ; it would become still higher and gradually fainter as the rate per second was further increased. Finally, at about 15,000 to 20,000 per second (according to the listener's age and acuity of hearing) the sound would disappear altogether ; and though the fairy might still be busily at work (provided she did not press so hard as to cause pain) the subject of her experiment would neither hear nor feel anything.

FIG. 1.

The amount of rhythmical pressure on the ear-drum necessary to produce the sensation of sound is astonishingly small. It has been estimated [1] that the weight of a single transverse slice of human hair $\frac{1}{1000}$ of an inch thick, say, of the thickness of a cigarette paper, rhythmically applied to the drum of the ear—e.g. 1,000 times a second—would be sufficient to produce the sensation of an audible musical note. If the pressures were increased (while keeping their number per second constant) the musical note would appear to be louder.

Sound, therefore, is only our way of recognizing small repeated pressures—within certain limits of frequency—on the drum of our ears. The musical pitch of the note heard depends on the number of pressures per second—the loudness depends on the extent of the repeated pressure changes.

In everyday life we dispense with fairies, and the repeated pressures which we normally " hear " are produced by rhythmical variations of pressure of the air which is in contact with our ear drums. These rhythmical variations of air pressure are due to sound waves, which are themselves due to some rhythmical disturbance of the air at the source of sound. If, for example, the air at any point is suddenly shaken, i.e. pushed rapidly backwards and forwards, as it is by, say, the movement of the diaphragm of a telephone or gramophone, or by the vibration of the soundboard of a piano, or of the " belly " of a violin, or of the parchment head of a drum—in every case each forward movement of the air gives rise to an invisible air-pulse or ripple, which travels outward through the air at the uniform rate of about 1,100 feet per second.

[1] R. L. Jones, " The Nature of Language " (Research Lab. of American Telephone and Telegraph Co. and Western Electric Co.), *Electrical Communication*, vol. ii, No. 1, July, 1923.

INTRODUCTION

The air-pulse or ripple is not carried by a current of air; this is fortunate, for 1,100 feet per second amounts to 750 miles per hour, and a current of air moving at that speed would have devastating results.

What actually happens, when still air is suddenly shaken, is in many ways analogous to what happens when a surface of still water is suddenly disturbed—as, for example, when we drop a pebble into a pond. In that case, a water ripple is formed and travels outward in all directions on the surface of the pond. The ripple is produced by the crowding together and elevation of a ring of water all round the spot where the stone fell in. A moment later the elevated water which formed this ring has sunk back, and in so doing has crowded and consequently elevated a slightly larger ring of neighbouring water immediately beyond the first, and so on. The elevated ring therefore travels outward, getting larger and larger in circumference, but the water at any point in the course of the travel of the ring only moves up and down. No water is carried with the ring.

So it is with sound waves in air—with this difference, that the crowding together of the air at the point of disturbance does not produce an " elevation " of surface but an increase of pressure, and that the individual particles of air—when a sound wave is passing—move to and fro in the direction of the travel of the wave instead of transversely up and down as in the case of the water ripple.

There is this further difference, that whereas water ripples form surface rings round the point of disturbance, sound ripples form layers or shells of high and low pressure alternately. These concentric layers entirely surround the source and travel outwards from it in all directions at the speed of 1,100 feet per second. In this respect the propagation of sound waves is more like that of light or of the etheric waves used in wireless telegraphy.

If the air at a source of sound be disturbed only once a second, it is evident from what has been said that the first layer or shell of high pressure will have travelled outwards 1,100 feet by the time that the second layer begins to follow it. In other words, the ripples will be 1,100 feet apart—measured " from crest to crest "—and the waves will be said to have a " wavelength " of 1,100 feet.

If the air be disturbed 100 times a second, instead of only

once a second, the ripples will be 100 times as close together, and the wave-length will now be 11 feet.

A sound due to 100 pressures per second corresponds to about G in the bass clef—a fairly low bass note. A sound with a frequency of 1,000 per second—and a consequent wave-length of 1·1 feet, say 13 inches—corresponds approximately to c''', a very high soprano note.

Fig. 2.    Fig. 3.

As a matter of fact the musical notes used in human song vary in wave-length from about 20 feet for the lowest notes of a bass voice to about 1 foot for the highest notes of a soprano.

There is a further analogy between sound waves and water ripples which may be useful to bear in mind. If we watch a family of ducks swimming on a smooth pond we shall see that each duck leaves behind it a Λ-shaped ripple in its wake, but that though these Λ-shaped ripples from different ducks constantly meet one another, they never interfere. The two ripples going, it may be, in opposite directions, pass through one another as if each of them were alone in the pond.

So it is with air waves, the air can carry any number of waves of different frequencies or of waves moving in different directions, simultaneously.

The Resonance of a Cavity

One other preliminary explanation remains to be made—namely, as to the nature of "Resonance".

Air is an elastic substance; it is for this reason that we make motor-car tyres of it—for the envelope of canvas and rubber, which is called the tyre, is only a prison wall to keep the airy pressed-gang, which really does the work of supporting the car, from escaping.

It follows that when a mass of air finds itself enclosed in a cavity, such as that of the human mouth and throat, the air as a whole behaves as an elastic mass or spring. If it is jogged in any way, it starts palpitating, invisibly, in and out of the mouth of the cavity—very much in the same way as the spring of a jack-in-the-box would jump up and down if suddenly depressed and then released.

INTRODUCTION

What actually happens is that, at the first moment of disturbance, a little of the air is jerked out at the mouth of the cavity, or a little extra air from outside is sucked in. In either case the air inside the cavity will then have a very slightly lower or higher pressure than the air outside. There will therefore be a return movement set up—from the high pressure side to the low pressure side—to re-adjust the difference.

But as the air, besides being elastic, also has mass of its own, it does not at once cease to flow as soon as the pressure is equalized inside and outside the cavity; it always overshoots the mark by a little—just as the beam of a balance, or the bob of a pendulum, overshoots its position of rest on returning from its swing.

In this way the original disturbance of the air inside a cavity results in rhythmical surging of the air in and out of the mouth of the cavity, each surging movement being a little less than the one before, till the air finally comes to rest. The rate at which this surging movement takes place—in other words, the number of surgings per second—depends mainly on three things.

First, on the volume of the cavity. The larger the cavity, the longer it takes for the difference of pressure between the air inside and outside the cavity to adjust itself. We may imagine the cavity as being like a concert hall, with the air for audience—the bigger the hall the slower will be the process of filling and emptying. A big cavity, therefore, makes for slow surgings or pulsations of the air at its mouth.

Secondly, the rate of surging depends on the size of the opening through which the surging takes place. The bigger the opening the more quickly the pressure differences can readjust themselves—just as, in a concert hall, the audience could get in and out more quickly if the doors were made bigger. And just as in a concert hall we might add more doors instead of enlarging the existing ones, so in an air-cavity we may add orifices, instead of enlarging the existing orifice, and produce the same effect.

Lastly, the rate of surging depends on the length of the neck of the orifice through which the surging takes place. We must remember that the movement—like that of any pendulum— is one of successive starting, accelerating, retarding, stopping, and of repeating these actions in the reverse direction. The time required to do this in the case of our air-cavity depends on how much air is set in motion.

If in our concert hall we prolong the sides of the doorway outwards, so that the doorway becomes a passage, and we imagine that passage crowded with people, all of whom have to " get a move on " before the filling or emptying process can start—it will be clear that the longer the passage, the slower the rate of filling and emptying will be.

Now, every time the air inside a cavity, such as we have been considering, comes surging out, it gives rise to an invisible ripple which travels out in all directions from the mouth of the cavity in the form of a sound wave.

If, therefore, the air inside a cavity is disturbed, it naturally tends to produce a series of sound waves which succeed one another at a uniform rate, depending on the volume of the cavity, the size of its orifice (or orifices) and the length of the neck or necks of these orifices.

The uniform rate of surging produces in our ears a musical note of a definite pitch, while the gradually reducing amount of the surging (as the pressure gets more and more nearly equalized) makes this musical note get rapidly fainter. If for example the air in a cavity is suddenly disturbed we get in fact a musical pop, such as is heard if we draw a cork from an empty bottle.

The variation of the resonant pitch of a cavity when the size of its orifice to the open air is varied may be effectively illustrated in this way :—Let the reader hold a glass tumbler (preferably one of thin glass) in one hand and tap the bottom of the glass from the outside with the other hand. The musical note heard is that due to the resonance of the air in the tumbler, since the glass is prevented from vibrating freely by being held in the performer's hand.

Now turn the tumbler so that its mouth faces the palm of the hand which holds it, and tap it again as before. It will be found that the resonant note is slightly lower than it was. If the mouth of the tumbler is now brought progressively nearer and nearer to the palm of the holder's hand—by bending the fingers—the resonant pitch (when the tumbler is struck) becomes progressively lower.

With a little practice a musical performer can easily play a tune on this simple instrument, by adjusting the distance between the palm of his hand and the mouth of the tumbler. The range of the instrument is a little more than one octave.

We have seen that the musical pitch of a resonating cavity

INTRODUCTION 7

can be varied in three different ways, viz. : by enlarging the resonator, which lowers the pitch, by enlarging the orifice, which raises the pitch, or by lengthening the neck, which lowers the pitch of the note produced by the resonant cavity. It follows from this that we can obtain the same resonant pitch from resonators of different sizes, provided we adjust the size of the orifice and length of neck so as to compensate for the difference of volume of the resonator.

One other point may be emphasized, namely, that since in cavities of the type we are considering, the air presses equally against all parts of the enclosing shell, we can replace the single orifice by two or more smaller orifices of equal total area without altering the resonance of the cavity.

This principle is actually made use of in the little instrument called the ocarina,

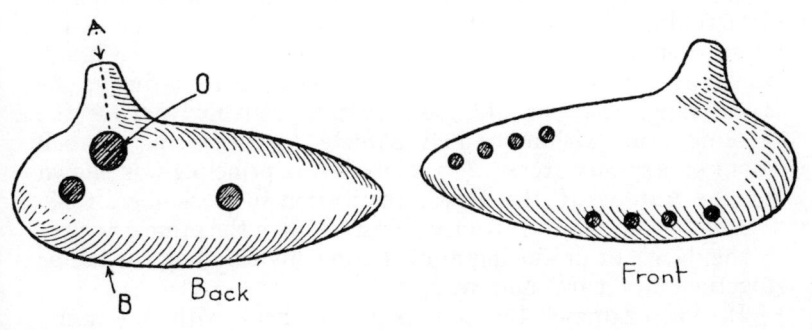

FIG. 4.

which consists essentially of a hollow pear-shaped resonator usually made of earthenware. The principal orifice has a

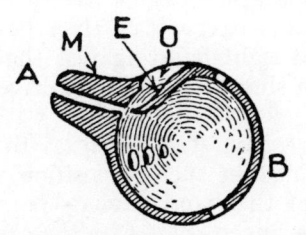

FIG. 5. Section on dotted line A of Fig. 4.

chisel edge at one side of it, against which a jet of air is directed by the mouthpiece M.

The effect of this is to produce a whistled note, of which the musical pitch is determined by the resonance of the cavity of the instrument.

Besides the principal orifice, there are 10 additional holes, so placed as to be capable of being closed or opened by the player's ten fingers. The lowest note is obtained by closing all the finger holes; the highest, by uncovering them all.

The ocarina is, I believe, the only well-known wind instrument which operates on the principle of the "Helmholtz" resonator—so called after the German Physicist who first systematically studied its properties.[1] It is for this reason that I have thought it worth while to describe it in some detail.

In its simplest form this principle may be illustrated by a bell-shaped resonator, 6 or 7 cm. in diameter, and about 8 cm. in length, with a whistle hole at the top of the bell. The tuning of the whistle may be lowered by a progressive closure of the mouth of the bell with the palm of the hand, the range being a little over one octave. Alternatively, the same range may be obtained by progressively varying the volume of air within the bell, namely, by immersing the bell more or less in water. A model on this principle was shown by the Author at the Royal Institution in December, 1928.

Another simple and effective illustration of the same principle is the device of producing musical notes by clapping the hands together in a particular way.

If, for example, the left hand be held with the palm extended upwards, and the right hand with the 1st, 2nd, 3rd and 4th fingers held side by side and then closed till the tips of the fingers touch the palm, so that the fingers and palm together form the largest possible cavity open at both ends, the resonance of this cavity can then be made audible by clapping the closed right hand against the open palm of the left hand, so that a sharp puff of air is driven into the tubular cavity.

To do this effectively, it is essential that the right hand shall be held inclined in such a position that the whole of the lower orifice of the hand cavity—i.e. the outer edge of the palm and little finger—closes at the same instant against the palm of the left hand. If the closure is progressive, owing

---

[1] See Helmholtz, *Sensations of Tone*, translated by A. J. Ellis, 1885.

to some portion of the lower edges of palm and little finger striking the palm of the other hand before the other portions, no popping sound will be produced.

Assuming that the reader has succeeded in making a musical pop by striking his right hand, made into an open-ended cavity, into the palm of his left hand, all that is necessary to vary the pitch of the sound produced is either to enlarge the upper opening, viz., that made between the thumb and the first finger, or to reduce the volume of the cavity as a whole by discarding one or more fingers, whilst always retaining the lower orifice formed by the little finger and its adjacent finger, the tips of which touch the palm of the right hand. With practice, nearly an octave and a half of musical notes can be formed in this way.

If instead of giving a single initial jog to the air inside a cavity (as we do when we tap it) we give it a succession of jogs—so timed as to coincide with the rate at which the air naturally surges through the orifice or orifices—then we shall get a much more vigorous and sustained production of sound waves. The musical note to which the cavity naturally responds is known as its resonant pitch.

Another simple experiment is that of blowing across the mouth of an empty bottle so as to awaken the resonance of the air within it. The resonant pitch can then be varied by pouring more or less water into the bottle, so as to reduce (more or less) the volume of air, while keeping the area of orifice constant. If the reader will then hum or whistle the same note as that given by the air in the bottle—holding his (or her) mouth close to that of the bottle—it will be found that the volume of the hummed or whistled sound is greatly increased by the resonance of the air in the bottle. If the hum or whistle could be passed *through* the resonating cavity by means of a second opening at the bottom of the bottle, the resonance effect would be even more marked.

If several musical notes were blown through the bottle at the same time, of which one was of the same pitch as that of the resonance of the bottle, the air in the bottle would pick out that particular note and " make much of it ". It will be well to bear this principle of resonance in mind, for it is the basis of all speech and song.

According to the late Lord Rayleigh—the greatest of all authorities on acoustics—the actual discovery of the relation between the musical pitch and the volume of a resonator was due to Liscovius about the year 1850, while that of the relation between musical pitch and the area of the orifice (for resonators without necks) was due to Sondhaus.[1] Helmholtz reinvestigated and clarified the whole subject so greatly that the spherical type of resonator which he used became known by his name.

RESONANCE OF A TUBE CLOSED AT ONE END

If the length of a cavity is substantially greater than its diameter, and if the mouth of the cavity is of the same order of size as that of its " bore ", a rather different effect is produced. The " cavity " has now become a " tube " closed at one end.

We can imagine this tube as packed with disc-like layers of air, just as disc-shaped biscuits are packed in a cylindrical tin—but with this difference, that each biscuit can be squeezed flat and can expand again when the pressure is released.

Any disturbance (a pressure in or a pull out) applied to the first layer—at the mouth of the tube—will then be communicated in turn to each layer till it reaches the last layer at the closed end of the tube. Here the motion will be reversed, and the impulse *in* will travel back towards the mouth of the tube and emerge as an impulse *out*. The air at the mouth of the tube has, in fact, performed half a complete vibration.

Under these circumstances it will be seen that the time taken for an impulse *in* to travel down the tube and emerge as an impulse *out* must depend on the *length* of the tube, not on its diameter. In other words, the resonant pitch of a closed-ended pipe—as distinct from a cavity of the Helmholtz Resonator type—depends simply on the length of the pipe.

There is another difference—namely, that the layer of air in contact with the closed end of the tube cannot move further down the tube when it receives the pressure of the layer next to it, nor leave the end of the tube when the pressure is reduced; the air column as a whole behaves, therefore, like a spiral spring with one end anchored at this point. Under these conditions " stationary air-waves " are set up in the tube, i.e. waves of which the air at a part of its length (in the present instance at the closed end of the tube) does not move at all but is only compressed more or less.

[1] *Pogg. Ann.*, li, pp. 235, 347.

INTRODUCTION

The formation of stationary longitudinal air-waves in a tube is analogous to the lateral waves which are produced in a rope fixed at one end, and shaken from side to side or up and down at the other; at the fixed end there is, obviously, no lateral or up and down movement, but only changes of tension, i.e. of pull on the point of fixture.

If a series of impulses, such as those of a musical sound, are communicated to the air in a closed tube, the air at the mouth of the tube will be " in step " with the sound vibrations when the wave-length of the sound is four times the length of the tube. This is easily realized when we remember that the original impulse which travelled down the tube and back—i.e. which had travelled twice the length of the tube—began as an impulse *in* and emerged as an impulse *out*, in other words it had only performed *half* a complete swing. A closed-ended tube, therefore, naturally resonates to a note of which the wave-length is four times the length of the tube.

If the tube is open at both ends, it behaves (as a resonator) rather like two closed-ended tubes of half the length placed back to back. The point of no motion but of maximum change of pressure—known as a ' node "—is then at a point half way down the tube; the wave-length of the resonant note is half the length of that given by a closed-ended tube of the same length—in other words, the wave-length of a tube open at *both* ends is twice the length of the tube.

Some Landmarks in Vocal Acoustics

In the year 1692, Sir William Temple—the husband of Dorothy Osborne, and the patron of Jonathan Swift, wrote his *Essay upon ye Ancients and Moderns*, in which the following passage occurs:—

"We pretend to give a clear account of how thunder and lightning (that great Artillery of God Almighty) is produced, and we cannot comprehend how the voice of man is framed—that poor little noise we make every time we speak." [1]

The nature of human speech was evidently a subject of active interest in those days, for, still earlier, in 1668, John Wilkins, D.D., Dean of Ripon, a Founder and Fellow of the Royal Society, had written a most learned and remarkable

[1] I have to thank Lady Hylton, of Ammerdown, for this reference.

work [1] in which he discussed the origin of languages and of writing, their imperfections, and the production of a universal philosophical language and language notation.

In Chapter X of his book, Wilkins attempts to give " a rational account of all the simple sounds that are or can be framed by the mouths of men ". He even devised a phonetic alphabet. Some account of his work will be given in our last chapter.

In the year 1779, the Russian Imperial Academy put the following questions as the subject of their annual prize [2] :—

(1) What is the nature and character of the sounds of the vowels *a, e, i, o, u,* so different from one another ?

(2) Can an instrument be constructed like the *vox humana* pipes of an organ, which shall accurately express the sounds of the vowels ?

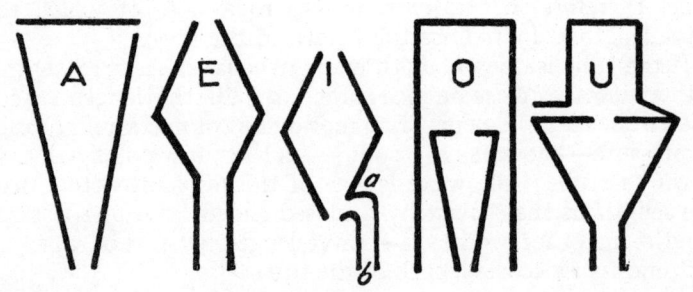

FIG. 6.

The prize was won by Professor Kratzenstein, who constructed a series of tubes of special form—suggested by observation of the form and dimensions of the human mouth when sounding the different vowels—and gave voice to his tubes by fitting them each with a vibrating reed (like the reed of a modern mouth organ—of which type he was apparently the inventor) through which air was blown into the tube by means of bellows.

In one instance the " voice " was due not to a vibrating reed but to a whistle, like that of an organ pipe or flageolet.

Fig. 6 shows (according to Sir David Brewster) the form (in section) of Kratzenstein's pipes.

[1] *An Essay Towards a Real Character and a Philosophical Language*, London, printed for Sa : Gellibrand, and for John Martin, Printer to the Royal Society, 1668.
[2] *Westminster Review*, vol. xxviii (1837), pp. 30–7.

INTRODUCTION

With these pipes "all the vowels could be distinctly pronounced by blowing through a reed into the lower ends of the pipes". It was also stated that "the vowel I is pronounced by merely blowing into the pipe a–b, of the pipe marked I, without the use of a reed".[1]

These tubes are said to have imitated "with tolerable accuracy" the five vowels, but they gave no indication of the acoustic principles underlying vowel formation.

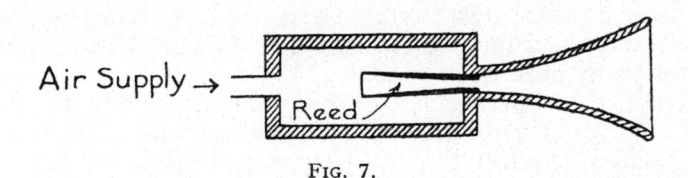

FIG. 7.

A more successful imitation of vowel sounds and an imitation of many consonants also was made about the same time by de Kempelen of Vienna.

His apparatus (shown diagrammatically in Fig. 7) consisted of a conical resonator, like the bell of a clarinet, fitted with a "free" reed like that of Kratzenstein, the reed being enclosed within a box supplied with air from bellows.

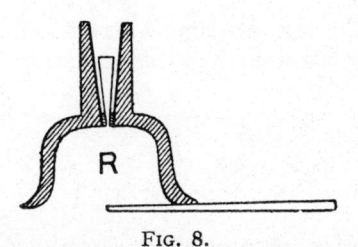

FIG. 8.

Different vowels were produced by progressive closures of the mouth of the "bell". The sounds u, o, and a could not be produced as sustained vowels, but only as transient sounds.

Fig. 8, copied from Sir David Brewster,[2] illustrates de

---

[1] *Letters on Natural Magic addressed to Sir Walter Scott, Bart.*, by Sir David Brewster, K.H., LL.D., F.R.S., V.P.R.S.E., MDCCCXXXII, p. 207.
[2] *Letters on Natural Magic*, p. 208. De Kempelen's own account appears in *Le Mecanisme de la parole suivi de la description d'une Machine parlante par M. de Kempelen*, Vienne, 1791.

INTRODUCTION

Kempelen's first model; it is here shown with a slide to close the orifice, but it is stated that the operator's hand was placed in various positions within the funnel. In a later model, the bell was made of elastic gum and was provided with two tin tubes which communicated with the mouth and acted as nostrils.

Apparently de Kempelen only produced one form of " plosive " consonant, namely *p*, but, as Brewster puts it, " by modifying the sound in a particular manner, he contrived to deceive the ear by a tolerable resemblance to those letters " (i.e. *t* and *k* and their voiced equivalents *d* and *g*) which were not actually present.

What the "particular" manner was we are not told; but that the articulation was not altogether satisfactory seems likely from the fact that de Kempelen never exhibited his apparatus in public. On the other hand there is the written evidence of an English witness, Mr. Thomas Collinson, that he had heard the machine articulate the word " exploitation " with the French accent!

It is further recorded that this apparatus could even produce such complete sentences as

Vous êtes mon ami.

Je vous aime de tout mon coeur,

but that it could not manage German, on account of the sibilants and terminal mutes of that language.[1]

Speech Notation

In any discussion of speech sounds, the difficulty at once arises that our present methods of spelling are not capable of indicating many of the speech sounds even of our own language. We use, in English, 13 or 14 separate vowel sounds, but we only have 5 symbols—*a, e, i, o, u*—with which to describe them. I have, therefore, throughout this book, made use of the convenient system of notation which is employed by the International Phonetic Association.

[1] Sir David Brewster, *Westminster Review*, 1837.

INTRODUCTION

In that system, the English vowel sounds are represented as follows:—

           i as in eat
           I   ,,   it
          ei   ,,   hay
(first part of the diphthong)
          e   ,,   men
          æ   ,,   hat
          ɐ   ,,   earth
          ʌ   ,,   up
          a   ,,   calm
          ɒ   ,,   not
          ɔ   ,,   all
         ou   ,,   no
(first part of the diphthong)
          u   ,,   who
          ʊ   ,,   put

The indefinite vowel sound, used in the word "the" of "God-save-the-King" is represented by the symbol ə. The pronunciation referred to is that of "Southern" or "Public School" English, as spoken by the present writer, which will be found recorded in Chapter III.

The first systematic investigation of the nature of vowel sounds—verified by their synthetic production by models—was published in 1829, by Robert Willis, M.A., F.R.S., F.G.S., Fellow of Caius College, Cambridge, in a very remarkable paper read in 1828 and published in the transactions of the Cambridge Philosophical Society.[1]

Willis observed that when the human mouth was set so as to pronounce a particular vowel, the mouth cavity gave rise to a resonant note of a particular pitch—due to the natural rate of vibration of the air in the mouth cavity.

He believed that it was the pitch of the resonant note of the mouth cavity which determined the vowel sound produced, and that the differences between the vowel sounds were essentially due to differences of resonance in the cavity which produced them.

[1] *Trs. Camb. Phil. Soc.*, vol. iii, pt. 1, x, p. 231.

INTRODUCTION

Willis further believed that each vowel was characterized by a definite resonant note of its own, and that this note was the same for men, women and children, and was independent of the notes which were produced by vibrations of the vocal cords. He made models to prove his theories, and showed that, by using a shallower bell than de Kempelen, he could reproduce all the five vowels, *u* (who), *o* (no), *a* (calm), *ei* (hay), *i* (eat), by progressive closures of the mouth. He also found that the same series of vowels could be produced by varying the length of the vibrating column of air in a single tube—the diameter of the tube being said to be immaterial. Willis' apparatus is diagrammatically shown, in section, in Fig. 9.

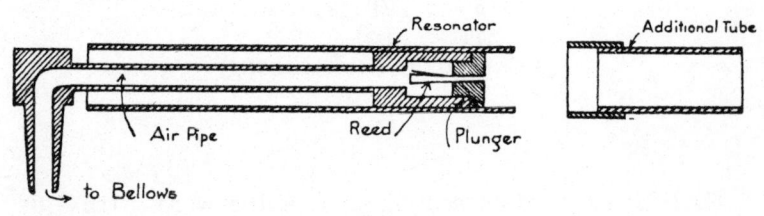

FIG. 9.

The resonator tube, 2 ft. long, operated as the cylinder for a piston or plunger which carried the vibrating reed. The piston rod was made hollow, and was bent downwards at about 2 feet from the plunger, and communicated with the bellows (not shown) which supplied air to vibrate the reed. In this way the effective length of the air column, between the face of the plunger which carried the reed and the open end of the resonator tube, could be varied from 0 to 2 ft., namely by sliding the tube relatively to the plunger. In the illustration the plunger is shown as pushed forward to within an inch or so of the open end of the resonator tube. An additional tube is shown ready for attachment, beyond the open end of the resonator tube, so as to increase its length if required.

In Willis' experiments the vowel sounds heard at different settings of the plunger were stated to be as follows :—

INTRODUCTION

Length of air column from face of plunger to open end of resonator tube—in inches.	Resonant pitch of air in front of plunger.	Vowel sound [1] heard on blowing air through the reed.
4·7	C_2	u (who) doubtful.
3·05	G_2	ɔ (all).
3·8	$\flat E_2$	o (no).
2·2	$\flat D_2$	ɑ (calm).
1·8	F^3	u (who).
1·0	D^4	æ (hat).
0·6	C^5	ei (hay).
0·38	G^5	i (eat).

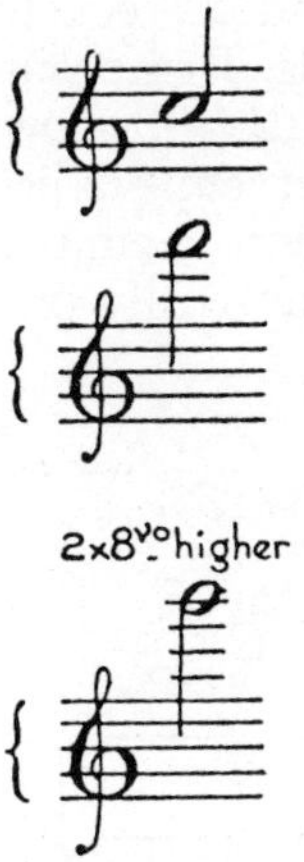

FIG. 10.

The attempt was made to repeat Willis' results, using as the variable resonator an apparatus belonging to Professor Daniel Jones, of University College, London, in which a reed is carried in the plunger of a tube about $1\tfrac{1}{8}$ in. diameter, and is arranged to be blown by mouth—through a hollow piston rod.

The only vowels which could be recognizably produced by varying the position of the plunger in the tube were

at $6\tfrac{1}{2}$ inches ɞ (earth) (not mentioned by Willis)
at $3\tfrac{3}{4}$,,   æ (hat) (compare Willis' o (no) at 3·8 in.)
at $2\tfrac{1}{4}$,,   ɑ (calm) to ʌ (up) (compare Willis' ɑ (calm) at 2·2 in.)
at $\tfrac{5}{8}$,,   e (men) (compare Willis' ei (hay) at ·6 in.)

There was a trace of i (eat) on blowing very softly with the plunger at about ·4 in., comparable to Willis' i (eat) at ·38 in. With this tube (at least) Willis' u, ɔ, o, were not produceable. But even though all the vowels may not have been produced (and there is good reason, as we shall see later, to doubt their

---

[1] The modern International Phonetic Association's notation has been substituted for that of Willis. The musical notation of three typical resonances has also been added to indicate their position on the pianoforte.

true production in the manner described) there can be no doubt that Willis laid the foundations of a rational theory of the nature of vowel sounds.

About the years 1834 to 1837 Professor Wheatstone, of King's College, London, constructed a talking machine, similar to that of de Kempelen, but with various original improvements. This device, shown (approximately) in Fig. 11, consisted of a leather cup-shaped resonator, with a slightly enlarged tubular stem, mounted in a wooden socket and terminating in a rearwardly-projecting reed. The wooden

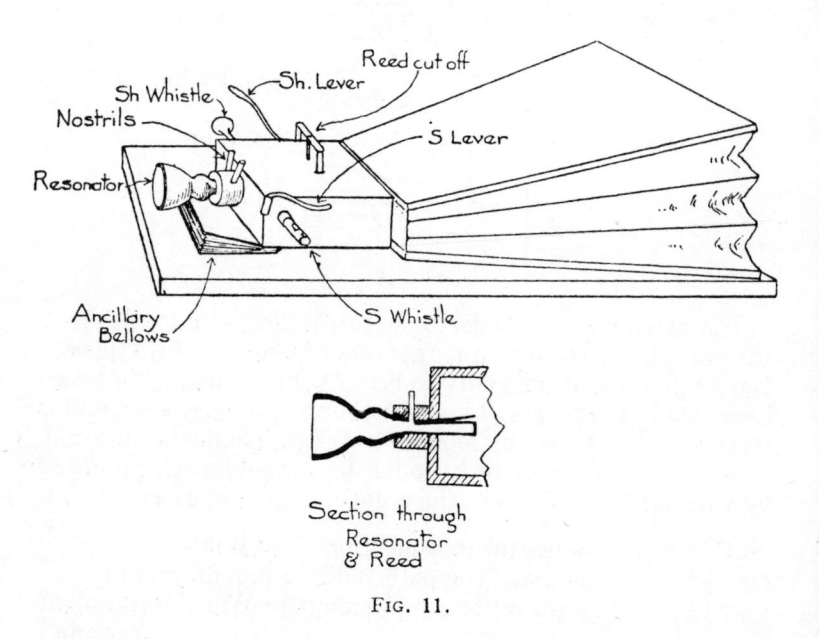

FIG. 11.

socket was attached to an air box into which the reed projected, and the box itself was attached to the bellows by which the reed and resonator were energized. The reed could be put out of action by a press button mounted on a lever at the top of the air box, so that the air then entered the resonator without passing through the reed. In this condition the apparatus produced whispered or unvoiced sounds.

Two separate whistle-like instruments were mounted in holes, formed on either side of the air box, the one producing

INTRODUCTION

a high-pitched hissing sound, like the letter *s*. The second whistle produced a sound like *sh*, by means of an air jet (from the air box) blowing into the small end of a short funnel-shaped tube, open at both ends and mounted axially in relation to the jet and about ½ inch in front of it.

Two small nostril tubes were mounted in the wooden socket of the resonator, so as to communicate with the interior of the tubular stem between the reed and the resonator. Auxiliary pressure-regulating bellows were mounted underneath the air box. The changes of resonance for producing the different vowel sounds were made by covering the mouth of the resonator, more or less, by hand.

The consonant *m* was obtained by closing and releasing the resonator mouth by hand while allowing the sound from the reed to escape through the nostril tubes. If the nostril tubes were closed, the closure and release of the resonator mouth produced the consonant *p*.

I have had the privilege of trying this apparatus, and have found that it can be made to articulate the vowels æ (hat), ʌ (up), ɔ (more), u (who), and also certain words such as pʌpʌ (papa), mʌmʌ (mama), hæm (ham), hæʃ (hash), hʌʃ (hush), sʌmʌ (summer), or other combinations of the vowel sounds mentioned with the consonants *p, m, h, s,* and *sh*.[1]

It does not seem possible to produce all the English vowels by manipulation of the mouth of the resonator, or to produce consonants other than those already mentioned.

If the accounts, already referred to, of the performances of de Kempelen's machine are to be believed, it would seem to have included devices which are now absent from Wheatstone's machine.

Wheatstone made an important contribution to acoustic theory by his discovery of what he called Multiple Resonance, i.e. the possibility of obtaining two or more resonant notes simultaneously from the same resonator. This is due to the fact that the air in a resonator—like the string of a violin or piano—can vibrate as a whole and also in " sections " *at the same time*. The vibration as a whole produces one resonant note (the fundamental); the vibrations in sections produce a higher note or series of higher notes (harmonics or overtones or partials).

[1] The apparatus was exhibited in operation by the present writer at the Royal Society Conversazione on 16th May, 1923.

Wheatstone thought that "vowel quality and multiple resonance are different forms of the same phenomena ".[1]

F. C. Donders, in 1858, determined the mouth cavity positions which correspond with the various vowel sounds, namely, by blowing through the mouth cavity with the glottis held open so as to produce whispered sound.[2]

The next important landmark in the field of vocal acoustics is the work of the great German Physicist, Helmholtz, to which we have already referred. Helmholtz investigated the natural resonance of small cavities—such as spheres—in which the acoustic effect is essentially different from that of a tube, whose length is large compared with its diameter. He also investigated the resonance of the human mouth cavity when producing the various vowel sounds.

He came to the conclusion that whereas vowels like a (calm), ɔ (more), u (who), ɒ (not), were due—as Willis had taught—to single resonances, the vowels æ (hat), e (men), i (eat), and the French vowels ö (peu) and ü (pu), were due to double resonance, i.e. to two separate notes, the one produced in the cavity behind the tongue, the other by "a constriction by the mid part of the tongue and the hard palate, like a bottle with a narrow neck" (*Sensation of Tone*, p. 107).

Helmholtz appears to have considered that the resonance of higher pitch, due to this "narrow neck", was formed by a tube rather than by a cavity of the Helmholtz type—a view that is to a certain extent supported by Mr. Benton's experiments (Appendix I).

In a resonator of the tube type, the rate at which air surges in and out of the mouth of the tube depends, as we have said, primarily on the length of the tube, not on its diameter. This is the principle involved in all the usual tubular wind instruments.

Helmholtz made many experiments in the reproduction of vowel sounds by resonators energized by air-blown reeds, or by tuning-forks vibrating at the mouth of the resonator ; but he does not appear ever to have tried the effect of energizing two Helmholtz resonators by means of a single reed.

---

[1] *Westminster Review*, loc. cit., p. 37.
[2] *Arch. f. Holl. Beitr. zur Natur & Heil-kde*, vol. i, p. 157.

INTRODUCTION

In 1873, Potter[1] described his experiments in which the vowels, as in

pipe (ʌi)
peep (i)
papa (ʌ)
pope (ou)
poop (u)
paper (ei)
water (ɔ)

were all produced by resonators formed of indiarubber hollow spheres energized by " free " metallic reeds such as those originally used by Kratzenstein.

In a " free " reed—it may be explained—a flexible tongue of metal is fixed at one end so that it lies across a long narrow opening in a metal plate, through which the air is made to pass. The reed is set in vibration by the air, so as to pass the air current in a series of puffs, but does not touch the sides of the

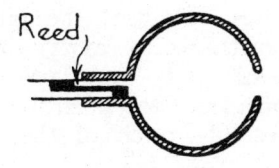

FIG. 12.

opening. In the " beating " reed which is commonly used in English organ pipes, the edges and the free end of the reed both overlap the opening through which the air passes, so that the reed (which is very slightly bent so as to curl upwards from the edges of the opening) alternately " beats " upon the edges of the opening and curls up slightly to admit the passage of a puff of air. The free reed behaves more like a swinging door, while the beating reed compares with an ordinary door which closes tight against its frame.

The free reeds of Potter's apparatus were fitted by short tubes to apertures cut in the hollow rubber spheres, to represent the fauces of the posterior part of the mouth, opposite apertures being cut to represent the lips.

[1] *Proc. Cambridge Phil. Soc.*, vol. xi, 1864–76, p. 306.

Different vowels were produced by "compressing" the indiarubber shell, when blowing through the reed, to make the shell take the same form as the mouth when producing a like sound. Potter apparently made no examination of the resonances of his compressed spheres, but, in the light of present knowledge, it may be said that his method of operation was probably truer to nature than that of any previous investigators.

In 1879 Graham Bell—the inventor of the first practical telephone—published his observations on the vowel resonances [1] and his conclusion that *all* the vowels were due to double resonance.

Between the years 1890 and 1896, Dr. R. J. Lloyd published his investigations of vowel resonances. He pointed out (1891) " the probability that every cardinal vowel derives one chief resonance from the anterior or oral part of its articulation, and another from the posterior or pharyngeal part ".[2]

He also studied the form of the sound waves—recorded phonographically when the vowels were sung—and deduced, from the curves thus obtained, the pitch of the various resonances present in the vocal cavity which produced them. His conclusion was that each vowel had (at least) two resonances, but that the identity of the vowel was not due to the absolute pitch of the resonances but to their mutual interval.

The following table—extracted from a more extensive statement at p. 251 of Lloyd's *Genesis of Vowels*, gives his results for the vowels in question. In the columns marked α, β, γ, δ and ε, he sets out the various resonant notes heard, and indicates them by their musical name, e.g. c¹♯, and by the number of complete vibrations per second (280 in the case of c¹♯) which produces them. The different columns refer to different parts of the vocal cavity in which the various resonances appeared to be produced.

The vowel symbols are those of the International Phonetic Association which have been substituted (as before) for those in the original paper.

---

[1] "Vowel Theories," *American Journal of Otology*, vol. i, July, 1879.
[2] *Phonetische Studien*, 1890–2. " Genesis of Vowels " (Brit. Assn. Paper, 1896), *Journal of Anatomy and Physiology*, vol. xxxi, p. 249. *Proc. Royal Soc.*, Edin., 7th Feb., 1898.

INTRODUCTION

Vowel (International Symbol).	Approximate English Keyword.	α posterior tube or cavity.	β anterior tube or cavity.	γ possibly in the trachea (windpipe).	δ possibly intradental	ε related to the anterior (front) tube or cavity.
i	marine	c^1♯ 280	f″ 2816	—	c^4♯ 2236	—
ɪ	pit	—	—	—	a^3♯ 1864	—
ei	rein	f′ *352*	c^4 *2212*	—	f^3 1408	—
æ (German ä)	there	d^2 *630*	f^3♯ *1508*	—	—	c♯ 2200
æ (Finno-Swedish ä)	man	g^2 *807*	f^3 *1431*	g^1 403	—	—
ɑ	father	g^2 *804*	c^3♯ *1115*	g^1 402	—	—
ɒ	hot (?)	e^2 *646*	e^3 *1342*	—	—	—
o (German long o)	note	d^1 *285*	d^2♯ *623*	—	—	—
ʊ	put	—	c^2 *528*	—	—	—
u	brute	e^2 *681*	e^1 *314*	—	—	—
ditto	ditto	a^2 *869*	d^1 *293*	—	—	—

FIG. 13.

(Note.—The vowels e (men), ɞ (earth), ʌ (up), and ɔ (all) are omitted).

It will be seen that in five cases Lloyd has recognized three separate resonances as being present together in the vocal cavities which produced those vowels; in four cases he recognizes two resonances per vowel and in two cases (ɪ as in pit and ʊ as in put) he finds only one. It will be seen later (Chap. III) that the great majority of Lloyd's α and β resonances are confirmed by my own observations and experiments. These are now printed in italics in the table.

Lloyd appears to have experimented also with models. He says (*Genesis of Vowels*, p. 249)—referring to the β resonances (due to the front tube or cavity)—" the assignment is fairly certain, because it can be confirmed by direct observations in whisper, by the behaviour of imitative cavities, and by careful measurement and calculation ". No record of the " imitative cavities " seems, however, to have been published.

In order that the reader may more readily appreciate the relation between the notes of the musical stave and the number of vibrations per second which go to produce them, I am inserting a table which will make the relationship clear.

The table also indicates the relation between the pitch of the sounds produced by resonance in the cavities of the human mouth, nose and throat, both in speech and in whispering, and the pitch of the notes which can be sung by the different types of human voice.

There is at present no universal musical standard of pitch. For example, the note called middle C on the piano, or the note called a', to which violins are tuned, are not actually the same in different countries, and have varied in pitch at different times. The pitch of the notes of all wind instruments also varies with the temperature of the air—rising about half a vibration per second for each one degree Fahrenheit rise in temperature.

Taking the violin a', which appears in the table as due to 430 vibrations per second, there is evidence that this note has been as " sharp " as 502·6 vibrations per second (at Heidelberg in 1511) and as " flat " as 395·2 at Trinity College, Cambridge, in 1759. Since then its pitch has steadily risen, till in 1874 it was 454 (Philharmonic Society, London), and even reached 457·5 in 1897. Orchestral pitch, which in 1899 was 438·6 in New York, was 440 in London.

The pitch adopted throughout this book is what is known as the scientific pitch, in which middle C is equivalent to 256 complete vibrations per second.

It will be seen that the table covers eight musical octaves, i.e. one more octave than the range of a grand piano. With three exceptions only the notes corresponding to the white notes on the piano are represented—in order to avoid overcrowding the diagram.

The successive octaves are divided by vertical bars. It may be pointed out that the " frequency " (i.e. number of vibrations

INTRODUCTION

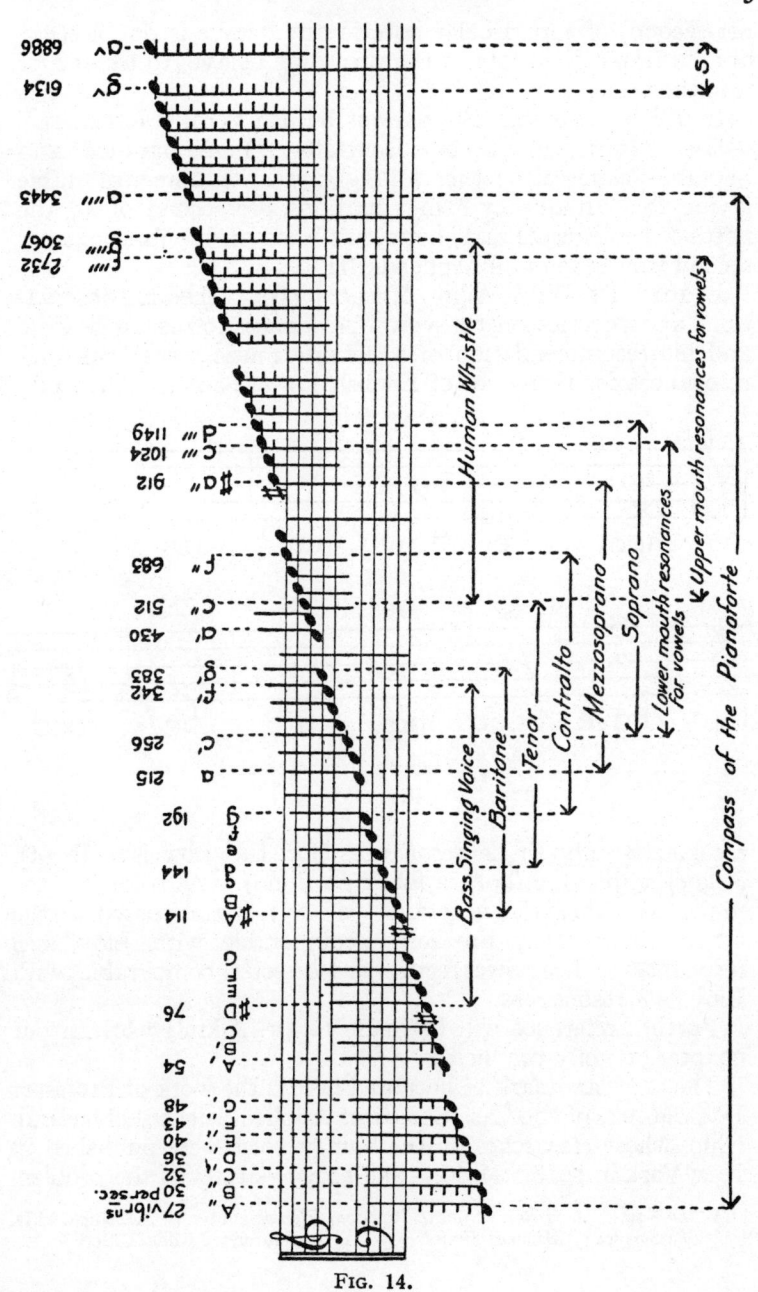

Fig. 14.

per second) of a particular note in any octave is double that of a corresponding note in the preceding octave, to the left of it in the table.

It will be seen that the various human vocal " Registers "—Bass, Baritone, Tenor, Contralto, Mezzosoprano, and Soprano—cover altogether four octaves. A numerical table giving the "frequency" in vibrations per second of all the notes of the musical scale between 16 and 3,864 vibrations per second will be found in Appendix II.

In 1910, Dr. W. A. Aikin, of London, published his observations and theories on the vowel resonances for use in singing, and his recommendation of a definite musical scale of oral resonances for the series of English Vowel Sounds. Dr. Aikin

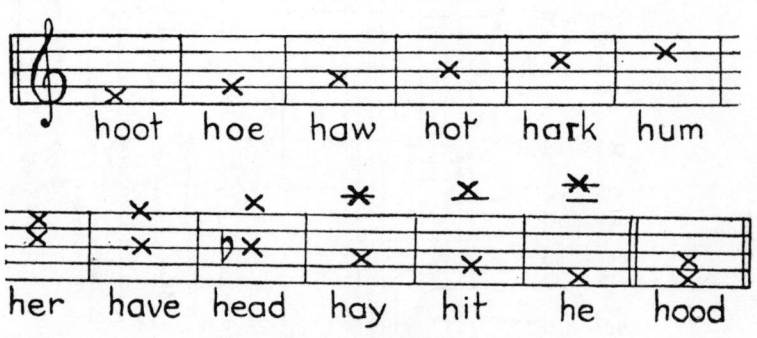

Dr. W. A. Aikin's Resonator Scale.[1]
FIG. 15.

recognized only single resonances for the vowels u (hoot), o (hoe), ɔ (haw), ɒ (hot), a (hark), ʌ (hum). As recorded, the upper series are all an octave too low; if transposed to the octave above they are fairly comparable with Lloyd's β resonances. The lower series are directly comparable with Lloyd's α resonances.

Further reference will be made to Dr. Aikin's work in our chapter on voice production.

The next landmark to be noted here is the work of Professor D. C. Miller, of the Case School of Applied Science, Cleveland, Ohio, whose researches on the human voice were published in New York in 1916.[2] Miller—like Lloyd—attacked the problem

[1] *The Voice; An Introduction to Practical Phonology*, by W. A. Aikin, M.D.
[2] *The Science of Musical Sounds*, by Dayton Clarence Miller, D.Sc.

INTRODUCTION

of vowel formation by a phonographic study of the wave form produced when the different vowels were intoned. He then subjected the characteristic curve—representing the complex wave form—to a process of mechanical analysis, so as to separate it into a series of simple waves, each of constant wave-length and amplitude.

By combining together and simultaneously blowing a number of organ pipes—each of which was designed to give a sound comparable in wave form with *one* of the series of simple waves deduced by the analyser—Miller was able to reproduce the vowel sound as originally intoned.

By the kindness of Dr. Miller I am able to show in Fig. 16 some typical groups of vowel-sounding organ pipes made in this way. The number of separate organ pipes (each giving substantially a single note) which are required to build up the effect of a single vowel sound intoned on a single note is certainly remarkable when compared with the simplicity of the mechanism —of reed and vocal cavity—by which the same effect is produced in the human voice.

Helmholtz had previously observed that a piano with the loud pedal pressed down would actually repeat many of the vowel sounds which were sung to it—various strings resounding to the various musical components which together made up the intoned vowel. Miller's groups of organ pipes can thus be compared, in each case, with the particular groups of piano strings which were set in sympathetic vibration in Helmholtz's experiments.

Miller's work confirmed Helmholtz's views that some of the vowels are due to double resonance, and that others, i.e. ɒ (not), ɔ (all), ou (no), u (who), ʊ (put), are due to single resonances. ɑ (calm) appeared to be produced in some voices by single and in others by double resonance.

C. Stumpf[1] studied the characteristic resonances of the vowels, and of the continuing consonants (*sch, ng, m, n, l, s, f,* and *ch*) by observing the changes of vowel or consonant character which resulted when resonances of a certain pitch (and over) were cut off by a form of sound-filter. By varying the musical pitch at which the cut-off operated, Stumpf was able to define the ranges of resonance which were characteristic of the various sounds. The results indicated that *ŏ, ä, ü, e,*

---

[1] *Berl. Ber.*, 1918, p. 351. *Beiträge Z. Anat.*, etc., vol. xvii, p. 181, 1921.

D

and *i* each had two separate resonance ranges—with evidence of a third still higher resonance range, except in the case of *i*; also that all the consonants named showed two or more resonant components.

With this brief and inadequate description of some of the landmarks of the past, we will now proceed to some preliminary observations on the vocal organs and their functions in speech.

Chapter II

PRELIMINARY OBSERVATIONS AS TO THE VOCAL ORGANS, AND THEIR FUNCTION IN SPEECH

The Vocal Organs and their Function

For the purpose in hand it will not be necessary to give more than a very rough outline of the various organs involved in the production of speech and song. The source of energy is the lungs (see Fig. 17). These are a pair of tightly packed

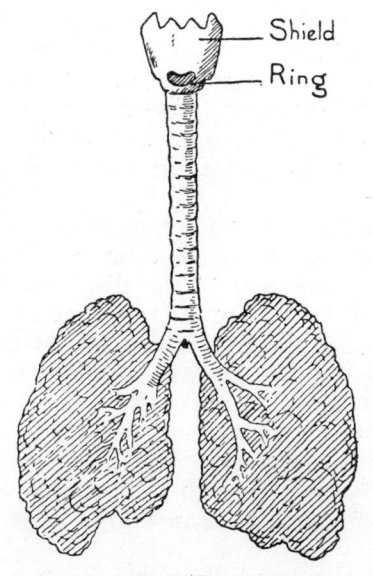

Fig. 17.

masses of minute air vessels each surrounded by blood vessels, which together form the dense foliage of an inverted branching system of air-pipes. Alternatively, if the reader prefers it, the whole arrangement may be compared with two clotted masses of tubular rootlets, supporting the stem of a plant having a tubular trunk and roots, and minute bladder-like root-endings.

It is well to emphasize the root-like and cellular structure of the lungs, so that it may be borne in mind that there is in fact no hollow cavity provided, such as might be expected to assist in the production of so-called " chest-notes ", or give rise to " chest resonance ".

The two separated masses of air-cells, and the branching air tubes which carry them, are closely packed within the flexible bony cage of the thorax, formed by the ribs ; the size and shape of this cage can be controlled by the operation of various muscles operating on the ribs. The floor of the " cage " is formed of a more or less horizontal flexible membrane called the diaphragm, which can be bulged up or down so as to vary the effective size of the cage from below.

The lung tissue is attached to the walls of its cage so that any variation of the effective size of the thorax reacts immediately on all the air cells. Contraction of the ribs, or the raising of the diaphragm, squeezes the air out of the cells as water is squeezed out of a sponge ; expansion of the ribs or depression of the diaphragm extends the mass of cells and thus creates a partial vacuum, which draws in fresh air through the windpipe.

In point of fact the action is not entirely analogous to that of a sponge, for the normal condition of a sponge is that of enlargement and we squeeze it to extract its contents, whereas the normal condition of the lungs is that of contraction, and it requires muscular effort to expand and fill them.

The relatively high air pressure which is necessary for loud voice production does require active muscular work. In that case the air is truly squeezed out of the lung cells by external pressure, as water is squeezed from a sponge. The lungs thus act mechanically as a (literal) pair of bellows, of which the volume and consequent pressure can be controlled with great exactness.

Acoustically, the lungs have no function except that of providing the requisite supply of air at the right pressure and at the right time for the service of the vocal cords and of the organs of articulation. They have no more resonance than ordinary bellows would have if they were packed full of damp bath sponges.

Indeed, from an acoustic point of view the human lungs are an almost perfect absorber of sound and destroyer of resonance. Their branching tubes—becoming ever smaller and smaller till they terminate in a multitude of infinitesimal air cells—act towards a sound wave like a shelving beach acts towards a wave of the sea. The wave gets broken up into an ever-thinning stream, which expends its energy in forcing its way up the beach. The energy of the wave is in fact mostly converted into heat by friction against the beach.

If instead of meeting a shelving beach the wave had struck against a vertical sea wall, most of the energy of the wave would have been reflected. Similarly, if the human lungs were a cavity like the mouth, there would be little absorption of sound, and consequently considerable reflexion of energy and the production of resonance.

It is fortunate that there is no such effect as chest resonance, for it would of course vary in pitch for every degree of inflation of the lungs, and would thus be a fatal bar to the uniform operation of the vocal cords. The lungs are acoustically neutral and therefore allow free action to the vocal cords.

The hollow vertical stem which grows out of the junction of the two main systems of lung "rootlets" is the windpipe or trachea. This is an air-tube, about ¾ inch in diameter and 8 inches long, leading up to the larynx or Adam's Apple, which may be felt as a hard lump in the front of the lower part of the throat.

The windpipe tube is flexible, but is kept in shape and prevented from expanding or collapsing by a series of rings of cartilage which surround and reinforce it—like the circumferential wire reinforcement of a garden hose pipe. In this part of the human air-supply system some resonance may perhaps be set up—the lungs behaving like the open end of a tube partially closed at the larynx; but inasmuch as the length and volume of the interior of the windpipe are practically constant (within about 5 per cent) it is certain that no appreciable resonance changes can be effected here.

At its point of junction with the larynx, the windpipe tube becomes rapidly flattened till the two flat sides ultimately meet—much as if the end of a rubber tube were squeezed between two fingers till the edges just touched. The meeting edges are thickened, and supplied with a complex system of muscles, so that they form, in effect, a pair of mobile lips—

not unlike the lips of the human mouth but of rather less than half the size, and lying horizontally, fore and aft, across the top of the windpipe instead of transversely and vertically as in the case of our own lips. These laryngeal lips constitute the so-called vocal cords.

Figs. 18, 19, and 20 represent photographs taken by Doctor G. Oscar Russell, of Ohio University, of the human vocal cords in action. In Fig. 18, the "lips" are drawn apart as in breathing; in Fig. 19 they are pressed together so as to vibrate (like the lips of a bugler) when air from the lungs is forced between them; in Fig. 20 the lips are shown in the act of vibrating at the moment of their furthest separation. The portions nearest to the front of the throat are shown towards the top of the figures.

It will be understood from the chart at p. 25 that in the various human voices these vibrations actually vary from about 40 per second (for a very deep talking voice) up to about 1,150 for a high soprano "top note".

The vocal cords are capable of a variety of movements and variations of size, shape and flexibility. In breathing they are opened wide apart, as already mentioned in relation to Fig. 18. In speech and song they are brought so near together that they appear to touch; their length and thickness also can be varied. The function of the vocal cords in speech is to act as a double reed like the well-known double reed of an oboe, or like the two lips of a cornet player, to produce a musical note of the required pitch.

In each of the cases mentioned—the voice, the oboe, or the cornet—the performer supplies air at a pressure sufficient to cause a small stream of air to force its way between the the contacting (or nearly contacting) surfaces of the two lips or reeds. In this way a vibration of the reeds is set up— by the passage of air between them—which results in the air stream being, as it were, chopped up into a succession of air pulses. If the reed-surfaces are drawn apart, as in Fig. 18, the air which passes between them is not set into pulsation, but passes through as a more or less turbulent stream.

In the case of the vocal cords, or the lips of a cornet player, the musical pitch of the note produced by the reed-action depends on the length, thickness and tightness (or pressure together) of the two elements of the "reed". The loudness of the note depends on the air pressure—with this proviso, that the muscular strength of the vocal cords or lips must be such as to resist the lung pressure, so that there may be a minimum leakage of air through the reeds between the pulses.

Dr. Russell (to whom I am indebted for permission to publish his photographs of the vocal cords in action) has also observed and demonstrated by actual photographs that in singing a series of different vowel sounds on the same laryngeal note (as, for example, in " intoning ") the laryngeal cavity actually assumes a different " expression " at each change of vowel sound.

These observations suggest that the interior laryngeal cavity prepares for the production of each vowel by assuming such a variation of form, in conjunction with the vocal cords, as will result in producing not only the note to be intoned, but also a particular selection of overtones or " partials ". Probably, the overtones produced are those which are suitable for setting up resonance in the cavities which are simultaneously formed in the mouth and throat—namely, by the positions of the tongue, lips, soft palate and epiglottis—when these are set so as to form the required vowel.[1]

On their upper side, the vocal cords form—when drawn together—the floor of a shallow cavity, of which the two sides (parallel with the vocal cords) are in-turned so as to form mobile flaps. These flaps are called the false vocal cords, or ventricular bands, to which reference has already been made.

Their function was, until quite recently, not fully understood; they appeared to act partly as a protection and as an airtight cover for the vocal cords. Experiments with models indicate that they also, by their variation of attitude, produce a small cavity, of variable resonance, immediately above the vocal cords. Such a cavity, co-operating with the fixed cavity of the windpipe, assists the action of the vocal cords in securing the required frequency of pulsation of the air which passes through them, and, in particular, produces the conditions

[1] L. P. H. Eijkman, of The Hague, has shown that in whispering the various vowel-sounds, the size of the opening made by the glottis varies directly with the frequency of the lower vowel resonance—the opening being larger for the vowels of high resonance. It is as if the glottal aperture took part in the tuning of the back resonator in order to save the tongue the trouble of making a tighter closure of the central orifice to produce the lower resonances, and vice versa.

of resonance which distinguish, for example, a whispered p, t, or k, from a whispered b, d, or g.[1]

Direct observations made in 1927 by Dr. Russell with a laryngeal periscope—by which the action of the false vocal cords could be observed during the articulation of the p, t, k and b, d, g sounds—confirmed the indications of my own experiments with models.

One other recently observed function of the false vocal cords may be mentioned here. In September, 1928, Sir James Dundas-Grant and I examined Mr. Strath Mackay, who has the peculiar accomplishment of being able to sing two notes at once. The higher notes (tenor register) are produced by the vocal cords; the lower notes, which normally vary with the upper notes so as to maintain a constant musical interval of 17 semitones (an octave and a fifth), appeared, from Sir James Dundas-Grant's observations, to be made by the bringing together of the false vocal cords, so that they vibrated like true vocal cords.

The observations were confirmed by a similar examination of my own throat while imitating (so far as possible) Mr. Mackay's double notes. Sir James was able to see the ventricular bands definitely in vibration while a very low note was being produced. It seems clear that in certain types of shouting—so as to produce a raucous sound—the false vocal cords are brought together so as to vibrate on their own account.

The normal pitch of the human voice, i.e. the average rate of the pulsations produced by the action of the vocal cords, depends as we have said on the length and thickness of the cords or lips themselves. The vocal cords of men are about $\frac{3}{4}$ inch long, as compared with $\frac{1}{2}$ inch in the case of women.

At puberty, a boy's vocal cords suddenly increase to double their previous size—with a corresponding lowering of the normal pitch of the voice. Those of girls increase only by about one-third, and the consequent change in the voice is much less.

The " cracking " of a boy's voice is presumably due to the unsuccessful attempt to produce the range of laryngeal notes, to which he was previously accustomed, by means of a reed, the length of which has suddenly been increased without the owner's knowledge !

[1] "The Nature and Artificial Production of the (so-called) Voiced and Unvoiced Consonants," Sir R. A. S. Paget, *Proc. R.S.*, vol. civ, 1927, p. 98.

Fig. 16. DR. R. C. MILLER'S VOWEL SOUNDING PIPES

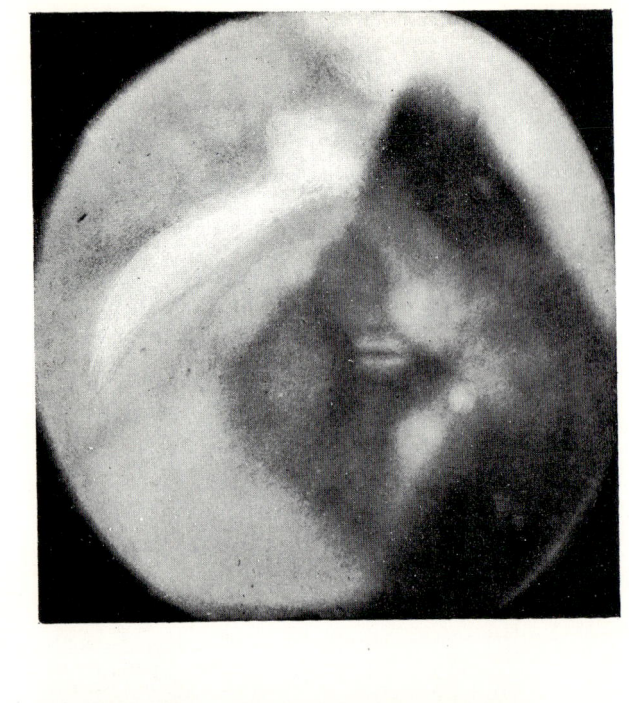

Fig. 18. NORMAL BREATHING POSITION OF VOCAL CORDS
Photo by Dr. G. Oscar Russell

Fig. 19. VOWEL Æ CLOSED
Photo by Dr. G Oscar Russell

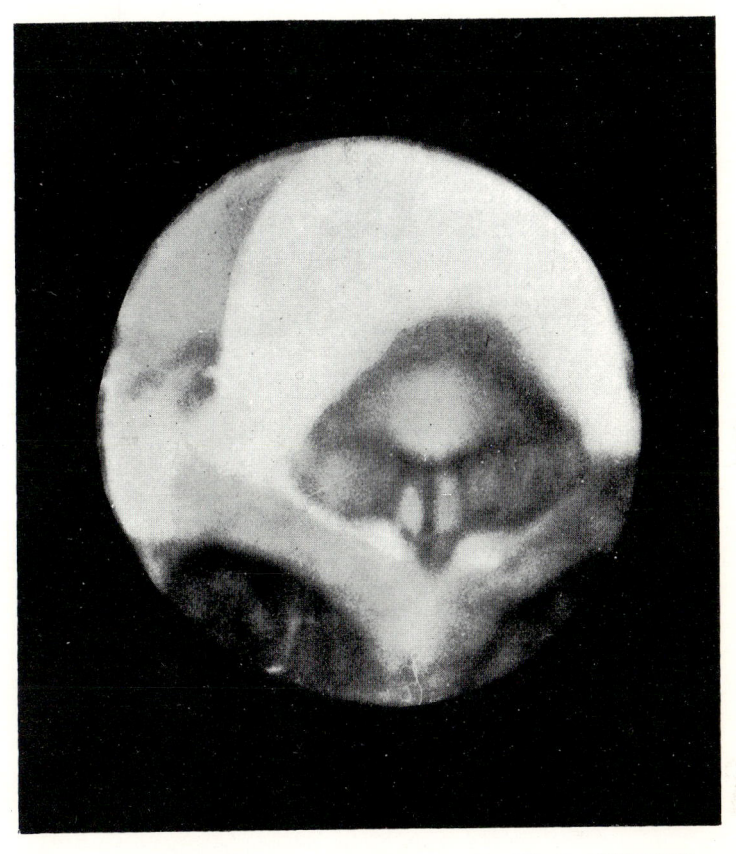

Fig 20. VOCAL CORDS AT THE MOMENT OF THEIR FURTHEST SEPARATION WHILE IN THE ACT OF VIBRATING

Photo by Dr. G. Oscar Russell

Fig 44. PLASTICINE MODELS ON LORD RAYLEIGH'S ORGAN

THEIR FUNCTIONS IN SPEECH

Immediately above the larynx is the cavity called the pharynx. (See Fig. 21.) The passage of this cavity can be obstructed by the miniature tongue or flap, known as the epiglottis, which can either lie flat against the back of the tongue, or be bent backward so as, more or less, to close the pharyngeal passage—as has been shown by Dr. Russell to be the case in the production of certain vowel sounds.

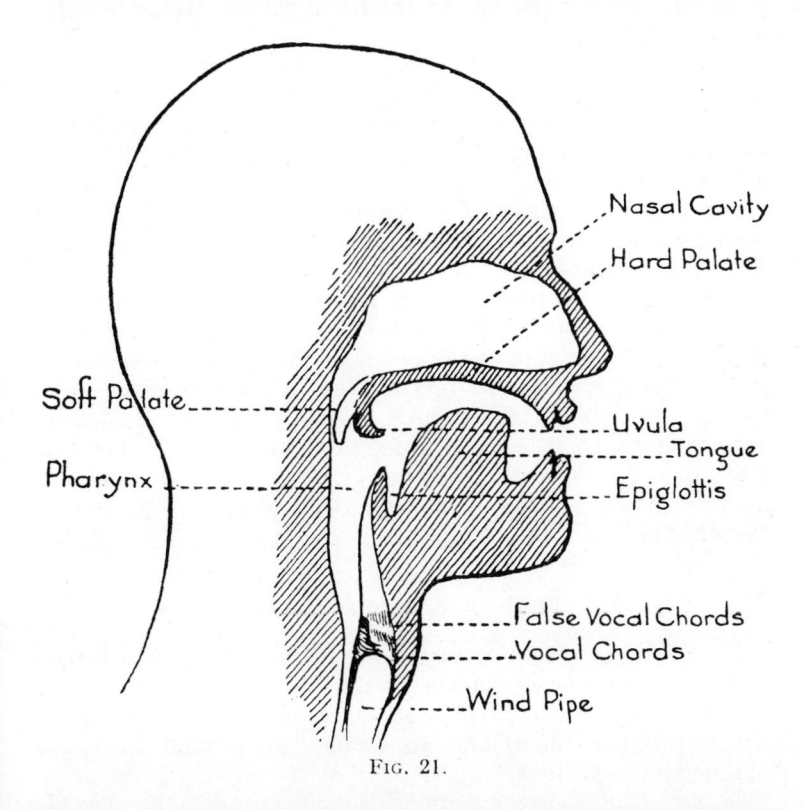

FIG. 21.

From the pharynx the out-flowing or pulsating air can take one or both of two courses. It may pass across the epiglottis, then over the upper surface of the tongue, and out at the lips. Or, it may pass upwards from the pharynx, behind the soft palate into the nasal cavity (above the hard palate) and out at the nostrils. Or it may take both courses simultaneously.

If the soft palate is pressed back—as indicated in plain

outline—the passage way leading to the nasal cavity is out of action, and all the out-flowing air passes through the mouth.

In speaking or singing it is easy to tell with certainty whether the passage behind the soft palate is open or closed—namely, by applying a rubber tube or stethoscope to either nostril, and listening at the other end. There is a sudden rush of sound, heard whenever the soft palate is moved forward so as to open the passage to the nasal cavity, which is quite unmistakable.

The tongue is a muscular organ, constant in volume, but highly and very rapidly variable in form. It can take a great variety of different positions inside the mouth, so as either to alter the shape of the cavity as a whole or close it altogether in different positions.

Beyond, and partially surrounding the tongue, are the teeth, which co-operate with the tongue in the production of certain consonants.

Finally come the lips by which the opening to air of the mouth cavity can be varied—from complete closure up to an opening of about half the bore of the inside of the mouth at its widest part. The lips may also function—to a lesser extent—so as to vary the size of the mouth cavity as a whole—namely, according as they are protruded, to enlarge the cavity, or retracted to reduce it. They may also form, as we shall see later, cavities of their own, for the production of certain consonants.

Types of Sound Produced

Having thus briefly surveyed the vocal organs we will now make a similar examination of the various types of sound which they produce, with a view to identifying the organs which produce them, and so laying the ground for more detailed observations.

Speech sounds are generally classified under the various headings of vowels (including diphthongs) and consonants. The consonants are subdivided into voiced—those which are normally produced with the accompaniment of a laryngeal hum—and unvoiced—those which are normally merely breathed or whispered. Thus, in the English language, v, ð (*th* as in that), z and ʒ (*zh* as in pleasure) are voiced sounds, while f, θ (*th* as in thin), s, and ʃ (*sh* as in share) are unvoiced.

The consonants are further subdivided according to the position in the mouth in which they are formed, and the type of articulating movement which produces them.

But though some consonants are voiced and some unvoiced in ordinary speech, all consonants, as well as all vowels, can be clearly and recognizably articulated in a whisper. In that case the vocal cords are separated so that the cavities of the throat, mouth and nose are supplied only with turbulent instead of with pulsating air. In whispered speech all consonants are "unvoiced".

It may be said that English and most of the European and Indian languages are based on whispered speech, and that phonation—i.e. the use of the vocal cords for producing a preliminary vibration of the air so as to cause a humming sound during the articulation of the vowels or "voiced" consonants—is only an auxiliary device. From this point of view the vocal cords are not really an organ of speech—their function is to give inflexion, melody, and emotional quality to speech and song, and to increase (as we shall see) the audible range at which the voiced sounds can be heard.

The effect of phonation, in acting as a carrier-wave for the whispered vowel sounds, was illustrated by a series of simple experiments which I carried out at my home in Somerset in December, 1923, with the aid of my daughter Sylvia.

The method adopted was as follows: I stood at a fixed spot in the park and whispered, as loud as I could, eight different English vowel sounds, in succession. My daughter, with a supply of pegs, marked in turn the furthest position at which each of the vowel sounds was just recognizable—the position at which each peg was inserted being the average of a number of trials of that particular sound.

The process was then repeated, with this difference, that the various vowel sounds were now spoken (phonated) in a loud tone of voice—but not shouted. The maximum range at which the voiced vowel sounds could be recognized was similarly marked.

The distances from the source of sound to the various pegs was then paced and recorded, as in the following table, a pace being approximately one yard (actually 3·075 feet).

The experiments were carried out in the afternoon, with a a light, north-westerly wind, the direction of speech being down-wind, the ground being flat grassland.

Vowel Sound.		Range.		Increase of range due to phonation.
Phonetic Symbol.	As in Keyword.	Unvoiced (in paces).	Voiced (in paces).	
u	who	26	363	14 times.
e	men	51	950	19 ,,
ʚ	earth	55	960	17 ,,
ou	know	57	960	17 ,,
ɑ	calm	66	960 +	14 + ,,
ei	hay	69	960	14 ,,
i	eat	93	740	8 ,,
æ	hat	118	960 +	8 + ,,

FIG. 22.

It will be seen that the effect of phonation was to increase the range from 8 to 19 times. So great an increase had not been expected, and, as will be seen from the table, the exact range of the voiced a (calm) and æ (hat) could not be obtained—for at a distance of 960 yards my daughter had reached the railway (with woods beyond) which forms the boundary of the park in that direction! Incidentally, it was noticed that, even at 960 yards, my daughter and I could speak to one another so as to be understood, though it is quite clear that none of the unvoiced sounds of speech could have been audible at that distance.

The other almost equally important function of the vocal cords is as we have said to give inflexion, melody and emotional quality to human speech.

In whispered speech we have the effects of a more or less turbulent air stream passing through the vocal cavities. The acoustic effects produced are constant and invariable for the same articulatory setting of the shape, size or obstruction of the cavities. There is no possibility of varying the tone of whispered speech—it cannot be inflected—its emotional quality cannot be varied, though it may be sounded with more or less emphasis, and with varying speed of articulation.

It may be pointed out that the production of a turbulent air stream, capable of causing audible sound in its passage through the vocal cavities, is not a necessary consequence of the air flow, but depends on the form of the jet-like orifice through which it passes into the throat and mouth. Thus, it is possible so to adjust (unconsciously) the opening of the vocal cords and surrounding parts of the pharynx that a lungfull of air may be rapidly exhaled, while the tongue and lips are moved as if articulating, without any audible sound resulting.

Thus, in a series of experiments, it was found possible to exhale, during articulation, at three times the rate of that normally used in speech, without producing any audible whispered speech sounds.

In voiced speech a new power is added, namely, that of combining the articulation with a hummed note produced by the vocal cords. The pitch of the hummed note can then be varied at will, without consciously varying the whispered speech sound which accompanies it.

In this way we obtain two new gifts—the gift of Vocal Inflexion, which adds emotional significance, emphasis and variety to speech, and the gift of Song.

We have asserted that the larynx is not (at least in our language) an essential organ of speech; but in order to be sure on this point, and to justify the assumption which has been generally (but not universally) made that the vowel sounds are essentially due to resonance in the vocal cavities, it was thought advisable to make a simple preliminary experiment.

This consisted in blowing with a pair of bellows into the mouth while shaping it as for the pronunciation of the succession of vowels **a** (calm), **ei** (hay), **i** (eat), **ɔ** (all), and **u** (who). It was found that not only all these vowels but also the remaining vowels and all the consonants, except the nasals **m**, **n**, and **ŋ** (*ng*) could be recognizably produced as whispered sounds by blowing air into or better still across the open mouth, while the larynx remained inoperative and the breath was "held" so that no air passed into the mouth from the windpipe.

It was plain, therefore, that all these sounds, when whispered, are simply produced in the mouth and throat. Exactly how they are produced, and what is the essential difference between the various speech sounds, were questions to which, as yet, no clear answer had been or could be given. There was evidently room for an intensive investigation of the acoustic nature of the speech sounds, and as all the essentials of these sounds were found in whispered (unvoiced) speech, it was generally obvious that the investigation should, in the first instance, be directed to the unvoiced sounds.

CHAPTER III

OBSERVATIONS ON THE VOWEL RESONANCES

My personal interest in vowel sounds dates from about the year 1887 when, as an undergraduate at Magdalen College, Oxford, I first noticed the almost startling effect of the changing overtones when a succession of different vowels is intoned on the same note.

The Chaplain at Magdalen in those days was the Rev. Horace Evelyn Clayton, M.A., his voice was melodious and resonant, and when he intoned the services in Chapel the harmonics of the note on which he was intoning varied with each change of vowel and performed bugle-calls of an almost militant character.

These changing harmonics were so loud and clear that it was only by a conscious effort that one could hear the fixed fundamental note from which they all sprang.

These observations were not followed up at the time, and it was only in 1915 that, as Secretary of Section II (Submarine and Electrical) of the Admiralty Board of Invention, I had occasion to make further use of the method of analysing sounds by ear.

During this period a few observations were carried out on the resonances of my own voice; but the times were not favourable for such peaceful investigations. They were, moreover, found to be difficult and to require complete freedom from disturbances, and a high degree of concentration on the part of the observer; it was necessary therefore to await a more suitable opportunity.

Eventually, in November of 1921, the occasion offered itself. Being alone in London, confined to bed with a slight chill, and disinclined to read, it occurred to me to try and listen to the whispered resonances of my own voice, as I had begun to do during the war.

The work required no appliances but pencil and paper, for though I have not got the faculty of recognizing instinctively the "absolute pitch" of any musical sound, I can always identify any note—within less than a semitone—by mentally comparing it with a fixed note which I literally carry in my head.

This head-note is a ♯g″ of about 812 vibrations per second—see Fig. 23—which I hear on tapping my skull just above either ear. Another independent head-note, b″ 966~—3 semitones higher than the first—is heard when I tap the centre of my forehead. These head-notes, which apparently are due to vibrations of portions of the skull, constitute two natural tuning forks, of seemingly invariable pitch, which I have used as my standard throughout these investigations.

FIG. 23.

The Unvoiced Vowel Sounds

At first the observations were very difficult—mainly owing to the fact that, to recognize the resonances of the whispered vowel sounds, it was necessary to hear these sounds not as vowels but as new musical effects heard for the first time.[1] The very fact of their familiarity as speech sounds made them almost impossible at first to analyse as musical sounds. Various expedients were tried such as putting one's head under the bedclothes, and stopping the ears so as to hear only internal sounds; indeed, I listened so hard to the sounds in my mouth that the strain produced a feeling of sickness. Gradually the perception grew, and as each vowel sound was whispered in turn, the combination was recognized of two faint but definitely musical notes—a different pair of notes for each vowel sound. The similar observations of Graham Bell and Dr. R. J. Lloyd were then unknown to me.

Having made a note of the resonances of the whispered and of some voiced vowels, I sent it to my friend Sir William Bragg, in case it might be of scientific interest. Sir William very kindly forwarded it to Professor Daniel Jones, of the Phonetic Department at University College, London, who then told me that the lower resonances of the vowels ɑ (calm), ɒ (not), ɔ (all), ou (no), u (who), and ʊ (put) were not generally recognized. It was largely owing to his encouragement that I was led to make a more serious study of the subject.

[1] The Audiogram of the Author's hearing as measured at the Bell Telephone Laboratory, New York, in 1927, is reproduced in Appendix III.

VOWEL RESONANCES

The next step was to classify the resonances heard and to see to what extent they were liable to vary at different trials.

The 14 vowel sounds of English—as spoken by myself in " Southern English " or " Public School " pronunciation—were then arranged in order so that their upper and lower resonances when charted on a scale of musical semitones gave, as far as possible, two continuous series.

The results are shown in the accompanying chart :—

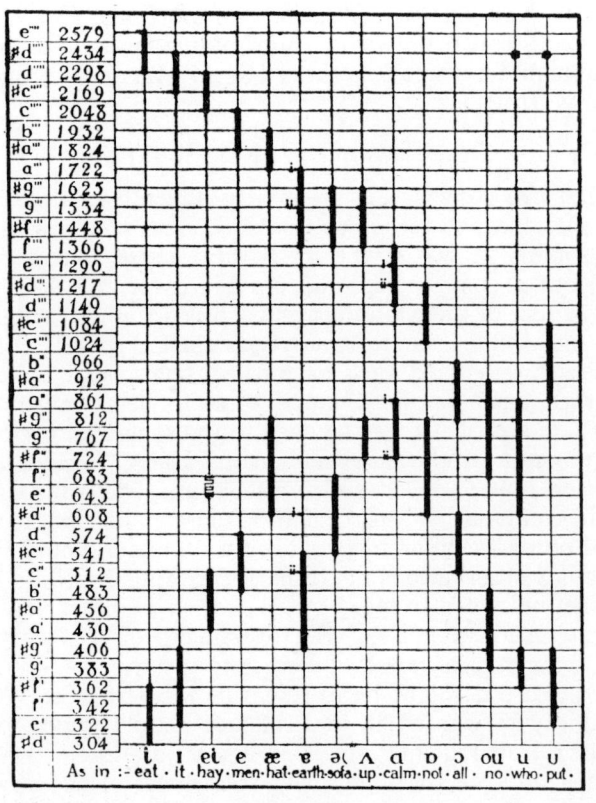

FIG. 24.

The vertical scale on the left-hand side of the chart represents a chromatic scale (i.e. a scale of equal semitones) extending over three octaves. The two thickened vertical lines, one above the other, which are drawn respectively over each of the

VOWEL RESONANCES

vowel symbols i (eat), ɪ (it), eɪ (hay), etc., represent the musical range over which the upper and lower resonances of that vowel were observed to vary at different trials. It will be seen that these variations cover a range of from 3 to 7 semitones in different cases.

It should perhaps be pointed out that, at the time when these observations were first made, I knew very little of the early history of the subject, which has been set out in a previous chapter.

Probably it is well that at the outset no attempt was made to master the subject; for if it had been, I should almost certainly have given up all hope of being able to carry it any further! Too much knowledge may sometimes also be a dangerous thing.

During the next three months the investigation of the vowel resonances of my own voice continued.[1] It appeared that it was possible to produce simultaneously two continuous series of notes due to resonance in the vocal cavities and that these series were practically independent of one another. One series had a range from about ♯d″ 608 to e″″ 2579, the other had a range of ♯d′ 304 to ♯a″ 912.[2]

Fig. 25.

The upper series was much more easily heard than the lower series—the upper notes being not unlike softly whistled or rather half-whistled notes not quite made to "speak". It was found that these notes could be made (all except the

---

[1] See the author's *Vowel Resonances*, International Phonetic Association (pamphlet), 24th March, 1922.
[2] The ranges of upper and lower mouth resonances shown in Fig. 14 on p. 25, are increased by 4 or 5 semitones, to include results obtained with other voices.

E

lower notes of the series) with the mouth in any attitude from wide open to nearly closed. The lower notes could only be produced by partially closing the lips. The pitch of the note produced appeared to depend mainly on the extent to which the tongue was moved up or down and forward or backward inside the mouth. The pitch was raised if the tongue was moved forwards or upwards, and lowered by moving it down or back.

The method of tuning the lower series of notes was less easy to follow, but was supposed to depend, in part, on movements of the back of the tongue; it evidently depended, to some extent also, on the size of the opening made by the lips or between the tongue and the roof of the mouth.

Various devices were tried for making the two series of resonances audible, such as tapping the front of the upper front teeth with the butt end of a pencil, drawing the breath rapidly in and out—for the upper series, and flicking or tapping the side of the throat to emphasze the lower series or releasing the breath suddenly by a glottal " click ". [1]

It was found that both resonances could be made quite audible by the music-hall trick of clapping the hands immediately in front of the mouth—so as to drive sharp puffs of air into it and so awake its resonances.

The best method of doing this appeared to be to hold, say, the left hand—with thumb and first finger widely extended and palm up—firmly against the chin, with the fingers pointing to the left, so that the edge of the palm, near the root of the thumb, formed, as it were, a continuation of the under lip. The palm of this hand was then gently but firmly clapped with the four fingers of the right hand, these fingers being held close together and in line with the fingers of the left hand. The effect of this manœuvre was to drive a sharp jet of air from between the palm of the left hand and the fingers of the right hand, into the mouth at each clap.

If the tongue was held up against the roof of the mouth (as if about to release the consonant K), a single note was produced, which varied in pitch according as the tongue was moved forwards, to raise the pitch, or backwards to lower it. A scale of about two octaves could be thus produced.

[1] The method of identifying vocal resonances by percussion of " Adam's Apple " was used by F. Auerbach in 1878. *Wied. Ann.*, vol. iii, p. 152. The method of tapping the cheeks and the use of an external air jet blown into the mouth were used by O. Abraham in 1916. *Z.S. fur Psychol.*, vol. lxxiv.

VOWEL RESONANCES

If the tongue was held in position for making a *vowel* sound, the *two* resonances of the vowel were heard together. Resonances of 1,448 vibrations per second [1] and over were faint, but still audible—the remainder of the vowel resonances could be made quite loud if the clapping was done correctly. It was discovered that, with a little practice, the two resonant scales could be independently controlled, quite apart from their vowel association. In this way it was possible, for example, to keep one note of either series constant, while the other series was made to execute a scale, or even to make both series perform scales in " contrary motion "—the one series playing up while the other played down !

The two series may be made to converge towards a note between 724 (f♯, treble clef) and 812 (g♯, treble clef) but I cannot be certain whether they actually come into unison (as I have stated in 1922) [2] or whether the sound produced at this resonant pitch, really consists of a single note of which no overtone was audible. The nearest *approach* of the resonances which I have been able definitely to detect was 812 for the lower resonance, and 912 (two semitones higher) for the upper. This produced a vowel rather like ɒ (not)— the mouth being then very nearly a plain tube, with the tongue flattened at the root as much as possible. A discussion on this point will be found in Appendix No. I.

Turning now to the vowel resonances themselves, it will be seen from the chart that many of the vowels in my own speech have either an upper or a lower resonance range in common. But in that case their other resonances are always well separated. For example, the vowels ɞ (earth), ə (as in Sof*a*, or th*e* King) and ʌ (up) all have an *upper* resonance between 1366 and 1625 or a semitone higher. Thus, 1534 would be a good average value for all three vowels. But their lower resonances are quite different, and form, as the chart shows, an ascending series, with steps of four or five semitones between ɞ and ə and between ə and ʌ respectively.

In the *lower* series, ɪ (it) and ʊ (put) have identical resonance ranges ; but their upper resonances are about fifteen semitones apart. In fact, the pair of resonances for each vowel is quite characteristic, and enables its pronunciation to be identified and recorded. Speech—so far as vowel sounds are concerned—

---

[1] See Fig. 24 at p. 42.
[2] "Vowel Resonances," International Phonetic Association, 1922.

46 VOWEL RESONANCES

could therefore be scored like music, the only difficulty being to find artistes to read and render the two-part score!

For example, the following sentence—which might have been addressed to Toricelli, the original discoverer (in the year 1643) of the weight and pressure of the atmosphere—as *whispered* in my own pronunciation, consists entirely of vowel sounds, counting *w* and *y* as vowels.

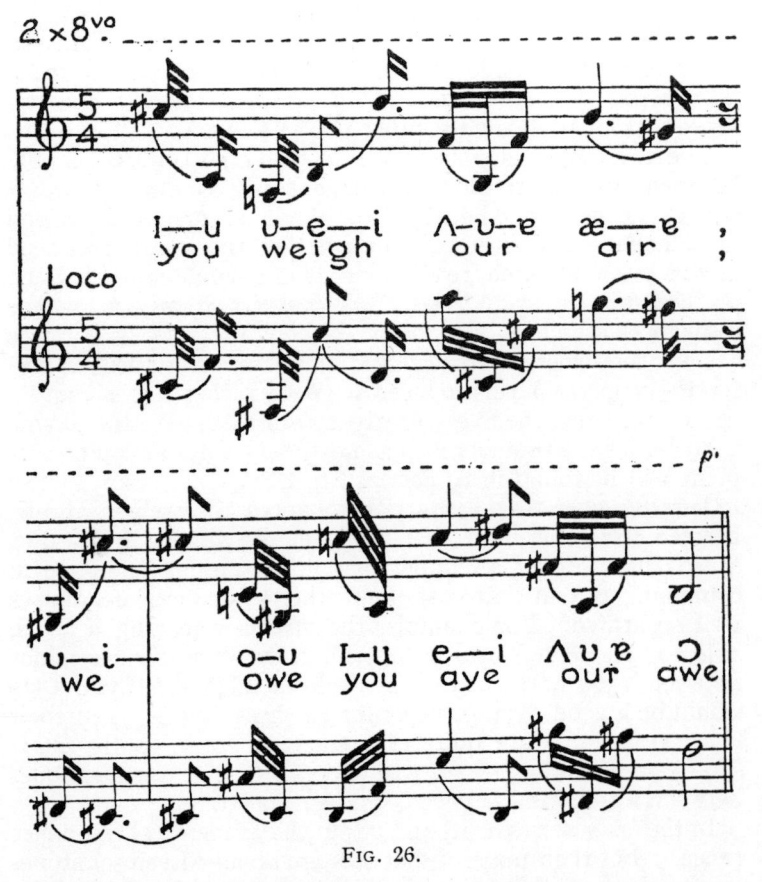

FIG. 26.

The resonances of these have been recorded, and are here transcribed in musical notation, as evidence, capable of verification, of the essentially musical nature even of whispered speech.[1]

[1] The faint, high resonances, which are also heard in many of the whispered vowels, are omitted in this transcription.

VOWEL RESONANCES

We now come to the question of the voiced vowel sounds—in which the resonances of the vocal cavities are energized by a laryngeal hum.

The voiced sounds, produced by the vibrations of the vocal cords, are quite independent of the whispered or half-whistled sounds due to resonances in the vocal cavity. This can be conclusively demonstrated by the device of whistling and humming at the same time. The pitch of a whistled note depends on the resonance of the cavity made between the front of the tongue and the lips; the smaller this cavity the higher the note; the opening of the lips is kept more or less constant. With practice, it is quite possible to whistle a scale up and hum a scale down at the same time, or to hum and whistle two parts in harmony [1]—or otherwise!

If we compare the series of vowel resonances already recorded with those found by previous observers, various differences will be found. An investigation of some of these may be of interest.

In Ellis' translation of Helmholtz' book [2] he gives a table of examples. The earlier observers only noticed a single resonance for each vowel. Even Helmholtz found no second "proper tone" for the vowels u, ɔ (more), ɒ (not), ʌ (up), and ɑ (calm). Neither did Dr. Aikin,[3] whose "Resonator Scale" shows single resonances for the vowels from ɑ to u, nor did D. C. Miller,[4] who by purely instrumental analysis arrives at the same conclusions. The question of single or double resonances will be dealt with in Chapter V.

On the other hand, Graham Bell believed that all the vowels were characterized by double resonance, and Lloyd, as we have seen, actually recorded them, for nearly all the vowels mentioned by him.

There are three reasons which, taken together, are probably sufficient to account for the discrepancies noted by Ellis in the vowel resonances recorded by different observers. In the first place those who were investigating (as they thought) single resonances may have actually heard either of the two

---

[1] At the Toronto meeting of the British Association, August, 1924, my daughter, now Mrs. Chancellor, who assisted me, joined in a quartette for two performers. She whistled the treble part and hummed the tenor, I whistled the alto and hummed the bass.
[2] *Sensations of Tone*, translated by Ellis, 1885, p. 109.
[3] *The Voice: An Introduction to Practical Phonology*, by W. A. Aikin, M.D.
[4] *The Science of Musical Sounds*, New York and London, 1916.

components which were really present. In the second place the resonant pitch of any given vowel is, as we have seen, not a fixed note. The actual pitch for each resonance may, and does, vary by several semitones at different trials or when the vowel is used in different words, or with different degrees of mouth opening. Lastly there is an unexpected difficulty in identifying by ear the actual octave in whch a whistled or half-whistled note should be placed in relation to notes produced by the vibration of the vocal cords.

We normally imagine that a whistled note is an octave lower than it really is. Thus Helmholtz's single resonance for u (173) is evidently written an octave too low and should be $173 \times 2 = 346$, which compares well with the lower resonance at 362 in my own voice. In the same way Dr. Aikin's transcription of the upper resonances must (as already mentioned) be transposed an octave higher, though the lower resonances which he records are correct.

The reason for the difficulty of identifying the octave of whistled notes arises, I imagine, from the fact that they are made by two different organs of naturally different ranges of pitch and that, in many cases at least, the observer cannot actually produce the same note by both methods. In my own case it is only by singing a high falsetto, that I can reach up to the lower notes of my whistling range [1]—the two series overlapping between about c″ 572 and ♯g″ 812. Thus, by comparing a low whistled note and a high (falsetto) voiced note, the absolute pitch of the whistled note can be made certain. Observers who either cannot sing so high or whistle so low must find a serious difficulty in comparing the two ranges.

Voiced Vowel Sounds

So far we have considered only the resonances of the vowel sounds when breathed or whispered. When, while shaping the vocal cavity as for the production of a whispered vowel, we bring the vocal cords into action, so that a laryngeal tone is superadded to the breathed vowel, a more complex effect is produced.

The resonances of the cavity as a whole are aroused not by intermittent disturbances due to the turbulent flow of air

[1] See Fig. 14 at p. 25.

VOWEL RESONANCES

through the cavity, but by a succession of sharp rhythmical impulses. These impulses succeed one another at a rate per second which may or may not bear a numerical relation to the natural rates of vibration of the air within the cavity.

There has been great controversy in the past as to this relation, but for the purpose we have in hand it is not necessary to enter into it now. We are concerned rather with what actually happens in the human mouth when a vowel is voiced. The experiment was tried of singing a chromatic scale to various vowel sounds in turn, and listening to the vowel resonances which resulted as the larynx note was progressively raised in pitch. The result was unexpected. In the case of vowels with a high pitched upper resonance like i as in eat (2298) or the French vowel u as in *tu* (2084) the same high pitched resonance could be heard throughout, while the larynx note was progressively raised by semitones through the octave from ♯G (102) to ♯g (204). Similarly, in the case of the vowel ɞ (earth), with resonances g‴ 1534 and ♯g′ 406, both resonances remained constant throughout the chromatic scale. In this case the lower resonances were heard by flicking the throat—between the ear and the larynx—while singing the successive notes of the chromatic scale.

When, however, the same experiment was tried with vowels of a lower upper-resonance, a different result was found. For example, in the case of the vowel ɑ, as in calm, with resonances 1149 and 724 the upper resonance was found to vary at each semitone rise of the larynx note, though the lower resonance appeared to remain constant. The upper resonances observed were as follows:—

Vowel Sound.	Larynx Note.	Upper Resonance.
ɑ as in calm	♯G 102	d‴ 1149
	A 108	♯d‴ 1217
	♯A 114	d‴ 1149
(lower resonance	B 121	♯d‴ 1217
♯f″ 724)	c 128	d‴ 1149
	♯c 135	♯d‴ 1217
	d 144	d‴ 1149

FIG. 27.

It will be seen that the upper resonance alternated between d''' and ♯d''' as the larynx note went up the chromatic scale. In the case of the vowel ou, as in the first part of the diphthong in the word " no ", the results were as follows :—

Vowel Sound.	Larynx Note.	Upper Resonance.	Harmonic Relation.
ou as in No	♯G 102	♯f'' 724	7th
	A 108	g'' 767	7th
	♯A 114	♯g'' 812	7th
	B 121	♯f 724 + ♯a'' 912	6th + O.
(lower	c 128	g'' 767	6th
resonance	♯c 135	f'' 683 or a'' 861	5th or O.
♯g' 406)	d 144	♯f'' 724	5th
	♯d 152	♯g'' 812 ⎫	⎧ Interval 2¼
	e 161	a'' 861 ⎭	⎩ Octaves.
	f 171	f'' 683	4th
	♯f 181	♯f'' 724	4th
	g 182	g'' 767	4th

FIG. 28.

In this case, therefore, the upper resonance varied from f'' 683 to ♯a'' 912, i.e. over a range of six semitones—corresponding exactly with the range of variation already observed for the (whispered) upper resonance of the vowel in question. It also appears that, of the 14 upper resonances heard, 10 were actual harmonics of the larynx tone, i.e. their frequency of vibration was a numerical multiple of that of the larynx note.[1]

In two of the remaining cases the relation, though not harmonic, was musically a simple one, namely an interval of 2 octaves and a fourth; in the last remaining cases there was apparently no simple relation between the larynx note and the upper resonance heard.

One further series of observations should be mentioned in this connection. It was seen that, in the case of vowels of

---

[1] The numerical notation of vibrations per second used is that of the " equal temperament " scale (as commonly used for the piano), in which the relation between the notes is not truly harmonic. For this reason the upper resonances do not appear to be exact multiples of the larynx frequencies.

high resonant pitch (2298, 2048, and 1534) this pitch remained constant while the larynx note was raised, by steps of a semitone at a time, from 102 to 204.

The experiment was made to see how far this condition lasted, and at what stage—in the musical relation of larynx note to upper resonance—the upper resonance began to vary with the rise of the larynx note.

A vowel with resonances 1366 and 406, which would be described phonetically as a " slightly advanced u "—was sung on a chromatic scale from ♯C 68 to ♯d′ 304—i.e. through a range of two octaves and two semitones. It was found that from ♯C 68 to ♯c′ 271 the upper resonance remained constant at 1366, but that, at the next rise of the larynx pitch (to d′ 287), the upper resonance rose to ♯f‴ 1448, and to g‴ 1534 at the succeeding larynx note (♯d′ 304). In this case therefore the upper resonance was constant until the larynx note had approached within 2 octaves and 4 semitones, after which the upper resonance became variable. Similarly, in the case of a vowel of resonances 1024 and 304 (a very forward variety of u) sung from ♯G 51 to e 161, the upper resonance was constant up to a larynx note of ♯G 102—the interval between larynx note and upper resonance being then 3 octaves and 4 semitones—after which the upper resonance became variable.

It thus appears that, provided the larynx note and the upper resonance are sufficiently far apart, e.g. not less than $2\frac{1}{3}$ octaves, the upper resonance is constant, while at a lesser interval it becomes variable. This may be because the higher harmonics of the larynx note—from the 7th upwards—form (as is well known) a continuous scale. Thus taking C (64) as the fundamental note, the harmonics (or bugle-notes) form the series :—

1	2	3	4	5	6	7	8	9	10	11	12
C	c	g	c′	e′	g′	♭b′	c″	d″	e″	♯f″	g″

Fig. 29.

At an interval approaching 3 octaves, therefore, there will always be a convenient harmonic within short range to which the upper resonance may conform ; whereas when the interval is less, the harmonics are much more widely spaced, and the upper resonance has to go hunting for the nearest harmonic to which to adapt itself.

It would seem that in some cases it fails altogether in its quest, and the upper resonance then becomes independent of the harmonics of the larynx note. We shall revert to this matter in connection with the question of voice production in Chapter X.

To confirm the view that vowel character is entirely a question of the pitch of the resonances of the vocal cavity, the experiment was tried of altering the resonances by adding artificially to the capacity of the cavity.

For this purpose a hollow resonator about 70 mm. (say $2\frac{3}{4}$ inches) long was modelled in plasticine,[1] with a mouth piece 27 mm. (about 1 inch) in diameter, shaped to fit against the operator's mouth, and with a smaller lateral orifice 7 mm. ($\frac{1}{4}$ inch) in diameter for the escape of the voice. The natural pitch of this resonator, with both its orifices open was C''' 1024. When this extra "capacity" was added during the breathing or voicing of various vowels the following effects were observed :—

ɑ (calm) with the added capacity became rather like ɔ (awe).
æ (hat) with the added capacity became rather like ɑ (calm).
ʌ (up) with the added capacity became a sound between ɞ (earth) and o.
ɒ (not) with the added capacity became rather like ɔ (awe).
ou (no) with the added capacity became rather like u (who).
i (eat) with the added capacity became rather like French u (tu).
eɪ (hay) with the added capacity became rather like ø (peu)
ɞ (earth) with the added capacity became rather like u (who).

FIG. 30.

In order to investigate more systematically the method by which the vocal resonances are produced, it was decided to make a vocal cavity entirely of plasticine, so that the effects of changing form might be studied in detail and under conditions which could be kept constant. An account of these experiments forms the subject of the next Chapter.

[1] A modelling clay, invented by Mr. Harbutt, which retains its plasticity over long periods.

Chapter IV

EXPERIMENTS WITH MODELS. (VOWELS)

The artificial vocal cavity with which the first experiments were made is shown in Fig. 31.[1]

It was, as will be seen, a very rough imitation of the interior of a human mouth and was approximately full size. It had a small mouth orifice and a fixed "tongue" (made by pushing up the floor of the model from below), but instead of the elaborations of soft palate—uvula—epiglottis and pharynx, it had a simplified bulbous back cavity, of approximately the same estimated capacity as that of the space between the vocal cords and the back of the hard palate of a small sized human mouth. The first model was found to produce two resonances, which were heard as faint, half-whistled, notes

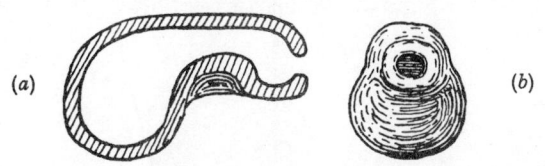

Fig. 31.—(a) and (b).—Original ɜ (earth) model, No. 1 (without larynx) : (a) Section ; (b) Front elevation.

when air was blown across the mouth of the model. The notes observed were ♯a‴ 1824 and ♯g′ 406, which, by comparison with the vowel chart on page 42, will be seen to be very near those of the vowel ɜ (earth), the lower resonance being just within the lower range, and the upper resonance one semitone above the upper range of the charted resonances. There were no means of voicing this model, but it gave a sound like a whispered ɜ (earth) when blown across.

At this stage no preconceived ideas were entertained as to how the two resonances were produced. The immediate object was to test the effects of various changes of shape and openings, such as might be produced in the human mouth and

[1] *Proceedings of the Royal Society A.*, vol. cii, p. 752 et seq.

throat. By finding out how to tune the model and make it give any desired pair of resonances, it was hoped to discover also the principles by which the corresponding process is performed in the human vocal cavity. At the outset the mistake was made of altering more than one characteristic at a time. My experimental notes show that, by raising the tongue upwards and forwards, reducing the projection of the lips and enlarging the mouth from 7 mm. × 8 mm. to 19 mm. × 8 mm. (say ¾" by ⅜"), the resonances were altered to ♯d''' 2434 and ♯f' 362. In other words the upper resonance had gone up 5 semitones while the lower one had gone down 2 semitones.

The model now was found to give, as would have been expected, a clear breathed or whispered 'i' (eat) when blown

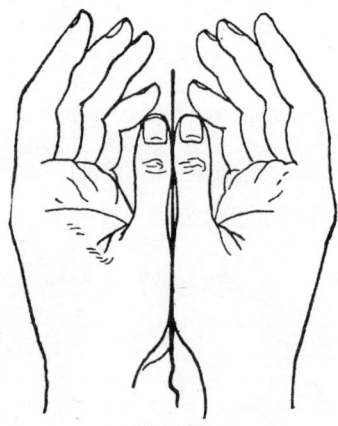

FIG. 32.

across the mouth. But how the resonances had been changed by the various alterations was not, then, clear.

A second similar model was made and tuned, by trial and error, to the resonances a''' 1722 and ♯f'' 724—corresponding to the charted resonances of æ (hat). This model also gave the correct whispered vowel when blown across the mouth; and a further improved æ on retuning, by trial and error, so as to raise the upper resonance one semitone to 1824 and lower the other resonance 3 semitones to 608.

At this point the experiments with plasticine models were interrupted, with a view to devising some convenient form of reed or artificial larynx to attach to the models, so that they

VOWELS

might produce "voiced" instead of whispered sounds. The construction adopted was suggested by the type of squeaker with which most boys have experimented, made by holding a blade of grass between one's two thumbs, so that it lies parallel with the thumbs and edgewise across the lenticular opening formed between them. (See Fig. 32.)

On blowing through the opening between the thumbs, the blade is set in vibration from side to side in the opening and produces a loud musical note.

In the present instance, the blade of grass was replaced by a thin indiarubber strip, and the gap, in which it vibrated, was a lenticular hole cut in a piece of paraffin wax—actually a candle end—shaped as shown in the figure. (See Fig. 33.)

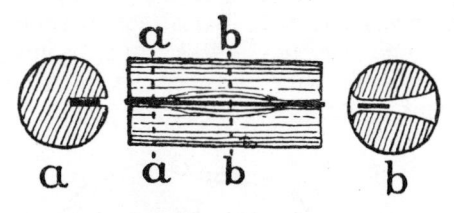

Fig. 33.

This "artificial larynx" was then joined up to a hole in the back of the model by means of a plasticine casing and passage, shown in section in Fig. 34.

It was found that, with this type of reed, the pitch of the reed-note could be varied over about one octave, by simply varying the air pressure by which it is blown—provided the rubber strip was of such length, and so fixed at either end, that its vibrating part was slightly longer than the width of the passage across which it lay. If the rubber strip was at all stretched, its note could be but little altered by variations of air pressure. With a well adjusted reed of this type it was quite easy to "hum" simple tunes by (unconsciously) varying the air pressure supplied by the performer's lungs to the reed.

When the artificial larynx or reed, just described, was attached to a hole made in the back of the "i" (eat) model, the resonances were found to have changed from 2434/362 to 2434/456 and the voiced sound, which was produced on blowing the model, was not "i" (eat) but more like a muffled ɐ (earth).

The reason, (which was not appreciated at the time), doubtless was that the air passage through the larynx was sufficiently large to act as a substantial orifice and thus raise the resonances of the back portion of the model till they were beyond the limits of those of the vowel "i" and within those of the vowel "æ". In the case of the model which produced the whispered æ (hat) this, when fitted with a rubber strip reed, gave a "fairly distinguishable" voiced æ, best heard as wæ wæ (like the first part of the word "whack") when the mouth opening was intermittently closed (partially) and released by hand during blowing. The resonances were 1824/608.

This same model was again altered, by "trial and error"—the upper resonance being lowered from 1824 to 1722 while the lower resonance remained unchanged at 608.

The vowel sound was now like ɞ (earth) though the upper resonance was one semitone higher, and the lower resonance two semitones higher, than those observed in my own voice. A section of this model is shown in Fig. 34.[1]

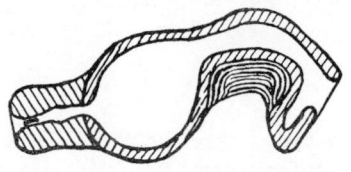

FIG. 34.

So far, the tuning of the models had been done by trial and error; there were always two audible resonances, but the principle on which the pitch of each of them depended was not understood.

A series of experiments was carried out to discover the proper method of tuning. The plan adopted was to make a succession of small progressive changes—e.g. of the mouth opening—and note, each time, the effects produced on both resonances. Similar trials were made by varying the position of the "tongue", up or down and forward or backward in the mouth.

In this way it was found, for example, that reducing the mouth opening lowered both resonances.

[1] In its original form the larynx was attached to the underside instead of in the rear of the back cavity. The fact of changing its position did not appreciably affect the vowel sound.

VOWELS

Again, a forward movement of the front of the tongue to the position shown in dotted lines at A (Fig. 35) raised the upper resonance and lowered the lower resonance. A backward movement of the back of the tongue to position B lowered the upper resonance and raised the lower resonance.

When both changes were made together the model was restored to its original resonances, so far as pitch was concerned, but the volume of the cavity, as a whole, was reduced while the passage way became lengthened; in consequence of this the resonances were less pronounced.

It was obvious that, from a voice production point of view, the passage way should be short and the resonators on either side of it large; also that the same pair of resonances (so far as pitch is concerned) could be made in different ways, so as to give more or less volume of resonance. It now became possible to tune a model systematically with a reasonable hope of arriving at the pair of resonances required.

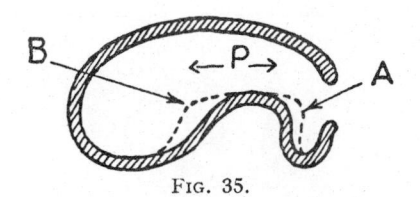

FIG. 35.

The attempt was next made to produce a model, giving the vowel ɑ, as in calm, with resonances 1217/767 or 724. It was constructed, in a less mouth-shaped form than the others, out of plasticine rolled out into thin sheets and built up into a hollow elongated box-shape, with parallel sides, getting wider towards the open end, and with a flat top and floor. A slight semblance of a tongue was formed by pushing up the floor from below. This model originally gave 1024 [1]/683—corresponding to the resonances of ɒ (not). It was progressively tuned—by varying the position of the tongue, the opening of the mouth and the capacity behind the tongue—till it gave the resonances 1217/812. The vowel sound was then a recognizable ɑ (calm)—the resonances of the model being—as will be seen—within the ranges actually charted for this vowel, though the lower resonance (812) was a semitone higher

[1] This resonance and the succeeding ones of this experiment were originally recorded as an octave higher.

than that originally intended. A section of the model is shown in Fig. 36.

This experiment, which was made about 23rd February, 1922, was the first in which a vowel-sounding model was designed, so as to give a pair of predetermined resonances.

FIG. 36.

In view of the experiments already described, in which vowel sounds made by mouth were modified by adding artificially to the capacity of the vocal cavity, a similar experiment was tried with the models which gave ɞ (earth) and a (calm).

The additional capacity used is shown at Fig. 37: its resonance, with both orifices open, was 1024.

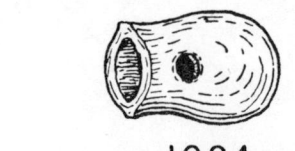

1024∼
FIG. 37.

FIG. 38.

This " capacity " was then attached to the mouth of the original ɞ (earth) model 1722/608, as shown in Fig. 38, and produced a " fairly well defined u "(as in who), the resonances being 812/342, which compared well with the charted resonances.

A similar capacity attached to the a (calm) model (1217/812) gave a fairly good o (no) with resonances 1084/383, the upper

VOWELS

resonance being 3 semitones too high while the lower resonance was correct.

It was found that a fairly good u could also be made by blowing, by mouth, through a rubber larynx attached to a single ovoid (egg-shaped) resonator (see Fig. 39), but that the production of the vowel sound then depended on the capacity given to the operator's mouth ! In other words the resonances

FIG. 39.

were partly produced in the cavity *behind* the artificial larynx. If the cavity of the mouth was reduced, the u sound was lost. When the ovoid resonator was blown by bellows, no u was produced; but on interposing a plasticine cavity between the nozzle of the bellows and the rubber "larynx", the u character was more or less restored. An additional resonator (giving 912 with both orifices open), was now attached in front of the ovoid resonator, and gave a fairly good u, whether blown by mouth or by bellows.

Finally, two separate resonators were joined, and systematically tuned, by varying the size of the front orifice and by cutting out or inserting transverse slices in the cylindrical portions of the two resonators, so as to vary the capacities of these resonators. At 608/362 this model, which is shown in Fig. 40, gave a good u.

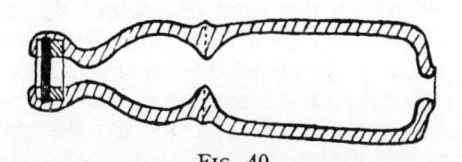

FIG. 40.

In this model the higher resonance (608) was produced by the back cavity and vice versa—an effect which also appears to occur in the human mouth in the case of the vowels ɑ (calm), ɒ (not), ɔ (all), ou (no) u (who) and ʊ (put).

The next model was one intended to give the vowel i as in eat. It was found that to obtain the high upper resonance

F

2298 to 2579, characteristic of i, the orifice between the back and front cavities should be narrow and that the front cavity should be short and open-mouthed.

Figs. 41 and 42 show two forms of this model, the latter one, Fig. 42, with the narrower internal orifice and resonances 2579/322 giving the better vowel.

Experiment was made with a rectangular model, built up out of rolled out sheets of plasticine, with the object of making a double resonator which could be easily reproduced in wood. The vowel sound intended was u (who). The resonances of the front and back cavities were made to match those of the former u model—which was taken apart for the purpose—and the two rectangular cavities when combined gave a good u. This was further improved by altering the capacity of the two resonators

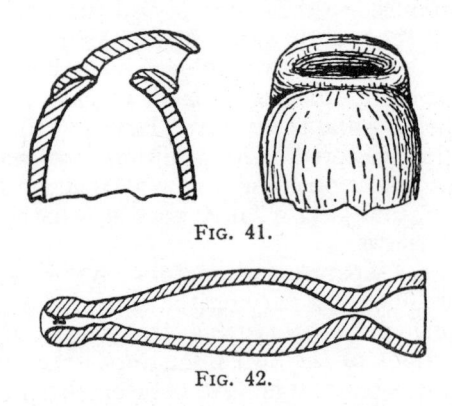

FIG. 41.

FIG. 42.

so as to give resonances of 645/383; the higher pitch being, as before, produced by the back resonator.

By this time the principle of vowel formation was becoming clear: there must be in effect two resonating cavities, each producing a separate resonance; provided these resonances are correct, neither the exact shape, cross section or length of the cavities are material; the two cavities behave like two Helmholtz resonators joined together in series.[1]

As a test of this theory, a model was designed to produce the vowel eɪ as in "hay" (first part of the diphthong), with resonances 2048 to 2298 and 430 to 512 respectively. The

[1] This statement is only strictly true (for full-size models) in the case of the vowels whose upper resonance is of the order of 1255 or lower. See Appendix I, Table 1.

model was made to a much smaller scale than before, and was built up from a back resonator of about $3\frac{1}{2}'' \times 1\frac{1}{2}''$ with an orifice $\frac{3}{8}''$ in diameter, which gave 512, and a small back orifice for the artificial larynx, and a funnel-shaped front resonator with a $\frac{3}{8}''$ back orifice giving 2048.

When these two resonators were joined so that their $\frac{3}{8}''$ orifices coincided, it was found that the pitch of both resonators had been affected by the junction. The front resonator had dropped in pitch by 2 semitones (from 2048 to 1824) while the back resonator had become lowered by 5 semitones (512 to 383).

The back resonance was then corrected, by enlarging the central (common) orifice, so as to raise its pitch by 4 semitones to 483; the front resonance was evidently raised too much by the enlargement of its back orifice, for it is recorded that the front funnel was "slightly lengthened" so as to give 2048.

FIG. 43.

The model—see Fig. 43—the resonances of which had been observed entirely by tapping the resonators—was now blown and gave a good voiced eɪ (hay) at the first trial; when the mouth of this model was closed by hand, air pressure applied to the "larynx", and the mouth closure released, closed and released again, the model articulated the word "Baby" (bei-bei).

This was the first of a series of models which were made, on the same principle, to produce the vowels ʌ (up), ɔ (all), ou (no), with resonances reversed (the upper resonance being produced by the back cavity), ɒ (not), e (men), ɪ (it), and ɑ (calm).

Fig. 44 shows a set of these models mounted on the late Lord Rayleigh's experimental organ at the Royal Institution, which was shown at a conversazione on 16th February, 1923.

To provide for the lowering of pitch which occurs—as already described—when two resonators are joined together, an allowance was made in the resonators *before* joining up, i.e. they were tuned higher than their ultimate pitch, and were finally corrected, after joining up, by adjusting the size of the central and front orifices respectively, or, in some cases, by pressing in the walls of the back cavity to raise its pitch. The alternative of enlarging the central orifice had a much greater effect in raising also the pitch of the front resonator.

Fig. 45 shows an ʌ (up) model 1534/812, Fig. 46 an ou (no) 406/861, Fig. 47 a second ou with resonances reversed 912/456, Fig. 48 an ɞ (earth) 1534/512 and Fig. 49 an ɑ (calm) 1366/724 from which the construction of the series will be readily understood.

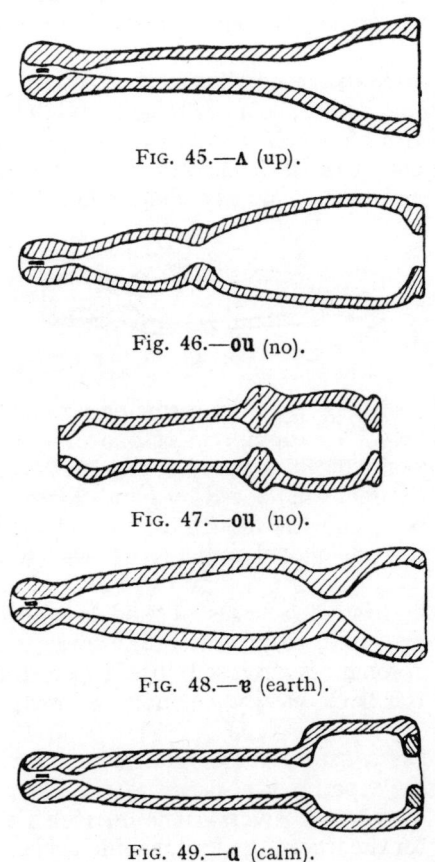

FIG. 45.—ʌ (up).

Fig. 46.—ou (no).

FIG. 47.—ou (no).

FIG. 48.—ɞ (earth).

FIG. 49.—ɑ (calm).

A word may be said here on the general effect of joining resonators in series, since this is an operation which must equally occur in the formation of vowels by resonance in the human mouth. The pitch of a Helmholtz resonator depends, as has already been explained, on the relation between the volume of the resonator and the size of its orifice or orifices, or, in the case of a bottle-necked orifice, on the length of its neck. Thus a smaller orifice or a longer neck both act as an acoustic impedance, so as to retard the natural rate of surging of the air in and out of the orifice.

If an orifice of a resonator A, which previously opened to the outer air, is joined up to the similar orifice of another resonator B, its freedom of action is at once limited, and in consequence the rate of surging of the air in A will be diminished, to an extent which depends on the characteristics of the resonator B. If B is very large compared to A there may be hardly any difference between the impeding effect of the air in B and that of the open air. The smaller B is made relative to A, the greater will be its effect on the resonance of A.

In the case of two resonators in series, with a larynx at the back of the back resonator (the larynx then acts as an almost negligible orifice), the maximum fall of pitch in the front resonator occurs when the front resonator is large, the back resonator small and the central orifice is large compared with the front orifice. A fall of 10 semitones was observed in one such case.

The least fall, in a front resonator, occurs when the front resonator is small, compared with the back resonator, and its front orifice is large compared with the central orifice.

In the case of a back resonator, the maximum fall occurs when the back resonator is large compared with the front resonator, and the central orifice is large compared with the front orifice. The minimum fall, for a back resonator, is produced when the front resonator is large compared with the back. In such case the relative size of the central and front orifices has but little effect. The action of resonators in series was investigated mathematically by the late Lord Rayleigh and his results are set out in his book on sound.[1] Further investigations by Mr. Benton appear in Appendix I of the present work.

It will be remembered that Willis, in his experiments, claimed to have produced the whole series of vowels by the use of a single cylindrical resonator of which the effective

[1] *Theory of Sound*, by Lord Rayleigh, 1894, pp. 189 to 192.

length could be varied, but that experiment with Professor Daniel Jones' apparatus did not support this claim.

In order to test this point further, a cylindrical resonator, 43 mm. internal diameter 21 cm. long, was made in plasticine, closed at one end and provided with a small aperture, in the closed end, for blowing the model.

The tube was progressively shortened, by cutting off transverse slices, 2 cm. in length, and the resonances were observed when the tube was blown after each reduction in length. The following observations were made :—

Length cm.	Resonances.		Vowel.
21	1084	383	ɜ (earth).
19	1217	430	ɜ ,,
17	1448	483	ɜ ,,
15	1534	512	between ɜ and æ (hat).
13	1824	608	æ (hat)
11	2048	683	æ ,,
9	2434	812	between ɜ (earth) and ʌ (up).

FIG. 50.

It will be seen that the plain cylindrical resonating tube produced two audible resonances.

Below 9 cm. the upper resonance became inaudible, but at 7 cm. a 1366 and 966 to 1024 was heard, giving a vowel ʌ (up), and at 3 cm. a 1625 and 1932, giving the vowel like ɪ (it).

If we represent by the letter n the number of vibrations of the fundamental given at any length between 21 and 9 cm., then the frequency of its overtone is in each case $3n$.[1] If we measure off with compasses on the vowel chart, an interval of semitones which corresponds to the relation of n to $3n$—namely 19 semitones—and apply this measure to the various vowels, it will be seen that the vowels æ, ɜ, ʌ and ᴜ can all be produced by resonances which have this numerical relation, e.g. æ at 1824/608, ɜ at 512/1534, ʌ at 1625/541 and ᴜ at 322/966.

These are, it is believed, the only vowels which can be fairly accurately produced by resonance in a plain cylinder of this

[1] In the case of the two lowest fundamentals, 383 and 430, the higher resonances recorded are 1 semitone lower than $3n$.

VOWELS

kind—the fundamental n, and its overtone at $3n$, taking the place of the two separate resonances of the vocal cavity.

These experiments were afterwards repeated (15.8.26), substituting a glass cylinder, 38 mm. internal diameter, for the former (plasticine) tube of 43 mm. diameter. The glass cylinder was closed by a cork plunger, fitted with a tubular piston rod, through which the resonator was blown. The space behind the plunger was packed with linen to avoid resonance there.

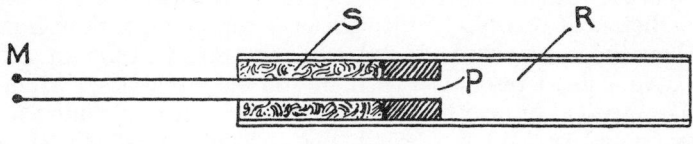

FIG. 51.

The resonances were found to be substantially the same as given by the wider tube, and the fundamental note and its overtone had the relation of n to $3n$, for all settings from 19 cm. to 7 cm. An additional overtone of $5n$ was heard at 21 cm. Below 7 cm. only the fundamental was recognized. It was found that when the resonator was blown *across* the mouth, at the various settings, the overtone was always about 1 semitone flatter than when the resonator was blown *through*. This difference became less as the resonator was shortened.

It was found that in blowing the resonator *across*, it was necessary to close the tubular piston rod at P, otherwise additional resonances were introduced.

To test the effects of a partial closure at the back of a cylindrical resonator, a brass tube, 37 mm. internal diameter and about 20 cm. long was closed by a plasticine disc 10 mm.

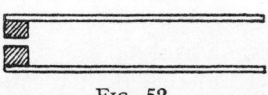

FIG. 52.

thick; it then gave a fundamental and an overtone of 3 times the frequency (541 + and 1625). A hole was then formed in the disc, as in the figure, Fig. 52, and progressively enlarged. It was found that, whereas the fundamental note was progressively raised from 541 + to 966, by gradually increasing the size of the hole up to the full bore of the tube, the original overtone (1652) remained substantially constant. With a back aperture of between 23 and 27 mm. diameter, the fundamental and overtone gave the frequency relation of n and $2n$ (between 812/1625 and 861/1722). This result may afford an explanation of a previous observation,[1] in which a single tubular resonator was found to produce a good ʌ (up) with resonances 1625/812, the overtone of $2n$ being possibly due to the effect of the larynx opening.

By similar experiment with an ovoid plasticine resonator, it was found that this also gave different resonances, according to whether it was blown through or across the mouth opening. When the model was tapped with the finger at its equator, it gave a single resonance without audible overtones. When it was tapped at or near either pole, or blown across the mouth, it gave n and $4n$. When it was blown through a small slit formed at the pole opposite the mouth, it gave n and $3n$ and $4n$—the actual resonances (for a cavity 60 mm. diameter × 105 mm. long with orifice 29 mm. diameter and a slit 10 mm. × 2 mm.) being 541, 1625 and 2169.

When fitted with an artificial larynx and blown, it gave a clear vowel sound between e (men) and ə (sofa), the e character being probably due to the 541 and 2169 (compare the charted 541/2048 for e) and the ə character to the components 541/1625, which are within the charted ranges of this vowel. The single ovoid resonator was in fact giving two vowel sounds simultaneously, by using a common lower resonance with either of two overtones respectively.

So far we have dealt only with single resonators, or with two resonators joined together in series or, as one might say, " driven tandem."

The experiment was tried of joining two resonators together in parallel, i.e. driven as a pair, and blown by a single larynx with a forking passage leading to the two resonators respectively, see Figs. 53 and 54.

The resonators were modelled in plasticine and tuned, by adjusting their capacity and size of orifice to air, so as to give the resonances 1534/812—corresponding to ʌ (up) and 2434/342 corresponding to i (eat).

In the case of the i model, the upper resonator formed a small funnel, connected to the larynx by a relatively long narrow passage; the only object of this arrangement was to

[1] Royal Society, loc. cit., p. 763.

VOWELS

bring the mouths of both resonators into line so that they could be opened and closed by hand simultaneously.

Both models produced recognizable vowels, but the i model no doubt suffered in quality by the presence of the upper passage which imported additional " parasitic " resonances. It was found that, in the case of resonators in parallel, there was practically no reaction of one resonator on another, such as occurred with resonators in series. It was, therefore, possible to tune the two resonators to their proper pitch in the first instance.

In the case of the i (eat) model, when the passage to the lower resonator was closed, so that only the upper resonator was in operation, a recognizable, whispered, i (eat) was

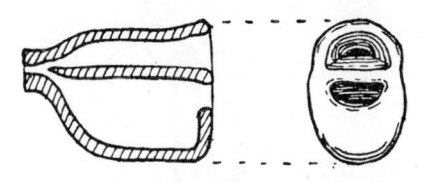

FIG. 53.

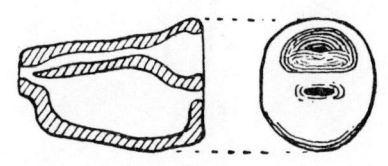

FIG. 54.

produced when the model was blown *without* a larynx. When, however, the larynx was replaced and the upper resonator blown by itself, the vowel was very poor and more like e (men)—the i sound being to a great extent lost. It was clear therefore that though the upper resonance (2298 to 2579) is highly characteristic of the vowel i (eat), the voiced vowel itself cannot be produced without the addition of the lower resonance (304 to 362).

It will also be seen that so far as vowel formation is concerned, Nature might have provided us with two mouths, side by side, instead of with a single cavity with the tongue in the middle of its length !

A further model was made, and attached to an organ reed, as shown in Fig. 55, the resonators being tuned to the frequencies heard in the vowel ɔ (all). This model produced a recognizable ɔ sound, but not so well as the resonators in series. A similar model tuned to the resonances of u (who) did not give the u sound—apparently owing to the presence of overtones in each of the two resonators.

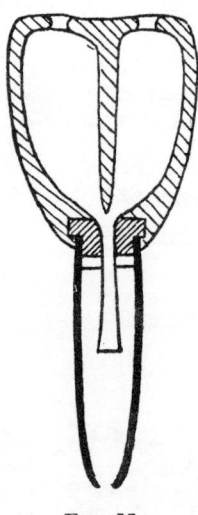

FIG. 55.

One other experiment may be mentioned in this connection, namely, that of inserting the artificial larynx between two resonators. The model thus made was shown at a Royal Institution Conversazione in February, 1923, and consisted of a small front resonator tuned to 912, and a larger back resonator tuned to 383, with rubber strip reed in the passage joining the resonators.

When this model was blown by an air tube attached to the back orifice (4 to 5 mm. in diameter) the model gave a vowel sound between ɔ (all) and ɒ (not). It seems not unlikely that the voice-like quality of the vox humana stop of the organ—in which the reed is enclosed within a relatively large air chamber, and opens out into a relatively small tube partially closed at the mouth—may be due to the same cause.

Material of Resonators

Many experiments were made to test the effects of different materials for the construction of resonators. Plasticine, glass, brass, cardboard, wood and india-rubber were all found to give almost equally recognizable vowel sounds, provided the tuning of the resonators was correct.

The quality of the sound (as distinct from the vowel character), was—as would be expected—affected by the material, being more " natural " in the case of the less rigid materials. When india-rubber was used as the material of the resonator, a difficulty of tuning was introduced, owing to the transparency-to-sound of the rubber walls. This had the effect of raising the resonant pitch, much as if an acoustically opaque resonator had been perforated with additional orifices to air.

To test this question more definitely the rubber tube was surrounded by a layer of plasticine $\frac{1}{2}$ centimetre thick. It was then possible to produce the vowel sounds of low-pitched resonance—viz., **i** (eat), by constriction of the tube by means of an adjustable clip at 3 cm. from its open end, and **u** (who) by similar constriction at $7\frac{1}{2}$ cm., after closing the mouth of the tube with a plasticine cap pierced with a 7 mm. hole. The question of acoustic transparency will be further considered later on, in connection with voice production.

Cylindrical Models

The plasticine models, though relatively easy to make and to tune, were also easily damaged. As it had been found that other materials produced satisfactory vowel sounds, it was decided to experiment with a metal cylinder and to substitute for the " central orifice " a ring-shaped plunger, i.e. a plunger with a hole through the middle—which could be set in any part of the cylinder, so as to make a constriction at that point.

By using a number of alternative plungers with different sizes of hole, it was hoped to obtain a model by which any vowel could be produced at will.

After some preliminary experiments with a glass tube and a perforated cork plunger, a model was designed with a brass tube and vulcanite mouth-piece and plungers, which were made up for me by Messrs. Griffin of Kingsway, see Fig. 56.

The plungers had each a single brass piston ring fitted round them which pressed against the inside of the cylinder, so as to keep the plunger in place. A metal rod with a pair of jaws at the end enabled the plunger to be gripped and moved to any position in the tube—the position being recorded by a centimetre scale, marked on the rod. This model, which was first shown in 1923 at the Royal Institution, gave a fairly good series of vowel sounds.

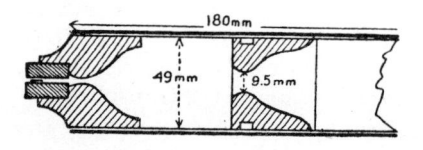

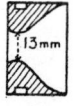

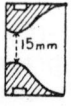

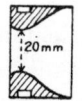

Fig. 56.

It was found that by moving the 20 mm. plunger in succession to 14, 12 and 15 cm. from the cylinder mouth, the model could be made to articulate the word "Ahoy", the h effect being produced by blowing harder.

Reference may here be made to a later variable vowel-sounding model with which experiments were made, in 1926, to test the resonance of the artificial vowels in comparison with those heard in my own mouth. The model shown in Fig. 57 was designed with the help of Dr. R. S. Clay, of the Northern Polytechnic, London, and was made by Messrs. Rushworth and Dreaper, Organbuilders, of Liverpool—to whom I am indebted for valuable help in connection with the application of the principle of double resonance to organ pipes, a subject which will be dealt with in a later chapter.

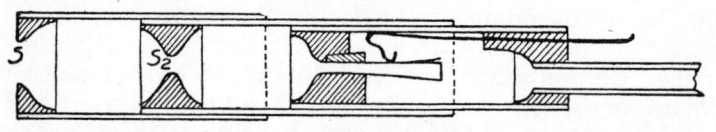

Fig. 57.

In this model the perforated plunger of the former design was replaced by a cork "tongue", fixed in position so as to give a lenticular orifice 25 × 18 mm.

The capacity of either resonator could be varied independently of the other—by sliding the plunger in the inner tube or by sliding the outer tube over the inner—while the size of the central orifice was kept constant throughout. In a later form, the cork tongue was replaced by a perforated stop (S2) as shown in Fig. 57.

The pitch of the larynx note—which in this instance was produced by an organ reed instead of by a rubber strip—could also be adjusted by means of the tuning wire which varied the effective length of the vibrating reed according to the position at which the curved end of the wire was made to press (downwards, in the Fig.) against the surface of the reed.

With this model the effect was tried of every possible combination of size of the two cavities, and the positions at which the best vowel-sounds were produced were recorded as distances from the mouth M of the front resonator to the centre of the tongue orifice O, and from O to the face of the plunger P, respectively.

The results are set out in the Appendix IV, where a comparison is also given of the resonances observed at the various settings with those recorded for my own voice.

It was found that all the double resonances observed in the model when set, by trial and error, to give the best vowel sounds, fell within the range of resonances heard in the human mouth when whispering the vowel in question. In some cases the model resonances were one, two or (in four cases), as much as three semitones below (but never above) those previously charted for that particular vowel. In each of these cases it was found that the vowel *could* be made at the same resonances as those of the model, though they were not normally made so low in my own voice. The fact that the central orifice in the model is small (18 × 25, lenticular aperture) may account for the abnormal lowness of some of the resonances.

It should be noted also that, in this model, the vowels ɒ not, ɔ all, ou no, u who and ʊ put, are all made with a full aperture of the front resonator tube, whereas in the human mouth they are made by a progressive closure of the lips.

Another point of interest is the relation between the different sizes of cavity which produce the series of vowels. Thus, in the case of the front resonator, its capacity varied from the minimum shown in position i (shown shaded in the drawing Fig. 58) to the maximum at position u. Similarly, that of the back resonator varied from the minimum at ɑ-ʌ-æ (shown shaded in Fig. 59) to the maximum at i It will be seen that,

72 EXPERIMENTS WITH MODELS

in the case of the front resonator, Fig. 58, the spacing of the different positions of the tongue is very uneven. There is a group of closely spaced positions at i, ɪ and æ, ei, e, then a gap before reaching ʌ and ɐ, then a gap of twice the distance to the closely spaced series ɑ, ou and ʊ, ɔ, ɒ, u.

In the back resonator, Fig. 59, the spacing is more even, but ɑ, ʌ and æ all occupy a single position.

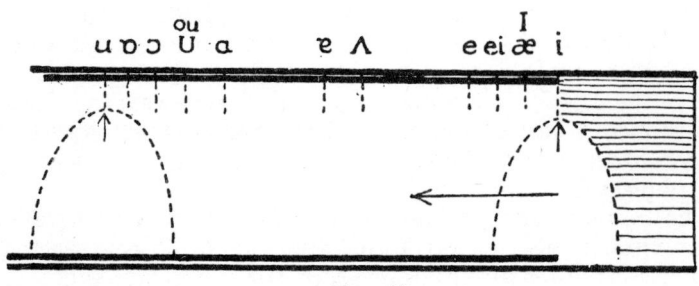

FIG. 58.

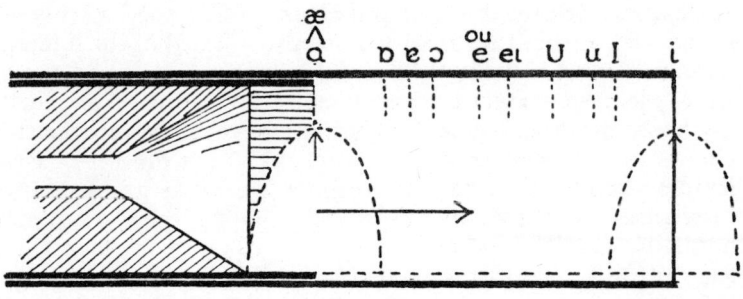

FIG. 59.

Whether we consider the tongue positions in the model or the actual resonances in the human voice, it is difficult to avoid the conclusion that the selection of resonances, which are at present employed for our vowel sounds, are not as well chosen and differentiated as they might be. It is an obvious mistake to use the same upper (or lower) resonance for two or three different vowels when, by a process of re-spacing, we might give each vowel an upper *and* lower resonance range which would be, both, characteristic of that particular vowel. The effect of such a process would be to alter the " pronunciation" of our vowel sounds so that they differed from one another much more than they do at present. They would then be less liable to be mistaken and easier to understand.

In view of the results obtained, it was now decided to make a set of cylindrical models in cardboard, energized by organ reeds instead of by rubber strips. These were made from cardboard tubing, about 44 mm. internal diameter and 2 to 3 mm. thick, such as is used for packing rolled documents. The tubes were fitted into corresponding tubular metal sockets, about 49 mm. internal diameter, 38 to 40 mm. long, connected by a conical piece to the "boot" of an ordinary organ reed. See Fig. 60.

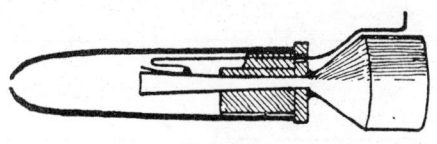

Fig. 60.

The experiments proved much more difficult than those with the plasticine models, owing to the inflexibility of the material and the consequent difficulty in tuning the resonances.

A note of these experiments, with illustrations of the models, will be found in Appendix V.

Electrical Resonators

In the course of the experiments with the plasticine resonators in series (April, 1922), the idea suggested itself, that as electrical resonant circuits (such as are used for "tuned" reception or emission in wireless telegraphy), are analogous to acoustic resonators, it might be possible to produce artificial vowels electrically, by substituting two suitably tuned electrical circuits for two acoustic resonators.

These, by the same analogy to the tuned circuits, might be electrically "coupled" in series or parallel and energized by some form of interrupter, which would fulfil the function of the larynx and supply energy to the circuits in rhythmical "puffs", so as to produce voiced vowel-sounds when the resultant current was passed into a telephone.

The matter was discussed with my friend, Dr. Eccles (then Principal of Finsbury College), who undertook to try the experiment, for which I gave him a set of resonance frequencies for the various vowels. But before he had been able to carry it out, the experiment was tried independently by Mr. John Q. Stewart, in the Research Laboratory of the Western Electric Company, of New York. Stewart's letter to *Nature*[1] gives a diagram of his circuits, which is reproduced (by permission) in Fig. 61.

Stewart followed D. C. Miller, and assumed that the vowels i (eat) to a (calm), required two resonators, and those from a (calm) to u (who) single resonators only. His double resonances were, as will be seen, coupled in parallel. The following is quoted from his letter: " Appropriate adjustments

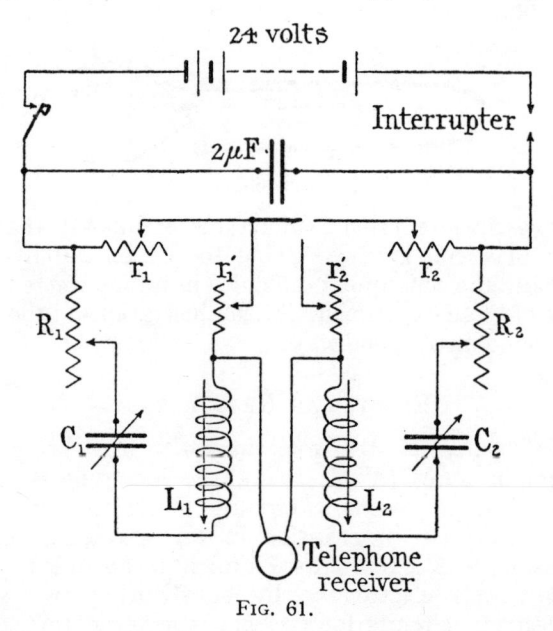

FIG. 61.

of the resonant circuits 1 and 2 were observed to result in the production of all the various vowels and semi-vowels in turn. Alteration of the frequency or damping at either resonant circuit was observed to result in alteration of the vowel produced. The frequency of interruption, which was the group frequency of the recurrent damped oscillations, was observed to determine the pitch of the vowel; but it did not determine what vowel was produced. It was found possible to produce the whispered vowels with interruptions that were non-periodic." It will

[1] 8th July, 1922, No. 2757, vol. cx, p. 311.

VOWELS

be seen, therefore, that the analogy between acoustic and electrical resonances appears to hold good in every respect—though the arrangement of resonators in series (instead of in parallel) has—so far as is known—not been tried.

One point in Stewart's results needs further explanation. Stewart believed that the vowels a (calm), ɔ (all), and u (who) were due to single resonance and he states, " The first three vowels (i.e., a, ɔ and u, in our present notation) are each characterized by a single train of recurrent damped oscillations ; the remaining three are characterized by two trains of recurrent damped oscillations." This apparent production of vowels

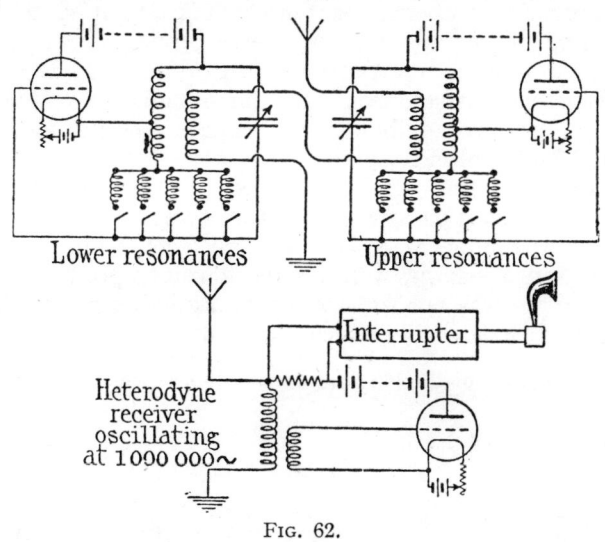

FIG. 62.

by single resonance is not in accordance with acoustic analogy, so far as my own experiments in vowel synthesis have gone.

The result of Dr. Eccles' experiments was shown by him at the Royal Institution in 1923 ; it differed in several interesting respects from Stewart's arrangement. Eccles' circuits are shown in Fig. 62.

There are two sending circuits each capable of giving different frequencies of oscillation of over one million per second—the *excess* above one million per second, corresponding to the resonance frequency for the vowel intended.

The receiving circuit was made to oscillate at exactly one million per second and therefore sent to the loud-speaker heterodyne beats (due to the difference of frequency between the sending and receiving circuits) at audible frequencies, corresponding to the excess over one million of the frequencies of the two sending circuits. These beats or difference-tones therefore produced, in the loud-speaker, the actual resonances characteristic of the various vowels—according as any particular pair of lower and upper resonances were switched on in the sending circuit.

The method of combining the two resonances was also of special interest. Instead of causing them to act together on a single telephone (as in Stewart's arrangement), Eccles caused his interrupter to operate on the sending circuit so that the upper and lower resonances were brought into action alternately at each interruption. He found that the effect of "persistence of audition" in the human ear caused the two resonances to combine into a single vowel-sound, as if they had been present together.

By the kindness of Dr. Eccles, I was privileged to demonstrate this apparatus, in a lecture given at the Institution of Electrical Engineers.[1] The vowels i (eat), ɔ (all), e (men), ɑ (calm) and ɞ (earth), were all recognizably produced; the vowel u (who) was not so good—possibly because the relative intensity of the two resonances was not correct.

[1] On the occasion of the Physical Society Jubilee meeting, 20th March 1924.

Chapter V

VOWEL SOUNDS, CONCLUDED—SINGLE OR DOUBLE RESONANCE ?

Up to this point we have left the question of single or double resonances in a very uncertain condition. My own observations all pointed to double resonances for the vowels a (calm), ɔ (all), u (who), while the very refined instrumental methods of D. C. Miller and the electrical experiments of Stewart indicated single resonances only.

As judged by ear, the double resonances of a, ɔ, and u are quite as clear as the others and are indeed easier than them to demonstrate by the clapping method ; the upper resonances of these three vowels are more audible owing to their pitch being lower, while the lower resonances—being comparable with those of æ (hat), ei (hay) and i (eat), respectively—are equally audible.

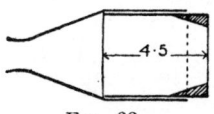

Fig. 63.

To compare the effects of single and double resonators in producing vowels of this class, two single resonators, made of cardboard tubing and tuned by adjustment of their length and orifice, were fitted to organ reed sockets, as used for the series of cylindrical double resonators. The one was tuned to D. C. Miller's frequency for ɔ (all), viz. 781, see Fig. 63 ; and the other to his frequency for u (who), 383. These two single resonators were then compared with my own double resonators for these vowels, 861/483 for ɔ and 812/322 for u. It was found that the single resonator at 781, gave a trace of the ɔ sound—being more like ʌ (up) at high reed frequencies and like ɒ (not) at low. The single resonator at 383 gave no trace of u sound—the sound produced being more like ɞ (earth) or French " eux ". On the other hand the double resonator gave a quite recognizable u.

The question was tested in another way, namely by making records of a given vowel by means of the Dictaphone and then altering the vowel character by varying the speed at which the cylinder was run when reproducing the original record. This method of phonographic transposition was originally used by Preece and Stroh [1] and by Herman [2] and was also employed by D. C. Miller.[3]

The present experiments—which were carried out at the offices of the Dictaphone Company, in London—consisted in recording the vowel ʌ (up) on a larynx note of 215, the vowel being intoned a large number of times in succession, at a constant laryngeal pitch, and then gradually slowing down the record when the Dictaphone was set for reproducing the record. The following results were obtained :—

ʌ (up) at 215 became ɑ (calm) at 203
ɒ (not) at 181
ɔ (all) at 152
u (who) at 108

the ʌ to u change having resulted from a 2 to 1 reduction of speed and consequently of the resonance frequencies recorded. This is exactly what would be expected from the charted resonances, where, by transposing the resonance ranges of ʌ 12 semitones down, they coincide closely with those of u. The other vowels ɒ (not) and ɔ (all) have been already observed to have resonances of the same average difference of about 10 semitones, but of progressively lower frequency; their formation therefore at intermediate speeds was also to be expected. Similarly the vowel æ (hat) recorded on a laryngeal note of 203 became a clear ʊ (put) at 108—i.e. when the note was lowered through 11 semitones.

Since it is generally agreed that the vowels ʌ (up) and æ (hat) are due to double resonance, the fact that they are transformed into ɑ (calm), ɒ (not), ɔ (all), u (who), and ʊ (put) respectively, by a simple change of speed of the record affords good evidence that these latter vowels are also doubly resonant.

These experiments were afterwards demonstrated at the Institute of Electrical Engineers, on 20th March, 1924, and before the British Association at Toronto in August of the

---

[1] *Proc. of Royal Soc.*, 1878–9, pp. 358–67.
[2] *Pflüger's Archiv.*, vol. xlvii, 1890, p. 251.
[3] *Science of Musical Sounds*, 1916, p. 232.

same year, the records being made audible by a loud-speaker horn, attached directly to the Dictaphone, by a short length of flexible metallic tubing.

The cumulative effect of these observations seems to point to the fact that the double resonances for a, ɒ, ɔ, u and ʊ really exist, as was originally maintained by Graham Bell and Lloyd.

Another observation of Lloyd, in his paper on the Genesis of Vowels,[1] may be of interest in this connection. He points out that, in the Fourier Analysis of intoned vowels (which was in fact the method used by Miller), it is useless to seek traces of a resonance of frequency n except when sung at a pitch of $\frac{1}{2}n$ or lower. Another paper "On the Fourierian Analysis of Phonographic Tracings",[2] mentions that, in the case of a vowel having two resonances differing only by about 300 vibrations per second, it is useless to look for any sign of doubleness in the reinforcements evidenced by the Fourierian Analysis, unless the vowel is sung below 150. Lloyd points out that records of the vowel O sung by Herman at 132 and Dr. Bocke at 128 both indicate double resonances.

In many cases Miller's single resonant vowels were sung at a lower pitch than $\frac{1}{2}$ the frequency of the lower resonance—in which case Lloyd's criterion does not apply. It is noticeable, however, that in Miller's figure 163, all the high pitched voices singing a (father) show single resonances, while the three voices of lowest pitch show clear double resonances. It is, of course, possible that in some voices the two resonances of a (calm), which are normally only 7 or 8 semitones apart, may come so near together as to appear, on analysis, as a single resonance range. But the resonances of ɒ (not), ɔ (all), ou (no) and u (who) are all normally from half an octave to an octave apart. In the case of these vowels, some other explanation must be sought for the absence of a lower resonance in ɔ (all) and of an upper resonance in ou (no) and u (who) from the results given by the Fourier Analysis of the phonographic tracing produced by the intonation of these vowels.

In the case of the vowel ɔ (all), to which Miller assigns a single resonance at 781, evidence of an unexpected kind is given of the presence of another resonance at about 512 by

---

[1] *Journal of Anatomy and Physiology*, vol. xxxi, pp. 233-4. I am indebted to Lord Rayleigh for the use of his father's copy of this paper.
[2] *Proc. Roy. Soc.* of Edinburgh, 7th Feb., 1898.

the ingenious toy " Radio Rex ". In this device a celluloid dog is made to jump out of his kennel when his name, " Rex ", is called. The mechanism is simple ; the dog is ejected by a spring inside the kennel. Normally the spring is held back by the pull of a small electro-magnet, which is kept supplied with current from a dry battery. The current from the battery to the electro-magnet passes across a loose metal bridge, which spans a vertical gap in the wire circuit ; this bridge is so designed that it chatters on its bearings when a note of about 500 vibrations per second reaches it, just as a teaspoon will chatter in its saucer if laid on the piano when the right note is played. It follows that when air-waves of 500 per second, or thereabouts, reach the kennel, the " bridge " chatters, and thus intermittently interrupts the current which supplies the energy to the electro-magnet. The magnetism, therefore, becomes reduced, so that the spring is enabled to reassert itself and eject the dog !

In experimenting with this toy, it was found that the reaction occurred when any of the notes ♯a' 456, b' 483 or c" 512 were played, either on the piano or on the ocarina. It was also found that the reaction of the word " Rex " was entirely due to the vowel sound e (men) and that if in his name other vowel sounds were substituted, e.g. as in " Reeks " or " Rooks ", the dog did not respond. The device was tested with simple vowel sounds and was found to respond to all vowels whose lower resonance, in my voice, occurred between 456 and 512 ; these include ei (hay) (weak response), e (rex), ɞ (earth), ɔ (all), and ou (no). On the other hand there was no response to either i (eat), ʌ (up), ɑ (calm) or u (who), the lower resonance vowels being either above or below the resonance range of the chattering bridge.[1] The experiment was also made of blowing the plasticine vowel models at a distance of 4 or 5 feet from the apparatus. The response was similar to that in the case of my own voice.

According to Miller's analysis, there should have been no response to ɔ. Rex, therefore, may be cited as a strong witness to the truth of this double resonance.

Two other observations bearing on the question of vowel resonance may be mentioned here.

The plasticine model giving the vowel ɪ (it), consisted of

[1] Modifications of pronunciation, so as to bring the lower resonance within the 456–512 range, produced the response.

SINGLE OR DOUBLE RESONANCE?

a nearly hemispherical bell-mouth, connected to an elongated back resonator by a small central orifice. The front resonator was made detachable, so that it could be withdrawn while the model was being blown. The effect was that on withdrawing the bell-mouth, the sound ɪ was entirely lost, the effect produced being more like a muffled ɞ (earth). The experiment indicates the important effect which the bell-mouth of a wind instrument may have not only in the volume of its tone, but also on its " vowel " character!

FIG. 64.

The other observation relates to the experiment of Helmholtz, which has been already referred to, of singing the vowel sound to a piano with the loud pedal pressed down, so that the strings are set into sympathetic vibration when a sound of their own pitch reaches them.

It was found that if instead of intoning the various vowels on a constant larynx note, the vowels were spoken on a rising or falling larynx note, there was still a quite definite vowel response—the resonances set up being, doubtless, those of the average of the overtones set up by the changing larynx note, while the two vowel resonators of the mouth were kept substantially constant. A similar but still weaker response for the vowels from æ (hat) downwards was obtained by whispering them well into the piano, ɑ (calm) and u (who) being the vowels most clearly reproduced.

RECOGNITION TESTS OF ARTIFICIAL VOWELS

So far the only independent evidence which has been produced as to the fidelity of the various models is the behaviour of " Radio Rex ", whose responses to the various vowel models were similar to the responses for the same vowels when intoned by the human voice.

An experiment of a different kind, proposed by Dr. Wilfrid Perrett [1] of the University of London, may be here referred to. Dr. Perrett suggested that in order to obtain an impartial

[1] Author of *Some Questions of Phonetic Theory*, Cambridge, 1919.

estimate as to the vowel character of the various models (of the plasticine double resonator series) they should be sounded from behind a screen in an indiscriminate order, and that an audience interested in phonetics, should be asked to record their impression of the vowel-sound in each case. The experiment was carried out at a meeting of the Philological Society, held at University College, London, about the end of 1922. It was made more difficult by the fact that the series of models included both long and short vowels, i.e. sounds which, like ɑ (calm) and i (eat), are normally prolonged, and others, like ɒ (not) and ɪ (it), which are normally curtailed in duration. When models giving these sounds are blown for equal lengths of time they are much more apt to be mistaken. The results of about 20 voting papers may be summarized as follows :—

ou (no) was heard as ou or u ; it was twice heard as ᴜ (put) and once as ɞ (earth).

i (eat) was recognized by all except 3 listeners, one of whom wrote ɪ (it) and the others ei (hay) and æ (hat).

ɑ (calm) was mostly heard as ɑ, 5 times as ɔ (all), and once each as ɒ (not) and ɞ (earth).

ɞ (earth) was generally heard as ei or e ; the model was afterwards retuned and its upper resonance lowered to distinguish it more from these vowels.

ɔ (all) was generally recognized ; 3 listeners wrote ou and one each ɒ (not) and ɞ (earth).

u (who) was recognized by nearly all. One listener heard it as ᴜ (put) and one each as ɔ and ou.

ei (hay) was recognized by nearly all. Two listeners wrote e (men), one i (eat).

ɒ (not) was heard by ten listeners as ɔ or ou, and by three as ʌ (up).

ʌ (up) was mistaken 6 times for æ (hat) and once for ɑ.

æ (hat) was mistaken 5 times for ɞ, twice for e and once each for ei and ɑ.

ɪ (it) was recorded as i (eat) by nearly all listeners, only one heard it as ɔ.

e (men) was recorded 6 times as ei, 3 times as æ (hat), and once each as ɞ to æ and as ɞ.

It will be seen that in almost every case the vowel-sound was either recognized or was recorded as a vowel whose resonances were of the same order of frequency as those of

SINGLE OR DOUBLE RESONANCE?

the model. The vowels of high upper resonances were mostly mistaken for others of higher resonance, while those of low upper resonance were mistaken for others of lower resonance.

The recording of vowel-sounds, detached from their normal environment of words, is difficult; it is not improbable that if the same experiments had been performed with the same series of vowel-sounds, intoned by voice, with the " short " vowels prolonged to the same duration as the " long ", the percentage of recognition might not have been greatly raised!

If further evidence of the reality of the artificial vowel-sounds is required, it may be found in the results (already recorded) of the variable double resonator.[1] It will be remembered that the capacity of the two resonators was adjusted so as to give the best obtainable series of artificial vowels, as judged by ear, and that the settings which gave these vowels were recorded. When the resonances of the two cavities were examined, at each of the recorded settings (corresponding to a particular capacity of the two resonators respectively), it was found that the actual resonances present corresponded in every case, either with resonances already recorded for the vowel in question, or with resonances so near to the recorded ranges that the vowel could easily be produced, in the voice, at those resonances.

Similar experiments have been made with the cylindrical models giving the vowels a (calm), e (men), i (eat), ɔ (all), and u (who), namely, by Professor L. H. Gray and Dr. Russell at Columbia University in 1927, and by Dr. C. S. Myers during the meeting of the British Association at Glasgow in 1928.

In the Glasgow experiment the artificial speech sounds tested comprised the vowel sounds a (calm), e (men), i (eat), ɔ (all), and u (who), and the consonants p, t, k, r, f/v, θ, (made by closure of a rubber tube resonator) and m and n, produced by differential closure of a cylindrical resonator with added nasal resonator.

The Jury consisted of Dr. Myers and twelve other observers interested in psychology or phonetics—including Miss Anne H. McAllister, of Jordanhill College, Glasgow, who afterwards analysed the results. The Jury turned their backs on the demonstration so as not to get any information from sight of the manipulations involved, e.g. the positions of closure and release, and the order in which the vowels and consonants

[1] See p. 71 (Chap. IV) and Appendix IV.

were produced was decided by giving them each a number and drawing corresponding numbered slips from a hat.

The result may be summarized as follows :—

The vowel a was correctly recorded nine times out of thirteen records ; e (men) was recorded six times as the long vowel ei (may) and once as ue, but not as the short vowel e ; i (eat) was correctly recorded four times out of ten and four times as e ; ɔ (all) was only twice recorded as ɔ, being generally heard as a (2), o (3), or u (2).

Better scores were made by some of the consonant models. p was correctly recorded eight times out of eleven, otherwise as f. t was only twice heard correctly, otherwise as f or p. k and r were both correctly recorded eleven times out of thirteen. f/v was correct four times—otherwise as r, and once as g. θ was correct seven times, the other records being f. m was correctly heard by all listeners. n was only once recorded correctly, being mistaken for m. The f-for-p mistake indicates imperfect closure ; the r-for-f/v and f-for-θ and m-for-n are mistakes which are common even in human speech.

It is evident that the range over which the resonance—whether upper or lower—of a vowel may extend is very considerable. Thus, in the case of my own voice, the resonance ranges charted in the first instance (20.2.22) varied from a single tone 2048 for the upper resonance of e (men) to a choice of six semitones for the upper resonance of ou (no) (638 to 912). Similarly in the lower series, a single resonance was observed for ʌ (up) (812) while ɞ (earth) was given a choice of six semitones (406 to 541).

Further observations have shown that these ranges can be considerably extended—even in the case of a single voice using what appears to be substantially the same pronunciation. Thus, from more recent observation (5.3.26) on my own voice, it appears that the lower resonances of all the English vowel-sounds can be varied over a range of eight semitones, i.e. over a musical interval of a fifth. The ranges of the upper resonances are not so uniform ; the following were noted :—
i (eat) five semitones, ɪ (it) six semitones, ei (hay) six to seven semitones, e (men) eight to nine semitones, æ (hat) six to seven semitones, ɞ (earth) six semitones, ʌ (up) seven semitones, a (calm) seven semitones, ɒ (not) seven semitones, ɔ (all) six to seven semitones, ou (no) eight semitones, u (who) ten to twelve semitones and ʊ (put) ten semitones.

SINGLE OR DOUBLE RESONANCE?

It will be seen that starting from i (eat), the ranges increase steadily to e (men), remain at about seven semitones from æ (hat) to ɔ (all) and then increase to ten or more for u (who) and ʊ (put).

Besides the two series of resonances which we have discussed hitherto, it appeared that (in some cases at least), additional components were present. Thus the first vowel chart of March, 1922, showed high resonances of 2434 in the case of u and ʊ and a faint additional component of 645 to 683 in the case of ei. Subsequent observations have revealed others of the same type as those of u and ʊ—the additional resonances and normal ranges of my own voice being shown in the revised chart, Fig. 65. These high resonances—which are apparently produced in the pharynx—are not controllable like the main resonances; they are also not characteristic, since the vowels may be recognizably produced by resonators (whether acoustic or electric) which do not provide for these frequencies. They are also relatively faint in comparison with the two principal resonances.

They can be varied to the extent of five or six semitones, by external pressure applied across the throat immediately above the larynx.

The pharyngeal resonances evidently play a definite part in the production of the vowel sounds, since most of the vowels are substantially altered in character by the application of external pressure on the pharynx while maintaining the position of the tongue. Thus (by transverse pressure on the throat immediately above Adam's apple) the vowel e (men) becomes like ɜ (earth); ɑ and ɔ become like ʌ; o becomes like æ (hat), while u becomes more like ɪ (it).

The modified forms are best heard by alternately closing and opening the mouth orifice with the hand, the position of the throat, tongue and jaws being kept constant.

The recording, by ear, of the resonances of other voices, is a matter which demands almost as much patience and a great deal more forbearance on the part of the subject than on that of the observer. For this reason my observations of voice resonances—other than my own—have been very limited. I am therefore the more indebted to three individuals, who have allowed their voice resonances to be recorded, namely, Miss M. Somerville of the British Broadcasting Company (English vowels), Mdlle Hélène Coustenoble, of the Phonetic Department,

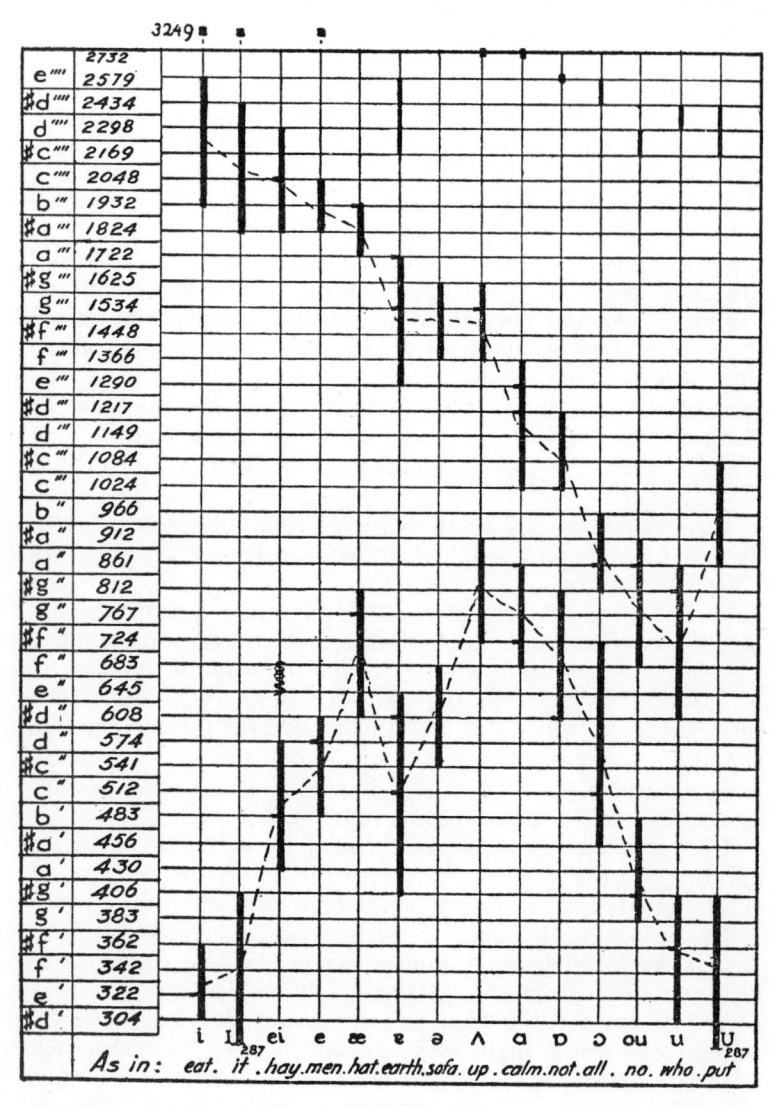

FIG. 65.

SINGLE OR DOUBLE RESONANCE? 87

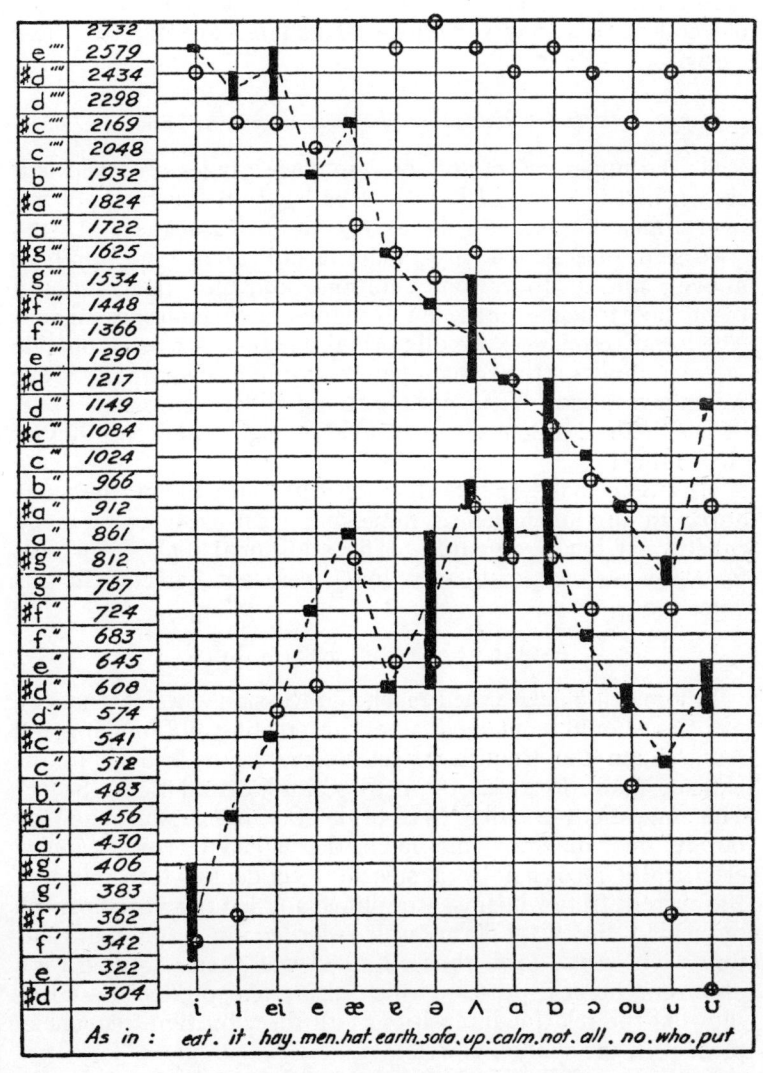

Fig. 65a.—O represents a typical resonance in the author's voice (for comparison). Miss M. Somerville's vowel resonances.

University College, London (French vowels), and Miss Tatiana Mosolova, late teacher of Russian and French in the School of Modern Languages, Oxford (Russian vowels); to these we will now refer.

OTHER ENGLISH VOWEL RESONANCES

Of the upper resonances or resonance ranges observed and shown in Fig. 65A, all but three fall within the range of my own upper resonances—the exceptions being æ (hat) at 2169 (two semitones above my range), ɔ (all) 1024 (one semitone above), and u (put) (one semitone above). The ei (hay) resonance touches mine, but extends two semitones higher. The lower resonances are all normally higher, six being outside my own ranges; the remainder are within or overlap my lower resonance ranges. The most striking difference is in u (put) of which the lower resonance range is eight semitones higher than mine!

Miss Somerville speaks very clearly, with about the same apparent pronunciation as mine, but with a somewhat more constricted back resonator. The additional high resonances for the vowels ɞ (earth) to u (put) were not detected in this voice.

AMERICAN VOWEL RESONANCES

Before dealing with the French and Russian vowel resonances, mention should be made of a very interesting and fundamental research on the English vowel resonances as spoken in the U.S.A., made in 1924, by I. B. Crandall and C. F. Sacia.[1] This investigation, like that of D. C. Miller, was made by purely instrumental methods—the spoken vowels being electrically recorded by a special " condenser transmitter ", the current from which was amplified and led to an oscillograph by which the wave form was recorded on a photographic film. The wave form thus obtained was then analysed by a photo-mechanical process, which ultimately produced a curve showing the relative intensities of all the vibration frequencies present in the spoken vowel.

From Crandall and Sacia's curves I have constructed the chart, Fig. 66 (representing the averaged results of the analysis

---

[1] " A Dynamical Study of the Vowel Sounds," *Bell System Technical Journal*, vol. iii, No. 2, pp. 232-7.

ANALYSIS OF VOWEL SOUNDS (MALE VOICES).
I. B. Crandall and C. F. Sacia.

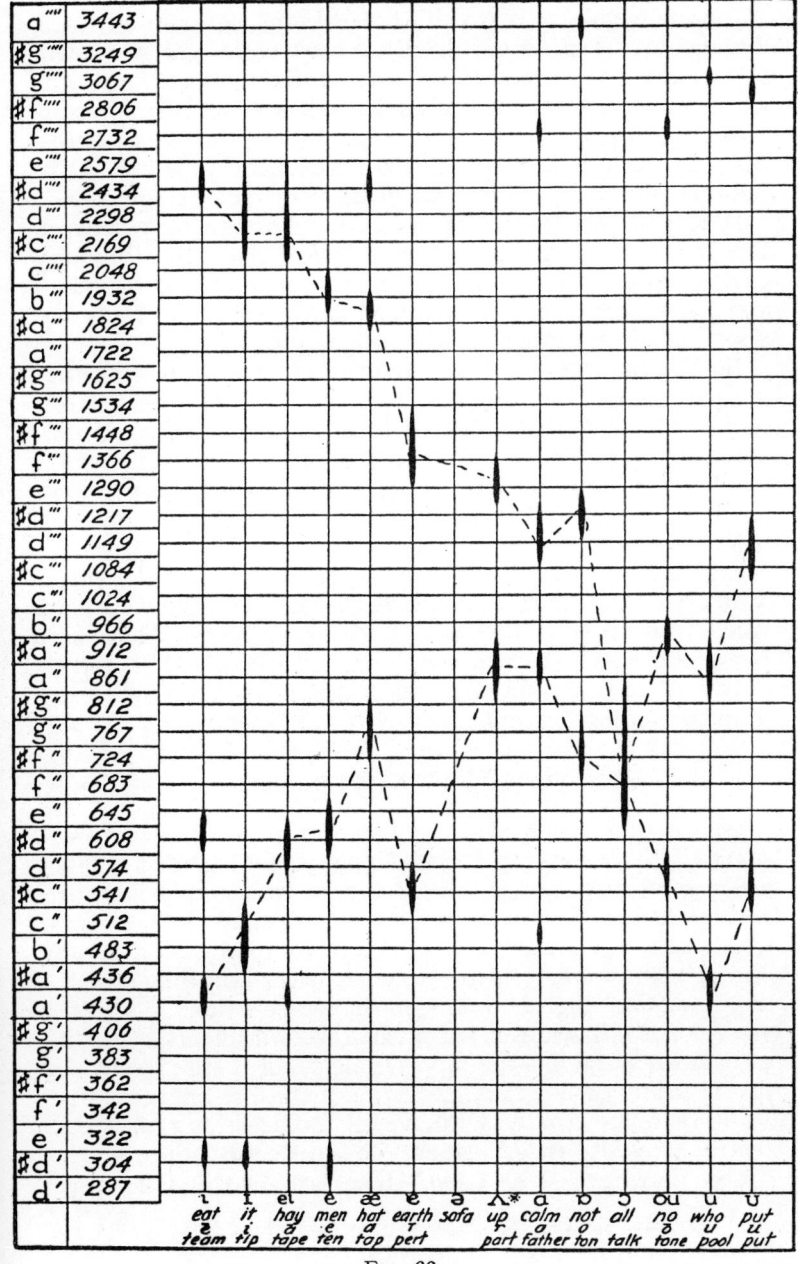

FIG. 66.

* As in American pronunciation of "part."

of four male voices), in which I have attempted to set out their findings in a form more directly comparable with my own. I have added the International Phonetic Symbols and key words above those of Crandall and Sacia. Their o (ton) corresponds to my ɒ (not), r (part) to my ʌ (up), ȓ (pert) to my ɞ (earth). The thickness of the vertical lines is roughly proportional to the intensity of the vibrations of that particular frequency.

It will be seen that there is a very close analogy between the two charts—the upper resonances being all within my charted ranges, except in the case of ɔ, for which Crandall and Sacia show a single extended range which overlaps my upper and lower ranges for the same vowel.

In the case of the lower resonances, the correspondence is equally good, but Crandall and Sacia find additional lower resonances for i (eat), ɪ (it), ei (hay), e (men), and ɑ (calm). They find additional upper resonances for the vowels æ (tap), ɑ (father), ɒ (ton), ou (tone), u (pool), and ʊ (put), all of which except æ (tap), are comparable with those heard in my own voice.

Crandall and Sacia's averaged results for female voices show a tendency towards higher resonances than those for male voices, especially in the case of the lower series. They show clear double resonances for ɔ (talk) at 1149/812, corresponding nearly to ɑ (calm) in my own voice. Further results by Crandall [1] accord even more nearly with my own.

French Vowel Resonances

We may now compare the resonances of the French vowel-sounds with those of the English language. Mdlle. Coustenoble's vowel resonances are set out in the following table (Fig. 67). If the frequency numbers of these resonances be compared with those of the chart on page 86, it will be found that only one of them, namely u (tout) comes within the range of the corresponding English vowel—in this case u (who). One other vowel, o (tôt) has ranges which come very near to the English equivalent ou (no)—the upper ranges of both resonances just touching the lower ranges of the English resonances. It is clear, therefore, that English vowels (at least as pronounced by the present writer) cannot do satisfactory duty in the French language! In i (*oui*) there are two audible upper

---

[1] "Sounds of Speech," *Bell Technical Journal*, vol. iv, No. 4, p. 611.

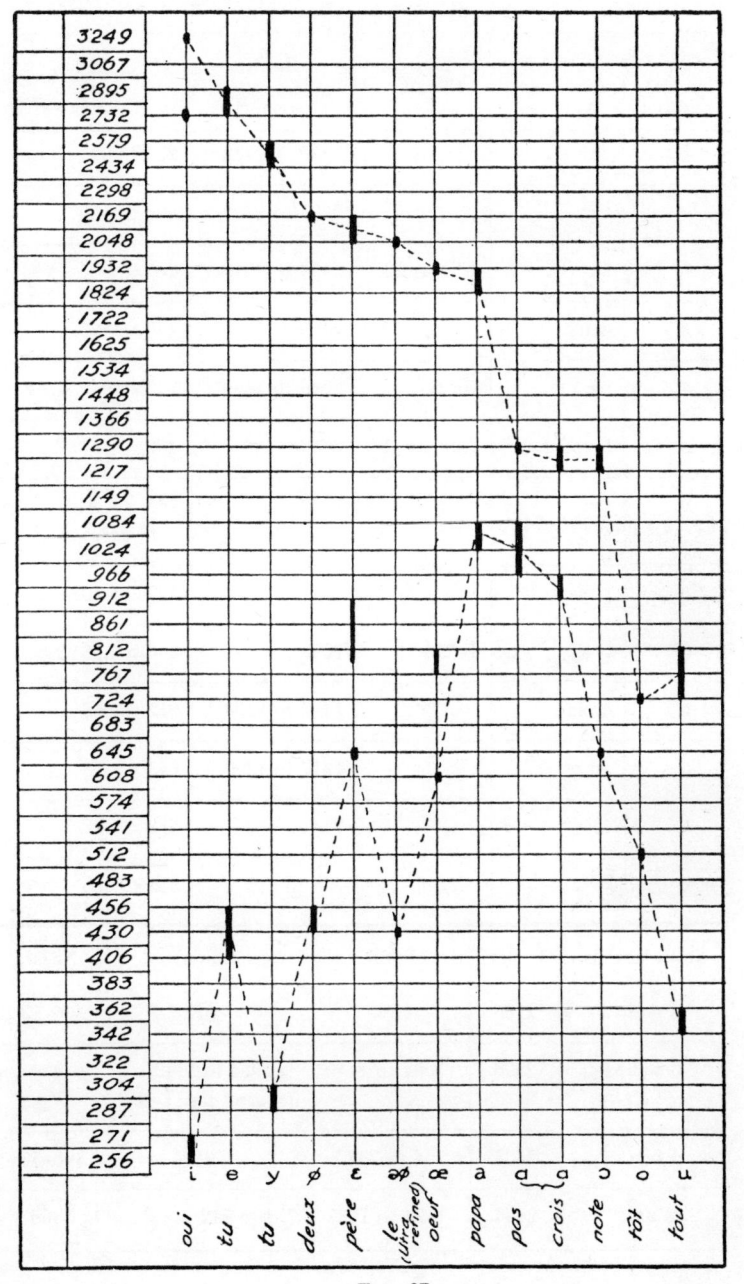

FIG. 67.

French Vowel Resonances
(Helène Coustenoble)

Vowel Symbol	as in :—	Phonetic Classification.	Front Upper Resonances.	Back Lower Resonances.
i	oui	Front	3249 + 2732	256 to 271
e	thé	,,	2895 to 2732	406 to 456
ɥ	tu	Abnormal [1]	2434 to 2579	287 to 304
ø	deux	,,	2169	430 to 456.
ɛ	perè	Front	2048 to 2169	812 to 912 + 645.
ə	le (ø like) [2]	Abnormal	2048	430
œ	œuf	,,	1932	767 to 812 + 608 to 645.
a	papa	Front	1824 to 1932	1024 to 1084.
ɑ	pas	Back	1290	966 to 1084.
ɑ	crois	,,	1217 to 1290	912 to 966
ɔ	note	,,	1217 to 1290	645
o	tȯt	,,	724	512
u	tout	,,	724 to 812	362 to 383

Nasal Vowels.	Upper.	Middle.	Lower.	Nasal.
ɛ̃ main	2169	1932	812	406–83
ɑ̃ temps	2895	1084 to 1149	1084 to 1149 ? no sep. res. heard.	430
ɔ̃ bon	2434	724 to 767	912	406–56
œ̃ un	2434	1824 to 1932	724 to 812	406

FIG. 67A.

[1] Combining the approximate tongue position of a front vowel with the mouth orifice of a back vowel.
[2] In "ultra-refined" or "precieux" pronunciation.

SINGLE OR DOUBLE RESONANCE?

resonances, while in ɛ (*père*) and ø (*veut*) there are two in the lower series—otherwise, double resonances appear to be the rule.

The nasal vowels are quite different. In forming these, as is well understood, the soft palate is drawn forward, so that the sound passes, in parallel, through the cavities of the mouth and nose. In the case of õ (*bon*) nearly all the sound passes through the nasal cavity—the back of the tongue being so much raised that it forms a nearly complete closure with the edge of the soft palate.

French Nasal Vowels

Vowel Sounds.	Upper.	Middle.	Lower.	Nasal.
ɛ̃ as in *main*	2169	1932	812	406 to 483
ã ,, ,, *temps*	2895	1084 to 1149	none heard	430
õ ,, ,, *bon*	2434	724 to 767	912	406 to 456
œ̃ ,, ,, *un*	2434	1824 to 1932	724 to 812	406

In all cases, except ã, four separate resonances were recognized; these have been classified as upper, middle, lower, and nasal. The position in which the upper, middle and lower series are formed has not been identified, but the series here called nasal, is almost certainly produced in the nasal cavity. The resonance missing in ã (*temps*) is of the lower series; when ɛ̃ (*main*) was changed to ã (*temps*), the lower resonance 812 of ɛ̃ was heard to rise to the pitch of the middle resonance of ã. When the change was made to the other nasal vowels, the lower resonance only varied over a range of about four semitones. It should be remembered that the nasal cavity is of a complex shape and that it is quite probable that more than one audible resonance is produced there. Although the cavity is fixed in shape the resonances might be capable of variation over a considerable range—due to variation in the size and shape of the neck of the back orifice formed by the soft palate, which acts as a downward opening trap door in the floor of the cavity. The variations of orifice which are made at this point are large compared with the size of the front orifice, formed by the two nostrils—the variations of resonant pitch may therefore also be considerable, especially in any resonance formed in the back of the nasal cavity.

RUSSIAN VOWEL RESONAN[CE]

Tatiana Mosolova).

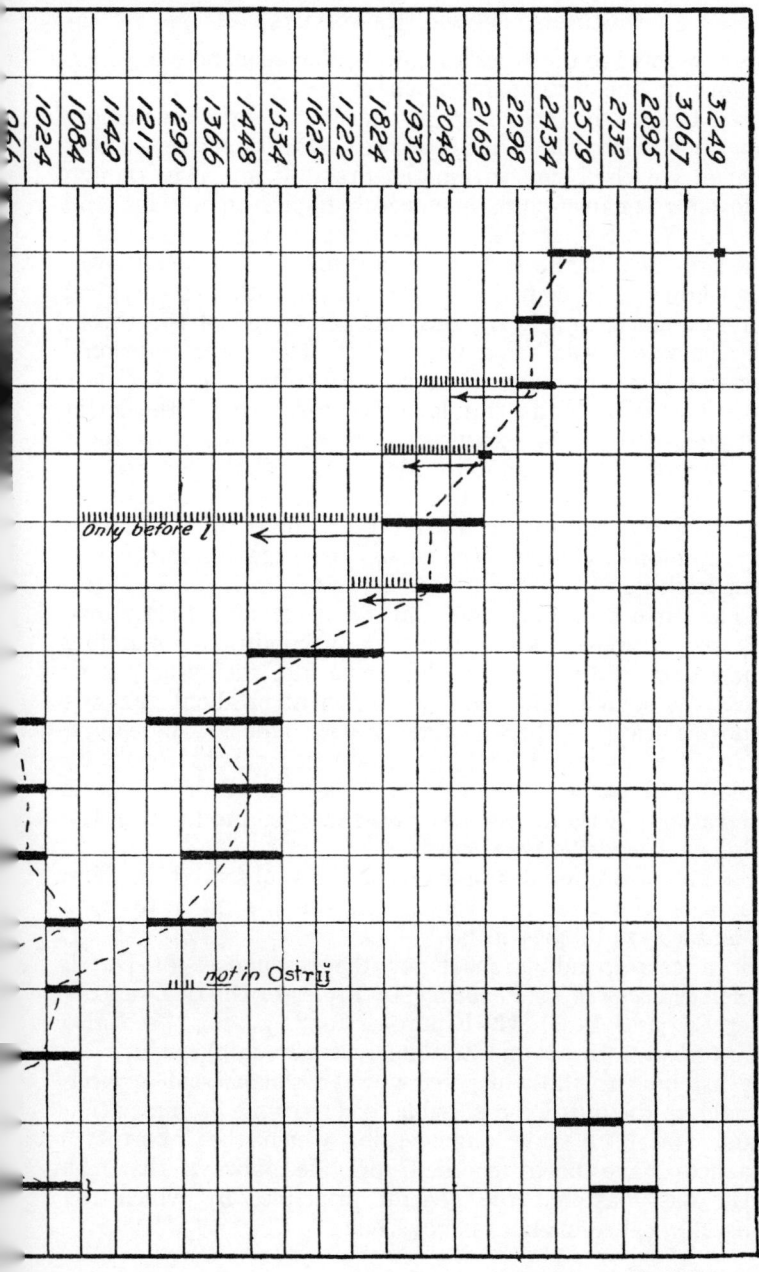

FIG. 68.

RUSSIAN VOWEL RESONANCES

We now come to the Russian vowels, the resonances of which are shown in the accompanying chart, Fig. 68.

It will be seen that they form, in the main, a series much more comparable with the English vowels—the upper resonances of eleven vowels, being within the range of my own, though the lower resonances are, in general, higher than mine and nearer to Miss Somerville's. The most striking difference is in the presence (in the Russian series) of two additional lower series (shown in broken lines) lower in pitch than the typical lower resonance, and heard only on percussion of the throat while the vowel was being whispered. The lower additional series was heard in many instances also, when the vowel was breathed or whispered—this latter is indicated by the letter b (for breathed). The exact position where these two lower series are formed has not been identified. That they are not all characteristic is proved by the fact that, in the case of the vowel ʌ, the vowel was accurately reproduced (in Miss Mosolova's opinion) by my voice, though the 322 resonance was absent from it.

It has since been observed that when listening to my own whispered vowel-sounds, under good conditions—standing in the corner of a room and whispering into the corner, so as to hear the sounds reflected—a component of about 242 was heard with nearly all the whispered vowel-sounds. These may, perhaps, be compared with the lower resonances found by Crandall and Sacia (181 to 304), already mentioned. It is conceivable that these low resonances may be produced in the windpipe—below the vocal cords.

The only additional upper resonances observed in Miss Mosolova's vowel-sounds were a 3249 in i, a 2434 to 2732 in u, and a 2579 to 2895 in ʊ.

For a corresponding chart for the resonances of Dutch vowels, see *Leerboek der Phonetiek*, by Professor Dr. H. Zwaardemaker Cz. and L. P. H. Eijkman, 1928, p. 103 ; see also *English Studies* (Swets and Zeitlinger, Amsterdam), p. 52.

By listening to the whispered vowel resonances of a pupil, it should, in the future, be possible to correct the pronunciation of any vowel, in any language for which the " correct " resonances have been recorded, provided always that the teacher has mastered the general principles by which the tuning of vocal resonances is governed !

SINGLE OR DOUBLE RESONANCE?
"NASAL" QUALITY.

Before concluding this chapter, mention should be made of another aspect of nasal resonance, viz. its supposed action in producing a "nasal" pronunciation in ordinary speech, as for example in the "twang" heard in English pronunciation in some parts of the North American Continent.

In listening to the resonances of my own voice, when imitating an American pronouncing the word "well" as wæ̃l, the æ̃ being not unlike the vowel in the French word *main* (mæ̃) or *vin* (væ̃), it appeared, on repeating the sound as a whisper, that there were additional resonances imported into the whispered sound when the twang was "put on", but that not all of these were affected if the nostrils were pinched during whispering. It was evident, therefore, that the effect was not wholly or even primarily nasal.

The resonances observed at a trial of the vowels æ and æ̃ (American) were as follows:—

æ as in hat.		æ̃ as in wæ̃ll
(loud)	1824 812	a new 2732 (unchanged on closing nostrils). persisted as 1824 (less audible). raised to 861–912. a new 1366 (lowered to 1217 on closing nostrils). a new 242 (throat resonance).

FIG. 69.

Similarly with the vowel i (eat) at 2434/383, this, when pronounced ĩ with a twang, gave 2434 as before, together with a new upper resonance of 3249 to 3864 (difficult to identify) and a nasal resonance, 1217–1366, which could be suppressed. There was also a low resonance of 242 heard with the nasal resonance besides two other low resonances, 383 (faint) and 287 (louder). These resonances were found difficult to identify, owing to the variability of the central orifice—made between the back of the tongue and the edges of the soft palate—and of the closure of the passage to the nasal cavity.

In order to test the possibility of producing a "nasal" quality in a vowel-sounding model, experiment was made with a resonator formed of a rubber tube (about 1 inch diameter), attached to an organ reed and fitted with a cork tongue, see Fig. 70.

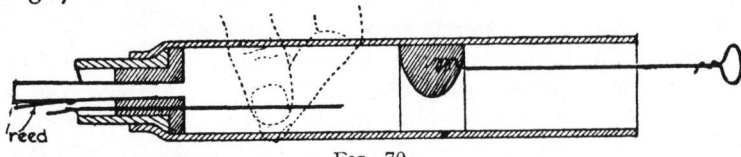

FIG. 70.

It was found that if, while the reed was sounding, the tube was suitably pinched, near the opening from the reed (as indicated in dotted lines in the figure), an appreciable twang was added to the vowel-sound. A similar experiment (substituting a rubber strip for the organ reed) was shown at Toronto, in August, 1924, but the nasal character was then less marked, owing to the poor quality of the reed note produced by the rubber strip.

This experiment indicates that a part, at least, of the so-called nasal quality of the pronunciation now in question, is probably due to a constriction of some part of the pharynx, so as to produce an additional resonator of high pitch, though the presence of nasal resonances seems also to be indicated. In this connection, the work of Mr. L. P. H. Eijkman should be mentioned.[1] After referring to the theory which has just been described, he says, "Now the additional resonating cavity of small size referred to is actually formed through the narrowing of the uvular aperture; for the smaller this aperture becomes, the nearer the palatopharyngeal folds [2] will approach one another, thus giving rise to a small resonance chamber, enclosed by these folds and the back wall of the pharynx. It would seem, therefore, that it is not the narrowing of the uvular aperture that actually causes nasality, but that it is brought about by the formation of a small resonance cavity in consequence of it."

THE EVIDENCE AS TO THE NATURE OF VOWEL-SOUNDS

We have seen that observations by ear of the principal resonances present in the human mouth, when the vowels

[1] *Neophilologus*, May, 1926, p. 277-8.
[2] I.e. the lower edges of the soft palate on either side of the uvula.

SINGLE OR DOUBLE RESONANCE ?

are whispered or sung, are confirmed by experiments with models. The same combinations of resonances in models give appreciably the same vowel-sounds, so as to be recognizable with a fair degree of certainty under test conditions such as those of Dr. Perrett's experiment.

The vowels are " our way " of appreciating the characteristic combinations of resonances, which are set up in the human vocal cavity, when the tongue and lips are set in different characteristic postures. The main result, at each posture, is to produce two principal resonances—a different pair for each posture.[1] The passage of turbulent air through the tuned cavities produces a combination of muted whistle-notes which we hear as a breathed or whispered vowel. The passage of rhythmically pulsating air (produced by the action of the vocal cords) " colours " the musical note by emphasizing—through the action of the resonators—such overtones, or harmonics of the larynx note, as lie within the resonance pitch (including possible overtones) of the resonators. Besides the two principal resonators, there are others—which we have not identified—giving non-characteristic, or at least less characteristic, additional resonances.

The resonances define the exact whispered pronunciation of the vowel-sound.

Considered as a musical instrument, the human voice is really a little orchestra of wind instruments—a reed (of the oboe type) and two, three, or four muted whistles (of the ocarina type). In whispered speech the reed does not play ; in voiced speech the reed plays *through* the ocarinas.[2] In the case of nasal vowels all four ocarinas are used—in other cases two only are essential.

True vowel-sounds can be obtained by single resonators, but only in cases where the nature and tuning of the resonator are such that its own fundamental note (n) and first overtone (2n, or 3n, for example) happen to coincide with the resonances

[1] The same pair of resonances may, however, in certain cases be produced in two different postures, viz. by counterchanging the upper and lower resonances.

[2] To test this analogy, an ocarina was muted with plasticine, applied to the whistle hole so as to reduce the whistle to a whisper, and fitted with a rubber strip reed over the mouthpiece. On blowing the instrument with all holes open, the resonance was 1290, and the " vowel " sound like a muffled ʌ (up), with 2 holes stopped 1084, and the vowel-sound like ɑ (calm), and with 5 holes stopped 812, and the vowel-sound like ɔ (all), with all holes stopped the sound was like the consonant m.

I

of a particular vowel. It follows that only those vowels which have a 2 : 1 or 3 : 1 relation between their resonance frequencies can be obtained in this way.

Since the form and consequent pitch of the vocal resonators remain substantially constant, irrespective of changes in the larynx note (except for minor adjustments, comparable to those of voicing an organ pipe), it follows that as the larynx note is varied and the vowel posture kept constant, different harmonics of the " successive " larynx notes will be emphasized by the action of the resonators. In other words, the notes will have a different tone colour, and their wave form, if studied by phonographic or oscillographic methods, will be found to be very different in the case of the same vowel sung successively on different laryngeal notes. Yet we instinctively recognize that they *are* the same vowel merely sung on a different note, not different sounds such as their wave form shows them to be.

The fact is that we unconsciously recognize the tongue and lip posture by their acoustic effects, and are primarily interested in the postures rather than in the wave form or tone colour which they produce.

My daughter (Mrs. Chancellor) has pointed out [1] that the effect of the double resonances of the vowels on our perception may be compared to that of binocular vision. In the case of visual impressions, our brain constructs a three-dimensional impression from the evidence of two two-dimensional images, taken from slightly different aspects. In the case of vowel-sound perception, we receive two acoustic images, one taken from behind the tongue, the other taken from in front ; from these two sound images we reconstruct a mental picture of the position or posture of the tongue which produced them.

[1] *Science Progress*, No. 73, July, 1924, p. 133.

CHAPTER VI

OBSERVATIONS AND EXPERIMENTS ON THE CONSONANTS

As compared with the vowel-sounds, the consonants used to be—acoustically speaking—a little known and rather neglected family. Phonetically, they had been studied in great detail, and the method of their production—by tongue and lip movement and position—was in most cases well understood. The linguists, too, had studied them minutely from the point of view of their gradual metamorphosis in the course of language development.

It was recognized that certain of the consonants—commonly classified as semi-vowels, i.e. **m, n, ŋ** (ng) ; **l, r** (untrilled) ; **w**, and **y**—were, in fact, nearly related to the vowels. They were considered rather as half castes, whose darker ancestry was unknown and of little genealogical interest. The remaining sounds, commonly classified as plosives—**p, b** ; **d, t** ; **k, g**— and fricatives—**s, z** ; ʃ (sh) ; **f, v** ; θ (th in thin), ð (th in this)— were usually treated rather as noises—i.e. unryhthmical vibrations—than as musical effects.

Thus D. C. Miller, writing in 1914, says,[1] " Words are multiple tones of great complexity, blended and flowing, mixed with essential noises. If with the vowel tone ă (mat) we combine a final noise represented by t, the word a + t is produced ; if to this simple combination, we add various initial noises, several words are formed, as : b + at, c + at, f + at, h + at, m + at, p + at, r + at, s + at, t + at, v + at. However, the study of noises may well be passed until we understand the simpler and more interesting musical tones." It will be seen that Professor Miller here includes even **m** and **r** amongst the " noisy and uninteresting " components of speech !

In the course of the original experiments with plasticine vowel models, many trials were made of manipulations of the models, during blowing—such as had been formerly carried

[1] *Science of Musical Sounds*, pp. 24–5.

out by Kratzenstein, de Kempelen, Willis and Wheatstone, with their bell-shaped or tubular resonators. It was found that a considerable number of different consonant sounds could be produced by the total or partial closure and release of the mouth or—in some cases—the central orifice of the plasticine double resonator models. It was also observed that the same manipulation did not produce the same consonant with all the models.

For example, complete closure (by the palm of the hand) and release of the models,[1] ei (hay), ɑ (calm), ɒ (not), ou (no), and u (who), produced p or b—followed by the vowel sound, according as the model was initially blown with high or low pressure; a partial closure (sufficient to allow the larynx to sound) and release of the same models, produced an m. Exactly the same (full closure) manipulation in the case of the models i (eat), ɪ (it) e (men), and ʌ (up) produced a sound like w—followed by the vowel! But if the palm of the hand was first moistened these models also could be cajoled into sounding p and b like the others.

Again, complete closure and release (under air pressure as before) of the central orifice of the ɞ model—see Fig. 48, page 62—by means of a plasticine plug on the end of a thin stick, gave p or b, according to the air pressure. By analogy to the human mouth and the principles of phonetics, it should have given t or possibly k, since the action was comparable to a closure of the tongue against the palate.

The conclusion was inevitable that these "plosive" consonants were not mere noises—they were the effects of the sudden appearance of musical resonances. Their different character was therefore due not to the position in the mouth (or in the vowel-sounding model) in which they were produced, but to the effects which their mode of production had on the resonances set up. Thus the different plosives were presumably due to the presence of different initial resonances—at the moment of release of the closed orifice which produced them—or to the different changes which the initial resonances underwent as the closure became fully released, or to both of these causes. From this point of view the apparently anomalous production of p and m or w could be explained.

It was noticed that all the p- b- producing models had convergent or cylindrical mouths. See Figs. 43, 47, 49,

[1] See Chap. IV, Figs. 43–9, pp. 61, 62.

whereas the models like ʌ (up), Fig. 45, or i (eat), Fig. 42, which, on release by hand, gave w sounds, had diverging mouths. It was therefore conceivable that these differences might produce different resonance changes as the mouths of the two classes of model were uncovered. The production of p and b by the divergent models, when the palm of the hand was moistened, might now be explained as the effect of a more airtight closure and a more sudden release, due to the liquid film between the operator's hand and the lips of the model.

The production of p and b, by closure and release of the central orifice of the ɞ (earth) model, Fig. 48, could not yet be explained, but it was seen to be analogous to another result of D. C. Miller,[1] in which a group of organ pipes—which together produced the intoned vowel ɑ—were made to articulate the word " papa ", viz. by the stopping and releasing of the air supply by pressure with the edge of the hand on the rubber pipe. In Miller's experiment, it was the sudden starting, stopping and re-starting of the vowel resonances which resulted in the consonant p ; evidently the same sort of effect had been produced in the present case.

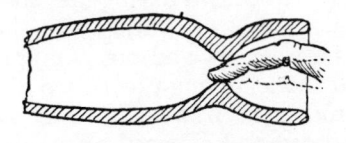

FIG. 71.

Further experiment was now made with this model (ɞ earth) and it was found that a variety of consonants could be obtained from it by small changes of manipulation.

This model was particularly convenient as it had an open mouth and an easily accessible central orifice, which could be reached by the fingers or thumb. It was found that when the central orifice was opened and closed by the ball of the thumb, as it had been, previously, by the plasticine stopper, the consonant was p at high pressure or b at low pressure, provided the thumb was given a uniform to and fro movement so as to cover and uncover the whole orifice in one operation. Any method of closure and release which altered this condition also altered the resulting consonant sound. If the central orifice was completely closed with the first finger, set at an

[1] Op. cit., p. 251.

angle, as in Fig. 71, and then partially opened by tilting the finger downwards, as shown in dotted lines in the figure, the consonant was like k or g—according to the degree of air pressure employed—while the vowel was u (who) instead of ʊ (earth), owing to the reduction in area of the central orifice by the finger and of the front orifice by the hand of the operator. If the first finger was pressed as before, against the upper edge of the central orifice, but so as not to penetrate into the orifice or to touch the lower edge, and was then sharply lowered to the opposite wall, a clear l, namely, as the syllable lu (loo), was produced; while if the finger was " waggled " up and down from one wall to the other the model said *ludl-ludl* (loodle-loodle).

The consonant l could be made in yet another way, namely, by inserting the first finger into the central orifice so as to close it by about two-thirds and then sharply withdrawing the finger towards the mouth of the model; this produced the syllable lʊ (rather like the *leu*- of the French word *leur*).

Finally, if the first finger was pressed less deeply into the orifice than for k/g, or l—so as to effect a partial closure, and was then gradually withdrawn during the blowing of the model, a sound like the syllable vʊ (rather like the French *voeux*), or intermediate between vʊ and mʊ, was produced. In the case of the similar model giving i (eat), see Fig. 41, yet another consonant was produced, viz. ð (as in thee)—when the central orifice was constricted and released by a plasticine plug.

It was clear that, in all these cases, the only physical effect had been to vary the acoustic resonances of the model in different ways—by varying the apertures of the orifices or, possibly also, in some cases, by introducing additional resonances by the formation of minor resonating cavities between the walls of the model and the operator's fingers or hand.

At this stage, therefore, the definite conclusion seemed justified that the consonant sounds—or at least all those which had been so far produced—were as essentially musical as the vowels, and that they should be capable of identification by the musical pitch of their resonances. Further, as there was every reason to suppose that the remaining consonants did not differ in kind from those already observed—which included semi-vowels, plosives and fricatives—it seemed likely that *all* the consonants should be capable of musical analysis and be reproducible artificially by models which produced the correct resonances and resonance changes.

Professor Daniel Jones had drawn my attention [1] to the work of Dr. Wilfrid Perrett—described in his book, *Some Questions of Phonetic Theory*.[2] There, in addition to observations on vowel resonances, Perrett had referred to those of the vowel-like " inverted (cerebral) ɽ in its extreme form as spoken in some parts of Somersetshire ".

Dr. Perrett had noticed two or three harmonics " reinforced at the same time ", but found that in whispering, it was most difficult to decide upon the pitch. Being personally very familiar with the sound in question, as I come from Somerset, I studied its resonances and then embarked on what turned out to be a very prolonged and, at times, very discouraging search for a method of reproducing them in a model.

The resonances heard, consisted of three principal ranges—an upper range extending over five semitones from 1625 to 2169, apparently made behind the tongue, a middle range of eight semitones from 1149 to 1824, made in front of the tongue, and a lower range of 342 to 406, made in the throat and heard on tapping the throat—besides two fainter nasal ranges, one at 192–215 and another at 767 respectively. These were apparently not essential, since the r sound could be made without using the nasal cavity. The upper and middle resonances covered, as will be seen, a very wide range ; the middle resonance was especially variable and was found to change its pitch by six semitones, according as the head was thrown backwards or forwards, while breathing or whispering the r sound ! Raising the head and throwing it backwards raised the resonances—lowering or throwing it forward lowered them.

It would weary even the particular reader—not to mention the general variety—if the succeeding experiments were described in detail. All that will now be attempted is to indicate the main results and to relegate any detailed observations of resonances and resonance changes of this and other consonants to Appendix VI.

The first difficulty to be encountered was that of tuning more than two resonators in series. For example, three separate resonators were made, in plasticine, with resonances—before joining—of 483, 1824 and 2048 respectively. The common

[1] 21st February, 1922.   [2] Op. cit., 1919, p. 99.

orifice of the back and middle resonators was 16 mm. in diameter and that of the middle and front 25 mm.; the mouth of the front resonator was large. When these three resonators were joined, the front resonator fell in pitch two semitones, the middle resonator fell twenty-six semitones, and the back resonator fell eleven! Moreover, the inner and back resonances were very difficult to detect. This was largely overcome by making small windows in the resonators and " glazing " them (so to speak) with patches of thin rubber sheet. These windows allowed the sound of the resonators to be heard through them and did not substantially alter the pitch of the resonator. Later in the experiments, very small holes were bored in the resonators, instead of inserting windows, so that the sounds inside them could be heard by " listening at the keyhole ".

A few experiments were made with three or more resonators in parallel; these were easy to tune, but the passages leading

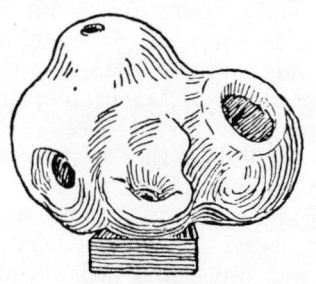

FIG. 72.

from the artificial larynx to the resonators caused spurious resonances, which interfered with the results. A resonator of this type giving the resonances for ð (as in thee), 2895, 1448 and 342, is shown in Fig. 72.

Besides the consonants already mentioned, the following were produced, accidentally, by the manipulation of the various models which were made in the attempt to produce the triple-resonant r :—n was produced, besides ð (thee) and k, by the models shown in Fig. 73.

This model had a flat rubber sheet roof covering the front two-thirds of the cavity, which was made trough-shaped; the floor of the model had a protruding tongue lying across the trough, beyond which was an open mouth. Thus the effect of raising the tongue could be imitated by depressing the rubber roof to meet it.

THE CONSONANTS

The **n** sound was made by pressing down the rubber roof, at the point indicated, so as to make an airtight joint between the roof and the tip of the tongue. It will be seen that so far as the tongue action is concerned, this model behaved like the human tongue in sounding **n**, except that the palate descended towards the tongue, instead of the tongue rising to meet the palate. There was no nasal cavity in this model

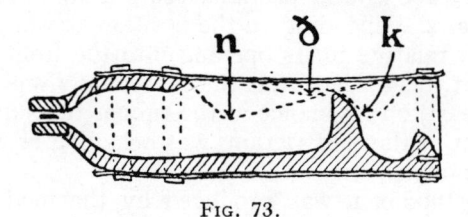

FIG. 73.

and the imitation of the continuous hum which passes out of the human nostrils must have been due to leakage between the surfaces of the tongue and the rubber. Pressure at the point ð produced the consonant ð (as in thee) : pressure and release at **k**, gave a clear **k**.

T and **d** were produced by manipulation of the model shown at Fig. 74, in which the three front resonators—two in parallel and one single—were connected to the common back resonator by two rubber tubes, C and V, which could be closed by pinching.[1]

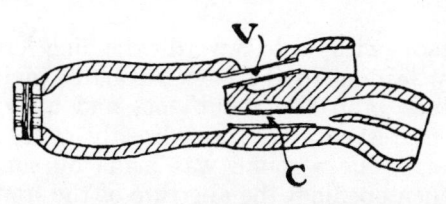

FIG. 74.

The **t** or **d** sounds were produced by pinching both tubes and then suddenly releasing tube V, while blowing the larynx of the model. High pressure gave **t**, low pressure gave sounds

[1] In this and other plasticine models fitted with rubber tubes, it was found that, in time, cracks developed in the material in contact with the rubber. The cracks tended to spread of themselves till the model ultimately separated in several pieces. This action was prevented by reinforcing the plasticine round the rubber tubes with turns of string embedded in it.

OBSERVATIONS AND EXPERIMENTS

more like d; the d was apparently improved by pinching the tube over a greater length than for t.

If the same resonator was closed by a perforated cap, so as to lower its resonance to 645, pinching the tube over a distance of 3 cm. (by two fingers on one side of the tube and the thumb between them on the other) gave a clear **ku** at high pressure or a sound more like **gu** at low.

Closure of tube C and partial closure and release of tube V gave a clear **zi**, depending on the position at which the tube was pinched, relative to its opening into the front resonator. In this case it was evident that the consonant **z** was dependent (in part at least) on resonance in the rubber tube and that the tube, in front of the constriction, was behaving as a resonator of very high pitch.

A more orthodox **n** was produced by the model, Fig. 75. This model contained an upper large front resonator tuned to 287 which acted as a nasal cavity, a smaller central front

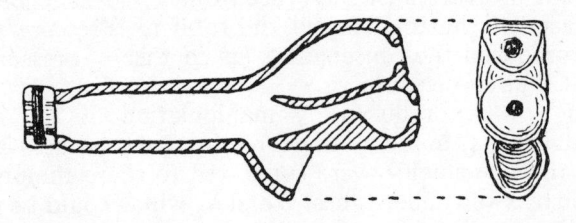

Fig. 75.

resonator (1290) with a backward-extending funnel-shaped passage (1625) leading to the back resonator giving 683 and a low resonance probably about 200, and a lower (vowel-sounding) front resonator (1824), directly connected to the back resonator. The n sound was made by simultaneously closing (and then opening) the aperture of the front resonator (1290) to the funnel-shaped passage (1625) and the aperture of the lower vowel resonator (1824) to the back resonator (683). In this manœuvre, the closing and opening of the lower aperture had a similar acoustic effect to that of raising the tongue to the palate—to form the closure, and lowering for the release, as in forming **n**. There are actually four resonances heard in **n**,[1] so that, provided they were properly

---

[1] 1448 to 2169; 1217 to 1366; 683; and 203 to 228.

THE CONSONANTS

tuned, the four cavities of this model might be expected to produce a good imitation of the natural sound.[1]

VARIATION OF CONSONANT RESONANCES

In the systematic examination which was made of the consonant resonances, the results of which are set out in Appendix VI, it was found that the various resonances varied in many instances over as wide a range as those of the vowels, but that the actual pitch heard at different trials of the same consonant depended on the vowel with which it was associated. Thus, in sounding the syllables it (eat), ʌt (as in utter) and ut (oot), the resonance changes were as follows :—

Consonant and associated vowel.	Throat resonance just before closure.	Front resonance just before closure.	Transient resonance at closure.
it	304	2579	3249 to 3443 (4 to 5 s.t. rise) 2169 (3 s.t. fall)
ʌt	362	966	1366 to 1722 (6 to 10 s.t. rise) 812 (3 s.t. fall)
ut	304	812	1217 to 1625 (7 to 12 s.t. rise) 812 (no fall)

FIG. 76.

[1] It was found (25.9.28) that tuning of the principal resonance of the consonant N can be varied from 1084 to 2732, i.e. through an interval of 16 semitones, without moving the point of closure of the tongue tip against the palate. The tuning in that case is accomplished by a vertical rather than a longitudinal movement at the back of the tongue relative to the palate, which thus controls the volume of the cavity behind the tongue. Similarly, the principal resonance of the consonant M may be varied from 683 to 2048 through 19 semitones, but the characteristic M sound is almost entirely lost when the principal resonance approaches the normal N resonance of 1625.

It will be seen that the front vowel resonance broke up, as it were, into two others—one of higher pitch and the other of lower or equal pitch—as compared with that of the front vowel resonance. But the final upper consonant resonances, which were heard at the moment of closure of the tongue against the palate, varied from 3443 to 1217, i.e. over a range of eighteen semitones, according to the vowel with which the terminal t was associated. The reason for this remarkable variation in the resonances of a single consonant, is no doubt that when the tongue executes a consonant gesture, either immediately before or after a vowel posture, it chooses for its gesture a site conveniently near to its preceding or following vowel position. The effect is that the same consonant may have resonances, which differ among themselves as much as the resonances of the vowel i (eat) differs from that of ɔ (all)!

If we examine the change of resonances which occurs in a particular case, it will be found that the changes themselves are also variable. Thus the upper transient resonance of it rises four to five semitones, while the lower transient drops three semitones, whereas the similar upper transient of ut rises from seven to twelve semitones and no falling transient is heard.

It is remarkable that though these transient resonances are of great importance in distinguishing many, if not all, of the consonants—so that if the resonant changes are not correct, either in point of musical pitch or rate of change, the consonant sounds all wrong or may even be unrecognizable —yet these resonances may vary very greatly for the same consonant. We shall refer to this question again later.

Resonances of a Rubber Tube

There is one very simple series of experiments from which so much information was gained that it may be well to refer to it in detail. It will be remembered that in the case of the model illustrated in Fig. 74, a z apparently, was formed by resonance within the rubber tube which connected the front and back vowel resonators. In view of this observation, an examination was made of the effect of closing and releasing a rubber tube at different distances from its open end, and also of making partial instead of complete closures at the same distances. The experiments were made with tubes of 6·5 and

THE CONSONANTS

13 mm. internal diameter, blown, either directly (to produce "unvoiced" sounds), or through a rubber strip larynx. It was found that various recognizable consonants could be produced in this way, and that for constrictions, up to about 50 mm., from the open end, tubes of 6·5 mm. and 13 mm. all gave similar results. At 65 mm. and over, the results with the two tubes were substantially different. The closures or constrictions were made by pressing the tube with the edge of a steel rule, while the resonances at the measured positions were mostly taken with an adjustable tube clip, substituted for the steel rule. The positions and resonances at which the clearest consonants were observed are set out in the table on page 110.

It will be seen that the consonants **p** and **f** are always found together—the one being made by a full closure and release of the tube and the other by a partial closure—whether at 0 distance, i.e. at the mouth of the tube or at 140 or 195 mm. from the mouth.

A similar relation was found in the case of the consonants **t** and **s**, and **k** and **θ**. If the tube was blown through a reed, the **f** became a **v** and the **θ** became **ð**. **p** and **t** generally remained as such, though **p** became more like **b** on blowing more softly.

The production of **p** and **f** at 0 and also at 140 and 195 was surprising, but, in view of Miller's experiments with organ pipes, seemed capable of explanation in this way. If **p** is heard when vowel resonances are started together suddenly, then any length of tube which naturally gives resonances corresponding to a vowel-sound, should give **p** in association with that vowel when the tube is closed and released at that length. In the table, it will be seen that at 140 mm. (full closure), the resonances were 1932/430, together with a faint 5790. Now 1932/430 form the vowel **e** (men) and in fact a whispered **e** could be heard on blowing across the mouth of the tube. The sudden energizing of these resonances, by the release of the tube, produced, therefore, the consonant **p**. Similarly, the closure at 195 mm. produced the resonances 2169/304, together with 1534. The 2169/304 produced an audible vowel, between **i** (eat) and **ɪ** (it), which was not much interfered with by the presence of the "extra" at 1534.

Trial was next made of the effects of constricting a tube in two positions, and it was found that a sound like ʃ (sh), could be got by constricting an 8 mm. tube at 120 mm. and 150 mm. A much better ʃ was made by constricting at 20 mm., with a

Distance from open end (mm.).	Diam. of tube (mm.)	Resonances observed at full closure.	Resonances observed at partial closure.	Consonant heard at full closure & release.	Consonant at partial closure & release.	Observations.
0	6·5	—	—	p	f	no distinctive resce. heard.
13	6·4	6134–6498	6886	ts	s	—
15	6·5	5790	—	t	s	—
20–35	13·0	—	—	dʒ (John)	—	full closure and partl. release.
40	6·5 & 13	2434	2895	k	ç (lecht)	—
65	6·5	1024–1084	—	t to k	s to θ	—
65	13·0	{ 1625, 6498	{ 1824, 2169, 5158	k	θ	clear consonts.
75	13·0	{ 1448, 4338	{ 1625, 4860	k	θ	clear consts.
80	13·0	{ 645 faint, 1448, 4596–5158	{ 1448–1722, 3443	t to k	f	clear f at 1534 partl. closr.
140	13·0	{ 430, 1932, 5790 faint	{ 271, 1217, 1932–2048 loud, 3249	p	f	p and f clear the 3249 may be 8vo. higher vizt. 6498.
195	13·0	{ 304, 1534, 2169	{ 271, 304, 342, 1149, 1625 loud, 2298	p	f	p and f clear Lower resonces. heard on tapping the tube. 8vo above 2298 possibly also present.

FIG. 77.

tube clip adjusted so as to leave a flat slit-like opening of 2 mm. inside the tube—and again, by finger and thumb at 45 mm. from the tube mouth. The finger and thumb constriction was made at right angles to that of the tube clip. Small changes in the finger and thumb constriction made marked changes in the resulting sound. Thus, at 54 mm.—instead of 45—the tube produced a clear whistled note 2169 ♯c''''. The measurements were taken to the centre of the constriction by finger and thumb and to the front edge of the tube clip respectively.

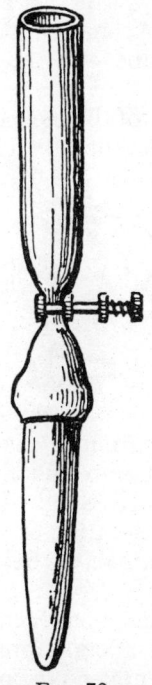

FIG. 78.

This result may suggest an explanation of the production of whistled notes by the human mouth in the absence of any chisel edge for the air jet to impinge on. The rubber tube whistle, however, would not speak when the air flow was reversed, as a mouth-formed whistle will do, on in-breathing.

The best ʃ (sh) of all was made by a finger and thumb constriction of the 13 mm. tube, at 22 mm., so as to leave a 2 mm. hole on one side of the tube, and a tube clip constriction, at right angles to the former, at 55 mm. The sound thus made was very like a natural ʃ (sh), such as is used in schools and, less frequently, in theatres for enforcing silence !

At a later stage (1924) a larger rubber tube—1 inch in internal diameter and 7 inches long—was fitted over the end of an organ reed so as to form a flexible resonator—the length from face of reed tube to open end of rubber tube being about 16 cm.

A good **ɑ** (calm) was produced by constricting the tube at 4·5 cm. from face of reed tube by means of an adjustable tube clip (see Fig. 78). With this arrangement it was found that a wide range of consonants could be formed by partial or total closure of the tube—by external pressure—in various positions.

Thus, complete closure of the mouth of the tube—by pressing its edges together with the thumb and first finger of both hands

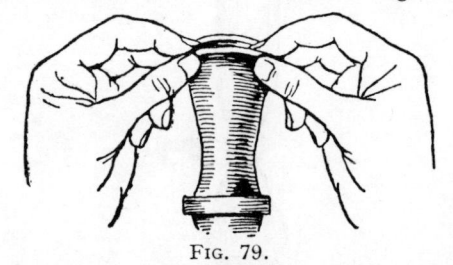

FIG. 79.

—followed by the application of air pressure to the reed and sudden release of the thumb and finger closure, produced a clear **p** heard as the syllable **pɑ**. If instead of completely closing the mouth of the tube it was *partially* closed and released in the same manner as before, the consonant was a sound between **w** and **v**.

When the tube was held between the thumbs and second fingers of each hand at 1 cm. from its open end, and a lip formed by bending the upper portion of the end of the tube backwards with the two first fingers, see Fig. 79, a clear **v** (va) was produced if the tube was slightly pressed—so that sufficient air passed to keep the reed in vibration, while, if the tube was more tightly pressed so that the reed no longer vibrated, the consonant was an equally clear **f** (fa).

s and **z** could also be produced—though with much greater difficulty—by compressing the tube at 2 cm. from its mouth and 1½ cm. from one side with the first and second fingers against the thumb of the left hand, while the rest of the cross-

THE CONSONANTS

section of the tube was closed completely by the thumb and first finger of the right hand. In this way a very small resonating cavity was formed against the left side of the tube which produced a z if the air flow was sufficient to operate the reed (ʌz) or an s if the compression was increased so as to reduce the air flow to a point at which the reed did not vibrate. The correct adjustment was difficult to find.

An alternative method was to constrict the whole width of the tube at 1·5 cm. from its open end between the first and second fingers of one hand and reinforcing the pressure with the fingers and thumb of the other hand. A minute change of position of the constrictions changed the sound from s to f— the latter sound being much more easy to produce and having (as it seemed) a much wider range of permissible resonance before it changed to the next lower consonant, namely θ (th) or ð (dh). These two sounds, θ as in thigh and ð as in thy, were easily produced by a partial closure at about 3 cm. from the open end of the tube according as the reed was in vibration or not.

The best t (tata) was produced by a clean-cut complete closure and release at 2·5 cm. from the open end—corresponding approximately to the ð or θ produced by partial closure. The closure could be performed better by laying the tube along the palm of the left hand and applying the edge of a paper knife across it than by pinching the tube between the fingers. Any leakage of air at the point of closure at once produced a θ sound.

After much searching a method was found of producing the triple cavity consonants ʃ (sh as in shire) and ʒ (zh as in plea*s*ure). The tube was held between the first and second fingers of the left hand so that the fingers crossed the tube at an angle of about 45° (pointing forwards) and so that the middle of the tube was constricted at about 5 to 6·5 cm. from its open end. The second (forward) constriction was made between the first finger and thumb of the other hand—applied at 1¾ to 2 cm. from the open end. As viewed from the end of the tube the two lines of closure made an angle of about 1½ right angles. To produce the ʃ or ʒ sound the two fingers of the left hand and the upper part of the tube were simultaneously squeezed between the right-hand thumb and first finger on one side and the second finger (reinforced by the remainder) on the other, see Fig. 80.

K

In this way a clear " ush " or a sound like the French " âge " were produced by variations of constriction. In this case also (as in that of **s** or **z**) the exact adjustment was difficult to find and the permissible limits of deviation were small.

At 7 cm. from the open end, full closure and release gave a clear **k** (ka)—the best result being produced by a clean cut closure as already described for **t**. A partial closure at the same position gave a clear untrilled **r**—a tighter partial closure —made with a $\frac{1}{2}$ inch metal rule held flat—at 9 cm. produced a guttural sound like the German word " ach ".

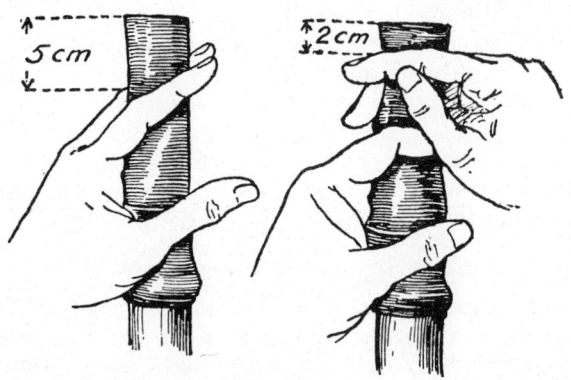

FIG. 80.

It will thus be seen that nearly all the principal English consonants (other than nasal sounds) can be artificially made by the simple expedient of compressing a rubber tube in the appropriate positions—corresponding to the positions of closure or constriction of tongue or lips by which the same sounds are produced in the human mouth. It is evident, therefore, that the sounds are in fact only the result of changes of resonance (with or without phonation) and as essentially musical in character as the vowels.

Classification of Consonants

In the accompanying table (Fig. 81) the various English consonant-sounds are classified, according to their method of formation, i.e. by full or partial closure—at different positions in the vocal cavity. The consonants of more forward formation are (so far as possible) placed above those of less forward position. The list, which contains forty-one separate sounds, is not complete; thus, it does not include the trilled **r**, or

THE CONSONANTS

the consonant—without a name—which many people make by a forward jerk of the soft palate for use in the word "tʌpns", (twopence). Neither does it include the series of sounds made by reversing the order of events in articulating the sounds written, ps, dz, tʃ, etc. These are made by the sudden release of the back orifice of a small resonator; their production is exactly comparable to that of the ʃ in the doubly constricted tube, substituting for the fixed partial closure at the back one which can itself be completely closed and released.

Many of the sounds included in the table have already been considered, it will suffice (it is hoped) if we now deal only with two general types, viz. the nasals m, n and ŋ (ng), and with the differences between the so-called voiced b, d, g, z, ʒ (zh), and ð (thee) and the unvoiced p, t, k, s, ʃ, θ (thin) classes respectively.

		Front.		Middle.		Back.	
		Full closure and release.	Partial closure.	Full closure and release.	Partial closure.	Full closure and release.	Partial closure.
VOICED.		p[1] ⎫ b ⎭	v	t[1] ⎫ d ⎭	l	k[1] ⎫ g ⎭	y (yes)
		—	z	—	—	tl (little)	—
		—	ð	—	—	dl (fiddle)	—
		—	ʒ	dʒ	r (un-trilled)	kl (fickle) ⎫ gl (giggle) ⎭	r (guttural)
		—	w	—	—	—	h
UNVOICED.		p	f	t	ll (Welsh)	k	ç (Scots "lecht")
		—	hw (hwen)	—	—	—	χ (Scots "loch")
		ps pʃ (option) pθ (ophthalmic)	s ʃ θ	ts tʃ (fetch) tr	—	ks (weeks) kʃ (action)	h
NASAL.		m	—	n ny (minion)[2]	—	ŋ (ng)	—

FIG. 81.

[1] The release or "offglide" of p, t, and k may be voiced or unvoiced. See Professor Daniel Jones' *Outline of English Phonetics*, § 766, p. 172.

[2] Minion may be pronounced mɪnyən but more often the n and y are combined into a single consonant ny.

Nasal Consonants

In listening to the resonances of whispered **m**, **n**, and **ŋ** (ng), it was found that they formed a series with a characteristic upper resonance, which rose by about seven semitones (i.e. a musical fifth) from **m** to **n** and from **n** to **ŋ** thus: **m** 1217 ♯d″, **n** 1824 ♯a‴, **ŋ** 2732 f″″.

With a rubber tube 25 mm. in internal diameter these resonances are given by constrictions at 80, 60 and 40 mm. from the open end. In the mouth, they are produced by the progressive reduction of the size of the cavity made behind the point of closure, namely the lips for **m**, the tip of the tongue against the hard palate for **n** and the back of the tongue against the soft palate for **ŋ**.

The cylindrical tube model, shown in Fig. 82, had a nasal cavity of resonance 724, connecting, by a 20 × 4 mm. rectangular aperture, with a main tube behind the fixed tongue. It was

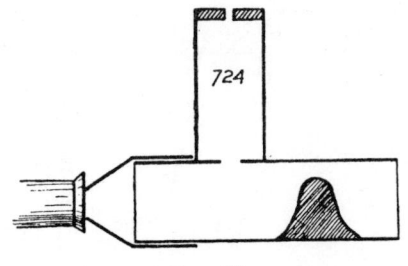

FIG. 82

found to produce a good **m** or **n**, according as it was closed at the mouth, by hand (for **m**) or at the orifice between the "tongue" and the opposite wall of the tube, by inserting the thumb (for **n**). The vowel-sound—due to the position of the tongue and area of the central orifice—was **ɪ** (it) when the tube was blown without closure. When the **m** and **n** closures were made in succession, the model said Minny, quite clearly. The tongue, in this case, was fixed; had it been made movable, it is probable that by bringing it back to the aperture, leading to the nasal cavity, and by providing means for closure—in that position—between the tongue and the tube wall, the consonant **ŋ** would also have been produced.

The **ŋ** sound was recognizably produced in this way with a 25 mm. diameter rubber tube resonator, projecting 160 mm.

THE CONSONANTS

beyond the reed opening, even without a nasal cavity—the effect of the continuing hum through the nasal cavity and nostrils being produced sufficiently well by leakage provided at the point where the rubber tube was constricted by hand. Constriction at the mouth produced **m** with a vowel like **æ** (hat) on release, constriction and release at 45 mm. gave **næ**, constriction and release at 65 mm. gave **ŋæ**, or the word "hang" on closure after sounding the vowel—the initial **h** being produced by over-blowing.

" Voiced " and " Unvoiced " Consonants

The other group of consonants to be considered, is that of **p, t, k, f, s, θ** and **ʃ**, commonly classed as unvoiced consonants and the corresponding series **b, d, g, v, z, ð** and **ʒ**, commonly called voiced. This classification is clearly not a fundamental one, since both groups can be readily distinguished when articulated in a whisper, i.e. both unvoiced. The audible resonances of the corresponding members of either group appear to be substantially identical though the lower resonances are, in general, louder in the so-called voiced series, and the upper resonances louder in the unvoiced. It is true that the two groups are usually distinguished—in ordinary speech—by being voiced or unvoiced respectively, and they may be reproduced in models by the same expedient—at least in the case of the continuing sounds **f, v, s z**, and **θ ð**.

It was found, however, that the consonant **f** could be humanly voiced without making it become a true **v** ; also that, in changing from the voiced **f** to the voiced **v** or, in a less degree, from the unvoiced **f** to the unvoiced **v** a slight forward movement of the throat could be felt above the larynx when sounding **v**, and a slight backward movement on sounding **f**. The action, if any, inside the mouth, could not, of course, be seen owing to the fact that all these sounds are made with a complete, or nearly complete, closure. To test whether the change from **p** to **b** was in any way due to lip action, a pair of fixed lips were made in plasticine—in the form of a ring, giving an opening of 18 × 22 mm., which could be held between the teeth. It was found that with this arrangement **p** or **b** could be made at will—voiced or unvoiced, and at high or low pressure—the opening and closing of the ring aperture being done with the finger or thumb, in the same manner and at the same rate, in each case, while the tongue was kept steady. Clearly then, the difference did not depend on lip action.

In order that the effect inside the mouth might be observed, a mouth stopper was made of a 45 mm. diameter cork, of which the centre portion was cut out and replaced by a glass window, an electric torchlight bulb was fitted to the inside of the cork (the leads being taken out through the cork window frame). With this device (shown in Fig. 83), the interior of the mouth could be easily observed, while articulating **p**, **b**—or **f**, **v**—the closures being made by the lips against the outer edges of the cork. It was found that no apparent difference was made either by the tongue or the soft palate in changing from **p** to **b** or from **f** to **v**, and that such difference as exists must, therefore, be made in the pharyngeal portion of the vocal cavity, That the nasal cavity is not concerned in the difference is further shown by the fact that all these sounds may be whispered.

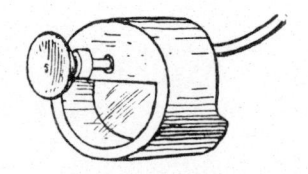

FIG. 83.

so that a rubber tube, led from one nostril to one ear, gives no sound. Under these conditions, the least opening of the passage leading to the nasal cavity causes a rush of sound to the ear.

It was found that when a fine jet of air was blown into the mouth, while forming the vocal cavities as for **f** and **v** and **θ** and **ð** respectively, a low resonance 362, was heard with **f** which was not audible with **v**, and a 383 (with 1366) for **ð** scarcely or not at all heard with **θ**. The essential differences therefore seemed to be due to pharyngeal resonance of some kind.

A rough model in plasticine was made of a mouth with soft palate closed to the nasal cavity and tongue lying flat; the pharyngeal portion consisted of a 1 inch diameter rubber tube, terminating in a funnel-shaped cork connection to an air supply tube of about 9 mm. internal diameter. (See Fig. 84.) With this arrangement there was no larynx, but a rough equivalent of the more or less opened

THE CONSONANTS

vocal cords could be made by constricting the tube by external pressure. With the pharynx tube slightly compressed, so as to give a relatively free passage to the air supply, complete closure and release of the mouth of the model, by hand, during blowing, gave a distinct whispered **b**, while partial closure of the mouth

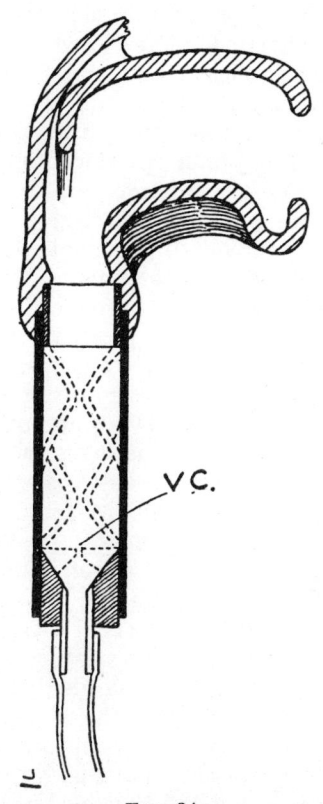

FIG. 84.

gave **v**—that is to say the "voiced" type of consonant in each case. When the pharynx tube was further compressed at the same point, so as nearly to close the passage to the air tube, the same manipulations of the mouth of the model gave a clear **p** or **f**, i.e. the "unvoiced" type.

A pair of permanent vocal cords, in plasticine, were next fixed, at the mouth of the funnel-shaped connection between the air tube and pharynx tube, as shown in dotted lines at VC in Fig. 84, so as to give a lenticular opening about 15 mm. long and 2 mm. maximum width. With this degree of opening of the vocal cords, the consonant at full closure and release was **p**. Enlarging the opening to 3·5 mm. width, gave **p** at high air pressure and **b** at low pressure; further enlarging the opening to 5 mm. width, gave **b** at high or low pressure.

The vocal cords were once more closed to a narrow width of about ·75 mm., giving a clear **p** or **f**, and the pharynx tube was constricted at various distances and with various degrees of closure. At about 1 cm. in front of the vocal cords, constriction up to a gap of 4 or 5 mm., produced no loss of the **p** or **f** sounds; further constriction, however, to 2 or 3 mm. gap, definitely changed the **p** or **f** into a clear **b** or **v**. This action would appear to correspond to a partial closure of the false vocal cords in front of the real ones. This same effect of converting **p** or **f** into **b** or **v** was produced by constriction at any point in the length of the pharynx tube, provided the degree of constriction was properly adjusted.

It was noticed that the change from the unphonated **p** or **f** to the unphonated **b** or **v** was always accompanied by a great increase of the whispered voice, due to resonance in the pharynx tube, when properly constricted. It was also noticed that if the constriction giving **b** or **v** was further increased, so as to give a nearly complete closure in front of the vocal cords, the **p** or **f** sound was restored, i.e. a certain minimum of acoustic connection was required between the mouth resonances and those of the air tube (with open vocal cords) or of the cavity formed between the true and false vocal cords in the case of a nearly closed attitude of the vocal cords themselves.

A simple model for the study of the whispered consonants—built up of rubber and glass tubes with tongue and vocal cords in plasticine—is shown in section at Fig. 85.

With this model it was found that with the fixed (plasticine) vocal cords wide apart (6 mm.) the consonant on closure and release of the mouth of the model was **bɑ**, which was converted to **pɑ** when the pharynx tube was constricted (as shown) at 2·5 cm. above the vocal cords. Conversely, with vocal cords near together (1·5 mm.) the consonant with unconstricted pharynx was **pɑ**, and with constricted pharynx **bɑ**.

It is clear therefore that there are two alternative ways in which a whispered **p** or **b** (and probably also the other

THE CONSONANTS

corresponding consonants) can be made—according to the degree of aperture at the vocal cords.

With the last-mentioned model a good **s** was produced by transverse constriction between the first and second fingers at $1\frac{1}{4}$ cm. This became appreciably an unvoiced **z** when the pharynx tube was pinched between the finger and thumb of the other hand—the fixed vocal cords having a separation

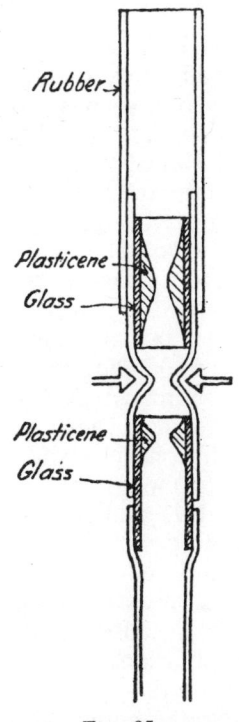

FIG. 85.

of $1\frac{3}{4}$ mm. Similarly, a θ (tha, as in thumb) made by a transverse constriction at $3\frac{1}{2}$ cm. became ð (tha, as in thus) and a **t** at $2\frac{1}{4}$ cm. became a clear **d** on constriction of the pharynx tube.

In view of the results obtained with models, the experiment was tried of compressing the human throat just above the larynx while whispering the various consonants of the so-called voiced series. It was found that by direct pressure on the front of the throat a whispered **va** became converted into a sound approaching **fa**, while **za** became a recognizable **sa**.

ð became "nasalized" by pressure immediately above the larynx, and became changed to **θa** by upward pressure nearer to the root of the tongue. **ba, da,** and **ga** were altered in character—losing the richness of their low resonances—but they never became **pa, ta** and **ka**.

Generally speaking, however, the change of consonant due to external pressure on the pharynx appeared to confirm the evidence of the models.

This at least can be affirmed, that the essential difference between the so-called unvoiced consonants, **p, t, k, f, s, θ, ʃ,** and the "voiced" series **b, d, g, v, z, ð, ʒ,** is one of resonance, and that the latter series are produced either by the acoustic effects of direct access to the trachea (in the case of a whispered sound) or to the effects of the resonance of a cavity formed between the true and false vocal cords.

It is interesting to note that with the model, the whispered voice (and the consequent **b, d,** effect) was loudest when the pharynx tube was constricted at 1 cm. from the vocal cords —i.e. in the position corresponding most nearly to that of the false vocal cords in the human throat.

The matter could be tested on the human subject by laryngoscopic observation of the pharynx through a mouth window with pharyngeal mirror attachment, while the subject articulated **p** and **b**, or **f** and **v**, against the edges of the mouth window frame, as already described.

I, later, had the privilege of seeing some of the results obtained by Dr. Russell, and of inspecting for myself the action of his vocal cords, false vocal cords and epiglottis during normal speech conditions.

Dr. Russell has developed what is, in effect, a pharyngeal "periscope", by which the action of the vocal cords, etc., can be studied with artificial illumination during normal speech. He has also taken an extended series of X-ray photographs during speech and song.

His results will throw much light on the operation of the vocal cords, the epiglottis and the tongue during phonation and articulation.

The varying "expression" of the laryngeal cavity as observed by him when different vowels are intoned on the same note has been already referred to in Chap. II, p. 33), as also

THE CONSONANTS

his observation that the epiglottis co-operates, in certain instances, in forming a constriction to produce the back resonator—for example, in the case of the vowel ɑ (calm).

As to voiced and unvoiced consonants, when whispered by Dr. Russell, it appeared that in the case of b and v the false vocal cords rose up and formed a cavity of comparatively small aperture above the vocal cords—the action being comparable to that obtained by constricting the rubber pharynx of the model shown at Fig. 84, as already described.

There has, up till now, been a great uncertainty as to the purpose and action of the epiglottis and of the false vocal cords in human speech. Dr. Russell's observations definitely show that they both act as essential organs of articulation.

Many of the consonants, as well as all the vowels, can be reproduced—so as to form continuous speech—in the device (due to the present writer) called the Cheirophone. In this, the resonating cavities are formed by the operator's hands, three fingers of which are made to represent the tongue, so that by their various positions and movements within the cavity, a tolerable resemblance of the vocal resonances may be produced. This device will be described in detail in a later chapter.

Besides the electrical experiments of J. Q. Stewart, already referred to, very important contributions to the knowledge of consonants, as well as of vowels, were made in about 1924-25 by Crandall.[1] A comparison of the resonances found by him by purely instrumental methods, and those which I had obtained by ear, is given in Appendix VII.

Audible Range of the Voiced and Unvoiced Consonants

In Chapter II, on the function of the vocal organs, an account was given of experiments made to test the audible range of the vowel-sounds. Mention may therefore be made of similar experiments, carried out on the "unvoiced" consonant f, θ (thigh), s and ʃ (shy) and their normally voiced relatives v, ð (thy), z and ʒ (pleasure).

In fairly good out-of-door conditions, with a moderate breeze and listening down wind, the following comparative ranges were obtained—the consonants being articulated by myself and identified by Miss G. M. Barker :—

[1] *The Bell System Technical Journal*, Oct., 1925, vol. iv, No. 4, pp. 586-626.

f, maximum range at which identification was certain about 45 yards; becoming unrecognizable at 77 yards—not distinguishable from θ (thigh).

θ, maximum range for certain identification about 79 yards; becoming unrecognizable at 96 yards—not distinguishable from s.

s, maximum for certain identification about 123 yards; becoming unrecognizable at 197 yards.

ʃ (shy), maximum for certain identification 320 yards; becoming uncertain at 326. This is much the most penetrating of the unvoiced sounds; it has more than twice the range of the best-carrying unvoiced vowel-sound.

Similar experiments were made with the corresponding "voiced" consonants, v, ð (thy), z, ʒ (pleas*ure*) with the following results:—

v, was certain at about 75 yards, uncertain at 153—about twice the range of f.

ð, was certain at about 220 yards, uncertain at about 400; say four times the range of θ.

z, was certain at about 500 yards, uncertain at 645—say three times the range of s.

ʒ, was certain at about 470 yards, uncertain at 700 yards—say twice the range of sh.

It will be seen that the effect of voicing the consonants f, θ, s and ʃ is to increase their range of audibility from two to four times—as compared with the ten to twenty fold increase of range which was found in the case of the whispered and voiced vowel sounds.

The weather conditions in these experiments were very similar to those of the experiments on the vowel ranges described in Chapter II—there was a light wind, never exceeding five miles per hour, blowing towards the speaker.

Nature of the Consonant Sounds

We are now in a position to state certain definite conclusions as to the nature of consonants. Consonants are due to resonances, like the vowels; but inasmuch as they are produced by movements of the vocal organs (like the diphthongs) their resonances are characterized, not only by pitch, but also by their change and rate of change in pitch. The consonants are all made by complete or partial closures of the front or back

THE CONSONANTS

orifice of the front resonator of the series which produce them. In every case there are more than two resonators in action.

The resonant ranges of the consonants are as extensive as those of the vowels, but in certain of the resonances, the actual pitch produced depends (as has already been explained) [1] mainly on the front resonance of the vowel with which the consonant is associated. The actual resonance changes of a given consonant may thus be very different when used with different vowels. The following additional examples may be given :—

Syllable	Upper Vowel Resonance.	Resonant Change in Semi-tones.	L. Resonance (upper).
il (eel)	2298	Fall of 5 semitones	1722
eil (ale)	2048	,, 3 ,,	1722
el (ell)	1824	,, 1 ,,	1722
æl (alleluia)	1824	,, 2 ,,	1625
ɐl (earl)	1534	Rise of 2 ,,	1722
ʌl (ultimate)	1534	,, 1 ,,	1625
al (arlington)	1217	,, 4 ,,	1534
ɔl (all)	912	,, 7 ,,	1366
ul (ool)	683	,, 11 ,,	1290

FIG. 86.

Here we have the same consonant characterized by a fall of five semitones or a rise of eleven semitones—according to the associated vowel, and a terminal upper resonance varying from 1722 to 1290, a range of five semitones. Yet if the terminal l be voiced by itself, as a continuing sound, it becomes quite unrecognizable. The resonant change is the real characteristic, in spite of its great difference with different associated vowels.

In this case the one constant characteristic is the movement made by the tongue, which rises rapidly from near its vowel position to touch the hard palate, and then falls with equal speed to the next vowel position.

We are, in fact, driven once more to the conclusion, already referred to at the end of Chapter V, that, in recognizing speech sounds, the human ear is not listening to music but to indications, due to resonance, of the position and gestures of the organs of articulation.

[1] See p. 107, Fig. 76.

CHAPTER VII

THE ORIGIN AND DEVELOPMENT OF SPEECH

CERTAIN of the conclusions to which we have been driven throw a definite light on the possible origin of speech. It may be of interest, therefore, to consider this question of Origin when viewed at a new angle.

Speech, we have seen, is essentially a musical phenomenon; yet, in our appreciation of it, we appear to be interested in the sounds only in so far as they give evidence of the positions and gestures of the organs of articulation which produced them. Very different sounds are naturally reckoned (for identification purposes) as identical, if they are due to similar articulation-gestures, though these gestures may (for convenience) be made in different positions in the mouth, according to vowels with which they are associated.

This fact points to the gestures as being the essential element of speech, and strengthens the conclusions of the philologists,[1] that " the earliest human language may be said to have been a language of gesture signs ".

ANIMAL GESTURES

We need not be surprised at this idea, for it is clear, when the evidence is studied, that gesture is a common method, in use throughout the animal world, for inducing action on the part of another individual. Professor Julian Huxley, whom I consulted on the question, has given me some interesting examples of animal gesture in connection with the courtship of insects and of birds.

Thus the male fly Empis approaches the female bearing gifts —actually a smaller dead fly done up neatly into an egg-shaped parcel !

Two exceptionally interesting examples of insect gestures have been recorded by Professor Dr. K. von Frisch of the Zoological Institute of the University of Munich.[2] von Frisch has shown that when a foraging bee has found good nectar,

[1] Compare the article " Philology," *Enc. Brit.*, 11th ed., p. 416.
[2] See *Aus dem Leben der Bienen*, Berlin, 1927, pp. 84, 89.

she gorges herself, returns to the hive, disgorges to the cell-charging bees, and then—instead of returning at once to the source of supply—she proceeds to announce her discovery to her colleagues.

This she does by performing a ceremonial dance of a peculiar character on the " floor " of the honeycomb. She runs round in small circles—clockwise, then counter-clockwise for several seconds, or, it may be, even for a minute or two at a time.

The surrounding bees all take notice ; they follow, and touch the dancer with their antennæ, so as to discover the lingering scent of the flowers which she has just visited, and they then fly out, independently, to hunt for flowers of a similar smell.

If the foraging bee has found good pollen, she also performs a dance, but of a different figure—a single figure of 8. The " 8 " is to be imagined as composed of two loops of equal sizes flattened (from top to bottom) so that the middle portion common to both loops—becomes a straight line. Over this course the dancing bee runs again and again, and, as she comes to the straight, she waggles her abdomen from side to side in a peculiar fashion !

I asked Professor von Frisch whether he could see any similarity between the action of these two dances and those of a bee in the presence of a plentiful supply of nectar or pollen respectively, but his answer was that no such similarity appeared. So, though the purpose of the dances seems clear, their origin remains obscure.

Among bird gestures supplied by Professor Huxley may be cited those of *Podiceps cristatus*, the Grasshopper Warbler, Savi's Warbler, and the Louisiana Heron, in which the male courts the female by presenting her with a sample of the nesting material.

In these cases—as in that of the spider—it need not be assumed that the gestures are intentionally symbolic, or indeed that they are intentional at all. From our present point of view it is sufficient that they are—in part at least—the means whereby the female is induced to accept her courtier.

In other instances I believe that birds do make truly symbolic gestures. In September, 1928, I had the opportunity—by the kindness of Lord and Lady Grey of Fallodon—of seeing a parrot (African grey) belonging to Lord Grey's sister, Mrs. de Coetlogon, which had evolved a gesture which meant " I want to be let out ". The gesture was performed as follows. The parrot held on to the bars of its cage with its beak and left foot, and pawed the air repeatedly, at about 100 beats per minute, with its other foot. It never made any sound while performing this gesture. The explanation given (which seemed a very probable one) was that the pawing gesture represented the action of feeling for its mistress's finger on which to perch as a preliminary to being taken out of the cage. The parrot had acquired the habit before coming into its present owner's possession.

It will probably be generally agreed that dogs communicate with one another, and with mankind, to a large extent by gesture. The bark or yap or growl signifies the emotional state, but purpose is expressed by action and expression.

I will give only one example which will serve as a type. At my home in Somerset we had a fox-terrier " Joseph ", who was especially devoted to our cook, Mrs. Wright. When Joseph wanted to be taken out for a walk, or thought it was time to be taken up to bed, he pulled Mrs. Wright by her skirt in the direction required.

I have to thank Mr. Gordon Bryan for the photographs here shown of Joseph pulling Mrs. Wright out of doors on a sunny day, getting her under way, and finally leading her across the stable yard towards the open country !

At the London Zoological Gardens I have personally observed mouth gestures (made without sound) by the Pig-tailed Monkey (Malay States) and by the Mandrill (West Africa), both expressive of pleasure. The Mandrill also shakes his head as a sign of pleasure. The Chimpanzees make some very expressive gestures when " asking " for food—in particular a projection of the lips, which is often coupled with the projection of the hands, and an open-mouthed gesture with the lips drawn back so as to show the teeth.

The monkeys make many vowel sounds, including i (eat), or ɪ (it), e (men), æ (hat), ɞ (earth), ʌ (up), ɒ (not), ɔ (all), ou (no), u (who), and ʊ (put), but, in my limited experience, I have not heard any one monkey make more than a few sounds of the complete series ! The higher apes appear to be much more silent than their lower relatives, but their gestures are eloquent. Of consonant sounds, the only ones I have observed are a soft-palatal release made by the Hamadryas Baboon, and a glottal release made by the Pig-tailed Monkey

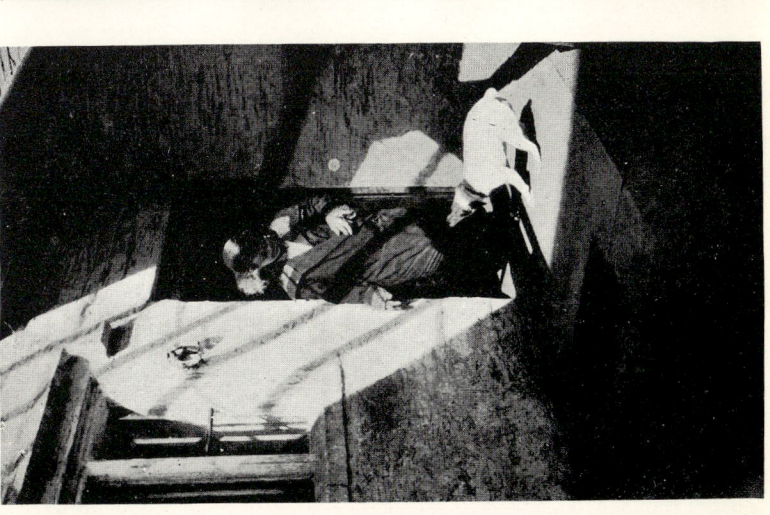

Fig. 87. "JOSEPH" AND MRS. WRIGHT

Fig. 88. "JOSEPH" AND MRS. WRIGHT

Fig. 89. "JOSEPH" AND MRS. WRIGHT

(Malay States), by the Chimpanzee and by the Sutty Mangaby.

The Siamang Monkey makes a sound very like **m**, by closing the mouth and inflating a bladder under the chin during phonation. The Japanese Ape makes a nasal sound, rather like the French nasal vowel **ǣ** (as in vin), while the Orang makes a sucking-in sound which might do duty as a consonant. The Chimpanzee makes a very human **he** (as in hen) or **hæ** (as in hat) when tickled. The beginnings of song are certainly present in the cries of some of the monkeys. Thus the Siamang monkey has a call, which I have recorded thus:—

FIG. 90.

the **ɐ** (earth) being very clear, and the **oũ** sounds being nasal Here we have words, music and rhythm—all combined!

At the Dublin Zoo, about 1924, I met Dr. Cross, who had made a special study of the sounds produced by the monkeys. He told me that one sound (of the **u** type) was a call of welcome. and that a newcomer to whom he made it had immediately established friendly relations with him when he addressed it with that particular call.

That the apes can be taught to articulate is proved by the success of Dr. William H. Furness[1] in teaching a young female orang-outan to say " papa "—which she finally recognized as her teacher's name—and the word " cup " which she used of her own accord, when ill, to express the fact that she was thirsty.

Professor Robert M. Yerkes, of Yale, in his book, *Almost Human*, concludes that the apes do *not* use language, and that the various sounds that they make are innate emotional expressions.

He makes the interesting suggestion that they may perhaps be taught to use their fingers somewhat as does the deaf and dumb person, and thus helped to acquire a simple-, non-vocal sign-language.

The most direct way to carry out Professor Yerkes' suggestion

---

[1] " Observations on the Mentality of the Chimpanzees and Orang-outans," *Proc. Amer. Philos. Soc.*, 1916, 55, pp. 281–90.

would be to put a young chimpanzee (for example) under the care of a deaf mute, with instructions to the keeper to " talk " to the animal freely by gesture, and to encourage it to imitate him, and to ask in sign-language for what it wanted. Such an experiment—given a sympathetic deaf-mute teacher, and a tractable young chimpanzee pupil—with adequate intelligence on both sides—would seem very likely to succeed.

That the higher apes have not developed speech is less surprising when one considers how little advantage speech would bring to them under their normal conditions of life. For conveying simple ideas, bodily gesture is probably quite as effective as speech—except only in the dark ; and as, at night, warnings, recognitions, challenges, and so on would naturally be expressed by emotional cries, there would seem to be little, if any, scope for speech in communities having the mental development of the apes—which is said to be equal at most to that of the human child of two years.

HUMAN GESTURE LANGUAGE

In Sir E. B. Tylor's *Early History of Mankind*,[1] he gives an interesting account of some comparatively modern uses of human gesture as a form of language. The most remarkable of these is the universal gesture language which was current until recent times among the native Red Indian tribes of North America. This was a silent language, by which all the different tribes, who met together on the plains, speaking widely different languages, could understand one another and carry on inter-tribal communications and negotiations. The gesture signs were very similar to those which are naturally evolved by deaf mutes, and were developed in several different ways.

Thus, the gesture might imitate the shape or outline of the thing described—as when a circle was drawn in the air to represent the sun ; or it might refer to a common movement of the thing described, e.g. as by making characteristic motions of the hand to signify those of a horse ; or the gesture might indicate an attribute of the thing or person described. For example, the British Prime Minister, Mr. Stanley Baldwin, having been popularly associated with his tobacco pipe, a tobacco pipe gesture might also come to mean " Prime Minister ".

[1] 1870 (American edition, 1878), chaps. 2, 3, and 4, also the same author's *Anthropology*, 1881, pp. 114-28.

Further information on this subject was obtained in New York in May, 1928, from General Scott, the leading authority on the Indian Sign-language. He pointed out that the Sign-language is still in the primitive root stage, and has apparently changed but little since historic times. There is evidence from the writings of Torquemada that the Tultecka and Chichimeka tribes " talked together by signs because their languages were different " prior to Aztec times.

In the Indian Sign-language there is no differentiation between parts of speech—the signs are based on imitation and analogy ; thus, such actions as prayer—hands up—and sleep —face resting on hand—are imitations, whereas time—indicated as if by drawing an imaginary thread backwards with the right hand from the closed left hand held downwards—or the word bad—indicated by a throwing away gesture—are due to analogy.

Spiritual ideas are signed by analogy, for example, the right hand with two fingers held up like a wolf's ear, means foxy, or wise—hence, a scout ; in this case, therefore, the sign in question is analogous to a verbal hononym having three meanings. Wisdom is signed by the wolf's ears moved laterally, as if hunting the ground ; the same sign coupled with the sign for sleep means a sleep-wisdom, i.e. a dream. Knowledge is signed by a small opening made between the crossed first fingers and thumbs held parallel, the opening then being enlarged by drawing the hands apart. Water is signed by the action of scooping up and drinking from the hand ; running water is signed by the sign for water, plus a forward rippling motion of the hand. Fire is signed by the fingers closed together, pointing upwards and opened suddenly, as if bursting into flame. The heat of the sun is represented by the open hands with fingers extended, as if pressing downwards.

Numerals are counted from the little finger of the left hand, held as if with a spear under the left elbow ; five is symbolized by the left hand help up, ten by the two hands dropped and closed ; six to nine are signed by the left hand plus additional fingers of the right hand.

The Cistercian Monks, whose vows precluded them from speaking to one another, are said to have evolved a gesture language, very similar to those already mentioned. It seems to be as natural to man as to the lower animals to express himself by pantomimic gestures when no other means are available.

ORIGIN AND DEVELOPMENT

The Emotional Language of Laryngeal Sound

Side by side with the development of gesture, there must have been a sister art—so to call it—based on the use of the larynx. The power of expressing the emotions by laryngeal tones is (as we have noted) almost universal among the higher animals, and it may be imagined that, in the early stages of human development, mankind roared and grunted and sung, on the one hand, to express his emotions, and gesticulated and grimaced on the other to explain his ideas. In some cases he may have used both methods together, as when a dog makes the threatening gesture of showing his teeth, and energizes or phonates this gesture by the addition of a laryngeal growl. Thus, according to *The Times* of 6th September, 1927, Mr. H. N. Ridley, of the Singapore Botanic Gardens, had observed that " Many of the smaller monkeys uttered a range of sounds that seemed to convey states of mind and to be a rudimentary kind of language. There were warning cries, as at the presence of snakes, calls to the young, sociable chattering, sex calls, and fighting challenges."

The Gesture Theory of Speech

What drove man to the invention of speech was, as I imagine, not so much the need of expressing his thoughts (for that might have been done quite satisfactorily by bodily gesture) as the difficulty of " talking with his hands full ". It was the *continual* use of man's hands for craftsmanship, the chase, and the beginnings of art and agriculture, that drove him to find other methods of expressing his ideas—namely, by a specialized pantomime of the tongue and lips. Mr. J. A. McMordie has suggested to me that the development of the arts and crafts also occupied the eyes, so that these were less available for recognizing gestures.

The apes, having (in their environment) no need of craftsmanship, thus escaped the necessity for a vocal language. As man developed in intelligence and technique, the need for more exact gestures became greater, while his hands became more occupied with the arts and crafts. Gestures, which were previously made by hand, were unconsciously copied by movements or positions of the mouth, tongue or lips [1];

---

[1] Dr. Gregory, of the Metropolitan Museum of Natural History, New York, with whom I discussed this theory, pointed out to me that it would be more probable that the mouth and bodily gestures were made concurrently at first and finally *superseded* by mouth gestures.

other gestures were developed—depending on any of the various instinctive methods of gesture formation of which some examples have already been given.

The origin of such a system of tongue and lip gestures may be inferred from an observation of Charles Darwin in his book *The Expression of the Emotions*, where, at p. 34, he writes: in relation to what he calls " serviceable associated habits " : " There are other actions which are commonly performed under certain circumstances independently of habit, and which seem to be due to imitation or some kind of sympathy. Thus, persons cutting anything with a pair of scissors may be seen to move their jaws simultaneously with the blades of the scissors. Children learning to write often twist about their tongue as their fingers move, in a ridiculous fashion ! "

The argument, then, runs as follows: Originally man expressed his ideas by gesture, but as he gesticulated with his hands, his tongue, lips and jaw unconsciously followed suit in a ridiculous fashion, " understudying " (as Sir Henry Hadow aptly suggested to me) the action of the hands.[1] The consequence was that when, owing to pressure of other business, the principal actors (the hands) retired from the stage—as much as principal actors ever do—their understudies—the tongue, lips and jaw—were already proficient in the pantomimic art.

Then the great discovery was made that if while making a gesture with the tongue and lips, air was blown through the oral or nasal cavities, the gesture became audible as a whispered speech sound. If, while pantomiming with tongue, lips and jaw our ancestors sang, roared or grunted—in order to draw attention to what they were doing—a still louder and more remarkable effect was produced, namely, what we call voiced speech.

Either effect—whispered speech or voiced speech—had this important property, that it enabled the mouth pantomime to be recognized by ear, so that, for the first time, mankind was able to impart information in the dark, or when he was was out of sight of the person with whom he wished to communicate.

Our ancestors must have soon found that *all* gestures of

---

[1] Professor Tilney of Columbia University, has pointed out (1928) that the speech centres in the human brain are a development of the hand-gesture centres.

tongue and lips were not equally suitable for this method of communication, and that, in particular, lateral movements of lips, tongue or jaw produced little or no audible change. It was therefore necessary to limit mouth pantomime to up and down, and to and fro movements—in other words, to operate in two dimensions instead of in three.

In this way there was developed a new system of conventional gesture of the organs of articulation from which, as I suggest, nearly all human speech took its origin.

This suggestion has often been foreshadowed. In the *Cratylus* of Plato on the origin of names [1] Socrates is represented as asking (amongst others) the following questions :—

" If we had no voice or tongue, and wished to make things clear to one another, should we not try as dumb people actually do, to make signs with our hands and head and person generally ? . . . And when we wish to express anything by voice or tongue or mouth, will not our expression by these means be accomplished, in any given instance, when an imitation of something is accomplished by *them* ? . . . A name then, it appears, is a vocal imitation of that which is imitated, and he who imitates with his voice names that which he imitates."

If instead of " voice " Plato had said " movements of his tongue and lips " this chapter might have been unnecessary !

The Tongue Track

Before considering in any detail this relation between the movements of tongue, lips, etc., which constitute the process of Articulation in speech, and the meaning that is attached to each individual group of movements, it will be well to look once more at the mechanism by which they are produced.

In Fig. 91 I have shown the approximate position to which my own tongue is humped to produce each of the vowels mentioned. This diagram may be compared with those previously given in Phonetic Transcription and Transliteration (*Proposals of the Copenhagen Conference*, April, 1925), or in A. Lloyd James' *Speech and Language*.[2]

The tongue is variable in shape but constant in volume; it follows that as its middle part is humped further back in the

---

[1] I have to thank Mr. Montague Francis Ashley-Montague of the Galton Society, New York, for this reference.
[2] British Broadcasting Corporation, 1928.

mouth, the tip of the tongue, just behind the lower teeth, tends to move backward.[1]

In my own mouth, the tip of the tongue lies close behind the lower teeth in the vowel i (eat) and moves progressively backward during the series ɪ (it), ei (hay), e (men), æ (hat), ɞ (earth), ʌ (up), ɑ (calm), during which it recedes about 10 mm. and still further from ɑ (calm) through ɒ (not), ɔ (all) to o (no) at 20 mm.—then it moves slightly upwards for u (who) and down again for ᴜ (put).[2]

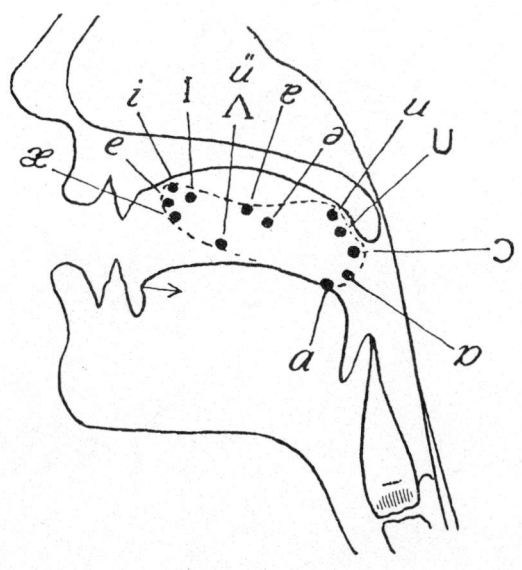

FIG. 91.

It will be seen therefore that in producing the vowel series i, e, æ, ʌ, ɑ, ɒ, ɔ, u, ᴜ, i, the middle part or hump of my tongue follows a ⬭ shaped course, while the tip of the tongue moves back and forth by about 20 mm., say ¾ inch. The lips maintain an approximately constant opening except at ɔ (all), o (no) and u (who) for which they

[1] This is incorrectly shown in Lloyd James' Fig. 3.
[2] Lloyd James' Fig. 4 shows the same tongue-tip positions for i and ᴜ.

are protruded and progressively brought closer together so as to reduce the mouth opening.

For the consonants, the approximate positions of the total or partial closures made by the tongue and lips—in my own case—are shown in Fig. 92. In many of these, e.g. s/z, t/d/n, θ/ð, ʃ/ʒ and r the tip of the tongue is active and takes part in the actual closures.

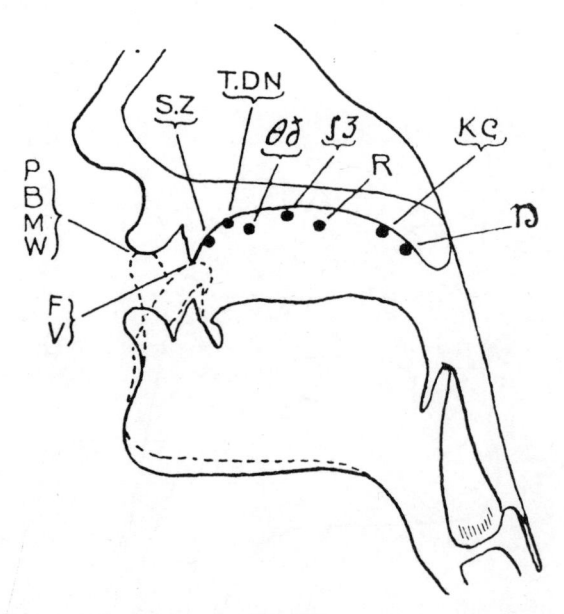

Fig. 92.

In the case of ʃ (sh) and ʒ (zh) the tongue actually makes two partial closures of which only the rearmost is indicated. In r (untrilled) the hump of the tongue goes to the position indicated, but with the tip of the tongue curled back towards the hump—while the sides of the hump are raised to touch the palate.

Mouth Pantomime

We can now form a mental picture of how the process of speech-making actually began, but an example or two will make the argument clearer. If the mouth, tongue and lips be moved as in eating, this constitutes a gesture sign meaning "eat"; if, while making this sign, we blow air through the vocal cavities, we automatically produce the whispered sounds mnyʌm-mnyʌm (*mnyum*), or mnɪʌ-mnɪʌ (*mnya*)—words which probably would be almost universally understood, and which actually occur as a children's word for food in Russian, as well as in English.[1]

Similarly, the action of sucking liquid in small quantities into the mouth, if "blown" as before, produces the whispered words sip, sʌp, according to the exact position of the tip of the tongue behind the lower teeth. It may be noted that the resonance changes produced by nearly all movements of the organs of articulation are the same, whether the breath is moving into or out of the cavities—in other words, we can whisper equally well on an in or out breath.[2] The transition from an in-breathing gesture to an out-breathing whispered or phonated speech sound is therefore a very simple one.

Professor Otto Jespersen[3] points out that "the vowel i (eat), especially in its narrow or thin variety, is particularly appropriate to express what is small, weak, insignificant, or, on the other hand, refined or dainty". He gives instances of this in various languages; he also refers to the observation[4] that in corresponding pronouns and adverbs, the vowel i frequently indicates what is nearer, and other vowels, especially a or u, what is farther off. Here we have an excellent example of the same principle. The small front cavity, made by the tongue, to express smallness—or the forward pushing of the tongue, to express nearness, both naturally result in the audible vowels i or ɪ; the withdrawal of the tongue to the back of the mouth to express farness or largeness, results in the vowels a, ɔ, or u. One of Tylor's examples (quoted by Jespersen) is especially interesting; iki, in Javan, means "this", ikɑ (a less forward tongue position) means "that", a little removed, while iku (retracted tongue and protruded lips) to indicate a distant object, means "yon, farther away".

Many of the invented words used by children—mentioned

---

[1] Tylor, in his *Primitive Culture*, 1903, vol. i, Chaps. v and vi (New York, 1877), refers inter alia, to *puf* (blow), *mu* (dumb), *kshu* (sneeze), and *nyam* (eat), but considers them all as derived from imitation of the *sounds* of the actions they represent.
[2] Except in the case of ʃ (sh) which becomes like ç (lecht) on an in-breath.
[3] *Language, Its Nature, Development, and Origin*, 1922, p. 402.
[4] See E. B. Tylor, op. cit., *Primitive Culture* (New York ed., vol. i, p. 220), and *Anthropology*, 1881, p. 128.

on p. 152 of Jespersen's book—seem capable of explanation on the same principle, such as **gön** (swallowing gesture) for " water to drink, milk ", **adi** (a tasting gesture) for " cake ", **dɛdɛtʃ** (galloping gesture made with the tip of the tongue) for " horse ". Professor Jespersen appears to have had an inkling of this relationship of gesture to articulation, for at p. 136, in speaking of the negative, he says " sometimes the *n* is heard without a vowel : it is only the gesture of turning up one's nose made audible ".

The following additional children's words may be mentioned **f(ph)im**, meaning " to smell ",[1] **min-nie** " sugar ", **da** " chair and sit down ", **by-la** " to put away toys ", possibly equals **bye-bye** " go to bed " and **la** " put down ", **by-nu** " to throw away permanently ", where **nu** may be a lip projecting gesture.[2]

Another adult example may be given, namely, in connection with the beckoning gesture—commonly made by extending the hand, palm up, drawing it inwards towards the face and at the same time bending the fingers inwards towards the palm. This gesture may be imitated with the tongue, by protruding, withdrawing, and bending up its tip as it re-enters the mouth and falls to rest.

If this " gesture " be blown or voiced, we get a resultant whispered or phonated *word*, like **edə**, **eðə** or **eðra** (according to the degree of contact between tongue and upper lip or palate) suggestive of the Icelandic **heðr**, the Hindustani **idhar**, and the Slavonic **ɪdeɪ**—all of which bear much the same meaning as our English word " hither ". If the same tongue gesture be finished more vigorously, the resultant word will end in a **k** or **g**, owing to the back portion of the tongue making a closure against the soft palate.

Thus, by unconsciously using the tongue, lips, jaw, etc., in the place of the head, hands, etc., pantomimic gesture would almost automatically produce human speech.

Synthetic Words

In March, 1927, I was in New York and met Dr. Neville Whymant, formerly Professor of Oriental Languages and Philosophy in Hōsei University, Tōkyō ; and sometime lecturer in Chinese and Japanese at the School of Oriental Studies, University of London. I happened to state in his

---

[1] Per the Rev. H. J. Langley.   [2] Per Lady Malise Graham.

OF SPEECH 139

presence my belief that i-i (made with a little mouth) and a-a or ɔ-ɔ (aw-aw) (made with a big mouth) were the original human words for " little " and " big " respectively.

Dr. Whymant added the interesting information that ɪ'ɪ was actually the primitive Polynesian word for " little ", while the archaic Japanese word for " big " was ōhō. In view of this apparent confirmation, I started to devise a number of fabricated words, descriptive of various simple actions, such as primitive man might have used. The process adopted was to make, in the first instance, a pantomimic hand gesture, descriptive of the action in question, and then to invent a corresponding gesture of the tongue and lips which might do duty in the place of the hand gesture, the correspondence being judged by " feel " rather than by sight.

When a satisfactory tongue and lip gesture had been evolved, it was then converted into whispered speech, by blowing air through the mouth, or into voiced speech by humming or grunting during the performance of the gesture of the tongue and lips, etc.

In the following table the fabricated words thus formed are set out, together with Dr. Neville Whymant's additions, in the fourth column, of some actual words with similar meaning, occurring in primitive Polynesian, Melanesian, Indonesian or archaic Japanese speech. In the column labelled Phonetic Resultant, the sounds produced by the pantomimic gestures are transcribed as originally recorded.

There are, however, a number of additional resultants, due to the same tongue and lip gestures, which might have been included, and which, in some cases, give an even better fit to Dr. Whymant's words in the fourth column. Thus, d, t, and n are all due to the same tongue gesture—the differentiations being made farther back. Therefore, " dra " for feel, stroke, might equally have been written " tra "—which closely resembles Dr. Whymant's " tura ".

Similarly, p, b and m are due to a single lip gesture, so that ðʌp, ðup might also be ðʌb, ðub—a closer fit to Dr. Whymant's ðubu. " Ledl-ledl " might equally have been letl-letl, so as to correspond with " lete-lete " to wave aloft, while pʌl written as bʌl or mbʌl, compares very closely with the actual words " bulu " and " mbulu ".

It will be seen that in every instance except one, Dr. Whymant has found actual words of similar meaning which

ORIGIN AND DEVELOPMENT

show phonetic relation to the fabricated words. For the present purpose only the closest "fits" given by Dr. Whymant have been included in this table.

SUMMARY OF TEN GESTURE WORDS, AND DR. WHYMANT'S SELECTION OF PROTO-POLYNESIAN AND ARCHAIC JAPANESE WORDS OF SIMILAR MEANING.

Meaning.	Pantomimic Gesture.	Phonetic Result.	Proto-Polynesian. Archaic Japanese.
Reach up	Tongue reaching up to *touch* palate	að, aθ, or ad	ada, adha-adaru, idaru, Arch. Jap.
Feel, stroke	,, feeling palate backward and downward	θra, ðra, lra, dra	tura, tula, tataru, Hazlewood 246.
Feel smooth, stroke up	,, feeling behind lower teeth and up behind front teeth	aɪl, ɔɪl, øɪl	-aila, -ɛɪla, -taira āri, ori, olo, oloi (Nine. Futuna) (W. Churchill Pol. Wand. 391).
Draw back suddenly	,, protruded and withdrawn	ærʌp, æðʌp	eðhupu, ðupi, (Indonesian), Brandstetter and Kern rap (Pol. Wand. 305) Aneityum.
Scrape	,, scraped between teeth	ðʌp, ðup, ðu	ðubu, ðuu (Indonesian), Brandst. and Kern.
Wave aloft	,, waved, touching palate	leðl-leðl ledl-ledl	lete-lete, vele-vele (Proto-Indones), Brandst. and Kern. lele.[1] (Hawaiian, Fijian) Pol. Wand. 421. Hazlewood 66.

[1] (Per Dr. Whymant) lɛlɛ in Fijian—the outer end of tree-branches in Samoan, Hawaiian, Tongan, Futuna, and Efate, either meteor or wind-driven.

OF SPEECH

Meaning.	Pantomimic Gesture.	Phonetic Result.	Proto-Polynesian. Archaic Japanese.
Shake (like a mat)	Tongue shaken (behind the teeth)	ᴅlɑ-ᴅlɑ	ore-ore (Japanese). ulia, urea. Fijian. Hazlewood 142. ruru-ruru, Rapanni. East.Isld. 299.
Stab or spear	,, protruded between lips and teeth	peð, pʌð, or possibly pʌl	bulu, mbulu (Indonesian), Brandstetter. m b a l e (Fijian), Hazlewood 241. pili (Hawaiian) Pol. Wand. 289.
Shoot (with bow and arrow)	,, reflexed, grip at back of tongue, and sudden release	ŏr-ki, ŏr-kui or dr-ki, dr-ku	koki, ikoki. (The initial K representing a strongly reflexed R) Author. Cf. çári (Skt.) arrow.
Pull down	,, reflexed and lowered	trɑ, trɔ	ndrei (Fijian), Hazlewood 30. tore, ataru (Japanese) Chamberlain and Ueda. Tr. Asiatic Soc. of Japan.

FIG. 93.

Another list of synthetic words, which was also submitted, later, to Dr. Whymant, is the following,[1] to which I have added the nearest confirmation found by him.

[1] Compare *Proc. Royal Soc. A*, vol. cxix, 1928, p. 168.

Action.	Gestures of Articulation.	Resultant.	Actual.
Sew	A grip with protruded lip—retracted and released (**pui**) followed by a new grip at a higher level (**s**) retracted (**r**) and brought forward to near the original starting point	**pui-sri** **b**[1] **zl**[1] **m**[1]	**fusɪ** ⎫ P.W. **vusɪ** ⎭ 292 (Tongan, Samoan, Fijian).
	Alternative to second part of gesture, grip (**s**) followed by lifting and protruding the tongue and finally curving it downward and back into the mouth	**-sla** **zr**	
Coil or Roll (towards oneself)	Initial back grip (**k**) followed by further depression of tongue (ɔ) lifting to near palate (ɪ) and bending back so as to touch the palate (**l** or **r**) before dropping (ʌ)	**kɔɪlʌ** (kawila) **g r**	**koeru** (Jap.) Engl. **kɔil** (coil) **kaviri** (Rapanni) E.I. 269.
Roll (away)	Tongue starts from **k, tl,** or **r** position and curves upward and forward (ɪ) down and back (ɔ) and up and forward (ɪ)	**tliɔe** **dr** **k** **r** æ (for ɔ)	**t'rie** (Indonesian) Skeat and Blagden.
Blow (thro' a tube)	A sudden (plosive) blast with lips protruded	**kɥ** (as in French *cui*) ŋ	**kɪ** (-rɪ) **ku** (Jap.) **hu** (Rapanni) (Easter Island, W. Churchill 274).

[1] The additional consonants inserted under the synthetic words are alternatives, due to the same tongue and lip gesture.

OF SPEECH

Action.	Gestures of Articulation.	Resultant.	Actual.
Dance up and down to and fro	Dancing action of the tongue	li-lɔ r r	li-lo Indo-Chin. P. Schmidt **lila**[1] (Skt.). **rere** (leap) E.I. 249 **lulla-by**.[2]
Plough	Tongue tip drawn back and scraped forward along the floor of the mouth	kɔri (r guttural) g g kɔi	**karia** (Fiji) Hay. 237. **keri** (dig) Pol. Wand. 347. **kei** (Marquesas) P.W. 347. **karsh**[3] (Ind. Iran.).
Strip grains from the stalk	Strip tongue between teeth	t h p or d h b	**tup**. Indo-Chin. P. Schmidt.
collect take a handful and scatter	tongue reflexed front grip between tongue, teeth and lips, tongue suddenly lowered and protruded.	r sɑ sə z	cf. Aryan **sɑ** (sow grain).
complete action as above	above actions in succession	θ'prsɑ ð b z say θʌpərsɑ (or equivalents in ð, b and z)	— No equivalent found.
Pick berries collect them bury in the ground	Front grip released tongue reflexed tongue tip buried between front of lower teeth and under lip	sp or sb r dvz or dvð	**tɑnɑ, tɑnum** (Tanna and Efate).
complete action as above	above actions in succession	sp'rdvz say spərdɑvz (or equivalents in t and ð)	**tɑðavu** (Fijian) Hazlewood 119.

FIG. 94.

[1] Game or enjoyment—per Prof. L. H. Gray.
[2] Dancing a child up and down, to and fro, to put it to sleep (author); also the Lithuanian **čiučiā-liulia** (*tchu-tcha-lu-la*) = lullaby.
[3] Per Prof. L. H. Gray.

With reference to the words **tana, tanum**, for bury in the ground, I find that **tan** can be made by a very similar burying gesture to that of **dvz** or **tvz**, but with slightly more open mouth—the initial t apparently represents an initial grip, like my **sp**. With these substitutions my **spərdavz** becomes **tərdavz**, not unlike the Fijian **taðavu**. I do not know whether such a tongue gesture as that of thrusting it behind the lower lips has been observed in any language, but I understand that tongue protrusion as an articulation gesture is known.

With reference to the words for " blow through a tube ", Dr. Whymant has pointed out that words beginning with **f** or **fu** are nearer the original sound—e.g. archaic Japanese **fŭkŭ**. This would indicate that the blowing action did not generally begin (as I assumed) with a sudden plosive release of the breath at high pressure, but by an increasing pressure so as to accelerate the dart in its passage through the tube.

As to the gesture of protruding the lips (to form the vowel u) it is interesting to remember that many unrelated races of primitive men commonly point with their lips (instead of with their hands) to indicate direction.

The following are some additional synthetic words with the nearest confirmations found :—

Action.	Gestures of Articulation.	Resultant.	Actual.
shoot with bow and arrow (alternative gesture).	lips protruded and drawn back, then closed, projected and plosively released.	oui-pɥ	i-pá (arrow) hhi-pa (Hoka) e-pa (throw spear. Pol.) Rivet 223.[1]
big	big mouth	o-o ɔ-ɔ	ōhō.[2]
little	little mouth	i-i	ɪ'ɪ, ɪtɪ.[2]
dig	tongue thrust down from contact with palate (ta) and thrown up and back (ri or di)	tari tadi	tari.

[1] Les Malayo Polynésiens en Amérique.   [2] See p. 139.

Action.	Gestures of Articulation.	Resultant.	Actual.
suck—sip	lips compressed and slightly protruded, breath expelled *instead* of drawn in as in sucking.	sʉp sup	suu susu sup, sip [1] (English).

FIG. 95.

Dr. Whymant has also given several other gesture-words from Proto-Polynesian, archaic Japanese and Chinese speech—from which I select the following :—

Come here	chê'rh lai	Compare Eng. *here*
	kochyra-e	
	haere-mai	
Swallow	gobu-gobu	
Eat	kai-kai	
	ŭmamma	
	koramuramu	
	kamu	
Drink	numu	
	nomu	
	minum	

In this connection I have attempted to devise synthetic words which might be equally applicable to the actions of eating, drinking and smoking, e.g. :—

        fypm or fypma
        u.b.n.   u n

        hyka   compare *hookah*
        f.u.g.

          ng   compare *hunger*

        dubna
        t p
        n

        um'ga
          k
          ŋ

[1] Author.

tumaga
d b k
n p ŋ

The **f** is intended to be bilabial.

I understand that such generalized words for all three actions are used in certain languages, but have not yet examined them. The following are some synthetic words for various methods of eating :—

Bite hard	ŋʌ (nga)	Compare Eng. *gnaw*
Eat with mouth full	gɒb (gob)	,, ,, { *gobble* / *gobbett*
Eat daintily	mniøm	,, ,, *mnyum-mnyum*
	pliøp (solid food)	
	tiøp (soft food)	
Taste (tongue to palate)	lɪʌ	
	nɪʌ ⎫	
	tɪʌ ⎬ (less dainty)	
	dɪʌ ⎭	

Gestures of Outline

Another series of tongue and lip gestures which may offer an interesting field of study are those suitable for symbolizing the shape of various kinds of plants and trees.

In Fig. 96 the attempt has been made to collect together some examples of these gestures which appear reasonably descriptive of the outline of various types of shoot, plant, tree, etc., and to give in each case the type of word which the gesture of articulation produces. The list of gestures might, no doubt, be greatly extended, while the resultant words of the present list must be multiplied many fold so as to include the other gestural equivalents of the consonants named in each case. Thus l might in general be replaced by **t, n, θ, ð** and often by **r**, though the tongue gesture which produces l is more truly a pointing up gesture. Similarly, **s** or **z**, as a jutting forward gesture—e.g. for the tip of a branch—may be replaced by **u** or **ub** ; **k**—indicating the root of the plant or tree—may equally be **g** or **ng**.

No systematic confirmation of these words has been attempted, though several—such as **laras, lila** and **astar**—

sound familiar, and one or two—such as that for **tsiau**—have been suggested by the consideration of actual words for certain plants. The gestures for short plants—made with the tongue

Up gestures

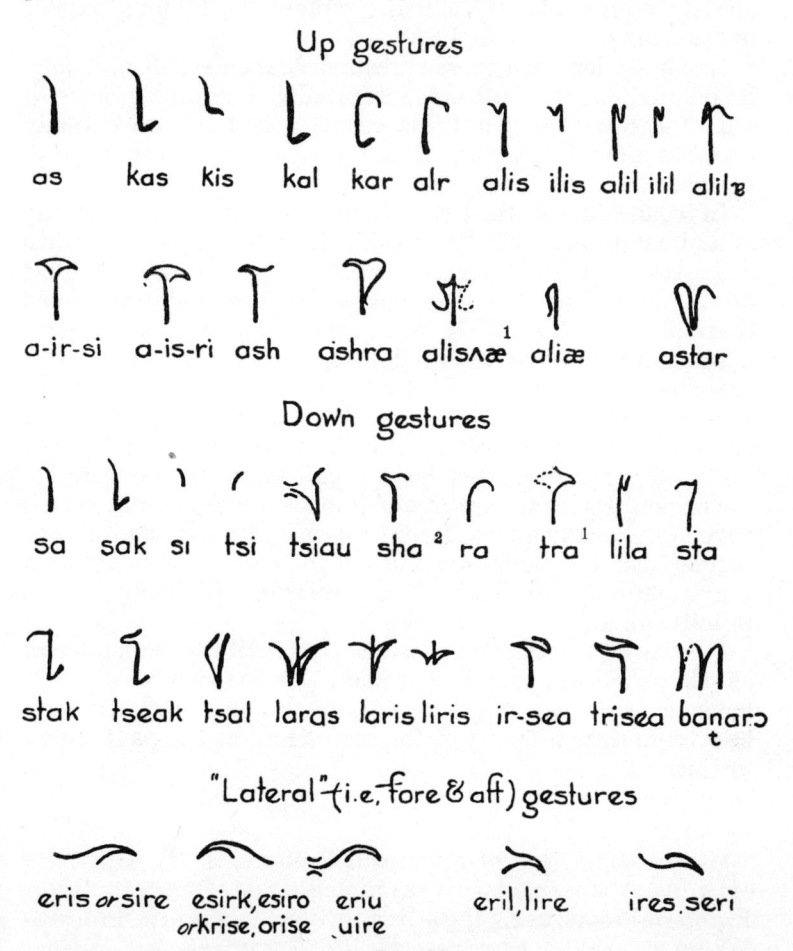

| ɑs | kɑs | kis | kɑl | kɑr | ɑlr | ɑlis | ilis | ɑlil | ilil | ɑlilɐ |

| ɑ-ir-si | ɑ-is-ri | ɑsh | ɑshrɑ | ɑlisʌæ¹ | ɑliæ | | ɑstɑr |

Down gestures

| sɑ | sɑk | sı | tsi | tsiɑu | shɑ² | rɑ | trɑ¹ | lilɑ | stɑ |

| stɑk | tseɑk | tsɑl | lɑrɑs | lɑris | liris | ir-seɑ | triseɑ | bɑnɑrɔ |
                                                                         t

"Lateral" (i.e. fore & aft) gestures

| eris *or* sire | esirk, esiro *or* krise, orise | eriu, uire | | eril, lire | ires, seri |

FIG. 96.

raised near the roof of the mouth—produce the vowel **i**. The tongue tracks are drawn, as before, for a mouth pointing to the left of the page.

[1] Only one side of the symmetrical outline is indicated by the tongue track.
[2] The **sh** is here treated as constituting a single tongue posture—though, in fact, it approaches the palate at two points simultaneously.

The tongue-track diagrams are divided for convenience into three classes—up, down, and lateral—the lateral movements—suggestive of spreading branches—being (as has already been explained) actually represented by fore and aft movements of tongue and lips.

In connection with these spreading branch gestures, it may be pointed out that **eril is** (substantially) the same gesture as **erin**, the Sumerian word for cedar, and that **sire** actually becomes **sidre** (cf. cedar) if the tongue momentarily closes against the palate on its journey from **s** to **r**.

In connection with Dr. Whymant's confirmation of my **i-i** and **a-a** or **ɔ-ɔ** words, Miss Hall, the head of a well-known girls' school near Pittsfield, U.S.A., informed me in 1927 of the interesting case of a boy of her acquaintance named Grenville Gilbert, of Ware, Mass., who up to the age of $3\frac{1}{2}$ to 4 years could not be induced to speak English, but used a language of his own. In that language **o-o** meant large; **i-i** (ee-ee) meant small, **ba** meant dog, **bojim** meant fall. It is remarkable that in this case the boy had hit on the same words for large and small as the early Japanese and Polynesians!

This and the examples of children's invented words, which have been already quoted from Professor Jespersen and others, suggest that the pantomimic use of the organs of articulation comes naturally to children, and therefore probably also to primitive man.

It is hardly necessary to assume that such Polynesian words as **ada** (reach up), **aila** (feel smooth) or **lete-lete** (wave aloft) have persisted unchanged since speech began; they may have been re-invented, owing to the persistence of the pantomimic instinct.

The Aryan Roots

At the suggestion of my friend Professor L. H. Gray, the experiment was made of examining a list of Aryan (Indo-European) roots, using the selection which appears in Professor Walter Skeat's *Etymological Dictionary of the English Language*. These roots, it will be understood, are not actual words, but " extracts " of words—i.e. the essential or qualifying parts of words (in different related languages) which appear to carry the meaning.

The first search disclosed some sixty words, not including their variants, in which the movement of the tongue and/or

OF SPEECH

lips and jaw required to produce the root-word appeared to have a symbolic or pantomimic relation to its meaning as given by Professor Skeat. Thus :—

agh or **angh**—choke, strangle (as in anguish)—is an evident tightening of the throat made by the tongue.

ad—(Latin, edo, eat)—is a tasting or eating gesture made by the tongue touching the palate.

an—breathe, as in animal—is the result of breathing through the nose.

ap and **am**—seize and take—are the results of the appropriate gesture of the lower jaw and lips.

wa—blow—is a blowing gesture.

kar—curve or roll—is made by a curving or rolling motion of the tongue—a downward motion of the back of the tongue (**ka**) followed by an upward and backward motion of the tip of the tongue (**r**).

ku—swell out, be hollow—as in cave—is made by a hollow mouth cavity, in which the air is made to resonate by the sudden release (**k**).

gar—devour, swallow, eat or drink greedily—as in gargle, is a swallowing or gulping gesture.

gus—choose, taste—as in gust, disgust, is a swallowing and tasting gesture.

ghar—seize, grasp, hold, contain, bend—as in girth, is a (**gh**) release at the back of the mouth, followed by a bending back or " containing " gesture (**r**). (Compare **kar**.)

ghu—pour—as in gush, in which the mouth is made as hollow as possible with protruded lips, suggests the idea of a bottle. Compare **ku**—hollow—the **gh** instead of **k** is suggestive of a flow through the cavity.

tank—contract, compress—as in thong, is due to two compressions in succession, fore and aft the palate.

da—give—seems to be an offering gesture made with the tongue.

dhugh (originally **dheughe**)—to milk, yield milk—is due to sucking and swallowing gestures in succession.

pa—feed, nourish—is a sucking gesture. **ma** is due to a precisely similar lip gesture, but with the lip closure prolonged and the nasal passage open.

pak—bind, fasten, fix, hold fast (our word pack)—is due to a release by the lips, followed immediately by a grip made at the back of the tongue.

pap, pamp—swell out, grow round (whence our word pimple)—tell their own story.

bhragh—break—is due to a bending back of the tongue (after the **b** release) followed by a lowering (**a**) and then a tightening or lifting of the back of the tongue (**gh**). It is as though one hand seized a stick (**b**) and bent it down (**r**), while the other hand forcibly lifted up the other end (**gh**) so as to break it in the middle.

mad—chew—is an eating gesture of lips and tongue.

marg—rub gently, wipe, stroke, milk—may be a rubbing or sucking and swallowing gesture, the rubbing being done by the tongue travelling back along the palate to form the (**rg**).

mu—bind, close, shut up, enclose—as in mute, is a closed mouth, opened to the smallest extent to produce the final (**u**).

righ, ligh (originally ri$\text{v}\chi$, li$\text{v}\chi$)—lick—are due to the gesture of licking the palate backwards.

rug, lug—break, bend—are due to the bending back (**r**), or grip (**l**), followed by the tongue-drop (**u**) and lift or grip (**g**) at the back of the tongue. Compare **bragh**, bearing in mind that the *tongue* positions of **u** and **a** are closely allied.

lagh—lie down—as in low, is formed by the tongue raised (**l**) and suddenly flattening out in the mouth so as to produce a partial back closure (**gh**).

wa, aw—originally **awe**—breathe, blow—are blowing gestures.

ud, wad—well, gush out, moisten, wet—as in water—are drinking gestures, such as would be produced by drinking out of one's hands.

war, wal—cover, surround, protect, guard—as in revolve, may be protecting gestures (**r** or **l**) made with the tongue following an *un*covering lip gesture (**wa**).

warg—press, urge, shut in, bind—is similar in gesture to **war**, but followed by a final grip at the back of the tongue (**g**).

wik—bind, fasten, hence our word vetch—is similar in gesture to **wark** but on a smaller scale. The initial lip gesture is rather a drawing-back (**wi**) than an uncovering (**wa**) and the withdrawing movement is transferred direct to the back grip (**k**).

sa—sow, strew, scatter—may be compared with **da**—give—but it starts with a small grip or cavity (**s**) made with the tip of the tongue between the back of the front teeth and the roof of the mouth, the contents of which are scattered by the downward tongue gesture to the **a** position.

OF SPEECH 151

sak, ska—cut, cleave, sever—possibly here **s** is the initial holding, **ak** or **ka** the action of cutting or breaking.

sar—to string, bind—again **s** may be the holding and **r** the bending or binding action.

sar, sal—keep, preserve, make safe, keep whole and sound—again **s** is the initial grip, while the **r** or **l** have the same meaning as in **war** and **wal**.

siw, su—sew, stitch together—if **s** is the initial holding, the lip action **iw** (**i-u**) may be the to and fro action of the hand which holds the needle. The needle in this case must be imagined as pointing forwards.

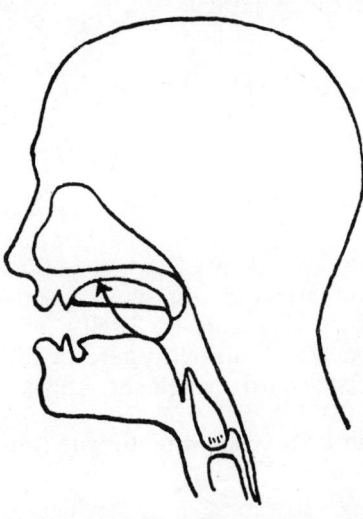

FIG. 97.

suk—to flow, cause to flow, suck—evidently a sucking or swallowing gesture.

skan—cut, dig—as in canal—**s** is the grip, and **k** a downward and backward gesture followed by a throwing up gesture (**n**). The action is that of a hoe rather than that of a spade.

skag—shake—here there is the grip (**s**) followed by a reduplicated movement (**k** and **g**) at the other end of the tongue.

skad, skid—cleave, scatter—this may be due to the grip **s**, followed by the rapid change from the **k** position to the **a** (or **ɪ**) and **d**. If the tongue track is studied it will be seen to be fairly appropriate to the idea of cleaving or scattering. See Fig. 97, and the tongue tracks :—

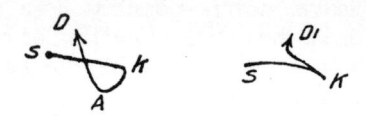

ska, skap—cut, hew, chop—the same argument may apply, **skap** substitutes a closure or holding action of the lips (**p**) at the end of the cutting action (**ska**)—in place of the upward throw (**d**) in **skad**.

skap—dig—compare **skan**, substituting an upward throw of the jaw, producing a labial **p**, for that of the tongue, which produces a palatal **n**.

sta—stand—here the tongue track is : [Fig. 98.] if the tip of the tongue be considered, or [Fig. 99.] if *closure* positions only are taken. The first of these may represent the action of sticking a spear or pointed stake in the ground so that it stands by itself.

starg, strag, strig, strug—stretch—here again **st** may be the hold, **r** the backward movement, and **g** the hold at the other end.

stigh—stride, climb, ascend—the tongue track in this case is something like [Fig. 100.] which possibly might do duty for the meanings in question, though it also apparently implies a return from the ascent !

sna—bind together, fasten—as in sinew, the tongue gesture (**sn**) here has a meaning comparable to that of the tongue and lip gestures in **siw, su**—only in **sn** the movement of drawing together is made from front (**s**) to back (**n**).

snar, snark—twist, draw tight, entwine, make a noose—here the **s** may be the hold, **n** the bringing together, **ar** the bending back, and **k** the final hold.

spa—draw out, extend, increase—the small cavity (**sp**) is suddenly enlarged to **a**.

OF SPEECH

spu, spiw—spit out—these are obvious.
smi—smile—probably a smiling gesture.
sru, stru—flow, stream—the tongue slides symbolically backward along the palate.
swad—please, be sweet (especially to the taste)—this appears to be a tasting gesture.
swap—sleep (Greek ὑπ-νος, Latin *sop-or*, Russian *sp-ate*)—here the **sw** may possibly represent the human eye which is closed by the **p** or **b** gesture, (Cf. **bhas**—shine, appear, in which the **swap** gestures are reversed)—in that case one would not expect the open-mouthed vowel **a**; **u**, as in Greek, would appear more appropriate.
swar, sar—string, bind—again **s** or **sw** may signify the initial holding, and **r** the backward bending or binding movement.
swal—toss, agitate, swell—on the same principle **sw** is the initial hold, or the initial small size, **a** is the enlarging, or, coupled with the **l** gesture, indicates the tossing or agitating.

In a recent review of Dr. Skeat's list of Aryan Roots, it was found that out of the first 100 roots listed by him, seventy-seven were clearly pantomimic; in twelve the gestures of articulation were not directly pantomimic, but were suggestive of a pantomimic origin, as for example **ark**, meaning "shine", where the reflexed and descending tongue may have reference to the sun's rays, and **kar**, meaning "burn", where the **ar** may have reference to the springing up, curving, etc., of flame. Only eleven of the 100 words showed no evidence of pantomimic origin.

Chapter VIII

VOWEL AND CONSONANT SYMBOLISM

The reader who has taken the pains to study the list of root-words given in the last chapter and has compared their meanings with the gestures of articulation which produce them, can hardly have failed to notice that they present some very interesting phenomena. There is a method in their madness.

The same gesture—say for example that of an initial **s**—is persistently associated with the idea of an initial grip of some kind, usually a grip in front. In the same way the grip of the back of the tongue against the soft palate which produces a **k**, **g**, or **ŋ** (**ng**) is either associated with such actions as swallowing, or it refers to a grip at the back. The consonant **r** is almost always associated with a backward movement of some kind—generally with a bending-back, from which it may be inferred that the original Aryan **r** was, like the Wessex **r**, made by bending the tongue itself backwards.

In the presence of such abundant material as that which the Aryan roots offer it is hard to know when to stop; it is hoped that the reader will bear with a brief résumé of the symbolism which has been observed in the case of the remaining consonants.[1]

Taking them in the order of their positions of closure (full or partial) from the front of the mouth backward we get the following picture:—

p, b, m and **bh.** These commonly denote closing containing or gripping actions—i.e. the act of closing the lips.

The same consonants also necessarily denote the reverse of these actions, i.e. bursting, expelling, releasing—viz. when the lip closure is released.

m seems to imply a continued closure—which is to be expected, since it is only by allowing the air stream to pass through the nose that the lips can be *kept* closed, and this form of closure inevitably produces the consonant **m**.

u, iw, i, y. Of these, the vowel **u** corresponds essentially to a projecting, pointing, directing, spouting gesture. Thus,

---

[1] See *Proc. R.S.*, loc. cit., pp. 162–8.

VOWEL AND CONSONANT SYMBOLISM

us, burn (jets of flame), **tu, thu,** or **ku,** swell, **du, duk, tuh,** lead, conduct—as in Duke.

iw, wi, as in **diw, tiw,** shine, and **wid,** see, are apparently miniature lip gestures imitating the human eye, but **wi** go, drive, is a pointing gesture. The vowel **i** (as already pointed out) corresponds to a little mouth and so produces such words as **mi** diminish.

s has already been considered, but two further examples may be forgiven, to illustrate a new point, namely, that the position of a consonant in relation to the word may also be significant. Thus, **la** means to be low, **las** means to be low *and* make a grip forward (**s**), i.e. to pick out, or glean (corn). **ku** means to swell, **sku** means to grip and then make a swelling action—in other words to cover or shelter.

th (θ) dh (ð). In these, the tongue tip seems to stroke the palate and back of the upper (front) teeth and the consequent meaning is that of smearing, kneading, etc.

t, d, n. Initial **t, d,** and **n** often appear not to be significant. It is as though they were used rather to draw attention to the remainder of the word like our use of the word " the ".

At the middle or end of a word, **t, d** often denote a stab or rise or closure in the middle, e.g. **sku,** cover, shelter, **skut,** spring out ;

n often denotes a continued closure in the same position. **d** and **n** also often relate to eating, tasting, etc., i.e. tongue touching palate, e.g. **mad,** chew.

r, dr, tr. As already mentioned **r** commonly implies a bending back, enclosing, etc. **dr, tr,** frequently denote running, flowing, or walking, the direction of the tongue movement being inwards towards the speaker, e.g. **ark,** protect ; **sru, stru,** flow ; **dra,** run.

l is the result (as is well known) of a tongue gesture very similar to that of **r**—the difference being that in **l** the tongue makes more of a point contact with the palate. **l** can, however, also be made with the tongue protruded and touching the front of the upper lip. It seems probable that in primitive speech the tongue was in fact protruded at times, as it still occasionally is among children. Thus, **lubh,** love, appears to be a phallic tongue gesture of which the receptive counterpart was **ka** or **kam**—also meaning love. Generally speaking **l** denotes movement, flow or rapid change of posture, as in **tal,** lift, **wal,** be warm, hot, boil.

k, g, nk, ng, gh, h. These are all made with a grip or constriction at the back of the throat. Hence **kak**, **kank**, **hang**, hang, **dak**, **tah**, **tang**, take, hold. **ma** is to think, **mak**—to think and grip back, i.e. to oneself—is to have power, be great.

The great majority of words in Dr. Skeat's list of 500 or 600 appear to be pantomimic. They are built up, much as the Chinese ideographs were, by the addition of separately significant elements. Thus, to give a final example from the Aryan roots, **la** is, as we have already said, to be low, **las** is to be low and grip in front, i.e. to glean ; **lag** is to be low and grip back, i.e. to collect ; **lagh** with a continuing grip at the back is to be low and stay there, i.e. to lie down ; **lad** is to be low and then spring up, i.e. to let go.

Prior Statements of the Gesture Theory

Sir E. B. Tylor, to whose *Researches into the Early History of Mankind* reference has already been made, evidently came very near to the formulation of this same theory of the Origin of Speech. Thus in talking of Heinicke's description of a 19 year old deaf mute's invented words, Tylor says : " some of these sounds, as ' mumm ' and ' schipp ' for eating and drinking, and perhaps ' beyer ' for the dog, are mere vocalizations of the movements of the mouth which the deaf and dumb make in imitating the actions of eating and drinking in their gesture language."

Further on, in contrasting gesture language and word language, he says : " These two kinds of utterance are capable of being translated with more or less exactness into one another ; and it seems more likely than not that there may be a similarity between the process by which the human mind first uttered itself in speech, and that by which the same mind still utters itself in gestures."

After the above was written, Professor L. H. Gray drew my attention to the gesture theory of language propounded by Wilhelm Wundt, in his *Völkerpsychologie*.[1] Wundt there definitely recognizes that it is the gestures of articulation (rather than the sounds) which are significant, and that the resultant sounds are " inwardly " associated with the gestures which caused them, so that the sound tends to evoke the same mimic gesture in the hearer.

[1] See vol. i, pp. 116, 126, 136, 332 (1904).

SYMBOLISM

He instances a group of words, in many different languages, referring to organs or acts, such as : tongue, mouth, eat, to be still, to blow, in which the sounds are due to a descriptive use of the organs, or to a pantomimic gesture made by them.

It does not appear that Wundt goes so far as to recognize pantomimic gestures—such as *tari,* dig—in which the object or act referred to has no relation to the organs of articulation— as when the tongue mimics the hands or the lips wink like the eye—but he clearly sees the principle of word-formation by pantomimic gesture of the organs of articulation, and the fundamental difference between this method and that of sound imitation (onomatopoeia).

In speaking of pantomimic gestures (*mimischen ausdrucksbewegungen*) Wundt includes the varying expressions of the face, which seem to me likely to have been of small importance in governing articulation as compared with the effects of direct pantomimic gesture performed by the organs of articulation themselves.

It will be seen that the theory which is now being presented as to the nature and beginnings of speech has been, in part, anticipated by Tylor and Wundt, but all three theories have, as it now appears, been anticipated by that of Dr. J. Rae. He wrote three articles in *The Polynesian* [1] published in Honolulu, and reference is made to these in Max Müller's *Lectures on the Science of Language,* delivered to the Royal Institution in 1863 [2] ; they are so remarkable that it has been decided to reprint them verbatim as Appendix VIII.

Dr. Rae points out that man is an imitative animal ; that the organs of speech, the lips, the tongue, the cheeks, etc., have resemblances more or less to the objects making up what we call the visible world ; that the lips, the tongue, the whole mouth assume different forms in the utterance of different syllables, and all of these forms may have resemblances to objects and actions external, though only so as to represent force, form and movement. Thus it follows that the primitive articulation and significant sounds only expressed force, form and movement ; on these the other significations were subsequently ingrafted.

In the Polynesian language every syllable has its own proper significance and force, even in the longest words.

[1] 27th Sept., 4th Oct., and 11th Oct., 1862.
[2] London, 1864, p. 10.

Dr. Rae considers the Polynesian language to represent the most primitive form of human speech, from which the Aryan languages were derived. Thus, he contrasts **mimi**, the voiding of urine, with Sanskrit **mih**, Greek **omicho**, Latin **mingo**. He also instances **umi** or **mi**, a rat-trap, and its analogy to the compressed human lips; the **u**, strictly a jutting out, when prefixed, stands for the other part of the trap. **umi**, ten, represents the fingers open (**u**) and closed (**mi**). In *umi-ki*, pinch, the **ki** denotes forcibly. In **emi**, to lessen, the **mi** is to squeeze, and the **i** means out.

He continues: " I could in a similar manner take up, one by one, all the syllables of which the Polynesian language is composed, dissecting each, and showing how its force depends on the configuration of the organs at the moment of pronouncing it."

In his article of 11th October, he points out that the pronunciation of each separate syllable indicates a certain configuration of the organs, and that a particular configuration has positive analogies, direct or indirect, with the actions or objects indicated. There is thus a real connection between the sign and the thing signified.

Similarly, **u** represents the nipple of the female breast, hence it means milk, or moisture generally; hence the word **ua** stands for the action of wetting, or rain. Dr. Rae contrasts this word **ua** with the Sanskrit **uda**, also meaning wet, hence our word water.

Professor Max Müller, while not scorning Dr. Rae's theories, evidently did not consider them of any importance, and they have since been lost sight of. Fortunately the British Museum Library has a bound volume of *The Polynesian* newspaper from which Appendix VIII has been transcribed.

Mouth Gesture in Modern English

Another later presentation of almost the same theory was given by Dr. Alfred Russel Wallace, in the *Fortnightly Review* for 1895.[1] In that article Wallace pointed out common cases in modern English in which the word is produced by an appropriate gesture of the tongue, lips or jaw, so as " to bring sense and sound into unison ". He instances such words as up in which the jaw makes an upward movement, and down

---

[1] I have to thank Sir Edward Hilton Young for this reference.

SYMBOLISM

in which the jaw gesture is downward, and the use of continuing consonants such as **f, l, m, n**, etc., for continuous motions such as fly, run, swim, move, whereas words for abrupt motions end with a stopped consonant, **b, d, g, k, p, t**, as in stop, hop, pat, stab, kick, etc. Wallace considers it " in the highest degree probable " that the pantomimic use of the various parts of the mouth constitutes " a fundamental principle which has always been at work both in the origin and in the successive modifications of human speech ".

As a simple preliminary test of Wallace's theory—as applied to the survival of gesture words in modern English, I took all the words of one syllable beginning with A in a Nelson's pocket dictionary. There were 22 words in all—simple words in common use—such as add, aim, air, apt, awe, axe—of these seventeen were clearly pantomimic, four were pantomimic, but less obviously, and one (ass) was doubtful. Of the seventeen pantomimic words may be instanced : add, aid, and, in each of which the tongue is lifted up to add itself to, or support the palate, and awe which is due to an open mouth—suggestive of fear and surprise. Of the less obvious class may be instanced : ask, which is due to a tongue grip in front of the mouth—(as)—which is, as it were, *transferred* to the back of the mouth (k)—the natural meaning of the gesture being "*grip to self*", which is at least consistent with the idea of asking, though more suggestive of taking ! In the doubtful case, ass, the tongue tip rises from a to make the grip s—possibly a foot-lifting gesture, since the early forms of this word appear to have been of the type as-l or as-n, i.e. a double rise of the tongue the first a little in advance (s) of the other (l or n). This, however, is pure hypothesis. It will be seen, therefore, that of these simple words in daily use a very high proportion are still due to a gesture of the tongue, etc., which bears a direct relation to the meaning of the word.[1]

In the *Archives de Philosophie* of 1924,[2] Marcel Jousse discusses the question of associated reflexes of sign language, speech gestures, and supplementary gestures, and reaches the conclusion (p. 233) that " le nom est l'essence de la chose, ou mieux son action essentielle, mimée sémiologiquement, concrètement—surtout, n'allons pas dire poétiquement ! "

---

[1] See also foreshadowing of the same idea in Logan Pearsall Smith's *English Language*, p. 102 (Thornton and Butterworth, London).
[2] Vol. ii, Cahier iv.

Gestural Limitations and Conventions

The limitation of gestures of articulation to two dimensions, to which attention has already been drawn, must surely have had important effects in developing pantomimic conventions of the organs of articulation at an early stage. It is possible that this limitation may have directly encouraged the use of the other organs of articulation—the soft palate, epiglottis and false vocal cords—of which the movements are performed unconsciously, in order to make up for the relatively small number of tongue and lip gestures which could otherwise be distinguished by ear.

Thus, the drawing forward of the soft palate in conjunction with the consonant gestures of **p**, **t**, and **k** gives three new sounds **m**, **n**, and **ng**. The epiglottis appears from Dr. Russell's X-ray photographs to assist in differentiating some of the vowels—more particularly ɑ (calm), from ʌ (up). The use of the false vocal cords has been shown above to be the essential factor differentiating a whispered **p, f, t, k, θ, s, ʃ**, from their relatives of identical tongue and lip gesture, **b, v, d, g, ð, z, ʒ**.

In the first instance, then, it may be imagined that man did not differentiate between the gestures of the lips which made **p/b**, or **m**, since each of these sounds is made by precisely the same lip closure and release. The same would apply to the consonants **t/d** and **n**, and to the group **k/g**, **ng**, since each of the groups is made by practically the same closure of the tongue against the hard or the soft palate respectively.

The first differentiation might be expected to be that between **p/b** on the one hand, and **m** on the other; similarly, **t/d** and **n**, and **k/g** and **ng**, since the **m**, **n**, and **ng** sounds represent the effect of a continued closure in the **p/b**, **t/d**, and **k/g** positions respectively during the process of humming through the nasal cavity.

It might therefore be expected that **m, n,** and **ng** would come to represent the long-continued or static forms of these three types of gesture.

The subsequent differentiation between **p** and **b** or between **t** and **d**, or between **k** and **g** would be expected to be of much later growth, since the differentiating mechanism in these cases resides, as we have shown, in the false vocal cords, which are not under conscious control. In so far as the difference is due to phonation, the voiced sounds **b, d,** and **g** might be

SYMBOLISM

expected to represent more weighty or emotional actions than the corresponding unvoiced sounds, **p, t,** and **k**. And besides these differences of articulation man has also commonly made use of differences of phonation ; thus in normal speech the two series of consonants last mentioned are *also* differentiated by being unvoiced or voiced.

Tone Language

One other method of differentiation should be mentioned here, namely, that of Tone, of which the Chinese language shows some highly developed forms. Thus, according to Professor B. Karlgren,[1] in ancient Chinese there were four categories of tone (" Cheng ") of which numbers 1, 2 and 3 differed only by their inflexion, i.e. by the manner in which the speaker's voice was made to rise or fall in phonation while speaking the word, while No. 4 differed both in the inflexion of the voice and also in the way in which the voicing was

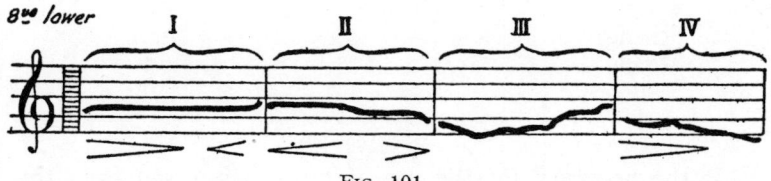

Fig. 101.

terminated. In Nos. 1, 2 and 3 the voice was prolonged and died out gradually ; in No. 4 the voice terminated abruptly.

The modern Pekinese language uses four tones, of which two versions are given—one by M. Courant in musical notation, and one taken by instrumental means by Professor Karlgren, from the speech of M. Ts'i Lien Teng.

Professor Karlgren's curves show differences of duration and pitch, which may be roughly indicated in musical notation as in Fig. 101. As the voice change is a gliding one I have indicated it by a curve rather than by separate musical notes. I have also slightly altered the spacing of the lines of the musical staff so that it corresponds to a true (vertical) scale of pitch in equal semitones, and allows for the fact that there are actually three semitones between the B and G lines, but only two between all the others ! (Another anomaly that we resignedly tolerate.)

---

[1] *Études sur la Phonologie Chinoise,* Leyden and Stockholm, 1915, p. 253.

The duration of the voice is (approximately) indicated by the length of the tone line—from which it will be seen that No. IV tone lasts about half the time of No. I when making the same articulation but in a different sense.

The maximum range of pitch occurs in No. III and amounts to just over five semitones. In the Canton dialect there are nine different tones, produced by different combinations of inflexion (even, rising or falling) duration (prolonged or abrupt) and musical pitch as a whole (high, medium or low). The actual tones used are as follows :—

Inflexion.	Duration.	Pitch.
Even	Prolonged	High
Even	Prolonged	Medium
Even	Prolonged	Low
Even	Abrupt	High
Even	Abrupt	Medium
Even	Abrupt	Low
Rising	—	High
Rising	—	Low
Falling	—	Medium

FIG. 102.

If the necessity for the use of tones has arisen from the lack of speech sounds, and if the lack of speech sounds in Chinese is due to the lack of consonants during thousands of years of gradual degeneration—then it may truly be said that the Chinese have paid dearly for the privilege of being careless in their articulation.

GESTURE IN POLYNESIAN AND ALLIED LANGUAGES

While in Washington during March, 1928, Professor Hrdlička showed me P. Rivet's study "Les Malayo-Polynésiens en Amérique"[1] and asked if I would examine the words which he gives—in the Malayo-Polynesian and in the North American (Hoka) languages—from the point of view of their articulation.

Rivet claimed that the existence of similar words in Malayo-Polynesian and in Hoka was evidence of immigration. Professor Hrdlicka suggested that if the words common to both families

[1] *Journal de la Société des Américanistes de Paris*, Nouvelle Série, t. xviii, 1926, pp. 141–278.

turned out to be gesture words, that fact might offer an alternative explanation: the words might have been independently evolved. I therefore examined Rivet's lists, noting—as before—the cases in which the gestures of articulation bore visible relation to the meaning.

Some interesting results are obtained. In the case of the personal pronouns it appeared that for the 1st person, forms like **ku ko kə** were found in Melanesian and Malayo-Polynesian and also (as suffixes) in Hoka. **k**, it must be observed, represents an " innermost " contact of tongue and cavity wall, and is therefore very appropriate for indicating oneself.

For the 2nd person, the words (or suffixes) were in **u** or **m**; e.g. **u, mu, mə, m**—which also occurred in both language groups. **u** and **m** represent lip pointing gestures, appropriate to indicating the person spoken to.

For the 3rd person, the forms (in both cases) were in **n**— such as **na, nã, nə, ny, n**. Here we have, as it were, a neutral or intermediate gesture such as—in hand pantomime—might be made by an outward pointing of the thumb for " He ". As a lateral tongue movement would be inarticulate, the upward movement **n** might naturally have been substituted.

In this particular instance the symbolism is so reasonable that it is easy to imagine that different races might have arrived at it independently. In Latin, for example, we find precisely the same method in use; ego, I, is made with the back grip **g**; tu, you, has the lip pointing **u**, while ille, he (there) has the upward tongue gesture **l** in the place of the Malayo-Polynesian-Hoka **n**. The demonstrative articles of form **t-, te-, de-, ta, ti-, θe-, se-, nia-, ne-, na-** are all comparable with the forms of the 3rd personal pronoun already mentioned (Rivet, p. 150). The numerous forms in **t/d** recall the observation we have already made as to the " insignificance " of initial t/d in the Aryan roots, and the possibility that it might be only equivalent to " the ". Indeed from the commencement of this study it was apparent that the consonant symbolism was practically the same as that which had been deduced from the Aryan roots.

Thus, the Polynesian suffixes in **k**—e.g. **mano** heart, **manu-ko** love, **mata** eye, **mata-ki** watch, look at—remind one of the Aryan **ma** think, **mak** (think + grip to oneself) be great, while the Indonesian suffixes in **p** (p. 167) in many words implying seizure or possession, recall the Aryan symbolism of **p** which has already been described, and which we still have in our words grip, grasp, snap, trap, clip, clap, crop, coop, etc. ; **ka** as a prefix is found in many words meaning eat and drink (p. 171), **ka** being, of course, a throat touching gesture.

Reduplication to indicate plurality, repetition or continuity is a purely gestural device which occurs in both families—we ourselves have grown out of it, but it lingers in children's words such as goody-goody, ta-ta, bye-bye, etc.

It is not possible to summarize here all the results of a study of the gestures of articulation of the words given by Rivet from Hoka, Melanesian, Polynesian, Indonesian, and (in some cases) Micronesian speech—which he groups under 281 heads of meaning, such as tree, joint, small, cut, etc., etc. About 80 per cent have been noted as showing a gestural relation to their meaning. These people were evidently given to mouth pantomime—as Dr. J. Rae clearly saw in 1862.

At p. 223 I came across **i-pa**, **hhī-pa** and **e-pa** as Hoka and Polynesian words respectively for arrow and to throw (spear) which compared well with one of the synthetic words (**oui-py**, to shoot with bow and arrow) which still awaited confirmation.

What appeared more interesting was that quite a large number of the words were not only gestural, but showed relationship to words of similar meaning in other languages —such as archaic Chinese, Semitic, English, and even ancient Sumerian ! Of 130 words which have been studied in Rivet's paper over 100 have been already noted as showing such relationships, the actual score being to Aryan 55, Semitic 34, Sumerian 10, archaic Chinese 3 !

I am not a linguist, and my only sources of information—up to date—have been Professor Hermann Möller's *Vergleichendes Indogermanisch-semitisches Wörterbuch*,[1] to which I was introduced by Professor L. H. Gray, Waddell's *Sumer-Aryan Dictionary*, vol. i,[2] which I have compared with Friedrich Delitzsch's *Sumerisches Glossar*,[3] and Professor Bernhard Karlgren's *Analytic Dictionary of Chinese*.[4] It can hardly be doubted that in the hands of a qualified linguist the harvest of relationships would be vastly extended.[5]

[1] Göttingen, 1911.   [2] London, 1927.
[3] Leipsig, 1914.   [4] Paris, 1923.
[5] I am aware that the authorities on whom I have relied do not command universal agreement among philologists, and that much new light has been thrown on the problem of " roots " since the work of Professor Skeat, for

SYMBOLISM

Mouth Gesture in Chinese

In May, 1928, I was at my home in Somerset and came across a dictionary of the Canton dialect [1] which I started to read, noting the gesture words. At the first reading the list of gesture words amounted to 750 entries ! The Canton dialect has lost far fewer consonants than the Pekin dialect, and its symbolism is therefore much more evident. The symbolism was identical with that of the Aryan, Semitic and Polynesian, etc., words which had already been studied—quite a number of the words were familiar !

I consulted Sir Denison Ross, who advised me to study archaic Chinese rather than modern Cantonese.

Karlgren's dictionary, already mentioned, proved a fertile source—about one word in four appears to be pantomimic. The whole dictionary has not yet been systematically studied, but, judging by the proportion of gesture words found there must be over 1,500 such words in all, of which over 400 are already noted. The differentiations of **m, n** and **ng** from the corresponding gestures **p/b, t/d** and **k/g**, is systematic and very interesting—the nasal consonants denoting continuing actions while the non-nasal denote sudden ones. Thus :—

yàm is to hold in the mouth—hence to contain or submerge (K. 62).
yàp (the same gesture but finished abruptly) is to close, join, take together ; or it may mean the lid of a box, or to cover (K. 71, 75).
an' means rest or peace—i.e. a continued enclosure (K. 236).
at means to pull up or eradicate (K. 237).
kam means a mirror, or example—i.e., the two lips held together represent the object and its image, or the example and its copy. (K. 376).
kap means to press from two sides, or to double, or it means pincers (K. 345).

Other instances might be added, but the series just given may suffice for the moment.

example, was first published. The researches of A. Meillet, K. Brugmann, and F. de Saussure, for the Indo-European question alone, would provide material for months of study. In particular, attention should be paid to the " Japhetic " theory of N. Marr, of Leningrad, which aims at linking up the early forms of Indo-European, Semitic, Caucasic, Basque, Elamite, Etruscan, and all the pre-Hellenic languages of Asia Minor and Greece.

[1] *A Tonic Dictionary of the Chinese Language in the Canton Dialect*, by S. Wells Williams, Canton, 1856.

The series of words for I, you, he, was studied—as in the case of the Polynesian and other languages mentioned on p. 163. Out of eight words for I given in Karlgren five are in ng—ˌngâng, 'ngâ (two characters both pronounced the same), nuong, ˌnguo—one 'd'ˈiəm [1] was only used by the emperor and the remaining two are ˌı and ˌı̈"o. These—like our word I—may well have lost an ng or a k somewhere. The words for You nearly all have ńźi—which is a clear tongue pointing (instead of a lip pointing) gesture—viz. ˌńźi, 'ńźię, ńźi̯"o, ńźi̯ak, ˌńźiung, the exceptions being 'ni and 'nâi. The words for He are in t, s, or t' s'—viz. tâ, si̯"o, ˌtśiän—the one exception is ˌı which is also used for I and, in this case as in that, has probably lost its significant consonants.

It will be seen, therefore, that a gesture symbolism for I, You, He, very similar to that of the Polynesian, etc., existed in archaic Chinese.

Homophones

Another principle which emerged from this investigation was that of what may be called "natural homophones". Chinese—even the archaic variety—is full of homophones, i.e. words of similar sound but different sense. The similarity of sound depends of course on similarity of the movements of articulation.

It was found that in many of these cases the different meanings attached to one and the same set of gestures (or words) were really due to different ways of interpreting them. For example, a rotary tongue-gesture, such as might be represented, say, by the tongue-track diagram ⟲ might obviously be construed in many different ways. It might mean to roll away or to bind round, it might mean an egg, or a circle or disc, or it might be interpreted symbolically to mean a year, or continuity, or even eternity! Thus it might happen that a word (in this case the all-vowel word ieâui, say) might be found with all those different meanings—even in the same language. So it comes that we find the archaic Chinese

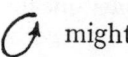

---

[1] d', t', n', and s', z', are made with the flat of the tongue instead of with the tip, as in d, t, n, s, and z.

SYMBOLISM

word **gʻiäu**—of which the tongue-track is shown in Fig. 103 (the tongue movement being completed by the lips) with the

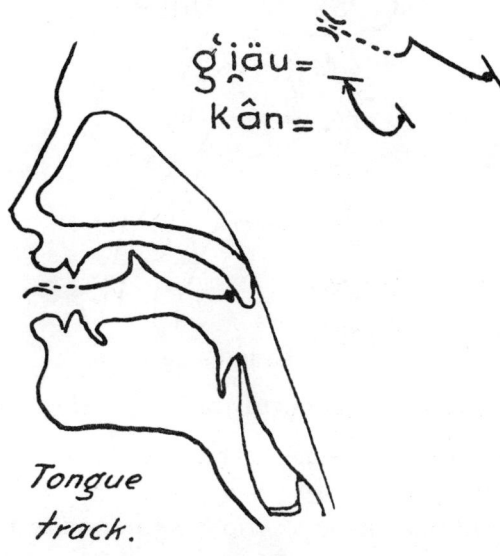

Fig. 103.

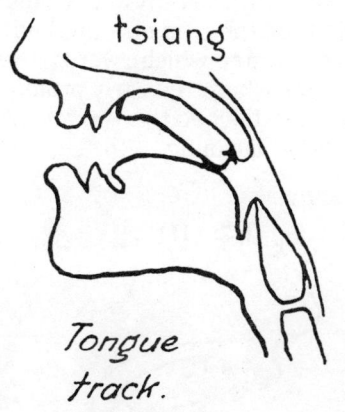

Fig. 104.

double meaning " curved up like the branches of a tree " or " to run or climb nimbly " (K. 359).

The first meaning treats the tongue-track as an outline, the second as a record of motion.

168 VOWELS AND CONSONANTS

daria
duria

Tongue track.

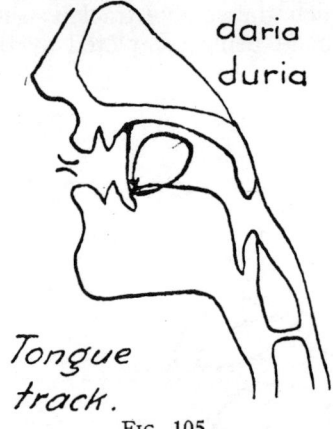

FIG. 105.

Similarly **kùn**, with the tongue-track ↰ (Fig. 106) means (inter alia) dawn (sun rising) hence, warmth of the sun; it also means trunk of a tree (K. 299).

RECONSTRUCTED PRONUNCIATIONS AND TONGUE TRACKS

Yet another principle, which seems worth mentioning, is that of the use of tongue-track study as a means of reconstructing a lost pronunciation, or the converse method of reconstructing the original action or form to which a word refers, by means of the tongue-track—in cases where the early pronunciation is known.

Thus in my first reading of the *Canton Dictionary* I came across the word **ts'ün** meaning "to sit cross-legged". Its tongue-track is:—

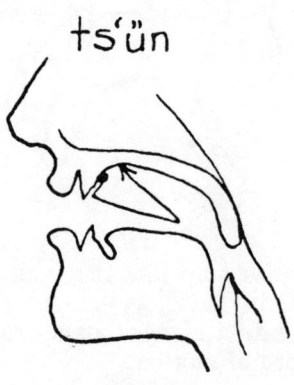

ts'ün

FIG. 107.

SYMBOLISM 169

This seemed at the time so poor a representation of the very gesturable action or posture of sitting cross-legged that it seemed worth while to try and improve it.

I tried the tongue gesture (Fig. 108) which gave a word which was transcribed ts'ʌøn—it might of course equally be dz'ʌøn, or dz'üøn, if the lips were partially closed, since the tongue position is the same in ʌ and u. Sir Denison Ross, to whom I put the question as to the *original* form of the word ts'ün, produced from Karlgren the archaic word dz'uən meaning to squat—the tongue-track of which is practically identical with that of Fig. 108. Other examples might be given of the same method of reconstructing the original sound " so as to bring sound and sense into unison ".

As to the converse principle of reconstructing the original gesture or outline, the following will serve as examples.

tsiang means (according to Karlgren) oar (K. 1061). The " gesture " is (Fig. 109)—see Fig. 104—if this be performed with the two hands, held outstretched one above the other—the movement being towards the performer—it will be found to represent very closely the gesture of paddling a Canadian canoe—the final tongue lift (**ng**) representing the action of lifting the blade out of the water. I venture to suggest that the original meaning of this word is likely to have been paddle rather than oar.

On the other hand ńźiäu meaning bent wood, oar (K. 222) and the word of similar gesture **tsiäp** (meaning oar, paddle, to row—K. 1057) with tongue-tracks which may be represented as (Fig. 110) are, as will be seen, flatter movements, more like those of rowing.

d''au' and **d'au'** (K. 588, 1234) meaning oar, pole, scull, to row, suggest a dropping of the hands **d'** followed by a gradual raising and reaching out **a** . . . **u**—also suggestive of rowing.

The only other rowing word given by Karlgren is **'luo** meaning long oar, to scull (K. 580) where **lu** suggests raising the hands and reaching out forward, with a retraction and lowering at **o**—the action in this case being suggestive of rowing (standing up) with a long oar, like that of a gondola, which is pushed forward for the working stroke.

I have ventured to give these various examples not because I consider them conclusive (which is far from being the case) but rather as indicating the method of investigation and as showing that all the four types of words for row, etc., are made by tongue and lip gestures which are at least consistent with the actions they describe.

Mouth Gesture in Sumerian

The next language to be examined was Sumerian—the oldest writing yet deciphered—on which two books were consulted, Dr. L. A. Waddell's interesting but highly controversial *Sumer-Aryan Dictionary* [1] and Friedrich Delitzsch's *Sumerisches Glossar*.[2]

The symbolism in Sumerian proved to be entirely on a par with that of the Aryan, Polynesian, etc., and archaic and modern Chinese words which have been examined. Thus, in Sumerian :—

ab is an enclosure-dwelling (D. 4).
al—a tongue-lifting gesture—means to protect, symbolizing the lifting up of the hand; compare the Aryan and Semitic al, meaning to grow up or be strong.
ama is mother or womb (D. 11) as in Greek ammia, mother—the same root a-m- occurs in Semitic with the same meaning.
kud is to cut (D. 126); the tongue gesture being identical with those of our English word cut and with the archaic Chinese word kât which also means cut. (K. 57).
munu—a tasting gesture—means salt, or something good (D. 193).
sa—a downward and outward tongue gesture which in Aryan meant to sow (corn) or scatter—in Sumerian means (inter alia) to show or set forth, or else to strike (D. 229). The hand gestures represented in each case are very similar.
se actually means corn or grain (D. 261).
ser is to bind, enclose (D. 262)—while in Aryan and Semitic ser means (amongst other things) to fasten together (Mö. 230) and the Aryan sar means keep, preserve.
izi means fire (D. 27), like the Aryan us, burn.

[1] London, 1927, Part I, A-F. [2] Leipzig, 1914.

Instances might be multiplied, but at the cost of overloading the argument. The interested reader will have no difficulty in finding further material in Delitzsch's Dictionary.

Mouth Gesture in Arawak

A remarkable confirmation of the gesture theory is found in the recent work of C. H. de Goeje of The Hague, in his study of the Arawak Language of Guiana.[1]

Mr. de Goeje has found, quite independently, that the Arawak languages are based on mouth pantomime (§§ 184, 185) so that there is an " inner and essential connection between the idea and the word " since the Arawak in speaking reproduces the thing or the event by making an imitative " gesture " with his organs of speech (§ 186).

North Guiana is so remote from Aryan, Semitic, Chinese, Sumerian and Polynesian lands that Mr. de Goeje's discovery of the same principle in the Arawak languages clearly strengthens the view that pantomimic gesture is the basis of all human speech.

The criticism has been made that the analogy which has been assumed to exist between the gestures of articulation and the pantomimic gestures natural to man is too fanciful to be real.

My answer would be that the subconscious mind of man is known to be essentially fanciful—as witness the symbolism of dreams.

The truth appears to be that for flights of Fancy we are all born fully fledged ; but most of us moult early, and our first gay plumage is not renewed.

Those who do not moult are plucked before their education is completed. The few who escape either fate are known as Poets.

Relation between Different Language Groups and Classification of Gestures

We have seen that, from a gesture point of view, many speech sounds which are different to the ear may be made by substantially the same tongue or lip gesture. A very small difference of adjustment—so as to produce a slight leakage

---

[1] *Uitgave van de Koninklijke Akademie ven Wetenschappen te Amsterdam*, 1928.

instead of a full closure, or a slight change of form in the surface of the tongue where it approaches the palate—may result in large changes of the consequent sounds.

In searching for relations between the words of different languages, it is necessary to bear in mind the various alternative sounds which may represent the same gesture. From this point of view the commoner gestures of articulation may be broadly divided into about seven classes which may be defined as follows :—

(1) Forward projection of lips (or tongue)—symbolizing shooting, thrusting, jetting, blowing or stretching out, bringing to a point. Lip projection may also refer to enlarging (as viewed from within the mouth)—swelling, containing, etc. The return-to-normal of these gestures may denote the reverse action.

The principal resultant sounds are :—

u/ü, pu, bu, fu/vu (bilabial f and v), wu, mu, or their equivalent in ü.

lb/lp, bl/pl and nm or mnm, all made with protruded tongue. In this series m, v, w, u/ü and possibly l may refer especially to continuing attitudes or states.

(2) Forward and upward movement of the tongue within the mouth—with or without reduction of the opening made by the lips—symbolizing smallness, reduction and upward direction or nearness. The return-to-normal may denote the reverse of these ideas or actions.

The principal resultant sounds are :—

i, ɪ, e, ü, also w, f/v (bilabial), b/p, m—associated with any of the vowels mentioned.

(3) Backward and downward movement of the tongue— with or without reduction of lip-opening—symbolizing large- ness, downward and backward direction, farness, or the reverse of these on return to normal.

The principal resultant sounds are :—

ɑ, ʌ, ɒ—less definitely ɐ, ø, æ.   ɔ, o and u with varying degrees of lip closure.

(4) Closure (complete or partial) of the lips—symbolizing closure, cutting, holding or constriction immediately in front. The release of these may indicate the reverse actions—i.e. opening, releasing, etc.

The principal resultants are :—

SYMBOLISM

p/b, m, f/v (used with other vowels than **u/ü**). Of these **m** represents continued closure, etc.

(5) Closure (complete or partial) of the front of the tongue (tip, or upper or under side adjoining the tip) against the upper front teeth or gums or the adjoining part of the palate—symbolizing a grip or thrust upwards or forward (but less forward than (4)) or a *small* movement (upward, forward or backward as the case may be) or the reverse of these on release.

The principal resultants are :—

s/z, ts/dz, θ/ð, t/d, st/zd, tθ/dð, n, tn/dn, tsn/dzn, tch/dj, sh (forward) ; also l (forward).

Of these, the sounds in **n** especially represent continued closures, etc.

(6) Closure (partial or complete) of the tip front or back of the tongue against the back of the hard palate—symbolizing lifting or pressing back or gripping (further back or lower than (5))—or the reverse on release.

The principal resultants are :—

l, ll, r, hr, tr, ꞔ, and forms of **t** and **n** approximating to **k** and **ng** respectively—the partial closures being commoner in this position.

(7) Closure (complete or partial) of the tongue against the soft palate—symbolizing a thrusting or striking, or gripping backwards or backwards and upwards (often **g** = gripping to oneself) or the reverse of these on release.

The principal resultants are :—

k/g, ng, x (loch).

Thus, from the point of view of origin, the forms **wuɪpeθ** and **müfmʌts** or the forms **axꞔi** and **ønglü** may (in each case) represent essentially the same word—because the tongue and lip gestures which produce them have the same sequence of position in the two cases—namely gestures of class 1, 2, 4, 5, in one case and 3, 7, 6, 2, in the other. The classification into seven divisions is, of course, only a rough approximation—a more exact classification could be obtained by a process of subdivision. It seems likely that useful indications of common origin may be obtained by classifying the common words of various languages according to some such numerical or equivalent system, so that similarities of gesture sequence may be made evident.

It will be seen that some of the consonant symbols occur in more than one class. In deciding on the approximate class number to be given to a particular syllable it will be necessary therefore to study not merely the sound (to judge of its position of formation in the mouth) but also the meaning of the word, so as to judge of the gestural meaning of the syllable in question.

SUMMARY OF THE GESTURE THEORY

Observations as to the actual resonance changes which occur in the production of the vowels and consonants show that we accept as identical sounds which are widely different, *provided* they are made by similar postures or gestures of the organs of articulation.

From this it is argued that the significant elements in human speech are the postures and gestures, rather than the sounds. The sounds only serve to indicate the postures and gestures which produced them. We lip-read by ear.[1]

Not only in the case of the Aryan roots—but in the Semitic, Sumerian, archaic Chinese, Oceanic (Polynesian), etc., North American (Hoka) and South American (Arawak), in modern English, and in the invented words used by children, we find the same principle at work. The sound of the word is frequently found to be due to postures and gestures of the organs of articulation which bear a pantomimic relation to the idea or action to which the word refers.

From this we infer that human speech arose out of a generalized unconscious pantomimic gesture language—made by the limbs and features as a whole (including the tongue and lips)—which became specialized in gestures of the organs of articulation, owing to the human hands (and eyes) becoming continuously occupied with the use of tools. The gestures of the organs of articulation were recognized by the hearer because the hearer unconsciously reproduced in his mind the actual gesture which had produced the sound.

At a much later stage in the development of speech, man—having (unconsciously) learnt the relation between articulation and the varied sounds produced by its different movements—may have attempted also the direct imitation of natural

---

[1] Miss Helen Keller, whom I had the pleasure to meet in New York, is able, though deaf and blind, to understand speech quite fluently. She lip-reads by touch, placing two fingers across the speaker's lips and her thumb under his chin.

sounds, so as to produce " onomatopoeic " words, such as pop, bang, crash, crack, hiss, sizzle, etc. These and similar efforts can only have been possible to man after he had become comparatively far advanced in the technique of speech.

Even so it must be admitted that his success as a mimic is by no means remarkable, and that such pretended animal words as bow-wow, cock-a-doodle-doo, etc., are but very feeble efforts in imitation. That this criticism is justified is surely demonstrated by the fact that most nations have a *different* form of word to imitate the same animal sound, for example, *kikeriki* in German, and *coquelico* in French, where we (equally inaccurately) say cock-a-doodle doo! In the art of onomatopoea the parrot is still far ahead of the human race; it would be interesting to know why.

The origins of human speech are so remote that, as has been already pointed out, it would be unreasonable to expect to find, now, any traces of the original sounds. The illustrations which have been given above (and which, from an anthropological point of view are all quite modern) are therefore not put forward as necessarily " genuine antiques ". If the principle of word formation by the voicing of unconscious symbolic tongue, lip and soft palate gestures has any real existence, it is likely to have operated at many stages in the long history of language development, though always without the conscious help of its human exponents.

Chapter IX

THE DEVELOPMENT OF DIFFERENT LANGUAGES

THE question naturally presents itself—if all speech is based on pantomimic gesture, how have the *different* languages arisen ?

The first answer is : Because almost every idea or action can be pantomimed in many different ways. Thus, deaf mutes have many different gestures for the same idea. Secondly, because every gesture can, as we have seen, be *construed* in many different ways.

Take, for example, the gesture of touching the palate with the tip of the tongue, as in forming the consonant l. At least three actions may be implied :—

(1) The tongue is raised.
(2) The tongue touches or presses the palate.
(3) The tongue is lowered or recedes from the palate.

Thus the word **al** (**ala**) *might* be expected to mean " to elevate " or " to touch " or " to come down from ".

Actually **al** means " *to grow up* ", as in Latin **altus**, or it may also mean *slack, weak, relaxed* (a receding gesture) ; it also means *sweet* (i.e. tongue touching the palate as in tasting). It has all these three meanings in both the Indo-European and Semitic languages.[1]

Again, the tongue-track of any given word may represent —as we have seen—either a *movement* or an *outline*—just as one could imagine a deaf-mute drawing a circle in the air either to imitate the motion of an air-plane looping-the-loop, or to indicate an outline the sun's disc.

SIMILAR WORDS IN UNRELATED LANGUAGES

It follows, therefore, that even the earliest human speech must have been full of homophones, with distinct or even opposite meanings—and that different tribes would naturally evolve different vocabularies. But things that are equal to the

[1] Möller's *Indogermanisch-semitisches Wörterbuch*, p. 6.

THE DEVELOPMENT OF DIFFERENT LANGUAGES 177

same thing are equal to one another—and as, according to our theory, the gestures of articulation of a word are (more or less) equal to the natural descriptive gesture for the idea which the word conveys, so we should expect that the words for similar ideas would be (more or less) equal in many different languages.

This is certainly a common occurrence in the few languages which I have so far examined in this connection. Thus, archaic Chinese and Sumerian are full of similar words of similar meaning—a fact already noted by Dr. Waddell (loc. cit. xxxii)—of these, one or two instances may be given.

Let us take for example the Sumerian word **tag**. This, according to Delitzsch, has seven distinct meanings—these are set out below. Similarly the word **dag** has three distinct meanings. In archaic Chinese there are a number of words in t-k or d-k which correspond very closely with the various Sumerian meanings of **tag** and **dag** respectively. The gestures of articulation which produce the words **tag** or **tak** and **dag** or **dak** are a downward thrust of the tongue tip t or d, followed by an upward and backward thrust of the back of the tongue against the back of the throat and the lower part of the soft palate—k or g. The tongue track is therefore of the type

↘↗ (Fig. 111) or ↘---↗ (Fig. 112) according as

one regards the gesture as a whole or the separate movements of the tip and back of the tongue respectively.

The natural meanings of the gestures—considered as a movement—would appear to be: to turn (e.g. a handle) ↻

(Fig. 113), to pull out and up, or scoop out ↺ (Fig. 114),

or to strike down and pull back (or pull or collect up) ↓₁ ↗₂

(Fig. 115). Considered as an outline, the track suggests

something rounded ↺ (Fig. 116).

o

THE DEVELOPMENT

The actual coincidences may be tabulated as follows:—

Word.	Sumerian.	Delitzsch.	Archaic Chinese.		Karlgren.
tag	1. Turn over	153	tiek	to hang down, droop	989
,,	2. Hit	154	t'‘åk	pierce, stab, break through	988
			d‘iek	attack, oppose, resist	987
,,	3. Pull out (as a fish out of water)	154	d'‘åk	pull out	988
			t'ɒk	pick, take away	987
			tək	obtain, acquire, get	980
tag-tag	4. Surround completely (used in connection with the body)	154	d'‘åk	sleek, fat	988
			t‘åk	sack, bag	1013
tag	5. Decorate	154 ⎫			
,,	6. Let go	154 ⎭	tiek	(bride) going to the husband's home. (? decorated and let go)	987
,,	7. Rage, be angry with	155	t'ɒk	criticize, blame	987
dag	1. Roam	131	d‘åk	cross over, pass	988
			tiek	go to, reach (same word as bride going to husband's home)	
,,	2. Tear down, Push in	132 132	d'‘åk	take away, destroy (same as pull out, Sumerian).	
,,	3. Bright, shining	132	i̯äu'	(derived root, d-g) sunshine, bright	988

Fig. 117.

It will be seen that every one of the ten distinct meanings of the Sumerian word **tag** or **dag** has a fairly close counterpart in archaic Chinese. Sumerian and archaic Chinese are both, from a linguistic standpoint, old languages—it might therefore be, perhaps, considered more natural that relationships should be found between them.

But even if we compare either of these languages with modern English the coincidences are abundant. Thus, the archaic Chinese **kap** means the cap of a seed or bud (K. 344). The gesture of articulation suggests a cavity (**ka**) closed (**p**) in front or on top[1] (see Fig. 118). There is (according to Delitzsch) no Sumerian word **kap**, but the corresponding word **ġab** means breast. In Latin we have **caput** (head)—in Indonesian Micronesian and Hoka we have (according to Rivet 238) **kapala, kapu-r-oro** (brain) and **kapa-i** head, in German we have **kopf**.

Of other archaic Chinese coincidences with English the following are some examples—(the references being to Karlgren):

  kât cut (57)
  d'i̯äu morningtide, moist (1183) (cf. dew)
  ki˜et take leave (440) (cf. quit)
  pa father (683)
  niep nip (670)
  tân dawn (966)
  k'âp cup (75)
  ma mother (592)

ma in archaic Chinese also means leech—which throws light on the original gestural meaning of the word, viz. the action of sucking.

The Aryan root word for love (receptive) **ka, kam**—which has already been referred to, finds its counterparts in archaic Chinese; **kâm** meaning find sweet, willing (K. 298) and **âm** meaning to desire (K. 1078). To these may be added Sumerian **ka**, mouth (D. 112) and **ġab**, surround, enclose (D. 209) (the same gesture as **kâm**, substituting g for k and b for m), and the Hoka **kam**, heart; Melanesian **gama**, intestines; Polynesian **ooma**, inclination for, joy (Rivet 162).

The other Aryan word for love—**lub**—is paralleled by

---

[1] If the speaker's face is turned upward.

archaic Chinese làu, love, lustful (K. 546) where the partial lip closure u takes the place of the full closure b. The Aryan root word siw, su to sew, stitch together, is paralleled by the old Chinese si̯əu', Japanese śū (siu) embroider (K. 822). The gesture word al or ar, meaning lift up or rise up is found in all the language groups which have been considered.

al, according to Möller, is derived from the pre-Indo-germanic a-l, Latin altus, high. In Semitic a-l means to stiffen (or strengthen) oneself inwardly (sich innerlich verdichten) a-l-l to be strong (Mö. 6). In archaic Chinese luâ means to pile up (K. 522)—(i.e. l = up, uâ = collect). In Sumerian al means to protect (D. 8) (i.e. to hold up a protecting hand) while alim means King or Highness (D. 9). In Hoka -ar- means to climb, mount up; in Melanesian 'ala'a is up, at the top of; in Polynesian ala or ara are to rise up (R. 118).

Two concluding instances may be given—based on the synthetic words li-lɔ (lilaw) and kɔira to which we have already referred.

li-lɔ dance up and down, to and fro	Sanskrit has lila—game enjoyment; English has fa-la-la, tra-la-la and lullaby (to dance a baby up and down, to and fro); Sumerian has liliz—believed to be a musical instrument (D. 171) but gesturally meaning " little down-up-down-grip-forward " ! Indo-Chinese has lilo, lilŭ, dance.
kɔira roll or coil back	English coil; Sumerian kur, bind (D. 128) kúr, sunrise (D. 121) (sun bending overhead); archaic Chinese has no terminal r but compare kʷâi, backbone, turn the back on (K. 439). Dr. Whymant gave koeru; Rivet gives koro as Polynesian for a running knot (R. 138).

Eology or Dawn Language

Many words of the international type are derived from a comparatively obvious gesture of the tongue and lips. These can be readily explained on our theory. But there is a residue of international words of which the gestural meaning is not at all obvious—for example the association of the sound ka with the use of a cutting tool. These deserve extended study, for they give evidence on the very interesting question of the origin of the different language groups.

OF DIFFERENT LANGUAGES

Thus, if it should turn out that words like **kât**, cut ; **au**, fire ; **teg, tok**, roof, dwelling, cover ; **pa, fa**, father, occur more frequently in unrelated languages than would be expected by chance, it might be inferred that these words common to many races were due to a common descent.

If, as I believe is the case, Anthropology inclines to the view that all the present races of men derive ultimately from one evolutionary source, it would naturally follow that their various languages also derived from a single primitive form of speech. The only alternative would be to suppose that the various races of men became differentiated before speech was evolved at all.

If we are to imagine a single original language—evolved by primitive man when he first became a craftsman—it will be a language very similar in construction to the sign-language of deaf-mutes and Red Indians—entirely innocent of grammar or parts of speech, or even of words as we know them. Eologic speech would be a matter of pure pantomime limited only by the necessity of suppressing the (vocally) inoperative lateral movements of tongue, lips or jaw, and relying on vertical or longitudinal movements. Such a language might well—like the deaf-mute sign-language of to-day—have been understandable to all races of men. That linguistic golden age has long since passed ; but it seems more than likely that it may come again, and indeed that it is approaching. We shall refer to this matter in a later chapter.

Voiced Speech and Song

So far—except in the discussion of Chinese Tone—we have spoken primarily of whispered speech—since this appears to be its simplest and most fundamental form. But, as man at the beginning certainly possessed the power of phonation, he must have discovered, very soon, that if he made an " emotional cry " with his vocal cords, while in the act of producing a speech gesture—which he well might do in order to draw attention to his gesture or to express his own impatience at not being taken notice of—the effect was to increase very greatly the range at which the gesture could be recognized, by sound. He must also have discovered that the same gesture could be voiced on a wide range of laryngeal sounds, without materially influencing its gestural character. This discovery was the beginning of two new arts—vocal inflexion and song.

The actual increase of range, by phonation, is, as we have seen, from ten to twenty-fold—in the case of the vowel sounds, and two to four-fold in that of the consonants—as compared with the audible range of the same sound when whispered.

It is surprising that this admirable invention has not been more universally adopted, and that, in all European languages at least, we still use a small minority of very inferior unvoiced sounds, such as **f, θ, s** and **ʃ** (sh), interspersed among the voiced sounds.

While it is true that, in the European languages at least, the larynx is not an essential organ of speech, but rather an amplifier and carrier of speech (since all the essentials of speech can be rendered in a whisper) it is yet equally true that the use of the larynx adds very greatly to the artistic and emotional qualities of speech.

Indeed, it may be said that even to-day the sounds which we make by the vibration of our vocal cords are a separate language altogether from that which we make by the movements of our tongue, lips and other organs of articulation.

The vocal cords supply the language of the emotions, and just as our facial expression "registers" pleasure, pain, surprise, fear, affection, and the like, so the lips of our vocal cords change their expression, and consequently produce changes of laryngeal sound as the air from our lungs is forced out between them.

It is the rising and falling of the pitch of the speaking voice which carries the emotional message, while the movements of articulation—remote descendants of the original descriptive pantomime made by primitive man—carry the intentional message which accompanies it. Except in its full-dress form —namely song—we have no notation for the emotional language; yet it has great importance, and deserves more attention than is yet commonly given to it in the teaching of language and of the arts of oratory and elocution.

INFERIORITY OF UNVOICED SPEECH SOUNDS

In whispered speech, the resonances are more or less constant —any deviation of more than a few semitones alters the pronunciation. Let the reader try, for example, to *whisper* the words and the tune of a song together. It will be found that only here and there can the whispered melody be made to fit the words; if the pronunciation is to be adhered to, the melody must be sacrificed; or if the tune is preserved, the pronunciation must be distorted.

The fact is that whispered speech cannot be inflected like voiced speech; it consequently lacks all those emotional qualities, which were inherent in the cries of love and hope and joy and fear and anger—with which our earliest ancestors expressed their feelings, before speech was invented. Voiced speech can and does, combine the emotional effects of phonation with the thought-symbolization of articulation. Whispered speech cannot be sung—the voiced melody is, perforce, suspended altogether whenever the consonants s or θ or f or ʃ (sh) appear in the text. It is only our uncritical familiarity which inhibits contempt for these weaklings in the family of speech sounds.

If an intelligent visitor (from some other world) to this planet, accustomed, let us say, to receiving and transmitting thoughts by telepathy, but having a good ear for music, were to listen to our speech for the first time, he would be horrified at its imperfections.

From the musical point of view, his artistic sense would be outraged by the sudden, purposeless cessations of the voiced melody—caused by the intrusion of the unvoiced consonants. He would resent these, as much as a human critic would if a violinist, in the course of his playing, were suddenly to reverse his bow and produce an "unvoiced" note with the back of the bow, about once in every dozen notes. Our planetary visitor would want to know why we did this—why we interfered in so extraordinary a way with the unity and melodic flow of the laryngeal instrument—why we were content to use (as it were) two concurrent coinages, one of which was permanently depreciated, to the extent of some 2,000 per cent, as compared with the other—and why we permitted ourselves to continue the use of speech sounds which were hard to hear, incapable of inflexion and totally lacking in vocal melody or emotional value. Personally, I can see no adequate answer to give him, except that we had inherited this state of things, and were so accustomed to it that it seemed natural and right.[1]

[1] It is interesting to note that in the Wessex dialect, as spoken in Somerset, the greater number of the s sounds are voiced so as to become z's, while f becomes v, and th (θ) becomes dh (ð). It has been observed that the Somersetshire dialect is better for telephonic purposes than standard English, probably by reason of its comparative freedom from unvoiced sounds.

COMPLEXITY OF VOCAL GESTURES

Another thing which would assuredly puzzle our visitor, would be the extraordinary complexity of the vocal gestures with which we express even the simplest element of thought. More than half the " words " we use consist of two or more syllables—yet there are literally thousands of monosyllables which might be made out of the vowel and consonant sounds which we employ, and which we do not yet use as words. Here there is evidently an immense waste of time and energy which had better be put to other uses.

The case, from our visitor's point of view, is even worse, for he would see at once, what we are yet apt to overlook, namely, that even our syllables are far from being true sound units. If we judge our syllables from the point of view of the postures and gestures of which they are composed, or of the combinations and changes of musical pitch which these postures and gestures produce (by the effects of variable multiple resonance) we find that each syllable consists of two or three separate actions of articulation.

Our classical method of division of speech sounds into syllables is neither fundamental nor trustworthy—the word " eats " is just as much a polysyllable as the word " eater "—it takes just as much time to say it—its rhythm (if we listen to it without prejudice) is one of two beats—a long and a short—musically it would be written ♩ ♪ (Fig. 119) ; why then do we call it a monosyllable ? *i - tz*

Here again, it would be difficult to explain ourselves to our visitor. Still he has served his turn in raising these questions, which we may now think over at our leisure ; let us take our leave of him and wish him a safe return to his native planet !

MUSICAL TRANSCRIPTION AND REPRODUCTION OF SPEECH

We have seen that the resonances of whispered speech are simple musical effects ; they are faintly heard owing to the relatively small disturbance which is set up by the mere flow of turbulent air through the cavities. Since they consist of musical notes, it follows that the resonances which constitute whispered speech should, as already shown, be capable of transcription in ordinary musical notation, and of orchestral reproduction by a combination of suitable musical instruments. The instruments for this purpose should preferably be of the whistle type and be capable of producing glides or " portamento " effects, since many of the changes of resonance that occur in connected speech, are progressive—i.e. the pitch of the notes varies gradually, and not by defined steps as in most wind instruments. They must also be capable of being muted, so as to give, what we have called a half-whistled tone. A very suitable instrument for the present purpose would be the Swannee Whistle, in which the pitch is varied by varying the position of a piston which slides inside the whistle tube. The whistle-note can also be muted—so as to produce the " half-whistled " notes—viz. by modifying the chisel edge, against which the mouthpiece directs the air-stream, and its opening to the air, by the addition of plasticine or modelling wax as described in Chapter XII. It is also possible that a somewhat similar effect might be produced by violins played with unresined bows.

Hitherto it has not been possible to collect the necessary performers, so as to attempt the production of whispered speech in either of these ways. For those of my readers who may wish to try the experiment for themselves, I have here transcribed—for three Swannee Whistles—the whispered resonances of Shakespeare's line (from Sonnets to Sundry Notes of Music) " Love, whose Month was ever May ".

The vowel sentence, " you weigh our air, we owe you aye our awe ", which was transcribed in musical notation at Chapter III, p. 46, should be reproducible, in the same way, by a pair of muted whistles or violins. The low F sharp in the lower resonance of the word " weigh " might be played as G, to bring it within the violin compass, without loss of vowel character.

Musical Reproduction of Voiced Speech

To reproduce voiced speech (as distinct from whispered speech) in this way, it would be necessary to blow the whistles *through* a reed like that of an oboe or clarinet. Whether any effect at all resembling speech could be obtained when each of the three resonators (whistles) was actuated by a separate reed, instead of all being energized by a single reed, experiment alone can disclose.

It is not suggested that chamber music of this type is likely

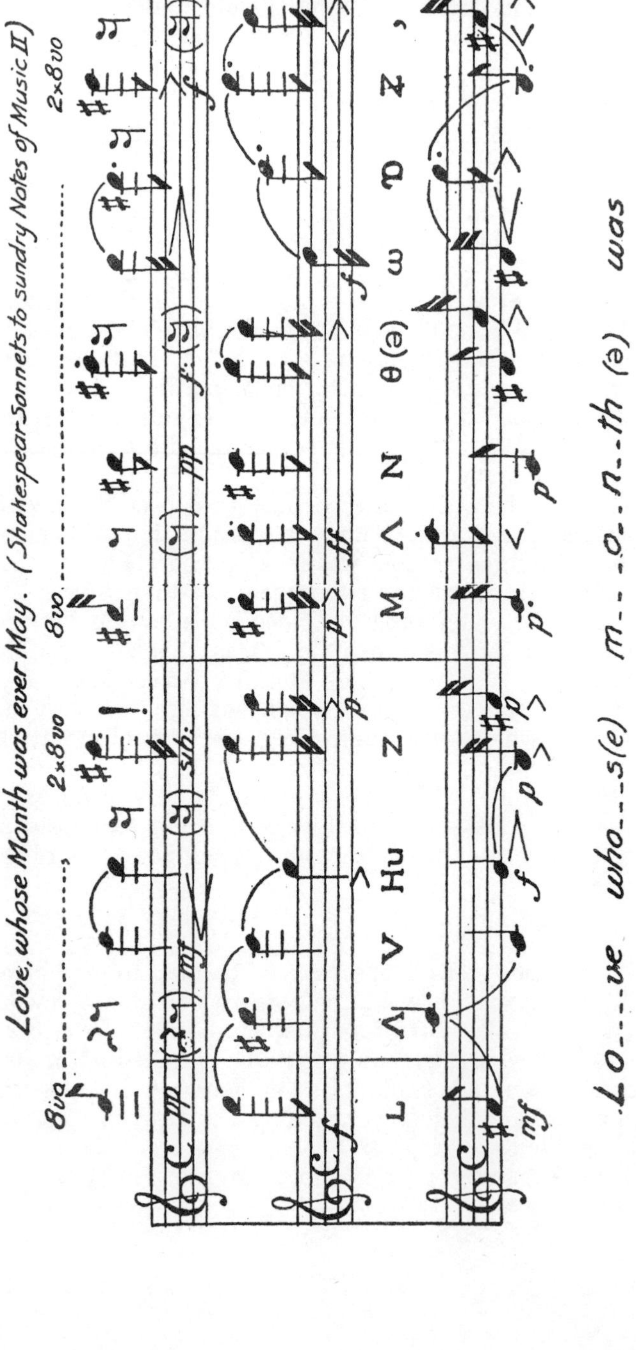
Love, whose Month was ever May. (Shakespear Sonnets to sundry Notes of Music II)
8va
2×8vo
8vo
2×8vo
L Λ V Hu Z M Λ N θ(ə) ω ɒ Z
Lo....ve who...s(e) m...o..n..th (ə) was

OF DIFFERENT LANGUAGES 187

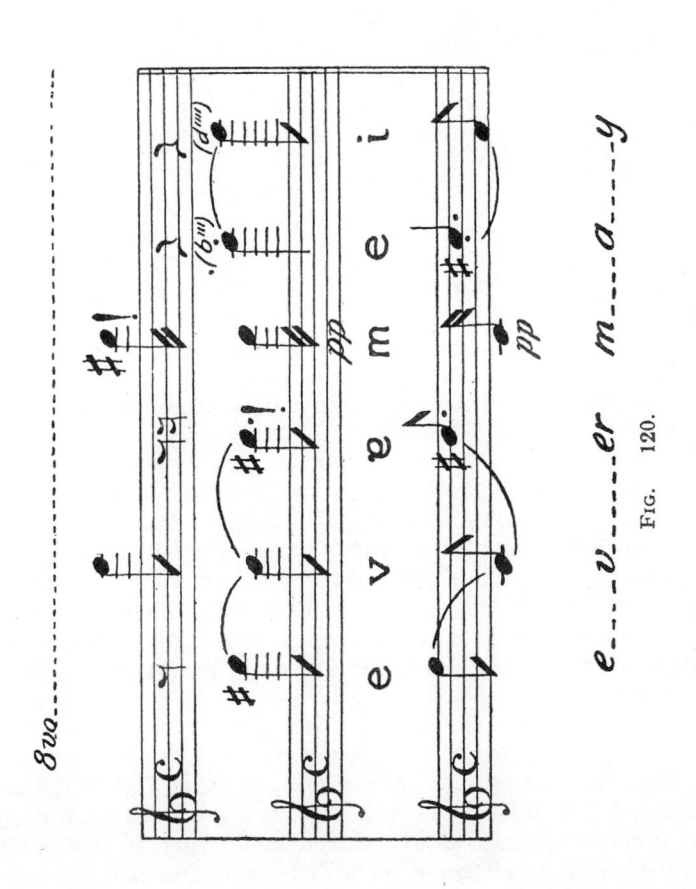

Fig. 120.

to supersede that which we at present enjoy, though it is conceivable that instrumental effects of high emotional value may be produced in the future by importing into music some of the sounds of human speech and song. At present the knowledge that human whispered speech can be scored as chamber music, for a trio of wind or stringed instruments, may serve certain useful purposes—it may remind us of the musical nature of speech—of its surprising and unnecessary complexity—and of the present duty which lies on every performer (especially of every performer in public) to perfect himself—so far as possible—in his art before inflicting himself on his audience.

Vocal Inflexion

In speech, as it exists, in most of the European and Indian, as well as in the Semitic and Corean languages, the larynx is, as we have said, not an essential organ. The inflexions of the voice are quite independent of the articulations of speech; thus, though the inflexions give emotional value, and are also even used for grammatical purposes—e.g. to indicate a question, by the raising of the voice—these uses are at most supplementary to that of articulation.

But there is another well-known group of languages—of which we have already given one example—called Tone-languages, including all the Chinese languages (except Corean), Japanese, all the Central and South African languages (except Swahili), Burmese and some Indian languages,[1] in which the larynx *has* become an organ of speech, and in which the meaning of a speech sound depends, not only on the articulation, but also on the type of laryngeal sound by which the articulation is energized.

These languages would seem, therefore, to have owed more in their beginnings to the laryngeal càlls, and less to the whispered articulation than those of the Indo-European family, unless indeed the necessity for using different tones of voice was a new invention, forced upon them by the multiplicity of homophones which developed in their language as the result of the gradual loss of consonants.

In the Tone-languages, the melody of phonation is tied to the articulation, and the combination of a particular pitch value with a particular articulation is necessary to define the word.

[1] I am indebted to Professor Daniel Jones for this information as to Tone-languages.

OF DIFFERENT LANGUAGES

On the other hand, in the uninflected languages the significance of tone inflexion is either psychologic—denoting the frame of mind of the speaker—or grammatical—as when the tone of voice is raised to denote interrogation. Inflexion of this kind is applied to a particular part of the sentence rather than to particular words. In Chinese, on the other hand, inflexion is an essential of speech, and it consequently follows that the language cannot be whispered!

The dependence of language on tone adds greatly to its complexity, and to the difficulty of devising a rational system of notation for recording it. In our own language, we make no attempt, in recording speech, to record also the inflexions of the voice—even though those inflexions may be of importance for indicating the emotional settings of the words used and almost necessary for enabling them to be understood, as a whole. At most, we indicate a raising of the voice at the end of a sentence by a question mark, ?, or we use notes of exclamation, !, or verbal descriptions of the tone of voice used, to assist the reader in mentally reconstructing the emotional background and consequent laryngeal cadence of the spoken words.

Since the object of speech notation is to enable the reader to understand and reproduce (so that others may understand) the original speech, it is obviously undesirable that the meaning of speech should depend in any way on an element which is not recorded in its notation. The ideal aim of language should, therefore, be to depend on articulation rather than on the " tone of voice " for its full meaning. In that case, inflexion (which undoubtedly adds musical beauty to speech) should follow some simple musical rules, so that the appropriate melody of inflexion may be correctly " extemporized " by the reader without the need of a separate notation for the purpose.

Linguistic Change

The gesture aspect of human speech may be of service in the science of linguistics, by affording a more directly mechanical explanation of the phonetic changes which are known to have taken place in the evolution of the present languages, from those of the past. If the gesture is the essential element, rather than the sound, it would be natural that different generations of men should make the same gesture in somewhat different ways, according to their temperament, conditions of life, vigour and culture. The gestures of speech, from this point of view, do not differ essentially from any other gestures of life—such for example, as the actions of walking or dancing or other common movements. We can tell a man or woman by their walk—we can even often tell a man or a woman's business or nationality in the same way, whether the man be a sailor or a policeman or an acrobat, or the woman a dancer or a mannequin. So it is with speech. National characteristics produce national mannerisms in the gestures of articulation.

From this point of view it might be expected that vigorous and uncouth nations would make vigorous and uncouth gestures of articulation, as in other ways. Their consonants would then tend to be full closures rather than partial, their vowel postures would be far apart—there would frequently be big changes of resonance in their articulation. They would say piper (pʌipə) or poiper (pɔɪpə) instead of paper (peipə). As such a race became more civilized and less bluff, the change would be seen in their manner of making the old gestures. The full closures would be less emphatically made, and would tend to become partial closures—the speaker's tongue or lips (less vigorously directed) would not trouble to finish out the gesture, but would only move sufficiently to indicate it.[1] In this way p and b would tend to become f and v; m also might become v or w; t or d might become θ or ð, k and g might become ç (Scots' lecht, or German ich) and χ (Scots or German loch) respectively—just as they did in the rubber tube experiments, mentioned in Chapter VI, page 108. It is almost self evident that the same gesture, which, when vigorously executed produces a full closure, may produce only a partial closure if made less vigorously.

Another obvious tendency, due to less energetic gesture, would be for the tongue to make its consonant gestures nearer to the spot where it had to be humped to form the associated vowel. Thus, closure after a broad ɑ or o or ɔ, would tend to be made in a position near the soft palate, so as to produce a k or g on full closure, or a ç (ich) or χ (ach) on a less vigorous partial closure. Conversely, the vowel postures of i, ɪ and e, would tend to be associated with the corresponding consonant closure, t, ts, θ and their voiced equivalents d, dz and ð. Similarly, an asperated vowel might tend to be

[1] Compare Jespersen, *Language*, p. 257, last three lines and p. 277.

followed by a back closure—producing **k**—rather than by a **t** or **p**.

In making big changes of vowel positions, as from **i** or **e** to **ɑ** or **ɔ**, the tongue of a less confident generation may feel the need of support on its journey and touch the palate at an intermediate spot, as in the well-known use of the articulated **r** in such phrases as here-and-there (hiə-ren-ðɛ′ə).[1] This action may actually be felt by laying the first finger along the palate and then articulating the words, so that the tongue makes its contacts with the underside of the finger instead of with the central portion of the palate. The sensation on the finger then suggests, very definitely, the action of some one cautiously crossing a stream, which is almost too wide to jump, and stepping lightly on a stone in midstream for the sake of safety in transit.

The difficulty of articulating the untrilled **r** is readily explained by the complex nature of the resonances and by the number and accurate formation of the cavities and connecting passages which are needed to produce the resonances correctly. It is interesting to note that in this and other cases, where substituted sounds are employed by persons who cannot articulate the original sound, the substituted sounds generally have very similar resonances, though they may be produced in a very different way. Thus, if I substitute for the untrilled **r**, a sound intermediate between **w** and **v**, the substitute maintains, in my voice, the resonances 1366 and 342, which are also heard (with other additional components) when I articulate the word "run" (rʌn). The same observation applies to the substitution of **f, v,** for **θ, ð**, their resonances are, as we have seen, very similar.

In these cases, the sound changes are evidently made by ear, not by consideration of the gestures of articulation. On the other hand, when a Chinaman says lun, instead of the English run, or a Japanese says Rʌndon for London—in both these cases the substituted sound is mainly due to imitation of the gestures.

It may be supposed that different races, with different cultural outlooks, will naturally pay varying degrees of conscious attention to the sounds of articulation. The more musical nations might possibly be expected to be more interested

---

[1] See Jespersen, *Language*, p. 290.

in the sounds and the less musical or more pantomimic to rely more on their unconscious realization of the gestures. In this way it may be imagined that different races might develop quite opposite methods of phonetic change, according to their respective cultural standards, and to the interest which they take in the sounds of speech as compared with its gestures.

The reader will understand that in what I have said above, as to the application of the gesture aspect of speech, to Linguistics, I am speaking as one who makes no pretence of any expert knowledge of that science. I have been tempted to venture thus far, only by the hope that the establishment of points of contact between students of Linguistics and those who may hereafter investigate articulatory resonance and gesture, may be of service to both parties in elucidating the truth.

The Improvement of the Technique of Speech

It is to be feared that the present tendency in English speech is not one that can be approved on first principles. It seems to be agreed by phoneticians that articulation is more slipshod, and that there is a tendency to substitute unvoiced for voiced sounds, owing to the saving of trouble involved. Thus, words like eggs, sounds, rubs, which were normally pronounced **egz, sʌundz, rʌbz**, are now often pronounced **eks, sʌunts; rʌps**, with an unvoiced **s**. This appears to be a really retrograde step, whether we consider it from the practical point of view of audibility, or from the artistic and emotional side of melodic or inflexional value.

Speech is at present our only way of expressing thought—it is probably our only way of accurate thinking. Without a language to think in, our thoughts would be as vague and formless as our ideas of quantity would be without the aid of numerals with which to symbolize and define the quantities in question. If so, then the perfecting and improving of human speech and language are essential to the perfecting and improving of the human powers of thought.

The question of improving language will be dealt with in a later chapter, but we may suitably refer here to that of improving the performance of human speech. Audible speech is, as we have seen, a purely musical phenomenon, due in the case of voiced sounds to the combination of the laryngeal music of the emotions with the gestural language of the organs of articulation, and in the case of unvoiced sounds to the changes of resonance which are heard when turbulent air passes through the gesticulating cavities. Articulation modifies the resulting sounds by varying the number and resonances of the cavities through which it passes, even to the extent of interrupting the sounds altogether, as in the case of the " plosive " consonants (**p; b, t, d, k, g,** etc.).

If speech is music—of a very refined and elaborate nature too—should we not take some trouble to master its technique, so as to be able to perform it reasonably well ? Yet, at present, very little stress is laid on perfection of articulation. The phoneticians appear cheerfully to accept every result of slovenly articulation as a new and interesting addition to their collection of sounds of the spoken language. The new slovenliness is faithfully recorded and taught to foreign students as the most up-to-date expression of colloquial speech.

Is this a safe attitude to adopt ? Let us contrast once more the case of music, and assume that slovenliness in execution was not only tolerated, but actually studied and encouraged and recorded by the musical critics as the very " latest thing " in the performance of the works, say of Bach or Beethoven.

Let us also assume that technical difficulties in execution were considered as unmixed evils, and as indicating the need for a simplification of the music in which they occurred. We should then have a very fair analogy to the present attitude of the public, and of many phoneticians even, towards spoken English to-day.

In the case of music it is easy to see that the attitude of indifference to technique would be fatal. The great works of the Masters would have to be revised and simplified so that all difficulties of execution were avoided—all music would then be such that any child could play any of it without difficulty. Music would, in fact, have reached its second childhood.

The Future of English

With us, English articulation is running the very same course, and we are rapidly losing sounds—substituting simpler gestures of articulation for the more finished, skilful, and expressive gestures of the past, and consequently reducing the numbers of colours in our articulatory palate. The end is not difficult to see if the tendency is allowed to continue unchecked. English will lose more and more sounds—words which were previously different will come to have the same easy sound, till, like the Chinese, we are ultimately left with a few beggarly hundreds of words, each of which has to do duty as the sole remaining representative of a whole family of departed sounds.

A language of many homophones is a language of doubt and ambiguity; it is haunted by the ghosts of its dead, and is a standing witness to the degradation and atrophy which inevitably follows when man ceases to take trouble or to endure conscious effort.

There is, therefore, good reason for urging that we should, in the future, pay definite attention to the technique of " articulation " as a necessary part of our racial progress and development, and learn to take an artistic pleasure in performing the gestures of our language with grace and skill.

Of course there will be change and development in the future as in the past; but it is evidently important that, in the case of a language so wide-spread as English, we should take care that the evolution of our language and of its pronunciation shall be carried out on a world-wide plan—not on a narrow parochial footing.

If things are left to themselves, it would not be long before the speech of Englishmen became unintelligible to citizens of the United States, and vice versa. In that case, the chief advantage of English—as a modern world-language—would have been wantonly sacrificed. It is in this respect that the art of Broadcasting, if wisely used, can be of priceless advantage to the English-speaking world.

Already, in England, a definite attempt is being made to set an example of good articulation and of artistic use of the language in the speech of the professional Announcers, whose voices will, no doubt, in course of time, be familiar to almost every citizen. What is needed is that there shall be a definite system of co-operation between all the English-speaking communities, with the object of eventually building up a world standard of English articulation and language.

Such a standard should, I suggest, be based not on the authority of former usage or of scholastic teaching, but on rational principles of euphony, precision, simplicity, directness, brevity, conformity between sound and symbol, and of all the other characteristics which go to make up a perfect method of symbolizing human thought by the twin arts (1) of phonation and articulation, and (2) of recording the results in writing.

Under such guidance, and with the stimulus of the universal interest of all English-speaking communities, the English language would assuredly take a new step forward—a step even greater (I believe) than that which it took between the times of Chaucer and Milton.

And with this improvement in their language, the English-speaking communities will have acquired an equal improvement in their powers of clear thinking, an advantage not to be despised.

Our present methods of symbolizing thoughts by the gestures of articulation, which we call speech, have all grown up out of hand and other gestures much as the Roman numerals did. In their case—as is well known—the i's represented a finger held up, v was an open hand, x was two hands crossed, and so on. Calculation in these symbols must have been extremely cumbrous and slow.

I believe that there are as great gains to be reaped in the technique of human thought by a systematic improvement of language as the inheritors of Latin culture gained in arithmetical facility by the adoption of the (so-called) Arabic numerals.

Supplementary Gestures

In one respect, the earliest language of man has probably survived to this day—namely in the gestures, of limbs, head or features—which all nations still employ, more or less, to supplement or replace speech. The shake of the head to indicate a negative, may be the substitute for a still earlier " waving aside " motion of the hand, but its great antiquity can hardly be doubted. A nod, a shrug of the shoulders, a smile, a wink, a kiss, are all forms of gesture language, expressing mental or emotional states with extraordinary brevity as compared with the method of words.

It has been said that the more highly civilized nations depend less on these gestures and more upon speech ; certainly in our own age and country, the use of gestural indication is declining. A public speaker who made use of the gestures which would be natural to a Southern European would appear to an English audience to be highly theatrical and insincere.

From the point of view of ease of record, gestures—as a means of communication—stand in the same category as vocal intonation: they are a language without an alphabet, and ought, therefore, to be avoided in all speech which is intended to be recorded in writing or by phonographic means. Otherwise the record will not adequately convey the speaker's deeper meaning.

As between man and man—or man and woman—the language of gesture will never be ousted by speech, however much it may be perfected in the future. A hand laid on the shoulder of a friend " speaks volumes "—as the saying goes—and far more eloquently than any words. The language of lovers, even the most civilized, would mostly make but poor reading if taken down in shorthand and published verbatim; yet, between lovers there is a more perfect expression of the subtlest emotions, and a more complete and mutual understanding of mentality, than between the very best of the articulate!

It will be no disgrace to human speech if, after all, it should turn out to be (as I believe it is) a branch of human gesture.

Chapter X

VOICE PRODUCTION

In the present chapter, the attempt will be made to indicate the bearing of the observations and experimental results, which have been already described, on the arts of voice production as applied to speech and song.

It must be confessed, at the outset, that in both these respects there is much which remains to be discovered, by further observation and experiment and especially by experiment with models. Still, there are certain principles, not hitherto fully recognized, which have been established, and which may be useful to those who are interested—either as teachers, pupils or exponents—in the arts of speaking and singing. To such as these this chapter is particularly addressed.

In speech—more especially in public speaking—the qualities of clearness and intelligibility depend, almost entirely, on the accurate production of the vocal resonances, which, as we have seen, are responsible for the audible effects of " articulation ". When a public speaker is incomprehensible (which occurs even at the meetings of the most learned societies) it is seldom, if ever, due to the fact that he is not speaking *loud* enough. The human ear is so sensitive that it can hear and understand speech though its loudness is reduced to one-millionth of the normal. The incomprehensible speaker is not understood because he is not making his vocal gestures, and consequently his vocal resonances, sufficiently precise. Thus, clearly *whispered* speech can be heard and understood by large audiences, even (as I have had occasion to prove) in parts of a hall of which the acoustics are known to be bad for normal voiced speech.

Again, excessive phonation—i.e. a too loud larynx note—combined with bad articulation, may be even more difficult to understand than if less vocal energy had been used ; for the laryngeal notes may cause echoes and reverberation, which mask the changes of sound due to articulation. For audibility in public speaking, the moral is : " Take care of the vocal gestures, and the voice will take care of itself."

One or two other general rules may here be referred to (though they form no part of the present investigation), such as :—

The larger or higher the auditorium, the slower should be the articulation. Otherwise the echo of each syllable, as it returns from the walls or ceiling, will clash with its successor. It should be remembered that the number of articulatory changes, which have to be made in producing a sentence, is much larger than the mere number of "syllables" into which we conventionally divide the words which compose it.

We must hear, not merely the syllables, but a sufficient proportion of their component changes, if we are to be certain as to their meaning. Consider, for example, the following passage of 74 words—comprising 140 syllables (i.e. an average of just under two syllables per word)—which may easily be spoken in half a minute :—

" The problem of giving telephone service is quite different from that of most business enterprises. The merchant, for example, may take more business in his store, without necessarily always increasing his facilities. The minute we take another subscriber, however, we add to our plant and plant investment. Similarly, in connection with the manufacturing industry, the manufacturer, for instance, is in a position to exercise very direct control over his activities. In the telephone industry, . . ."

Here (if I have counted them correctly) there are 313 changes of articulation in the 140 syllables which form the 74 words. The changes of articulation in this case succeed one another at an average rate of 626 per minute. Actually they are formed more quickly than this, for the average rate does not allow for the pauses which the speaker makes between his phrases.

Taking for convenience 600 per minute, i.e. 10 articulatory changes per second (which would correspond to a slightly slower rate of speech than our postulated 148 words per minute), these will be interfered with by echo if the preceding sound returns a tenth of a second later. Sound travels, as we have said, about 1,100 feet per second, so that an echo " lag " of a tenth of a second, represents the effect of an echo-path—from speaker to wall or roof and thence to the listener—of 110 feet. In an auditorium where such length of echo-path is possible, the speaker must therefore go more slowly than 150 words per minute—otherwise, if the ceiling and walls of the auditorium are hard (so as to act as reflectors of sound) his words will be difficult to understand.

Another useful rule—more particularly for speakers with an ear for music—is to avoid, in speaking, the use of a larynx note, which corresponds to the natural resonant note of the air inside the building. When such a note is present, the speaker's larynx tone becomes suddenly magnified and " built up " by resonance, whenever its frequency of vibration coincides with that of the air in the building; on the other hand his articulation changes get no such advantage and becomes masked by the continuing resonance. Generally speaking—whether in resonant buildings or in broadcasting (where electrical resonance is commonly introduced intentionally) a speaker should phonate less and articulate more than when he is speaking under conditions of less resonance.

Speech for the Deaf

The results now under consideration have a bearing which may be worth mentioning, on the problem of teaching the deaf to speak by visual and tactual observations of another speaker. It would appear that, since the essentials of speech are all to be found in the whispered form, it would simplify the problem if, in the first instance, the pupil were introduced to whispered speech as a separate art. There are so many sounds in which the vocal cords are not used, that it must surely complicate the initial problem if these sounds are treated together with others in which the vocal cords are used. Whispered speech, on the other hand, is perfectly homogeneous. If whispered speech were taught in the first instance, the art of phonation would then follow naturally, or could be taught concurrently as a separate subject. It could then be applied to the two separate purposes, viz., of phonation (in the case of vowels, diphthongs and voiced consonants) on the one hand, and of vocal inflexion on the other.

It seems probable that, by dividing the subject in this way, the deaf pupil might obtain a much clearer conception of the purpose of phonation (as distinct from articulation), and a much better grasp of the principles of vocal inflexion —on the correct use of which the naturalness of speech in any language or dialect so largely depends. Speech learnt without the aid of hearing could hardly become *natural* until the pupil had learnt something of the art of phonation as a means of expressing his or her emotional state. I believe that this art could be learnt, so as ultimately to become instinctive.

I have been confirmed in this opinion by the results of an afternoon spent in the company of Miss Helen Keller (to whom reference has already been made) on 26th February, 1927, at her home at Forest Hills, New York. Miss Keller learnt to speak by the usual method of combining articulation and phonation from the start—she was not separately interested in phonation, and her vocal inflexion is consequently monotonous. I discussed the question with her and found her keenly interested.

It appeared that she could whisper, and she recited a short poem first in voiced and then in whispered speech; this I wrote down and " scored " for vocal inflexion by drawing a wavy line which rose and fell as my own voice rose and fell in pitch when I spoke the words.

This score was made readable to the touch, by pricking along the wavy line from the back of the paper so that the line of pricked holes appeared in relief. After a preliminary practice in rising and falling voice inflexion, Miss Keller was able to repeat the poem, using the rising and falling voice inflexion as recorded on the " score "—with a consequent gain in naturalness and emotional value.

It seems also possible—though this has not yet been put to the test—that the teaching of the postures and gestures of articulation might be made easier by the use of models, indicating the general form of resonators to be aimed at in each case.

In Miss Keller's case she was able to recognize change of pitch in the larynx note of my voice by feeling the vibrations of my throat. For those who have sight but not hearing, much the better plan would be to adopt some method of making the pitch of the larynx note visible on some sort of " frequency " scale.

One instrument of simple construction for this purpose is the Phonoscope of Professor Joh. Georg. Forchhammer, of the Metropolitan School, Copenhagen, which was in practical use as early as 1887. In this, the note whose pitch is to be made visible is sung into a mouthpiece which communicates the vibrations to a sensitive gas flame. The flame, therefore, rises and falls with the vibrations of the note sounded. The light of this flame is thrown onto a revolving cylinder, mounted on a vertical axis and having twenty-one separate "scales" printed round its circumference. Each scale consists of a given number of equally spaced black squares with white spaces between, the lowest scale having the smallest number of black squares and consequently the largest spacing between squares. The scale next above has more squares and the next still more up to the twenty-first scale. The cylinder is uniformly turned by clockwork and under these conditions each scale presents a different number of black squares passing uniformly per second.

The effect of the rhythmically flickering light is to make the scale whose number of squares passing per second corresponds with the number of flickers per second stand out *as if the squares were at rest* (the well-known stroboscope effect), while all other scales appear blurred or in motion. The apparent motion of the scale is in the direction of the actual movement of the cylinder or in the contrary direction—according as the note sung is flatter or sharper in pitch than the corresponding pitch of the scale in question. The scales (of black squares) actually used correspond to the vibrations of the notes of a chromatic scale extending over nearly two octaves. With this apparatus, a deaf person can see the effect of a note hummed into the apparatus and can then match it with a note of his own.

Other more recent devices, serving the same purpose with greater exactness, are the Optical Sonometer of Adam Hilger, Ltd., Rochester Place, Camden Town, London, N.W., the Osiso of Mr. J. W. Legg, of the American Westinghouse Co., and the Oscilloscope as used by Professor Robert H. Gault, Ph.D.[1]

Voice Production in Song

In song, our aim is in many ways more complex than in the production of speech. There is articulation—as in speech—combined with laryngeal inflexion—as in voiced speech—but the inflexion has become elaborated and formalized, so that it no longer rises and falls in pitch by progressive "glides", but by defined steps or musical intervals. Moreover, the range

[1] *Archives of Otolaryngology*, U.S.A., Feb., 1926, vol. iii, pp. 121–35.

or compass of inflexion, and the rate of change of pitch are both enlarged, as compared to most normal speech.

The purpose of song—as compared with speech—is to appeal more especially to the emotions. In song, the emotional language appears in a new and startling guise dressed in its best, and leaping athletically from tonal point to point—as compared with the slipshod glides of intonation in speech.[1]

The relation of song to speech—so far as vocal inflexion is concerned—is therefore very similar to that of the descriptive dance as compared with the common actions which it portrays, or to the relation between the same sequence of ideas as expressed in poetry or in prose. Every time we speak or sing a rhyme, our tongue and lips necessarily repeat the postures which produced the sound on which the rhyme is formed. Poetry, from this point of view, is the art of pantomimic dancing, performed with our tongues and lips—melody is another kind of ceremonial dance performed—in time rather than in space—by the action of the vocal cords.

A further aim, in song, is to secure an increased amplitude or intensity,[2] on the one hand, so as to reach a larger audience, to penetrate the orchestral screen in opera, or to produce the greatest sense of power and emotion; to this we must add, on the other hand, an equal contrasted power of reducing the volume of sound to a minimum on any given laryngeal note.

All these elements—articulation, inflexion, range, control of amplitude—must be combined with the arts of phrasing, i.e. the appropriate variation of the duration of each note sung (or voiceless syllable whispered), and of varying the resonant quality and the amplitude or loudness of the sounds produced, so as to give the desired emotional effect. It is evident, therefore, that good singing is a highly artificial and accomplished phenomenon, depending on many forms of control, and on the artistic and emotional character and power of expression of the singer.

In venturing to make some remarks on voice production in song, I would point out that these constitute at most a commentary, made in the light of such experiments and conclusions as seemed to have a bearing on the subject. My results are far from being sufficient to enable anything

---

[1] See I. A. Richards, in *Psyche*, July, 1927.
[2] "That intensity, which is the culmination of his art," W. Shakespeare, *The Art of Singing*, p. 14.

approaching a complete theory of voice production to be built up at the present time. They do, however, point to certain facts, some of which are directly contrary to views which are more or less current among singers and teachers of singing. In order, therefore, that truth may further prevail (if only in a small part of the field) reference will now be made to certain of these current theories, in order that they may, if possible, be corrected. They are as follows :—

(1) That the lungs are a resonator ;

(2) That chest and head notes are due to selective resonances in the chest and head ;

(3) An ultra fallacy (not generally current, but widely published) that the voice is produced by resonance in the sinuses ;

(4) That the hard palate and teeth act as sound-boards ;

(5) That sound, inside the mouth, can be thrown or directed forward or backward, up or down ;

These five fallacies may now be considered in order.

FIG. 121.

(1) *The lungs as a resonator*. We have seen in Chapter II that the cavity of the thorax, which surrounds the lungs, is entirely filled by the lung tissue of minute air cells and blood vessels and their connecting air tubes, and that there is, in fact, no cavity connected to the windpipe such as might act as a resonator. On the contrary, it was pointed out that the lung tissue, with its finely subdivided passages and air cells, is especially adapted to act as an absorber of sound. It is true that on singing, in what is known as the chest register, the chest—and trunk generally—may be felt to vibrate. This is no doubt due to the fact that when powerful vibrations are set up by the vocal cords (amplified by resonance in the vocal cavities) the air is set in vibration, both above and below the point at which the air current is rhythmically interrupted. Thus in the model shown in Fig. 121, a resonator placed behind the rubber strip larynx, was found to operate sufficiently

to produce a vowel sound in combination with another resonator in front of the larynx.

The effect of vibration—i.e. of rhythmical changes of pressure—set up behind the human larynx, will be to cause pressure changes on the walls of the windpipe, bronchial tubes, etc., which will tend to shake these walls ; the resulting disturbance even reaches the framework of the thorax and is felt at its outer surface. Such an effect will diminish rather than increase the resonance of the windpipe, by utilizing the sound energy to do work in shaking the walls of the air passages along which the sound waves travel.

The only function of the lungs in singing, is to supply air at the right pressure, of the right volume and at the right time, to the vocal cords and organs of articulation. The windpipe—in which the lungs act as an open end—may, as we have said, have a resonance of its own, though no characteristic pitch has so far been detected with certainty.

(2) *Chest and headnotes.* As the resonances behind the larynx are not variable, it follows that the variations which produce chest notes or head notes, must be sought elsewhere. They will be considered later, in connection with the resonances of the vocal cavity.

(3) *Voice production by resonance in the sinuses*—i.e. the nasal cavity and its annexes. As to this, it is only necessary to point to the conclusive evidence that phonation is due to the action of the vocal cords.

According to Dr. V. E. Negus, F.R.C.S.—who has made a special study of the vocal organs of men and animals—the larynx was originally a means of breath control, rather than of phonation ; its purpose was to act as a valve by which the air could be locked inside the lungs, so as to stiffen the thorax and thus give a more rigid anchorage for the muscles of the arms and shoulders (or their equivalent) when a special muscular effort was demanded of them. As to their present action in producing phonation, there can be no doubt.

By the courtesy of Sir Arthur Keith, I was introduced in 1923 to Dr. Negus, who was then working at the Royal College of Surgeons, and who demonstrated the larynxes of various animals (including monkey and man). He showed that by attaching an air supply pipe to an excised larynx, preserved in spirit (provided it was not too old so as to have become stiff), it was possible to make it phonate. The experiment was

VOICE PRODUCTION

tried with a preparation of tongue and larynx as shown, approximately, in section in Fig. 122, and I found that, by varying the pressure (by hand) on either side of the excised larynx—as if to press the edges of the vocal cords more or less together—and by adjusting the air pressure (by blowing the larynx by mouth through a tube), it was possible to vary the larynx note by at least an octave and even to make it hum a tune.

In this experiment there were no resonators and no sinuses, yet there was a controllable phonation, due to the combination of controlled air pressure and laryngeal pressure.

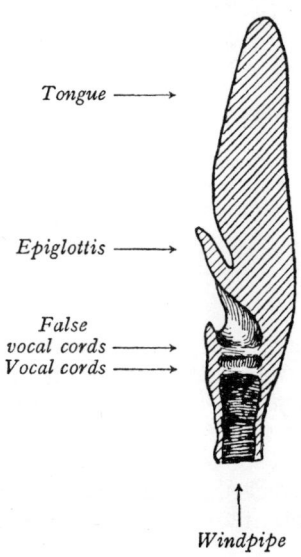

FIG. 122.—Section (approx.) of prepared tongue and larynx.

The range of the living vocal cords is very much greater than those of an excised larynx—due, no doubt, to the great variety of adjustments of length, tension (possibly also of edge to edge pressure), thickness, etc., of which the living organs are capable.

It may be mentioned that in the case of the living larynx, lateral pressure lowers the note, whereas the note of an excised larynx was raised. Frontal pressure on the living larynx lowers the range still more than lateral pressure.

A Model of the Vocal Cords

The action of the vocal cords may be imitated very simply in a model by cutting a transverse slit about $\frac{1}{2}$ to $\frac{3}{4}$ inch long in the wall of an india-rubber tube, of say $\frac{3}{4}$ inch internal diameter, and closing the tube near one end of the slit by means of a solid plug, as shewn in Fig. 123. If air is then blown into the tube by its other end, so that it forces its way out through the slit S, it is possible, by suitable adjustments, to make the edges of the slit vibrate so as to produce a musical note.

The adjustments required are (1) as to the tension of the edges of the slit and (2) as to the resonant conditions of the air tube or of the cavity (if any) into which the slit opens. Thus it was found that, with the slit open to the air, no

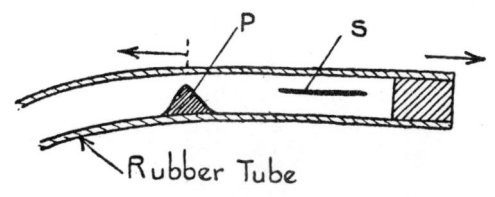

FIG. 123.

phonation could be obtained with any variations of tension —produced by pulling the rubber tube from either end of the slit, as shown by the two arrows—unless the air tube was of a suitable length, or unless it was partially stopped (by means of a plug P inserted in the tube so as to form a constriction to the air passage) at the correct distance from the slit, and thus set up resonance of the right frequency in the air supplied to the slit.

By adjusting the position of the stop so that the slit vibrated at minimum tension, it was possible to raise the pitch of the note produced by about 7 semitones, viz. by progressive increase of tension of the edges of the slit, without altering the position of the stop.

The note produced in this way was pure and musical but apparently lacking in overtones; it was found not to be so good for energizing a vowel-sounding model as an organ reed, or as the laterally vibrating rubber strip which was used in the earlier experiments. Both the slit tube and the prepared human larynx were much less sensitive to changes of air pressure than the vibrating rubber strip type. For example, the human larynx gave no change of pitch from the lowest air pressure at which phonation began up to about twice that pressure. Further increase of pressure raised the pitch up to a maximum of 4 to 5 semitones. The rubber slit was even more constant under variations, the note merely becoming louder as the pressure was increased.

Constriction of the air tube ($\frac{3}{8}$ inch diameter) which supplied the prepared human larynx, at a point 3 to 4 inches behind the vocal cords, lowered the pitch of the note by 5 semitones; the lowering became less as the point of constriction was further removed.

Effect of the Larynx on Vowel Sounds

In experimenting with a slit tube artificial larynx attached to a vowel-sounding model (of which the two resonators were kept constant in pitch) it was found that variation of the frequency of the larynx note actually produced changes of vowel-sound; thus, the vowel i (eat), at 256 and 2434, was not recognizable when the larynx note was 483, but was clearly recognizable when the larynx note was raised to 541. It seems evident from this experiment that there is a relation between laryngeal frequency and vowel resonance frequency, and that to this extent the theory that the resonators are separately excited at each laryngeal impulse is not tenable. It seems probable that the note given by the slit tube form of reed is less complex than that given by human vocal cords, or by a vibrating rubber strip, and that for this reason the slit tube larynx will only give clear vowel-sounds when the frequency of the reed is related (within limits) to the vowel resonances; thus, in the case mentioned above, the vowel was recognizably produced when the reed frequency was within a semitone of the octave above the lower vowel resonance.

In the human larynx (even after preservation in spirit) the conditions for vibration are so favourable that the aid of resonance is not essential to obtain phonation—but it seems almost certain that the *range* and control of pitch obtainable in speech and song do depend to some extent on the proper adjustment of the resonance of the cavity into which the vocal cords open. Adjustment of the resonance of the windpipe does not seem to be physically possible.

VOICE PRODUCTION

So far we have taken the view that the larynx is not an organ of speech, but rather an organ of phonation. Some further observations of Dr. Russell appear to show that this view is not strictly true. He noticed that when different vowels were sung on the same larynx note, the attitude of the vocal cords varied from vowel to vowel.

Thus, i (eat) was made with longer and sharper edged cords than ɪ (it), while the cushion of the epiglottis, i.e. the front wall of the laryngeal cavity, moved inwards in the direction of the vocal cords, and the cords themselves became more rounded in passing to the vowels of lower resonance. It is indeed quite conceivable that the vocal cords may adjust themselves so as to give a note rich in the particular overtones which are required to energize the resonators which the tongue and lips have prepared for them.

The Range of Laryngeal Notes

I have made a number of experiments on the range of my own laryngeal notes at different times, from which it appears that it varies during the day. On rising in the morning, the range is greatest—about 4 octaves and 2 or 3 semitones—in the evening the range is reduced to about 3 octaves and 9 semitones, from about a 54 to ♯f″ 724, i.e. a reduction of 5 or 6 semitones, as compared with the morning range. The maximum range so far recorded is 4 octaves 10 semitones, on 2nd November, 1924. Such a range is abnormal and is due to the accidental production of higher falsetto notes (above ♯g″ 812) by some conditions of the vocal cords which cannot be reproduced at will. A more normal maximum was 4 octaves 6 semitones, from ♯d 38 to a″ 861.

It should be understood that these wide ranges of laryngeal tones do not represent a compass suitable for singing. In my case the lower notes are too faint and the upper notes (made falsetto) are too feeble and too squeaky for use in song. The observations seem worth recording, however, as evidence of the power of the human vocal cords to produce vibrations extending over a very wide range of frequency.[1]

---

[1] Sir Felix Semon, in a discourse at the Royal Institution on 13th March, 1891, described the laryngeal action of a soprano whose singing voice had a range of 4 octaves. Réthi and Fröschels (*Pflügers Arch. f. d. ges. Physiol.*, vol. cxcv, pp. 333, 1922) have recorded a range of 5 octaves. See Geiger and Scheel, viii, p. 466, Berlin, 1927.

VOICE PRODUCTION

For singing purposes, the normal range of the human voice may be taken as about 2 octaves and 2 semitones for a soprano, 1 octave 10 semitones for a contralto or tenor, 1 octave 9 semitones for a baritone, and 2 octaves 2 semitones for a bass. Broadly speaking the vocal cords get longer and thinner to produce higher notes, while the cavity into which the cords open gets smaller or more open-mouthed.

In all voices certain ranges of the notes are made by a different method of adjustment of length, thickness, length of slit and tension of the vocal cords, and/or of the size and shape of the resonating cavities immediately adjoining them; these different methods of adjustment constitute the so-called registers. Their action is not fully understood, and it is evident from photographs (taken with the laryngoscope) of different subjects that the methods of adjustment used may vary individually even for the same type of voice—soprano, contralto, etc.[1]

Laryngeal Tone Quality

In the experiments now in question, systematic investigation of the registers has not yet been possible, but it may be of use to place on record the following isolated observations.

A vowel-sounding pipe, consisting of an organ reed and two resonators of variable capacity but constant central and front orifices, was set to give the vowel e (men). It was found that with a fixed reed note (271), a wide range of different qualities of voice—apparently comparable to head notes, chest notes, etc.—could be produced by small changes of capacity of the back resonator. During these changes the vowel-sound itself remained appreciably constant. It will be observed that in this case the reed remained unaltered and the reed note was constant. The change of quality in this particular experiment, therefore, was due to differences of " pharyngeal " resonance.

In another series of experiments, a 2 inch diameter rubber tube was attached to an organ reed and fitted with a cork " tongue " and set at 5 inches from the mouth of the tube; the vowel-sound was a. It was found that a louder and more " forward " production of the vowel-sound was given by

[1] See for example some remarkable photographs taken by Dr. French, of Brooklyn, and shown by Sir Felix Semon, loc. cit., pp. 21–4.

bending the tube so as to constrict it behind the tongue, thus forming a third resonating cavity 3—suggestive of the action of the epiglottis in the human pharynx. A very good ɑ (calm) with a forward production, was given by substituting a cork

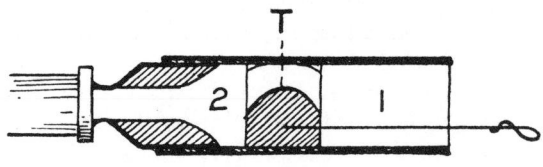

FIG. 124.

stop S for the rubber tube constriction C, the tongue T being in contact with the conical mouth of the stop S, so as to reduce the size of the cavity 2.

The resonances were of the order of 966 for 3, 1932 for 2

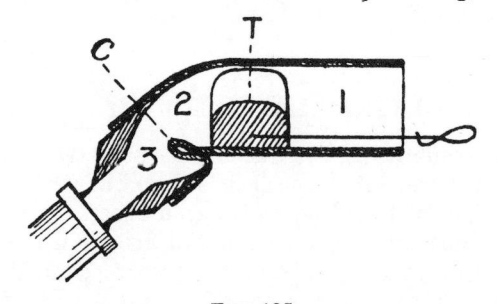

FIG. 125.

and 430 or lower for the space between 3 and the reed. The mouth and throat resonances heard on breathing ɑ (as if for a similar " forward " production) were 512, 966 and 2579—corresponding to the resonances of ɔ (all)—which compare

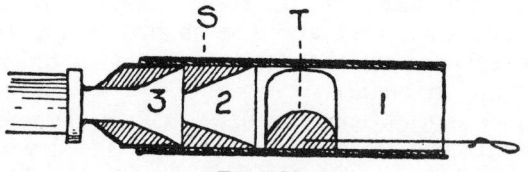

FIG. 126.

with those of the rubber tube model. In this case also it is probable that the addition of a cavity, giving a resonance of the order of 2000, was the cause of the " forward " production.

VOICE PRODUCTION

A further experiment made with the rubber tube resonator described in Chapter VI may be mentioned in this connection. When the rubber tube was constricted, either by an external tube clip or internally by means of a cork tongue, so as to give the vowel α (calm) it was found that, if the tube was further pinched immediately in front of the opening of the reed tube, a definitely nasal twang was given to the vowel sound. This experiment confirmed my personal observations that the typical American twang is not due to nasal resonance but to a constriction of the pharynx.

There can be no doubt that a great deal of the quality of the human voice depends on the pharynx, or rather on the resonating cavity behind the tongue. The greater part of the energy of the voice is known to lie in the lower resonances of its vowel sounds (see for example the experiment with " Radio Rex ")—so do its audible characters of richness or " forwardness " or nasality. Nobility of tone would seem to depend almost directly on the volume of the back resonator.

The experiments which have just been described, though much too incomplete to constitute proof, appear to support the view that resonance is an important element in the quality of the voice production apart from its function in defining vowel character. In the human vocal cavity it is even conceivable that the false vocal cords—which produce a small cavity immediately in front of the vocal cords, comparable with the cavity 3 of Fig. 126—may have some share in determining the quality of the sound produced, apart from vowel and consonant character.

(4) and (5) *Soundboard action of palate and teeth, and direction of sound in the mouth.* It is a well ascertained physical principle that waves—whether of sound in air or on the surface of water, or of light in space—cannot be reflected (so as to take a definite direction) except from surfaces which are large compared with the wave-length (measured from crest to crest) of the undulation which falls on them.

A mirror reflects light because of its polished surface, but only so long as its surface is large compared to the wave-length of the light which falls upon it. If the mirror were made smaller in dimensions than a wave-length, the light would envelop it and pass on—just as a wave in the sea would ignore a single upright post, standing in its path. On the other hand a continuous line of posts, longer from end to end of the line than the distance between one wave and the next, will act as a barrier, and the wave will be reflected back by it.

In voice production, the wave-lengths employed vary in length from between 14 feet and 3 feet, in the case of a bass voice, to between 4 feet and just under 1 foot for a soprano. If by a " soundboard " in voice production is meant a reflector, such as is suspended over pulpits to throw the speaker's voice down amongst his audience, then the palate of a basso profundo would need to measure 20 feet either way (if not more) to be effective on his lower notes. A soprano might be able to manage with a palate of, say, 6 feet square, and teeth (if these are to be included) of the same length! The soundboard and reflector theory is therefore not tenable.

Chapter XI

MOUTH RESONANCE IN RELATION TO LARYNGEAL PITCH.

We have seen, from the experiments with models, that the cavities of the mouth (except in the case of high-pitched resonances) behave generally like Helmholtz resonators. One of the qualifications of such a resonator is that it shall be small compared with the wave-length of the vibrations which it produces.[1] The inside of such a resonator is then entirely filled with palpitating air which presses rhythmically against all parts of the containing walls; there can be no *direction* of sound against one part or another of the interior of such a resonator. And so it generally is, without doubt, in the case of the human mouth. If the resonator is large (within the permissible limits of size) larger *amplitudes* of vibration may be set up than if it is smaller, though the musical pitch of both resonators may be the same if their orifices are properly proportioned to the volume of their cavities.

When a resonator is being energized, the air inside it is stirred into vibration by the rhythmical impulses due to the action of the vocal cords. The vigour of its response will then depend, to some extent at least, on the relation between the rate per second at which the air in the resonator would naturally vibrate (if given a single push) and the rate per second at which it is being actually and repeatedly pushed by the laryngeal puffs. If the resonator is tuned so as to be in proper relation to the vibrations by which it is energized, the response will be greater and more continuous than if it were not so tuned.

This fact probably affords the explanation for the rule that, in singing, the tongue and throat must be kept mobile. So far as resonance pure and simple is concerned, flexibility can be of no advantage—indeed the more yielding the resonator the less efficient it will be. The object of flexibility is probably to enable the organs to hunt instinctively for the position of

[1] See Appendix I.

best resonance (within the possible limits of variation of the vowel resonance) at each change of the larynx note on any given vowel, or at each change of vowel on a given note.

The sensation of forward production may thus be due to the fact that, when the resonators are properly adjusted, a bigger amplitude of vibration (especially of the " overtones " or vibrations of high frequency which give brilliance to the voice) is felt within the front cavity of the mouth. Such a hunting action of the tongue and throat (if it actually occurs) would be very analogous to the operation of " voicing " an organ pipe, so as to get the best relation between the reed and its resonator.

One other experiment may be mentioned here, namely as to the action of the soft palate in connection with the different forms of production.

If, while singing a given vowel—say α (calm)—on the same note all the time, the character of the voice production be changed in various ways, it will be seen that the soft palate assumes many different attitudes. These can be easily studied by illuminating the inside of the mouth with a small electric light.

We shall refer again to this matter very shortly.

Nasal Resonance and Vowel Production

There has been and still is, great controversy as to whether or not the passage to the nasal cavity should be opened (by the forward and downward movement of the soft palate) during the singing of vowel sounds. Whether the passage is open or shut is very easily determined (as we have said)—by the observer or by the singer personally—namely by the use of a stethoscope, held to either nostril, so as to lead the sound to the ears. Another and cruder way of trying the same experiment, is to close the nostrils intermittently (by pinching them) while singing the vowel. If the nasal passage is open, the closure of the nostrils produces a marked change in vocal quality ; if the passage is already closed, the further closure of the nostrils makes no perceptible difference. This further indicates that when the nasal passage is closed by the soft palate, there is no appreciable leakage of sound into the nasal cavity and that it is essentially inoperative.

Of the few well-known singers with whom I have tried either

of these experiments, all have proved *not* to be using the nasal cavity in vowel production.

The experiment was tried of adding a nasal cavity to a plasticine double resonator. There was an appreciable increase of sound (especially if the nasal resonator was in tune with the reed note), without much change in the vowel character. Similarly, it was found that, in several vowel models, increased volume could be obtained by making a small orifice to the air in the back resonator (so as to give a direct exit to the back resonance) though with some loss of vowel character.

In the human voice, it seems probable that greater volume may be obtained by opening the nasal passage, but at the cost of adding a constant group of nasal resonances to those of every vowel sound. This, to my ear, gives a disagreeable monotony to all the vowel sounds.

On the other hand, it may be possible that (as is claimed by Mr. Weston, a voice-trainer, of Boston, Mass., with whom I have discussed this question) the soft palate can be so adjusted as to vary the opening to the nasal cavity, so as to tune its resonance and regulate the proportion and pitch of the nasal resonance in each case, and thus gain volume while avoiding monotony.

The only point on which I can speak with confidence in this matter is that several very good singers—male and female—do not use nasal resonance at all in producing their vowel sounds.

In this connection, we may also consider the question of the nasal consonants **m**, **n** and **ŋ** (ng). It is well known that these may be produced with or without "nasal" quality, though the normal production of all three consonants is, of course, through the nasal cavity. It will also be remembered that in the case of one of the rubber tube vowel models, **m**, **n** and **ŋ** (ng) were all made without the use of a nasal cavity, namely by nearly complete closure of the tube at the front, centre, or close to the reed opening, and that the continuous hum—which is an important characteristic of all three sounds—was produced by leakage at the closure. The same effect can be produced in the human voice, but the articulatory change is certainly less defined than when these sounds are made as in normal speech.

To test the cause of variations of nasality, when singing the sound **m**, experiment was made with the windowed mouth stop and internal lamp, already described at p. 118. It was found that when **m** was intoned without nasality, the palatal arch was broad and flat as in Fig. 127, whereas when the production was changed to a strongly nasal **m**, the arch became more Gothic—being narrowed at the base and drawn up to a point as in Fig. 128. The two figures indicate the appearance as seen through the window of the mouth stop.

The nasal stethoscope experiment was also tried in the case of the various consonants, as used by myself in normal speech. It was found that **m** (as already mentioned) was normally nasal, but not always; for example, in the word " transmits ", where I make the **m** very short, there was no opening of the passage to the nasal cavity. **n** and **ŋ** were always nasal, **ð** (as in this) was variable, e.g. in the word " that " **ð** was occasionally nasal, to the extent of an almost instantaneous " tap ", formed

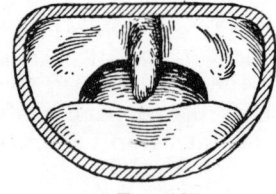

FIG. 127. 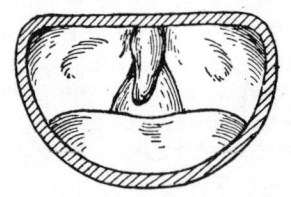   FIG. 128.

by a momentary opening of the passage at the beginning or end of the **ð** sound; **gl** showed a similar " tap " at the end of the sound; **kʃ** (as in action) was sometimes nasal but not normally; so also was **y** (yes). **h** was sometimes nasal, sometimes not. In my brother's voice, it was nasal in **hi** (he), **hu** (hoo) and **hɪt** (hit) and non-nasal in **hei, he** (as in hen) and **hæ**. In my own voice H was nasal with the vowels **ei** (not always), **e** (not always), **ɑ** (not always), **æ, ɐ, ʌ** (occasionally).

H was not nasal with the vowels **i, ɪ, ɒ, ɔ, ou** and **u**. In my own voice, the vowel—

ɑ before **n** or **ŋ** is generally nasal.
ɑ before **rt** as in " articulate " is generally nasal.
æ before **m** is not nasal.
æ before **n**, as in " and ", is nasal.
ʌɪ as in " by " is, sometimes.

These experiments show that many of the consonants, in which nasal resonance was observed when whispered for experimental purposes, are not nasal when employed in normal speech; they further show that the presence or absence of nasal resonance does not make any appreciable difference to the audible vowel or consonant character of most of the speech-sounds.

As a test of nasal resonance in singing, the following nonsense words may be sung, to the tune of " Ye banks and braes of bonny Doon ". The first four lines contain no nasal consonants, and should be capable of being equally well sung, with the nostrils free or pinched, by singers who do not employ nasal resonance on their vowels. On the other hand, the last four lines contain a nasal consonant (m, n or ŋ) in every word and may serve as a test of the extent to which nasal resonance is necessary in singing these sounds.

I (*without nasal consonants*).

Hard by the shores of far Brazil
 We rode for pleasure years ago,
Led forward ever by the will
 To brave each risk, to fight each foe.

II (*with nasal consonants*).

No roaming more! In time nigh spent
 Mere strength grown faint, new prudence strong;
And now from home my mien unbent
 Must amble near my mate—in Song!

In comparing the action of the tongue (in vowel formation) with that of the artificial constrictions made in the vowel-sounding models, it has hitherto been assumed that, in the human voice, the central orifice is entirely due to the position and shaping of the tongue. This assumption is not strictly true, for, in certain cases at least, observation of the illuminated interior of the mouth, shows that the lower parts of the soft palate—on either side of the arch of which the uvula forms the depending keystone—may co-operate with the back part of the tongue. In these cases the central orifice is formed by the palatal arch itself, with its foundations resting on the back of the tongue. It is only in certain forms of production—namely those of a more strident or nasal type—that this action occurs; it seems to be associated, in the vowel ɑ (calm), with the development of a high pitched resonance 2579, together with the normal vowel resonances which are but little altered by the change of attitude of the tongue and soft pillars or curtains of the palatal arch. Fig. 129 indicates roughly the appearance of the palatal arch and tongue during this operation; the corresponding sectional view (taken from the left-hand side of the subject's mouth and exaggerated in height towards

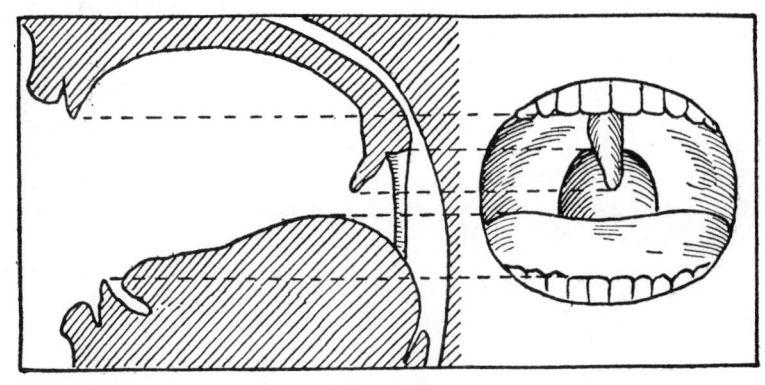

Fig. 129.

the front, so that similar parts may be joined by dotted lines in the two views)—may enable the organs to be more easily identified.

Another question in connection with the nasal consonants is

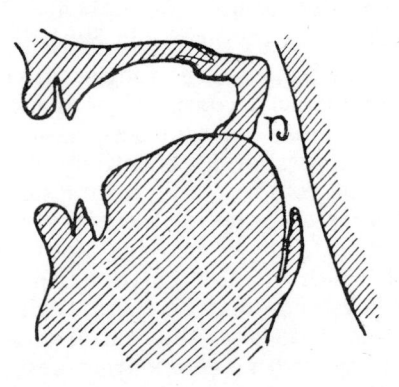

Fig. 130.

as to where, exactly, the high-pitched resonance—about 2434, of the sound ŋ—corresponding to 1625 in n and 1084 or lower in m—is formed.

When the tongue is pushed back into the k position and the

soft palate drawn forward to meet it, there is obviously no mouth cavity available.

The most probable explanation (though at present, so far as I know, it lacks confirmation) seems to be that the high-pitched resonator is formed between the back of the tongue and the back of the upper part of the soft palate which produce the cavity marked ŋ in Fig. 130.

Leakage of Sound through Cavity Walls

There is another phenomenon already referred to, in connection with the models, namely, transparency to sound, which may have a bearing on voice production. It will be remembered that it was found feasible to listen to the resonances of interior cavities, by forming india-rubber sheet windows, through which the resonant pitch could be heard. The following experiment shows that a considerable volume of sound passes out through the skin of a singer's cheeks and throat.

Pinch the nostrils and keep the lips closed ; it will be found that under these circumstances, a succession of fairly loud notes of short duration can be made—the air from the lungs being forced through the larynx so as to fill the mouth at each note and being returned to the lungs at its conclusion. The moral would appear to be that, to utilize this sound-leakage, the singer's throat should be bared and held well up, so as to expose the maximum surface of " window ". This operation may raise the resonant pitch of the back resonator (since leakage through the walls of a resonator is equivalent to enlarging its orifice), but the effect may be neutralized by the greater volume given to the back resonator, by the more erect attitude.

Conditions of Best Resonance

How are the best resonant conditions to be obtained in the human vocal cavities ? The answer given by our theory is : by forming the cavities so that they operate as a pair of resonators of the maximum size, properly tuned in relation to the larynx note by which they are being energized. As there are two distinct ways of tuning Helmholtz resonators, it follows that a big resonator with a big orifice may have the same pitch as a small resonator with a proportionately smaller orifice ; but the larger resonator with the larger orifice will produce the greater volume of sound. There should be the maximum of resonating cavity and the minimum of passage between resonators.

In the accompanying Figs. 131 and 132 (from X-ray photographs taken by Dr. Russell) this principle is well illustrated.

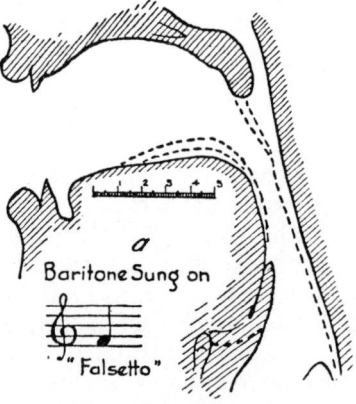

FIG. 131.

In Fig. 131 showing the vowel a sung, falsetto, on f' (342 ~) by a baritone, there is a very large front orifice due to a well-depressed tongue, a rapid convergence to a narrow constriction just above the epiglottis, and a similar rapid divergence to the

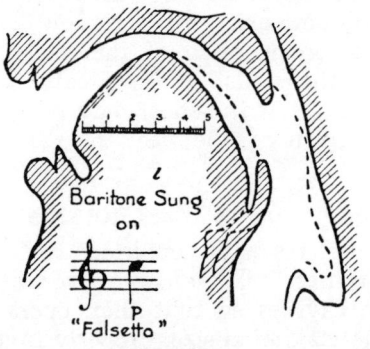

FIG. 132.

cavity immediately above the vocal cords. Even so it seems possible that by humping the tongue more directly towards the back of the throat (instead of somewhat upwards towards the passage leading to the nasal cavity) a further increase of volume in both mouth and pharynx might have been obtained.

LARYNGEAL PITCH

In Fig. 132 showing the vowel **i** (eat) sung, falsetto, on c" (512 ~) also by the same baritone, the tongue is well humped towards the hard palate, so as to leave an aperture only ¼ inch deep between the tongue and the palate. The back resonator is very large, but is, in this case, constricted in an unexpected way at about its middle by the backward projection of the epiglottis. The front resonator forms a diverging funnel.

As to the total volume of the resonating cavities and the opening of the mouth itself, I speak with less certainty than as to the shape of the resonators.

It seems highly probable that, to give uniformity of production throughout the range of the vowel sounds, the *total* volume of the resonating cavities should be constant, and the mouth opening (to air) should vary as little as possible between different vowels.

The vowel changes then become those due to the shifting of the central orifice, together with the additional lowering of the resonances brought about by partially closing the front orifice (mouth) for the vowels ɔ (all), **ou**, and **u**.

As to the degree of mouth opening to be used, for all the other vowels, it may be said that assuming the cavities to have been made as large as possible, and the mouth opening at least as large as the central orifice, there is no acoustic advantage in opening it wider. Such further opening will, in fact, alter the tuning and distort the vowel sound by raising the resonant pitch.

Flexibility of the tongue, soft palate, etc., it will be remembered, was considered to be of use in so far as it enabled the vocal cavities to retune themselves automatically at each change of larynx note or of vowel sound, so as to obtain the conditions of best resonance. Actually if a singing exercise be performed on a single vowel sound, the tongue will be seen to rise and fall slightly in the mouth as the larynx note is raised or lowered.

From this point of view the fixed resonator scale, advocated by Dr. Aikin,[1] would not appear to be desirable, as it is inconceivable that a single fixed resonance for each vowel would give the best resonance throughout the chromatic scale. The merits of Dr. Aikin's method would appear to be : (1) that by drawing the singer's attention to the audible resonances of the voice, the singer is led to increase the size

[1] See Chap. I.

of the resonating cavities and reduce the useless passage-ways, i.e. to produce the conditions, shown diagrammatically at A, rather than those of B. (2) that by separating the upper vowel resonances into a musical scale, Aikin secures a more defined and distinct series of vowel pronunciations than that due to a chance selection of vowel resonances.

But to give the best resonance on every note of the laryngeal scale, the resonator scale itself must be capable of being transposed to some extent.

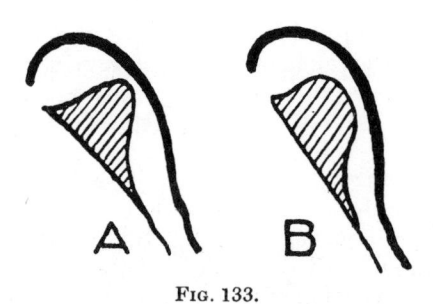

Fig. 133.

Vowel Sound in Relation to Pitch of Larynx Note

In Willis'[1] early experiments—referred to in Chapter I—he found that when the pitch of his reed was high, some of the vowels became impossible to produce.

Willis recognized the cause—namely, that the reed impulses were more frequent than the natural rate of the air pulses in his resonating tube, and he also recognized that the same effect occurs in the human voice, more particularly in the case of women's voices, owing to the higher pitch of their larynx notes. To test this point further the following experiment was made :—

The vowel sound u (who) was sung on an ascending scale of larynx notes and the vowel sound tested at each change of note by closing the aperture between the lips with the fingers (during phonation), so as to produce the vowel with interruptions of the consonant b. It was found that the bu sound thus artificially made changed progressively from bu to bᴜ (as in book), bo, bɒ (as in boss) or bɔ (bore) as the larynx note

[1] See p. 15, Willis, loc. cit., p. 240.

LARYNGEAL PITCH

was raised, while the vowel posture was kept as far as possible constant. Tabulating the results, we have :—

Laryngeal Frequency.	Vowel Heard.	Observations.
512	ɒ as in (not)	512 is a lower resonance of ɔ
483	ɒ	483 ,, ,, ,, ɔ
430	ɒ to ɔ (all)	
406	ou first part of diphthong	406 ,, ,, ,, ou
342	ʊ as in (put)	342 ,, ,, ,, ʊ
322	u as in (who)	

FIG. 134.

Unless the vowel was artificially interrupted in the way described, the ear did not notice the loss of the u sound; it probably recognized that the tongue was still in the u posture. It seems unlikely that a true u sound can be sung on any note above, say, ♯g″ 406,

FIG. 135.

since a resonator cannot be energized by impulses of a higher frequency than its own—just as a boy on a swing could not be kept going by giving him a succession of pushes at a higher rate per minute than that of the natural rate of the swing. If, therefore, good pronunciation is required in singing, composers should not demand of the vocalist that any vowel should be sung on a note higher than the lower resonance range of the vowel in question. For bass voices this rule raises no difficulties, since practically all the notes of a bass are below the range of the vowel resonances. A tenor should not be asked to pronounce an ou (no), u (who), ʊ (put), i (eat), or ɪ (it) on his highest notes, while the contralto is still more limited. Finally a soprano must not be expected to pronounce any vowels, except perhaps ɑ (calm) and possibly ʌ (up), ɒ (not), and æ (hat) on her highest notes; it would seem to be a physical impossibility to do so.

On the other hand experiment with models shows that the vowels of high upper resonance can be *recognizably* produced on a reed note which is higher than their lower resonance.

In this case the vowel is recognized by its upper resonance alone.

Most singing at the present time would appear to be learnt by imitating the voice of the teacher through unconscious adaptation of the pupil's vocal organs, by practice, and by observation of other singers.

It cannot but be of advantage to the art that its fundamental principles should be better understood; it is hoped that even the very incomplete observations of this chapter may be of some help towards laying the foundations of a more reliable theory, and that they may stimulate other investigators.

Abnormal Speech

A consideration of the principles involved in phonation and articulation, and of the behaviour of models, can hardly

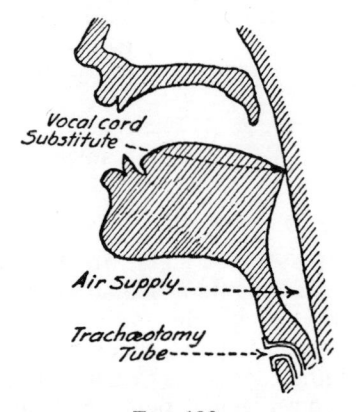

Fig. 136.

fail to be of service in the study and treatment of the various abnormalities of speech which occur in practice.

Thus, an experiment in which an artificial larynx effect was produced by simply stretching a plain rubber tube till its sides touched, and blowing through it, gives the clue to an interesting case of recovered phonation after removal of the larynx which I was privileged to investigate in New York in May, 1928.

The subject, a patient of Dr. Lee M. Hurd, M.D., was examined by X-rays, and it then appeared that he first drew air into his pharynx and the upper part of his gullet (æsophagus); he then humped the back of this tongue against the back of his throat, so as to imprison the air, and finally expelled it between the contacting edges of the hump of the tongue and the back of the throat so as to produce a reed-action at this point.

The exhaling action was produced by a downward and inward collapse of the front part of the throat—the diaphragm and chest muscles being fixed during the process of phonation.

The reed-note thus produced was low pitched (somewhere about 64 ~) and was not yet variable, but it was otherwise quite natural and effective for voiced speech. The subject was able to articulate all the vowels and consonants (except **h**) effectively. As to **h**, it seemed likely that, as **k** was producible, a sound sufficiently near **h** would be obtained by a partial closure at the same point as for **k**.

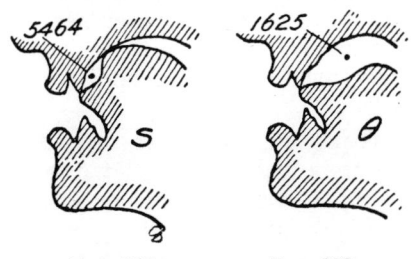

FIG. 137.   FIG. 138.

Similarly, the study of the resonance essentials of the various vowel and consonant sounds may be of service in the voice—or speech—training of persons suffering from abnormal formation of, or injury to, the organs of articulation. Thus, the knowledge of the resonances which are required to produce the missing speech sounds may suggest to the vocal trainer alternative ways of producing them, or new ways of producing similar resonances.

Take for example the simple case of the lisp, in which the subject substitutes a θ for an **s**.

The typical resonance of **s** is between 5000 and 6000 ~ — made by a small, short cavity formed by the tongue just behind the teeth; the typical corresponding resonance of θ is 1625, made by a much larger cavity due to a lower and more retracted humping of the tongue. The position of the tongue tip may be the same in both cases. See Figs. 137 and 138.

Obviously, therefore, what is needed to convert a θ into

an **s** is to raise the hump of the tongue towards the front of the palate so as to reduce this cavity till the **s** resonance appears.

The consonant **k** is made by a closure and release of the back of the tongue against the soft palate. Now let the experiment be tried of making the consonant **t** (with the tip of the tongue against the palate, just behind the front teeth) and repeating the gesture while moving the point of closure further and further back from the teeth. A variety of **t** sounds will be formed in this way: but, by the time that the point of closure is as far back as the tip of the tongue can possibly reach, the consonant sound will be found to be not **t** but a quite recognizable **k**.

Similarly, while **l** is normally made by touching the palate with the tip of the tongue and sharply withdrawing it, a sound almost identical with **l** can be made by protruding the tongue and touching the outside of the upper part of the front lip. A quite good transient **r** can be made in the same way—the two edges of the tongue being closed against the two sides of the upper lip.

Dr. Russell has pointed out to me that in the case of cleft palate speech (where a true plosive release of the lips or tongue is impossible owing to the pharynx being *always* open to the nasal cavity) a close imitation of the plosive consonants can be made by combining the appropriate tongue or lip gesture with a glottal release to give the plosive effect.

A somewhat similar effect can be produced in the Cheirophone (see p. 241) where plosive sounds, which would not be possible to produce owing to the leakage of air past the operator's fingers, may be imitated by closing and suddenly releasing the air supply behind the artificial larynx simultaneously with the moment of release by the fingers which take the place of the tongue.

This method is identical with the production of the **p** and **m** sounds in Professor D. C. Miller's organ pipe groups which reproduced intoned vowel sounds. The closure and release of the air supply behind the pipes produced the same consonant effect as if the mouths of each of them had been covered and uncovered simultaneously.

The consonant **s** is normally made—as has been explained—by resonance in the small cavity made behind the front teeth, to which, strictly speaking, should be added a further and fainter resonance (about 2732 in my voice) made by the cavity formed by the lips in front of the teeth.

A very similar sound can be made *without* the aid of the tongue, namely by drawing back the under jaw and lip, so that the front teeth overlap the underlip, which then takes the place of the tongue. The upper lip can then form a cavity—in co-operation with the *outside* of the underlip—so as to form s-like sounds by partial closure, or sounds like t or n by full closure.

In this connection may be mentioned the forcible conversion of an unvoiced (i.e. whispered) v into f, or of a whispered b into p, by applying external pressure across the front of the throat just above the larynx. The method may be found useful in teaching deaf mutes the difference between the so-called voiced and unvoiced consonants in whispered speech.

In every instance it is the resonances of the cavities—their rise and fall, both in pitch and in volume of sound—which determine the speech sounds that we hear.

In cases of surgical excision of the tongue (in whole or in part) one of the immediate effects is to alter (lower) the natural resonance of the vocal cavity by increasing its volume.

It seems reasonable to suppose (though I do not know that the experiment has yet been tried) that this condition could be remedied. If the volume of the mouth cavity were reduced by effectively lowering the roof of the mouth by means of a plate—so as to compensate for the lowering of the floor due to the removal of the tongue, the original volume and resonance might be restored. In other words, the roof of the mouth would then bulge downwards instead of the tongue bulging upwards. Such a procedure might also make it possible for the remaining portions of the tongue muscle to make contact with the artificial palate in cases where this would not be possible otherwise.[1] Happily, owing to the success of radium treatment in cancer of the tongue, cases of surgical excision are becoming rare.

An interesting application of the principles of articulation under abnormal conditions occurs in the art of Ventriloquism. Here, the main object aimed at, is to produce clear articulation, without visible movements of the speaker's lips, cheeks or

---

[1] I am indebted to Sir Lenthal Cheatle for the opportunity of observing the phonetic effects of the surgical removal of the tongue in the case of a patient at King's College Hospital, Denmark Hill, London.

throat—in other words an object exactly opposite to that of a speaker who desires to be understood by the process of lip-reading.

Since, in the matter of vocal resonance, we are dealing mainly, at all events, with resonators of the Helmholtz type, it is usually possible to substitute a reduction of volume for an enlargement of the aperture and so obtain the same resonant pitch as before. For the same reason, children can produce similar resonances to those of adults. The ventriloquist, therefore, can form a complete range of vowel sounds while maintaining a small and constant degree of mouth opening. The lowering of resonances, produced by the small mouth opening, is readjusted by a reduction (made by the tongue and throat, etc.) in the volume of the resonating cavities.[1]

In Ventriloquism, a difficulty of another kind, arises in the case of the labial consonants **m**, **p**, **b**, **f**, **v**, which cannot be normally articulated without visible movement of the lips. This difficulty, however, may be overcome, by keeping the lips immovable and only slightly apart, and the teeth sufficiently separated, so that the tip of the tongue can be inserted between them, so as just to close the space between the lips. In this way, by protruding or withdrawing the tongue between and behind the inner surfaces of the lips, the performer produces practically the same acoustic effects as if the lips themselves had been brought together or separated. In this way **m**, **p** and **b** are formed without visible lip movement. **f** and **v** which, as we have seen, are produced by partial closures, corresponding to the complete closures and releases of **p** and **b**, are then produced by a partial closure by the tongue of the space between the lips—the tongue being pressed against the inside of the lower lips, but so as to be just clear of the upper lip.

The rest of the art of ventriloquism is concerned with maintaining the immobility of the throat and cheeks, with the mimicry of sounds and voices, and with various practical applications of the methods of suggestion, by which the audience are induced to believe that the sounds which they hear are coming from some other source than the performer's mouth.

[1] It will be found that a complete range of vowel sounds can even be produced with a perforated mouth-stop, with an aperture of about $\frac{1}{2}$ in. diameter, held between the lips, or with the tip of the tongue touching the palate, just behind the teeth—the necessary adjustments being instinctively made to correct the resonances.

LARYNGEAL PITCH

Sounds such as those of human speech are—as we have already seen—mostly of long wave-length, compared to the size of the cavities which produce them. The consequence is that the sound waves travel outwards from the speaker's mouth in all directions, and not at all in a directed beam of sound as they would from a large trumpet. They are reflected by floors, walls, and ceilings, and, the final result is that the audience, being quite unable to locate the direction of the sound at all exactly by ear, readily accept the suggestion of the performer as to the location of its source.

Chapter XII

ARTIFICIAL SPEECH AND SONG

WHILE it may be reasonable to assume that some of the results which have been described in previous chapters will eventually be capable of practical application, it must be admitted that such applications are, as yet, in their infancy. Still, as " infant welfare " is now recognized as worthy of intensive study, an account of the first attempts in the use of multiple resonators may be of interest.

The general method of producing speech-like sounds—by combining two or more resonators in series and/or parallel, so tuned as to give the resonances heard in the (human) sound when unvoiced, and by energizing the resonators rhythmically for the production of voiced sounds and unrhythmically for producing unvoiced sounds—forms the subject of the author's British Patent No. 214,281.[1] The same document, to which the interested reader is referred, illustrates typical methods of reproducing the various vowel and consonant sounds and gives examples of the application of the principles to such purposes as the construction of talking signal or motor horns, actuated by air-blown reeds, syrens or whistles, or by electrically vibrated diaphragms. It also describes methods of applying the same principles to the manufacture of organ pipes and the like, so as to produce vowel-like musical sounds, or to toys designed to imitate human speech, or animal noises. In the latter case, the correct resonances are obtained by imitating, with the human voice, the animal-sound in question, and then observing the vocal resonances when the same sounds are repeated in a whisper.

No attempt has yet been made to devise an instrument capable of producing connected speech " synthetically ". The great variety of changes of resonance which are required for this purpose would, almost inevitably, necessitate a complicated mechanism. If the mechanical production of connected speech

[1] The corresponding U.S.A. Patent is not yet issued (Sept. 1929).

is required, it is obviously simpler to start with human speech and reproduce it by phonographic methods.

The first crude attempt at the artificial production of a sentence, by the principles which have been described, was made in September, 1923, by an "orchestra" of seven performers, each supplied with a separate mouth-blown vowel or consonant resonator. The sentence selected (as being within the capacity of the models available) was "Oh mother, are you sure you love me". It was performed in this way:—

Oh (o-ʊ) by partial closure of the mouth of the o model during blowing, to give the terminal ʊ sound.
Mother by manipulation of a model producing the sounds th, dh.
are by the ɑ (calm) model (the r not being sounded).
you by partial closure, during blowing, of the i (eat) model, to give terminal u.
sure by an unvoiced sh model, immediately followed by a voiced vowel on the ɔ model (the r not being sounded).
you as before.
love by manipulation of the ʌ model—the l being made by a flicking of the thumb in the mouth of the front resonator and the v by an almost complete closure of the mouth of the model.
me by manipulation of the i (eat) model.

Signal Horns

One obvious application of the method was for the production of talking signal horns for various purposes. Thus for motorcars a talking horn appeared to have certain definite advantages. The human sense of hearing is probably more alert to voice-like sounds than to any others, and it is a common experience of motorists that, in the last resort, a shout is often more effective in attracting attention than a much louder and more raucous blast on the horn. It seemed likely, therefore, that a signal horn, designed to produce a voice-like "Hi!", or any loud cry, might be made actually less noisy and unpleasant than an ordinary horn and yet be more effective.

Experiment was made as to the various methods of energizing a device of this kind. The air-blown reeds, commonly used in motor horns, which are operated by squeezing a rubber ball, were found to be quite effective. These reeds do not differ from those used in organ pipes, except that the metal strip, which operates as the reed, is usually thicker and therefore stiffer in the motor horn type and requires a higher air pressure to set it in vibration.

Experiment was made with various types of electrically actuated diaphragms, to test whether these could be substituted for a reed to energize the air of a multiple resonator, attached in the place of the horn. It was found that those types in which the diaphragm was set in motion by percussion of the electric bell type, were not capable of producing vowel sounds. The action of the hammer blows on the diaphragm results in the production of very high harmonics of its fundamental note; these being higher in pitch than the natural frequencies of the vowel, resonators have no power to energize them. The

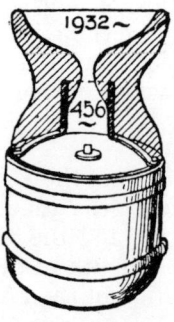

FIG. 139.

consequence is that the sound of such a diaphragm is but little altered in character by passing through a vowel resonator. On the other hand, a diaphragm which is electro-magnetically vibrated (without mechanical contact)—as in the case of the telephone—is sufficiently free from high harmonics and if vibrated at a laryngeal frequency, can be made to energize vowel or consonant resonators. A diaphragm, actuated by a phonographic record, of the laryngeal note required, would presumably act in the same way.

Experiments were made with the electro-magnetic mechanism of a horn, which was supplied by the courtesy of the Clear-Hooter Company, of Birmingham (England). The first experimental (hand-manipulated) signal horn to be made with electro-magnetic " larynx " was designed to articulate the signal cry " away ! " The arrangement is shown in Fig. 139,

ARTIFICIAL SPEECH AND SONG

in which the resonators only are shown in section. The double resonator was made of plasticine, built on to the cylindrical metal socket, to which the horn is normally attached. The proportions of the back resonator were adjusted, so as to give the resonances 1932 and 456. With these it was found that the vowel

(i) ɪ was given on full opening, by hand, of the front resonator.

(ii) e was given on nearly full opening.

(iii) ʌ was given on partial closure.

(iv) ᴜ was given, or rather w, on nearly complete closure

The successive operations, iii, iv, ii, i, then articulated the word " away ". This model (which was afterwards dismantled, for other experiments) was originally shown at the British Association meeting at Liverpool, on 17th September, 1923. The articulation was quite recognizable, but was somewhat overwhelmed by direct leakage of sound from the back of the diaphragm through the thin metal casing which enclosed the electro-magnetic actuating mechanism. In later models this objection was largely overcome by sound-insulating the casing as a whole, but, so far as articulation is concerned it would appear that the reed-actuated models give the better results.

Vowel-sounding Organ Pipes

About the same time as the experiments on the " Away " horn, similar trials were made of the application of the double resonator method to organ pipes, at the organ building works of Messrs. Rushworth & Dreaper, at Liverpool. To them must be given the credit for having carried out the first pioneering work in applying double resonance to organ pipes.

It is true that organ pipes with a central constriction had been used before, but never for the purpose of producing a definite vowel sound, or with any intention of producing definitely tuned cavities. Thus pipes of the type shown in Fig. 140, have been used by German builders—with a transverse diaphragm, pierced by a small central hole. The object of the diaphragm with its central hole was (as I was informed by Messrs. Rushworth & Dreaper) to reduce the volume of sound of the pipe, and the separate cavities formed by the division were, as will be seen, not stream-lined. Such a constriction would give but little vowel character and, indeed, was not used for that purpose.

Another form of constricted pipe is the better known "coned gamba", of which the typical form is shown in Fig. 141. Here again the constriction was not made for the purpose of obtaining a vowel quality, though it was known that any alteration of the length of the upper cone, produced an alteration of the quality of the sound. There was no attempt at tuning the portions of the pipe above and below the constriction, and the lower portion was not stream-lined towards the reed.

In the present experiments, trials were made with resonators in series and resonators in parallel, made in wood or organ pipe metal. It was found that good vowel-quality could be

Fig. 140.

got by series or parallel resonators, but that though the parallel arrangement allowed the separate resonators to be more easily tuned, they were less convenient to manufacture and took up more space. As to materials—good vowel-quality was obtained with either wood or metal—the latter being (as would be expected) rather more brilliant in character. The tone of a metal pipe could be made to approximate towards that of a wooden pipe by forming windows in the metal wall and covering these with leather patches.

It was found that the combination of two resonators in series had an unsuspected effect on the reed—in making its note stable over a much wider range of frequencies than would

ARTIFICIAL SPEECH AND SONG

otherwise be the case. Thus it was found that in one case the reed pitch could be varied continuously over a range of 1½ octaves—by variation of the effective length of the reed, by means of the tuning wire. With the same reed and a cylindrical pipe of similar length and capacity, there would have been various points of instability and discontinuity in the series of reed frequencies produced as the effective vibrating length of the reed was progressively reduced. Typical pipes

FIG. 141.

made at this time (November, 1922, and May to September, 1923) are shown in Figs. 142 and 143. In Fig. 142 the tuning was adjusted by the telescopic arrangement shown. In the case of the wooden pipe, the adjustment was made by means of the movable stop with a wire handle, in staple form, extending beyond the mouth of the model. The back resonator could be independently tuned by varying the aperture of a "nasal" orifice, shown just below the movable stop—see Fig. 143.

A set of three wooden pipes of this design were shown on an experimental organ, supplied by Messrs. Rushworth and Dreaper, at the British Association meeting already referred to —together with a corresponding set of *vox humana* pipes for comparison. These—see Fig. 144—consist of single resonators, with an adjustable mouth, they were found to give a much more nasal and less vowel-like tone than the double resonators. The vowel character was between ʊ and ə.

Fig. 142.   Fig. 143.

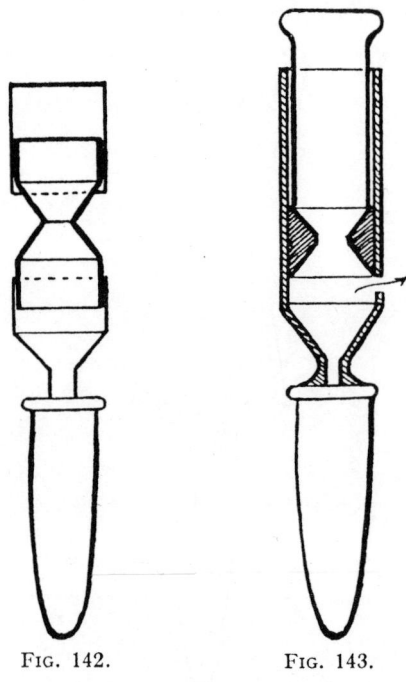

It is possible that resonance behind the reed, viz: in the metal tube which encloses it, may assist in producing a vowel-like character, but it would not be expected that much effective action of this kind would be obtained, owing to the fact that the cavity behind the reed is entirely cut off from the pipe in front at each vibration of the reed onto its seating. A pipe made as in Fig. 142, was tried in the organ at St. Paul's, Knightsbridge, on 31st May, 1923, and when used with the tremulant, was found to give a very human quality, the vowel was ɑ (calm).

ARTIFICIAL SPEECH AND SONG

Experiment was made with a plasticine model to test the possibility of obtaining effective vowel character with pipes of substantially larger dimensions than those of the human mouth. It was found that though vowel-like sounds could be obtained by larger double resonators—the vowel quality was not so good as that of the mouth-sized models, owing to the appearance of additional resonances in the larger cavities. Resonances of high pitch such as the 2298 of i (eat) could not

FIG. 144.

be obtained with a front resonator of greater depth than about 33 mm—say 1⅜ inches.

With the plasticine models, trial was also made of the effect of adding a nasal cavity. It was found that so far as volume of sound was concerned, the addition was only effective (as compared with the effect of piercing a hole in the back resonator) in the case where the resonance of the additional cavity was in unison with the reed frequency. The addition of a nasal cavity did not have any marked effect on the vowel character.

This coincides with the experience that, in singing, the vowels may be produced with or without nasal resonance.

For the practical utilization of vowel-sounding pipes, two alternative methods suggest themselves. (1) A complete stop of sixty-one pipes might be made with their resonances all tuned to give (so far as possible) the same vowel throughout the scale. (2) The twelve semitones of the octave might be divided up between twelve separate vowels—the same in each octave. Thus the chromatic scale might run as follows:—

Note	c	♯c	d	♯d	e	f	♯f	g	♯g	a	♯a	b
Vowel	u	o	ɔ	ɒ	ɑ	ʌ	ɐ	æ	e	ei	ɪ	i

It is evident, however, from what has already been observed, as to the relation between the larynx note and the vowel

Fig. 145.

resonances, that in the higher octaves, the vowel sounds will not all be of equal efficacy.

A few experiments were tried with other methods of energizing the resonators. A free reed of the harmonium type—as used in Kratzenstein's original experiments—was tested with a plasticine double resonator, tuned to the resonances of ɔ (all). It was found to give a vowel character not materially different from that of the beating reed, as used in English organ pipes. Trial was also made of a whistle for the same purpose.[1] The arrangement, which is shown in Fig. 145, consisted of a double resonator in plasticine, tuned to the resonances of u (who).

[1] One of Kratzenstein's vowel-sounding pipes was energized by a whistle instead of a reed.

ARTIFICIAL SPEECH AND SONG

The rubber-strip larynx had been removed and replaced by a whistle mouthpiece and chisel-edge (also in plasticine) as shown. The resonances were 406/812, with a faint additional 1932 heard on tapping or blowing across the mouth of the front resonator. It was found impossible to locate the 406 and 812 resonances, as they seemed equally loud in either resonator. The whistled note was a mellow 406—with an u quality, rather like the call of an owl. This note could be raised by six semitones, to 574, by forming additional holes in the walls of the front resonator; these operated like the finger holes of an Ocarina; the vowel character changed progressively from u to ʌ, as the holes were uncovered.

A similar model was made, tuned to the resonances 645/1149, corresponding to those of ɒ (not). In this model the higher resonance was easily located in the front resonator, thus indicating that the pitch of the whistle note depended, as might be expected, on that of the resonator to which it was

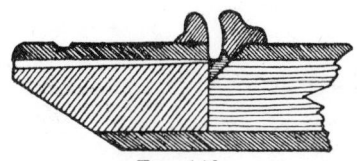

Fig. 146.

directly attached. The whistle note had an appreciable vowel character. No wooden or metal pipes have hitherto been made on this principle.

Whistle-mute for Swannee Whistles, etc.

In connection with the production of whispered speech, by a number of whistles—as referred to in Chapter IX—trials were made of various forms of mute for converting the whistle sound of a Swannee whistle into a breathed sound. The whistle was not easily muted, and it was found necessary to bridge over a large proportion of the whistle-hole with a plasticine cover, in order to prevent the whistle from speaking at any part of its range, according to the position of the plunger. For a whistle with a barrel of about 29 mm. external and 18 mm. internal diameter, the best effect was obtained by a cover, having a transverse slotted opening 3 to 4 mm. by 32 mm., extending over the whistle hole, as shown in Fig. 146.

With a mute of this type, a single Swannee whistle could be

made to produce many recognizable sounds, by tuning the instrument to the upper resonances, in succession, of the sounds required. In particular, it was noted that a " plosive " lip closure or opening of the air supply, gave a good **t** at 2169 whistle frequency and an appreciable **k** at between 966 and 1625. It is possible that the cavity of the player's mouth may have acted, to some extent, as a lower resonator.

The Wow-wow Mute

The so-called " wow-wow " mutes for cornets and the like, which in recent years have appeared as additions to the varied equipment of the Jazz band, appear to be based on the principle of multiple resonators, so tuned as to give speech sounds. In a typical form the device consists of a hollow cylindrical metal box, with opening at both ends ; one end is tapered to

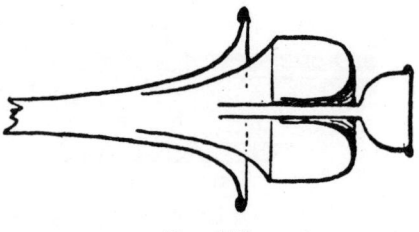

FIG. 147.

a nozzle, provided with an eternal cork ring, so that it can be made to fit tightly inside the bell of the instrument ; the other end is made re-entrant, so as to form the bearing for the tubular stem of a hemispherical front resonator, which can therefore be set so as to project more or less in relation to the cylindrical cavity.

When the cornet, or other instrument, is blown the larynx note is determined by the action of the player's lips and the effective length of the trumpet tube. The vibrations thus produced, pass into the cylindrical resonator and thence by the tubular stem into the cup-shaped front resonator. The vowel-like sound produced in this way can be varied by the player, as in the case of the " away " experimental horn, by covering and uncovering the mouth of the front resonator by hand, while the " larynx " of the instrument is in action.

ARTIFICIAL SPEECH AND SONG

Adjustable Vowel-sounding Models

It was thought that if a simple form of multiple resonator could be devised—such as that already described at p. 69—of which the resonances could be varied independently and recorded by some form of scale marked on the instrument, such a device would be of use in the teaching of phonetics and linguistics. The arrangement shown diagrammatically in Fig. 57 (p. 70) had the advantage of enabling scales—for setting the capacities of both resonators—to be marked on the exterior of the reed cylinder and the stop cylinder respectively.

The first experimental model, which was made by Messrs. Rushworth & Dreaper, was found to give good imitations of all the English vowels, even with a single central stop of fixed orifice and an open mouth. The artificial vowels made by a device of this kind, have one advantage over those made by phonographic methods, namely that the vowel-sound is constant, irrespective of the air pressure at which the model is blown and (to a certain extent also) of the pitch of the reed note. On the other hand, phonographic records of vowel sounds may, as we have seen, be modified or even completely altered in vowel character by changes of speed in recording. A further possible advantage of the adjustable model is that the effect of small changes in the position or attitude of the tongue or in the opening of the lips can be directly illustrated.

The Cheirophone

During the earlier experiments with variable resonators, the idea suggested itself that a variable cavity—comparable to that of the human mouth—might be made by the human hands, so that by connecting this cavity to some form of artificial larynx, a succession of different voice-sounds might be produced. Thus, if the two hands be clasped at right angles to one another, so as to enclose the largest possible volume of air within the cavity thus formed, and the second, third, and fourth fingers of one hand (say the right hand of a right-handed person) be withdrawn inside the cavity, but still held together side by side, these three fingers will divide the cavity into two parts. The double cavity thus formed may be considered as analogous to that of the human mouth and the three fingers be made to function (more or less) like the human tongue.

ARTIFICIAL SPEECH AND SONG

Thus movement of the three fingers—which we may call the "tongue fingers"—towards the palm of the hand to which they belong, becomes comparable to drawing the tongue backwards in the mouth, while an outward movement of the tongue fingers will imitate a forward movement of the tongue, as if to articulate the vowel i (eat). The palm of the other hand then becomes the palate against which the tips of the tongue fingers operate. The proper place for the artificial larynx in this analogy, would be in front of the wrist of the tongue hand, but as we are dealing mainly with Helmholtz resonators, the shape of the resonating cavities and the position of the air supply should not be of prime importance. The artificial larynx was therefore inserted, for convenience, between the thumb and first finger of the tongue hand, while the thumb and first finger of the palate hand operated as the lips of the vocal cavity.

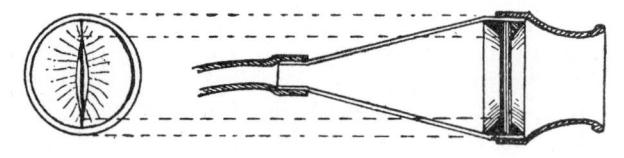

Fig. 148.

The larynx with which all the earlier experiments were tried was of the rubber strip variety; it was mounted at the end of a conical metal tube—to provide an air capacity behind the reed—and terminated in a short tubular handle, designed to be held with an airtight grip between the thumb and finger of the tongue hand as already explained. The general arrangement was as shown in Fig. 148,[1] the artificial larynx being blown by mouth through a rubber tube.

In later models an organ reed operated by foot bellows was substituted for the mouth-blown rubber strip reed—the arrangement of tubular handle, to form the pharynx of the cavity, being the same as before.

All the English vowels could be imitated by various postures of the tongue fingers and apertures of the thumb and first finger of the palate hand, u and ʊ being the poorest and the vowels of medium resonant pitch, e, æ, ɞ, ʌ, ɑ, being the best in quality.

[1] For further structural details, see British Patent No. 237,316.

ARTIFICIAL SPEECH AND SONG

With the arrangement described, no unvoiced sounds could be produced, as the larynx was always in operation, but a number of voiced consonants were produced.

The attitude of the two hands, prior to clasping to form the cavity, is shown in Fig. 149, where the position of the hollow handle is indicated by the dotted ring within the thumb and first finger of the right hand. In this position the clasped hands represent a mouth pointing upwards with its chin towards the right.

i (eat) was made by a very forward posture of the tongue fingers, so that their tips were within half an inch of the "lips," formed by the arching of the thumb against the first finger of the palate hand, and almost in contact with the "palate".

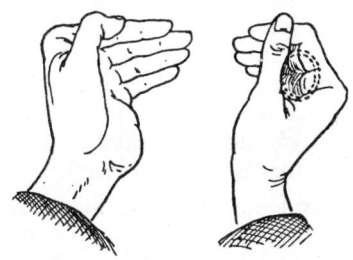

FIG. 149.

ei (hay) was made by slightly raising the knuckles of the tongue fingers, so as to enlarge the front orifice between their tips and the surface of the palate hand.

e (men) was made by bending the tongue fingers rather more than for ei, so as to enlarge the front cavity, the central orifice being about the same as for i (i.e. a small orifice).

æ (hat) was produced by a very open mouthed posture, the tongue fingers being drawn right back while at the same time the palate hand was lowered to increase the aperture.

ɞ (earth) required the tongue fingers to be withdrawn till the second and third fingers touched the palm of the tongue hand, the palate being withdrawn so as to give a space of about three-quarters of an inch between the knuckles of the first joints of the tongue fingers. Rather exact adjustment of this space was required to give the correct resonances.

ʌ (up) required hardly any change from ɐ of the posture of the tongue fingers, but the palate needed to be lowered as for æ (hat).

ɑ (calm) was given by the same posture of the palate hand as for ʌ and æ, but the side of the second finger of the tongue hand had to be pressed against the mouth of the pharynx tube, so as to make an extension of the tube, the other two fingers being held as in the case of ʌ (up), but with the knuckles somewhat more raised.

ɒ (not). In this case the attitude of both hands was the same as for ɑ (calm), only the two outer tongue fingers (the third and fourth) were lowered towards the palm of their own hand.

ɔ (all). For this—the most difficult of the vowels—the second finger of the tongue hand was held as in producing ɑ (calm), but the remaining fingers of that hand were closed tightly, both laterally against each other and inwardly towards the palm; the palate hand being held as in the case of i (eat), so as to make a large cavity with a medium orifice in front of the back cavity, with very constricted orifice, formed by the tongue hand.

ou (no). This sound was made practically like ɔ changing into u, only the cavity of the tongue hand was made (so far as possible) larger while retaining the constricted orifice so as to lower slightly the back resonance. The terminal u sound was made with the palate hand by sliding the fingers of this hand in the direction of the knuckles of the tongue hand, while keeping the thumb of the palate hand pressed against the outside of the thumb and the surface of the finger nail of the tongue hand. This had the effect of closing the "mouth" of the front cavity and lowering both resonances.

u and ʊ could not be produced clearly, owing to the impossibility of forming the requisite low resonances. The u sound, made as described for the terminal of the diphthong ou (no), was the nearest attainable approach to these vowels.

As to consonants, l was easily made by touching the "palate" with the second and third fingers of the tongue hand and sharply withdrawing them. A good unvoiced r was made by nearly closing the mouth of the pharynx tube with the side

ARTIFICIAL SPEECH AND SONG

of the bent-up second finger of the tongue hand. This effect was afterwards repeated with a plasticine cap with a small lateral orifice, giving the half-whistled resonances 1625 to 1824 and 1024 to 1149—varying according to the air pressure employed. ð (as in thee) was made by a nearly complete closure of the three tongue fingers against the palate, in about the same position as for forming the vowel i (eat). v was made by a nearly complete closure made with the knuckles of the first joints of the three tongue fingers against the palate. m was given by a nearly complete closure of the three tongue fingers against the " lips ", formed by the edge of the palate hand between the thumb and first finger—the humming sound due to leakage taking the place of the nasal resonance. n was given by a similar closure of the tongue finger tips against the middle of the palate. ŋ (ng) was practically impossible to produce—the best imitation was got by a nearly full closure of the mouth of the pharynx tube, somewhat similar to that for the untrilled r, but made by keeping the closing finger parallel with the mouth of the tube, so as to open and close it with a piston-like motion. In the r closure and release, the movement of the finger was transverse to the mouth of the pharynx tube.

The plosives, p, b ; t, d ; k, g ; could not be well produced by the hands alone, owing to the difficulty of obtaining the full closures without leakage on which these sounds depend. The best p and t sounds were obtained by suddenly interrupting and releasing the air supply by external pressure on the air tube, while making the appropriate gesture with the tongue and lip fingers ; k was (like ŋ) not producible.

The voiced consonants b and d were easier to produce, the d being due to the same gesture as for n but more completely closed. The g made by the ŋ type of closure was very poor. z was made, though not easily, by a nearly complete closure of the three tongue fingers close to the lip edge of the palate, while the " mouth " made by the thumb and first finger of the palate hand was made small by sliding the ball of the thumb up the first finger as far as the second knuckle.

It will be seen that a large proportion of the voiced sounds were found to be producible so that by selecting words containing these sounds the device could be made to imitate connected speech.

The following sentences have been produced (in public) on different occasions:—

" Hullo London! Are you there? "
" Oh Leila, I love you."
" A happy New Year."
" I hope you have all enjoyed the Paper." And the sentence (for use when gagged in the dentist's chair) : " Easy there, you're on the nerve." (British Association Paper on nature of speech, Toronto, 1924.)

The manipulation (except where otherwise stated) is not difficult, but practice is needed for the production of new sentences.

The air control, by mouth, is very much easier, though no doubt less dramatically effective, than that by foot bellows. It was remarked that, with mouth blowing, the pitch of the rubber strip reed could be quite instinctively controlled by varying the lung pressure—so as to make the reed hum a recognizable tune—thus indicating that a similar control may possibly be occurring in the case of vocal intonation and song.

The cheirophone effect can be reproduced without apparatus by the expedient of forming a reed, or artificial larynx, by means of the operator's own lips. Thus it is possible, with a little practice, to produce a continuous hummed note, due to the vibration of the lips, and to vary the pitch of the note by varying the tension of the lips themselves—possibly with simultaneous variation of the air pressure from the lungs.

If the operator's lips are held against the opening between the thumb and first finger of his tongue-hand, and are then caused to phonate, movements of articulation made with the hands may produce quite life-like speech sounds. Alternatively the lip vibrations may be performed more readily with the aid of a cornet mouthpiece combined, as before, with a suitably shaped hollow handle. A device of this type was shown at the Glasgow meeting of the British Association in 1928.

Miniature Vowel-sounding Models

The successful production of the vowel *ei* by resonators of reduced size, indicated that full scale models were not necessary, provided the correct resonances were secured by a proportionate reduction of orifice to compensate for the reduced capacity

ARTIFICIAL SPEECH AND SONG

of the resonators. Experiment was therefore made with wax or plasticine models of much reduced scale—the smallest of these being about one-tenth of the life size cavities of the human mouth.[1] With these, appreciable breathed or whispered vowel sounds were obtained, but the vowels of low front resonance were very difficult to produce, owing to the necessary smallness of the orifices required to tune them.

It is evident that if two models are made of similar proportions but to different scales, the volumes of the resonators will vary as the cube of the scale of dimensions. Thus, if one model be made half the size of the other, its length, breadth, and depth will all be halved and its cubic capacity will therefore by $\frac{1}{2} \times \frac{1}{2} \times \frac{1}{2}$, i.e. $(\frac{1}{2})^3$, or $\frac{1}{8}$ of the capacity of the larger model. For the small model to have the same resonances as the larger, its orifices must also be $\frac{1}{8}$ of those of the larger model. But then, if the scale of the orifices is reduced, like that of the resonators, to $\frac{1}{2}$, the area of the orifices will only be reduced by $\frac{1}{2} \times \frac{1}{2} = \frac{1}{4}$, instead of $\frac{1}{8}$, while the length of neck of the orifice will be reduced by only $\frac{1}{2}$. To maintain the resonances, it is therefore necessary to reduce the area of the orifices as much again, so that the *areas* of the smaller resonators shall be in the right relation to the *volumes* of the resonators. To give an example: if we compare two models, one of 8 in. length and the other of 2 in., i.e. a reduction in scale of 4 : 1, the capacities of the smaller resonators will be as 4^3 : 1, or 64 : 1; the orifices of the smaller resonators must therefore be 64 times as small as those of the larger model, though its all-over dimensions are only $\frac{1}{4}$ of the first.

It will be seen that with miniature models the orifices become exceedingly small in comparison with the resonators, so that the resulting resonances are very faint. On the other hand, small increases in scale of size produce a correspondingly big increase in the requisite size of the orifices to give the same resonances; it is therefore not difficult to adjust the scale of size according to the purpose in hand.

In Fig. 150 are shown typical miniature models, giving whispered vowel sounds. These were from 50 to 57 mm. (2 to 2¼ inches) in length, and their orifices varied from ·5 to 1·5 mm. in diameter. The first of these was tuned progressively

---

[1] The very small models were made to test a question put to me by Col. Mervyn O'Gorman, as to the speech powers of the Fairies ($\frac{1}{12}$ life size) who were presumed to inhabit the Queen's Dolls' House !

248   ARTIFICIAL SPEECH AND SONG

to give ɪ, e, æ and ɐ, by small variations of the front orifice and capacity of the back resonator. The second model gave a clear whispered ɑ of 1149/812 to 861.

Models on a reduced scale might be suitable for incorporation in talking dolls and other toys for producing speech or animal sounds, provided that in the case of voiced sounds produced by a reed, the energy of the reed is reduced so as to be in scale with the volume of the resonators. If the reed be too loud, the resonances due to the cavities become insignificant in comparison with the reed note, and the voice effects are lost. On the other hand there is a limit of size beyond which the scale of dimensions cannot be enlarged, without jeopardizing the resonances—namely that at which the dimensions of the model become large compared with the

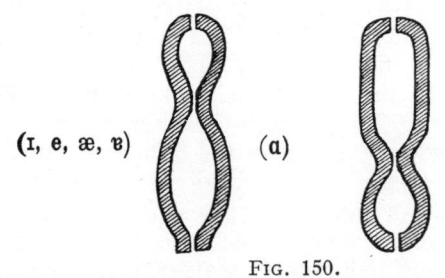

(ɪ, e, æ, ɐ)   (ɑ)

Fig. 150.

wave-length to which they are designed to respond. The shortest wave-lengths in the vowel resonances are 10–12 cm. (4 to 5 inches for the high resonances of i (eat) and i (it). It was found actually not feasible to make an i sounding model with a front resonator much larger than 4 cm. deep by 6 cm. across the mouth. If Gulliver had really been as large as he looked, during his visit to Lilliput, his speech-sounds would have been formidably changed. On the other hand, if the Lilliputians were really as small as they seemed to Gulliver, it is probable that they could only talk in whispers!

CHAPTER XIII

THE ADVANCEMENT OF LANGUAGE AND ITS NOTATION.

SHELLEY, in his *Prometheus Unbound*, wrote these words: " He gave man speech, and speech created thought, which is the measure of the Universe."

Shelley makes bold claim for speech, and puts it even before thought; whether in this he was guided by poetic insight, or only by poetic licence, is beyond our present inquiry; but that there is indeed the closest connection between speech and thought will hardly be disputed. As Max Müller put it, " To think is to speak low. To speak is to think aloud." [1]

We have seen that speech is essentially a matter of symbolic gestures of the organs of articulation—a ritual dance—or gesture code—by which we strive to give outward and visible form to our thoughts (or some of them) so as to define and symbolize them in our own minds and inform the minds of others.

From this point of view, words bear much the same relation to thought that numerals bear to our ideas of quantity. In primitive language, the words used probably represented actions or things or simple qualities—abstract ideas may have been incapable of expression; but as mankind advanced in culture and power of thought, he needed—and consequently devised—a more precise and elaborated code, wherewith to express himself. Unfortunately man, even in his more cultured stages, was largely unconscious of his own problem— he accepted the language as it was spoken by his fellows, ignored its imperfections and made the best use that he could of it.

Great thought has, in the past, been given by the best minds to the analysis of the structure of the various languages used in literature—to the arts of grammar, syntax and the like. More recently, there has been an essentially scientific investigation of the evolution of languages and of the laws of growth and

---

[1] *Lectures on the Science of Language*, vol. i, pp. 438–9.

change by which new languages are developed. Yet there still is but little active interest taken in the problem of making the existing languages more perfect for their purpose—more directly expressive of the thoughts which they connote.[1]

ARTIFICIAL LANGUAGES

Effort of this kind has been mostly expended on the invention of new artificial languages, such as Volapuk, and its successors, Esperanto, Ido, etc. Some of these—especially Esperanto and Ido—have made considerable progress, and are used (more or less) by large numbers of people, but there is, I believe, little evidence that any one of the existing synthetic languages will become generally used as a "universal language".

Esperanto and Ido are both inflected languages, being derived from the various European languages—they are, therefore, from a linguistic point of view "old-fashioned" languages, already out of date! Nevertheless, the study of these, and other, synthetic languages may be of service in raising the question of the efficiency of the old existing languages in comparison with their new synthetic rivals, and in turning the minds of thinking people towards the neglected problem of how best to symbolize and record the results of human thought.

The ideal Universal Language would—in the light of our present theories—probably be one in which the words were primarily based on symbolic gesture of the organs of articulation.[2] Such a language might be more natural and more durable than one of a conventional vocabulary, and certainly easier to learn and remember.

In this connection may be mentioned the action of the British Association, who, in 1919 appointed a Committee "To study the Practicability of an International Language", under the chairmanship of the then Secretary of the Royal Society (Sir W. B. Hardy), following on the appointment of a similar committee by the International Research Council at Brussels in the same year. This latter committee has its headquarters at the offices of the National Research Council, in Washington, U.S.A.[3] Some of the subjects under review

[1] See O. Jespersen, *Language*, p. 49.
[2] I am indebted to Dr. Eccles, F.R.S., for this suggestion.
[3] See *A Short History of the International Language Movement*, by Professor Albert Léon Guérard, London and New York.

by this committee—for example the new sciences of "synthetic or applied linguistics", are of direct interest to our present aims and may possibly result in popularizing the idea (which, at present, is certainly not popular) that even the best of the present languages are capable of, and indeed deserving of rational improvement.

Improvement of Existing Languages and of Methods of Notation

This idea was more familiar and acceptable in the past than it is now. As early as 1664, the Royal Society appointed a committee for improving the English language. The Society's minute of 7th December runs as follows : It being suggested that there were several persons of the Society whose genius was very proper and inclined to improve the English tongue, and particularly for philosophical purposes, it was voted that there be a committee for improving the English language ; and that they meet at Sir Peter Wyche's lodgings in Gray's Inn. Unfortunately this committee seems never to have presented its report !

Dr. John Wilkins

A more successful result followed the personal efforts of Dr. John Wilkins—whose work has already been referred to in Chapter I. Wilkins attempted to build up a rational synthetic language and also to invent an ideographic notation for human thought—i.e. a notation which represented the sense (not the sound) of the ideas to be recorded. With such a notation—which may be compared with the ideographic characters used in China and Japan—persons talking different languages could all read and understand the same script. In reading it aloud, they would "translate" the sequence of ideas represented by the script into their own language. It was a gallant attempt which might have had great results for the intellectual and material good of humanity if only there had been a sufficient number of interested persons—in different countries—to work out the method and secure its adoption as a universal medium of communication. Wilkins was in advance of his time—he was even in advance of our own ; but he may be useful, even now, to point the way, either to the invention of the perfect synthetic language, or to the scientific improvement of those which have already grown up without the conscious guidance of mankind.

At p. 378 of his book, Wilkins shows a series of thirty-four faces (with the mouth and throat in section in most cases) each articulating a separate speech sound, and adds a " lesser Figure " consisting only of the chief outlines representing the organs of speech—by which the characteristic attitude may be recognized. He also gives separate letter symbols for all the English speech sounds—as for a mouth facing to the right.

Thus :—o (our o as in no) has the " lesser figure "

ʊ (our u or ᴜ as in who or put)   is

ɑ (our ᴅ or ɔ as in not or all)   ,,

i (our i or ɪ as in eat or it)   ,,

y (our ʌ as in up)   ,,

FIG. 151.

Voiced consonants are distinguished from the corresponding unvoiced sound by a projection at the back of the sign for the tongue, thus :—

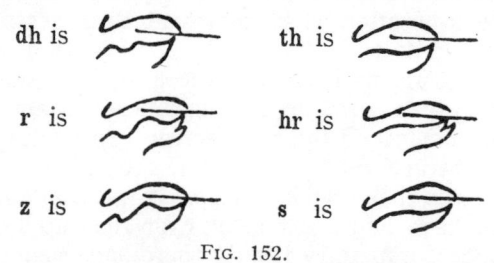

dh is   th is

r is   hr is

z is   s is

FIG. 152.

While it must be admitted that Wilkins' " lesser figures " are not in every case adequate, they represent a system which could without difficulty be developed so as to indicate the speech sounds with a high degree of certainty.

But besides analyzing and devizing a notation for the gestures of articulation and for the speech sounds to which they give rise, Wilkins also went deeper and endeavoured to

AND ITS NOTATION

analyze and dissect the ideas which they are used to convey, and thus to build up a synthetic Philosophical Language. He then found that the existing languages (he specially considers Latin) are by comparison very incongruous—abounding in what he calls "improper and preternatural Rules" of inflexion, declension, gender, syntax and so on, and consequently unnecessarily difficult to learn.

Wilkins is so original, so clear in his vision and so ingenious in his methods that one is tempted to describe his work in detail—but that would overload our Chapter.

Alexander Melville Bell's Visible Speech

In much more recent times (1867) Alexander Melville Bell, Professor of Vocal Physiology, Lecturer on Elocution in University College, London, published his *Visible Speech: the Science of Universal Alphabetics*, and his *English Visible Speech for the Million*. Bell's notation, like Wilkins' "lesser figures" indicates—though in a clearer and more conventional manner—how the tongue, lips, soft palate and vocal cords are to be placed to form the various vowels and consonants.

Thus: the symbol ⌒ denotes what I have called the hump of the tongue, the sign being used in different positions to indicate correspondingly different positions of approach or closure in a mouth directed towards the reader's right.

Fig. 153.

For example, C —directed towards the back of the throat—denotes a humping towards the back. The additional symbol | conventionally indicates a closure, so that ⊂| represents the consonant k. The same symbol in the position ∪ represents the point of the tongue up (in contact with the palate) and represents t. In the position Ɔ the symbol (somewhat inconsistently) represents a closure of the lips (instead of the tongue) and thus represents **p**.

The corresponding " voiced " consonants are denoted by the same symbol with an added stroke, thus :—

$$\exists = \text{G} \quad \text{W} = \text{D} \quad \ni = \text{B}$$

The same closures with soft palate open are denoted by a wavy line, thus :—

$$\exists = \text{NG} \quad \text{W} = \text{N} \quad \ni = \text{M}$$

The vowels are all denoted by a vertical stroke (which symbolizes the closure of the vocal cords) with the addition of a tongue sign ⌒ or ⌣ in the appropriate position. Thus ɪ (it) with tongue humped forward and high is denoted by ⌈ while ɑ (calm) in which the hump is backward and downward is represented by ⌋. Lip-rounding is conventionally, and not very appropriately, denoted by a cross-stroke. Thus : ⌉ tongue humped high at the back denotes ə (as in -tion, -tious, -er) while ⌉ i.e. the same tongue posture with lip rounding represents ʊ (good).

Bell's system, though it was highly praised by the eminent phonetician Alexander J. Ellis, F.R.S., and by other contemporary authorities, never came into general use. Bell laboured under many disadvantages of technique—there were no X-ray photographs or pharyngeal periscopes in 1867, and some of his data were consequently uncertain. But he produced a notation by which *any* speech sound could be recorded to be recognizably reproducible, at sight, by another reader—and not merely speech sounds but even such unalphabetical articulations as a yawn, a hiccough, a wheezing cough, a growl, or a clearing of the throat and nose! As a general notation for *all* human speech, Bell's Visible Speech is manifestly superior to any extended alphabet which can be evolved by mere modification of the haphazard alphabetical notation which we have inherited from the distant past.

MUSICAL, ALPHABETIC AND GESTURAL NOTATIONS

The alternative method of recording speech, namely, by recording the resonance changes by which the movements of articulation are in fact recognized—is more difficult to carry out. Our ears are not yet trained to analyze speech sounds as musical effects, and probably only those who have a specially good ear for music could ever learn to identify mouth resonances.

Since, however, the identification of the actual resonances is the only certain way of notationally recording a speech sound, it would seem desirable that all teachers of phonetics should be trained to make the analysis by ear. Incidentally it may be pointed out that mouth and nose resonances are most easily heard when the articulation is unvoiced, so that—even in dealing with an unfamiliar speech sound—in the case of a voiced sound it should be analyzed and taught, first in the unvoiced condition, and then voiced after the correct whispered articulation has been secured.

The confusion and ambiguity which still exists in our methods of recording and identifying speech sounds is indicated by the Proposals of the Copenhagen Conference which met in April, 1925.[1] There is in fact no system—only a number of attempts to extend the existing alphabet by the invention of additional symbols or by the modification of existing letters. It is thus necessary to know the speech sounds by ear before they can be read or identified.

It can hardly be disputed that the notation of speech sounds should be such that any reader who is generally acquainted with the notation should be able to read a new sound " at sight " so as to be able to reproduce it (if he is skilful enough) without having heard it before from the lips of another speaker.

There are, as we have seen, two possible methods of forming such a notation.

(1) A systematic notation for tongue, lip, soft palatal and false vocal cord postures or movements.

---

[1] *Proposals of the Copenhagen Conference*, Oxford, 1926.

(2) A musical record of the resonance changes which the postures or movements produce.

The present notations depend on neither of these methods, though they doubtless aim at recording tongue postures, etc., namely, by reference to those of other well-known speech sounds.

Scientific Improvement of Language

So far as existing languages are concerned, the argument for applying scientific method towards their rational improvement, may be put thus: Any imperfections of an existing language which cause difficulty (whether conscious or unconscious) in the process of coding thought into speech, or decoding speech (whether oral or written) into thought, are a stumbling block to the intellectual and material progress of the people who speak the language in question. The greatest power of clear, accurate and rapid thought and perception will belong to the communities whose language most closely follows and most accurately symbolizes the successive stages of thought.

If the argument is a good one, it follows that we shall do well to study our own language with a critical eye, and not to be too content to preserve old forms which are manifestly anomalous or imperfect, or too conservative to adopt newer and better ones, if by these means the language may be improved for our use.

The absence of a word meaning his-or-her, or he-or-she, has been frequently felt in the present work—the need for new words common to either sex becomes greater as fields of activity become more and more competitive. Similarly, there is a crying need for words meaning he-she-or-it-*here* and he-she-or-it-*there* like the uses of *hic* and *ille* in Latin. Take, for example, the following replies given in an examination on the technique of Infant Welfare [1] :—

" When a baby has finished its bottle, you should screw its head off, rinse it thoroughly under the tap, and put it away in a cool place."

" If a baby doesn't thrive on fresh milk, you should boil it."

Here the fault was not all with the candidates—the poverty of the language is in part to blame.

It has been pointed out, for example,[2] that whereas the

---

[1] Quoted by Lord Asquith in a broadcast talk from London, July, 1926.
[2] *The Meaning of Meaning*, by C. K. Ogden and I. A. Richards, 2nd edition, 1927, p. 118.

conception of being in contact with the upper surface of another object is expressed by the word "on", we have no corresponding word for contact with the under surface ; such instances might be multiplied.

Anyone who has ever attempted to describe in words, even the simplest structure or shape or movement or incident, so that there may be no ambiguity in the description, will have realized how poor language still is even to represent thoughts which, in themselves, are relatively simple. Indeed, it is probably not an exaggeration to say that of all man's powers, that of expressing his thoughts by the symbolization of speech or script has been least of all subjected to the scientific method of rational improvement and development.

Or take the class of Homophones,[1] the origin of which we have already discussed. Professor Jespersen [2] considers that Homophones are not objectionable unless they are of the same part of speech, thus, he argues that know and no, knows and nose, knew and new have little chance of being mistaken ; these, however, form only a small proportion of the whole. Even granting that active mistake is unlikely in some cases, would not "one thought, one sound " be a better rule—would not the thinker's mind be freer if there was no need to guard against a possible risk of mistake ? To give an analogy : there is a certain disadvantage in the use of the same symbol o to denote the vowel-sound in no and the arithmetical symbol called nought or zero, or in the use of the symbols i, x, v, etc., to denote also Roman numerals. In using these ambiguous symbols, the mind has to be on the look-out lest it be trapped into a symbolic pun—it cannot give its whole attention to the thought and express it instinctively.

If Homophones are to be eliminated, there will be scope for the invention of many new words with which to enrich our language. In other instances a small change of pronunciation will suffice as a complete remedy.

Another obvious imperfection of English (and doubtless most other languages) is the unnecessary length of many words and the gross neglect of monosyllables. I have pointed out elsewhere [3] that with the thirteen English vowel-sounds (i.e. excluding the indefinite ə as in sof*a*, or th*e* King) and twenty or more consonants—each of which may be used at the

[1] See Dr. Robert Bridges, S.P.E. Tract II, Clarendon Press.
[2] *Language*, p. 286.   [3] S.P.E. Tract XXII, p. 31.

beginning, or end, or both, of any of the vowels—there is the possibility of forming over 5,000 words of one syllable, very few of which are at present in actual use. Any new invented words should, therefore, be monosyllables, unless some very good reason—e.g. of analogy to a corresponding or complementary existing word—can be shown to the contrary.

Now let us consider very briefly the question of verbal inflexions, i.e. the modification of the sound of a word—generally, but not always, of its terminal sound—to denote its number (singular or plural), person (masculine, feminine or neuter), case (nominative, accusative, genitive, etc.), or tense (present, past, conditional, future, etc.). The languages from which English was developed, were highly inflected—like modern German, for example, still is ; but, for reasons which lie beyond our present scope, the greater number of these inflexions were dropped, to the great simplification of the language.[1] The new turn which our language then took was analogous to that which had long before been taken by the Chinese, whose words are all simple and uninflected, and who, so to speak, indicate the number, person, case, tense, etc., of their words, by their order in the sentence.[2] It is said that, in Chinese, the order of the words is always strictly logical. English, though far more inflected than Chinese, has fewer inflexions and a more logical order of words than any other European language.[3] But it still bears the burden of many relics of barbarism—burdens which make our language needlessly difficult to learn and to speak, and add in no way to its beauty or utility. Consider the present tense of the verb to go : I go, you go (thou goest has been dropped), we go, you go, they go— for all of these persons and numbers, the single word " go " is used, whereas in the earlier languages, the verb was differently inflected at almost every stage. But when we come to the third person singular we still say he " goes ". It is a useless and unreasonable complication. If " go " will do for all the other persons and numbers except the third singular, why not let it do also for that person and number—as it does in the case of the word can : I can, you can, he can. I will only give one other example—the present tense of the verb

[1] G. M. Trevelyan's *History of England*, Chap. 8, pp. 131, 132.
[2] Jespersen, *Language*, p. 369. Karlgren, *Sound and Symbol in Chinese*, London, 1923, p. 76.
[3] J. R. Lowell, *Among My Books*, 1st Series, p. 293, wrote with reference to German : " The language has such a fatal genius for going stern foremost."

to be, which in our present standard English runs : I am, (thou art) you are, he is, we are (ye are), you are, they are. What a makeshift we have here—and how inferior to the West Country form : I be, you be, he be, we be, ye be, they be.

The genius of the English-speaking people—the inventors of English—was swift and practical, it made wonderful changes in a very short period,[1] by which the language became immeasureably simplified and more direct and expressive.[2] Unfortunately, the initial effort of our rude forefathers has not been kept up. Literature, and above all the invention of printing, stepped in, and, like the Gorgon's Head before the court of Polydectes, turned all who saw it to stone. There have been hardly any essential improvements in English since the time of Caxton, while in the matter of spelling, we have gone measurably backwards.

Only off the beaten tracks of literature and grammar, are improvements in the true English spirit to be found : " he do," instead of " he does," like " I be " (of which I have already spoken) are simple cases in point.

When the foundations of a better English are laid—as I hope they soon may be—by a scientific examination of the merits and deficiencies of our language, in all its forms, it will almost certainly be found that our standard English of to-day has much to learn, in linguistic science, from many of the rural dialects, which it is apt to despise.

Articulation and Pronunciation

Let us now leave the forms of words and their order and meaning, and turn to the question of pronunciation.

We have seen that even our vowel sounds—as pronounced in Southern English—are not as well separated as they might be. A small change of pronunciation in certain cases—so as to make both the upper and the lower resonances characteristic —would almost certainly make them easier to recognize and distinguish. The consonants, being the acoustic result of

[1] See Trevelyan's loc. cit.
[2] Jacob Grimm writing in 1851 spoke of English as the language "which by sheer making havoc of all old phonetic laws and by the loss of all flexions has acquired a great force and power, such as is found perhaps in no other human language . . . like the English people it seems destined to reign in future even more than now in all parts of the earth". O. Jespersen, *Language*, p. 62.

active gestures of the organs of articulation, are more uniform in character, since the exact position in which the gesture is made does not produce any noticeable acoustic difference.

The important thing is that the rising generation should become interested, as early as possible, in the finished execution of these gestures, so that their articulation may be clear and graceful, and their speech made pleasant to hear and easy to understand.

In this connection war should be waged on such degenerate tendencies as that (to which attention has already been drawn) of dropping phonation in the terminal z sound of such words as cabs, sounds, eggs, loaves, loathes, etc., so that they are made to end in an unvoiced hiss. Rather should we encourage the use of additional phonation for the sake of making our language more musical, more artistic, and more audible. We have a long way to go!

At the present time, if anyone were to pronounce every syllable in English with care and finish, his speech would be considered affected and absurd—however easy it might be to understand. This attitude toward the technique of articulation is surely a mistake. We do not think it affected or absurd if a musician plays every note which the composer has written in his composition—indeed, we should be rightly indignant if he left any of them out and thus blurred the composer's meaning.

We need a new movement in Phonetics—a movement to raise the standard of technical skill in articulation, and to preserve our language from phonetic decay. The world-wide development of Broadcasting has given the spoken word an ascendancy such as it has never had since writing was invented. It is high time, therefore, that we begin to " mind our p's and q's ", and to study systematically how the English-speaking peoples can obtain the greatest benefit from their heritage of a common language. We have a splendid foundation to build on—as old Jacob Grimm, and such impartial authorities as Professor Jespersen and Professor Karlgren have not hesitated to admit. Thus in the little book (*Sound and Symbol in Chinese*) from which quotation has already been made, Karlgren describes English as " the most modern, the most ' practical ' of all the Indo-European stock."

We cannot for ever arrest our language—let us see therefore that we train it to grow in the right direction.

Accentuation

Another matter needing rational treatment and reform, is that of accentuation. Random accentuation—the stressing (whether in duration or in loudness of articulation, or both) of one or other of the syllables of a polysyllabic word, is a useless addition of complexity to our language. It is especially open to objection in that our system of notation, in spelling, gives no indication of these stresses. If they are to be encouraged and retained, then we should, in reason, adopt a system of added accents to indicate the stressed syllables. A far better way would be to make accentuation serve a really useful purpose, namely that of indicating the *first* syllable of every word. In connected speech we make no systematic pauses between words—we make them between phrases and between sentences—and we frequently run our words into one another just as closely as we pack our syllables in the articulation of polysyllabic words.

If then, the rule were that in all words of more than one syllable, the accent should be on the first syllable (as in fact it is in a large number of English words) the accentuation would be of great assistance and advantage in marking the divisions between words, and saving the listener the mental effort of sorting out and subdividing the string of successive syllables into their correct verbal groups. There can be no doubt that if the tendency to accentuate the first syllable were systematically encouraged, our language would become easier to understand. It is objected, I know, that certain polysyllables (like " laboratory ") are difficult to understand or liable to be mistaken (for " lavatory ") if the accent is retained on the first syllable, and in this case it has been recommended [1] that the accent should be transferred to the second (thus, " labóratory "). My reply would be twofold : (1) If the word láboratory is properly articulated, there is no difficulty at all in understanding it or in distinguishing it from lávatory ; (2) if láboratory is too difficult a word to articulate, which is denied, then let us adopt its common abbreviation " lab " and use this instead. Abbreviations which are unambiguous, such as bus for omnibus, bike for bicycle, and phone for telephone have much to recommend them.

[1] See Recommendations of the B.B.C. Committee, 1926.

262 THE ADVANCEMENT OF LANGUAGE

In the United States the tendency seems to be to accent the first syllable of polysyllabic words, and to add a secondary accentuation thus, lí-brá-ry—where, in England, the pronunciation would be lí-brary or even lí-bry—and díctionáry, where an Englishman would say díctionry. Personally I see no objection to the use of secondary accentuation, since the risk of mistaking a single doubly accented word for two separate words (owing to each of its accentuated syllables being mistaken for the beginning of a new word) would be very remote. But the single accent on the first syllable would seem to be the ideal arrangement.

Vocal Inflexion

The question of accent leads naturally to that of vocal inflexion or intonation—to which we have already given consideration. The argument here is that, as it is of prime importance to keep our system of language notation simple, and as we have at present no notation for intonation, and rightly do not want to have one, we should avoid any reliance on tone as a significant part of our speech. On the other hand, a variation of laryngeal tone during speech is artistically most desirable—for the avoidance of monotony. Those of my readers who have seen the Capec Brothers' play " R.U.R." and heard the effect of the monotonic speech of his Robots, will have no doubt on this point. Intonation should therefore be encouraged as an auxiliary and decorative art in speech, but it should be based on simple rules, so that every foreign reader with any pretence to knowledge of the language may be able to " extemporize " the appropriate intonation—without the need of any auxiliary notation for the purpose.

Notation

We now come to the thorny subject of notation and spelling reform. Our present-day alphabets are derived, as is now well known, from a prehistoric picture writing. In the so-called Pictograph the pantomimic hand-sign was made to record its own track and thus produce a descriptive symbol whose meaning could be read by others.

The Chinese ideographs and the Egyptian hieroglyphs were both developed from picture writing.

The remarkable similarity between certain pictographs used

AND ITS NOTATION 263

by different nations almost suggests that their emigration from the cradle-land may have started at a period after the invention of Pictography. See for example the signs for mountain :—

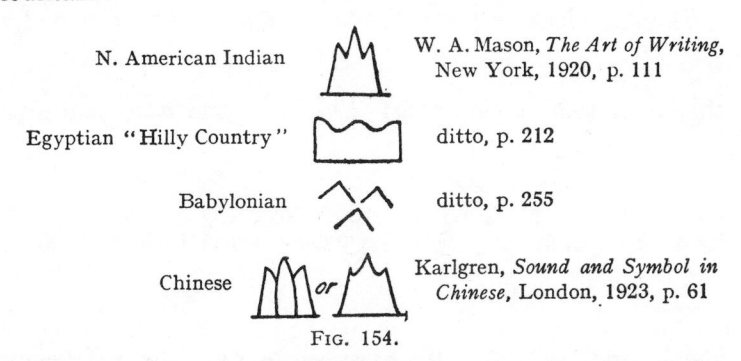

N. American Indian	⛰	W. A. Mason, *The Art of Writing*, New York, 1920, p. 111
Egyptian "Hilly Country"	⌒⌒	ditto, p. 212
Babylonian	∧∧	ditto, p. 255
Chinese	⛰ or ⛰	Karlgren, *Sound and Symbol in Chinese*, London, 1923, p. 61

Fig. 154.

The invention of numerals is a branch of the same art, and refers to the gestures by which the numbers were expressed. Thus the early "Arabic" symbols (origin uncertain) for 1, 2, 3, viz. ӏ Ձ Ӡ [1] have an obvious relation to the gestures,

ӏ = tongue held up—giving the Aryan word **oin**, Semitic **ahad**

Ձ = two lips (opened) „ „ „ bi- „ p-
(protruded) or **du-**

Ӡ = tongue between lips „ „ tri, „ thl-

The symbol 4 is related to the Indian Cave-inscription sign ᛉ, the Nānā Ghāt sign ⊬, and the Ghobār sign ⌐ .

These, it seems to me, are all forms of the sign for a hand with the thumb closed across the palm (the hand, in the Ghobār sign, being held pointing across the body). The gesture word associated with this sign appears to be **ku** (hand projected forward) + **at** (barred across) = **kuat**.

Similarly the signs for five, ५ (Devanāgari) and ५ (Ghobār) are conventional pictographs of the hand as a whole—

[1] See *Encyc. Brit.*, xi ed., vol. xix, p. 867.

giving rise to the root **p-m**, Semit. χ**-m** (Mö. 200). (Compare the old Chinese sign for hand [1] ᛞ .)

The signs for 6, e.g.  ⟨ (Nanā Ghāt) and the cave sign ⟨ then represent a closed fist ⟨ , with one *additional* finger held up thus 🖐 = ⟨ = 5 + 1, which by analogy should produce words like **s-p-m**, **s-b** or **s-v**. These, I believe, do not appear in Indo-European, which instead has words in **s-g**, while Semitic has **s-d**. A nearer approach is the Zend word **Khshvash** which suggests **kub** + **ash**, i.e. 5 + 1.

The signs for seven, such as ⟩ are not suggestive, but it may be noted that 1 + 5 + 1 might naturally be pronounced **s-ab-t** or **s-ab-n**.

Eight—the divisible number—is pantomimed by making a mouth cavity **u**, **o** or **o**—and dividing it in the middle by an upward tongue gesture—giving **ot**, **ut**, etc.

If the gesture is made with the two hands—with finger and thumb tips touching respectively so as to make an enclosure, and this is then divided in the middle by bringing the finger and thumb tips together—we also get a " figure of eight "— thus 🤝 from which the

FIG. 155.

symbol ∞ or 8 might readily be derived.

---

[1] Karlgren, op. cit., *Sound and Symbol in Chinese*, p. 44.

The Devanāgari sign ⊂ (meaning 8) seems to suggest the cavity halved.

Nine—Sanskrit *navan*—suggests an earlier **nab** (5) + **ban** (4)—the **n** in **ban** representing the thumb across the palm like **t** in **kuat**. The symbolism of the signs— 2, 3, 5 & 9 — is not evident; can 5 represent 9 5 + 4?

Ten—derived from early forms like **dek**—may well refer to the two hands held together—as if to cover something—compare our word deck, German *dach* (roof).

In the ideographic stage the meaning of the symbols became extended, so as also to denote abstract ideas—an eye dropping tears thus comes to mean grief—a heart in a window means anxious, one leg over a precipice means dangerous—and so on.

Then comes the stage of the syllabic pun—in which the symbol is used not to express an object or action or idea, but to denote the sound of the word which it signified. The symbol thus becomes a sign for a sound. Finally comes the stage when the sign no longer denotes a complete syllable, but only a portion of it—as we should say a vowel or a consonant.

The first intention of systematic spelling was no doubt to represent the sound of the spoken word, but spelling, in English, was never an exact science, and even as late as Shakespeare's days, had no peculiar sanctity such as is now claimed for it by many authorities on English. Words were spelt as they were pronounced, or as the writer fancied they should be spelt, and the language certainly did not suffer by this latitude since it was under these conditions that it reached the highest pinnacle of its fame. But printing and scholasticism and Johnson's *Dictionary* stereotyped our spelling, as literature did our language. Indeed by the misguided efforts of pedantic scholars, the spelling was in many cases made more difficult and actually less accurate—as when the old English words "ancor" and "ake" were provided with a superfluous and silent **h** and became "anchor" and "ache", while dette and dout became debt and doubt—to the discomfort of all subsequent generations!

We are now at the stage when the sounds of many of our words have changed so much from those of earlier times that the spelling is but a symbol of the word itself, not of its sound. The original spelling was, let us say, a phonogram—a writing of the sound of the word; the present spelling, if it deserves a Greek title at all (which I doubt), should be called a paleologogram—a writing of the ancient form of the word. It is as though a grown-up person, requiring a passport, were to present a photograph of himself taken at the age of two as a means of identification.

Spelling Reform

It is surely obvious that this state of things cannot be allowed to continue indefinitely—for if it were so continued, we should arrive, in time, at a state where the spelling bore little or no relation to the sound of the word it represented. What then should we do—now? The most practical course would appear to be a twofold one; first, we should allow and encourage the utmost freedom in spelling, such as our Elizabethan ancestors enjoyed in the heyday of English speech; second, we should teach all the rising generation the use of a true phonetic alphabet, such as that of the International Phonetic Association, to which reference has already been made. Very young children should begin with the phonetic alphabet—it is immensely easier for them to learn and encourages an immediate interest in reading and writing " without tears ". When the child has thus learnt the pleasures of reading and writing, it will be time enough to introduce him to the imperfections and anomalies of our present methods. The differences will not be so great as to cause much difficulty in reading books in the present standard spelling, and, provided that formal accuracy in spelling is not required in examinations, the young student will have little difficulty in shouldering the burden of both systems.

The great advantage will be that we shall have planted the seed which in another generation will grow up as the perfect plant—a rational spelling, which will enable anyone, of any nation, to read English at sight so that it may be understood.

I would ask the reader to consider how great an impetus to the extension of English and of Anglo-Saxon ideals such a reform would bring about. English is already the most widely spoken language, it would be well nigh universal but for the extraordinary difficulty of learning it from print, and of transcribing it in writing—owing to the anomalies and inconsistencies of our spelling. We owe it to our language to be actively interested in its welfare and advance, and to take steps to remove this clog on its activities, as soon as possible.

In no other direction should we tolerate the handicaps which we suffer by our spelling. English has (as we have said) thirteen vowel sounds, or fourteen, if we include the indefinite sound ə as in " sof*a* " or " th*e* King "—sometimes called the " after-dinner vowel ".

For these thirteen or fourteen fundamental sounds we have five symbols—a, e, i, o, u, i.e. about one symbol to every three vowels, or " three men one vote ". Let us translate this state of things to the region of Arithmetic and see how we should fare if the ten cardinal numbers (including zero) were allowed but four symbols between them. 1, 2, and 7, being somewhat similar in appearance, might be represented by 1 ; 6, 9 and 0 would all be written 0 ; 3 and 8 would both be 3, while 4 and 5 would share the last symbol, 4 ! There is no greater absurdity in this scheme than in that which we suffer daily as a matter of course in the notation of our vowel sounds.

The attempts at spelling reform which have been so far made—more especially in the United States—do not seem to me to go sufficiently to the root of the matter. Thru is certainly better than through, but labor is no better than labour as a spelling for the word in any of its common pronunciations in England or America.

For this reason I do not advocate simplified spelling, or indeed any other particular system at the present time. I plead for a period of liberty, coupled with the teaching of the phonetic alphabet to all English-speaking children, and the laying of the foundations of a literal " English-speaking Union " directed towards the improvement of the language and the ultimate standardization of its pronunciation.

Can we do anything now to arouse interest in the problems of improving our language and method of notation and to break down the wall of ancient custom and scholastic authority which, at present, separates our language and spelling from the living world of science and progress ?

What is needed is the application of the experimental method —the interesting of many minds in the problems we have been considering—the trial of alternative solutions—and the encouragement of a scientific attitude on the part of all lovers of English, such as will lead them to welcome its further and more perfect development.

An Experiment in English

A possible method of making a start has suggested itself which I am tempted to describe here, in case any of my readers may be moved to give it a practical trial. Let us imagine the formation of a real or fictitious circle of narrative Story-tellers—comparable in form, if not in matter, with those of the *Decameron*, the *Canterbury Tales*, or the original idea of the Pickwick Club. Their avowed object is to make practical trials in the rational improvement of English, and to embody these in their stories. The circle includes one or more expert narrators, a professor of Linguistics, an authority on early English, a foreign student of our language—who sees difficulties and anomalies to which familiarity has blinded us—a poet, to watch over matters of music and rhythm, and finally the man in the street—brought indoors for the occasion—to supply the leven of common sense.

The first story must certainly be a good one, and well told—so that the Printed Proceedings of our Circle may find readers—but it will include some typical difficulties of our language, whether of construction, verbal inflexion, the lack of a suitable word or the existence of a homophone. These are then objected to by one or other of the members ; the Circle considers the objection, and resolves on a remedy which is thereafter to be adopted in all future proceedings.

The second story then begins, and is carried on with the aid of the new improvements already agreed on. If the story-teller makes a lapse—as he certainly would be liable to do—he is called to order, and invited to correct his expression. Other imperfections of language, noted in the second story, are then discussed as before, and further improvements agreed, and so on. Thus, by a gradual process, the readers of the Proceedings would be led to take an active interest in the idea of applying reason to the form and structure of English and afforded an opportunity of testing the improvements suggested in a practical fashion. The writers, on their side, would obtain, at the least, a new insight into the true merits and demerits of our language and—whether their particular solutions are ultimately accepted or not—will have been instrumental in carrying out a useful and stimulating linguistic experiment.

The personnel for such an experiment will need to be carefully chosen ; the writers—unless they are expert parodists, with an almost impersonal command of form and style—will need to be young, for to a mature writer, whose language has become a part of his personality and methods of thought, the use of new forms and new words could present intolerable difficulty. Still, there is plenty of youth to be found in the English-speaking world, and adventure, fit for youth, in the experiment itself.

Education in English

When, and by whatever means, interest has been finally aroused, so that active steps may be taken with general assent, the first advance will (I trust) be that the National Education systems of all the English-speaking communities shall pay far more attention than at present, to the history and structure of their *own* language, and to the broad principles of linguistic science and phonetics. That every child should begin with the phonetic alphabet, has been already advocated ; let them follow up with a sufficient study of their own language, its origin and development and future needs, so that they may be able to express themselves in the present, and see how to do it yet better in the future. In this way, we shall pave the way for a scientific and rational cultivation and improvement of our mother-tongue, which will make it as much better than at present, as the modern scientific breeds of wheat are better than the wild cereals from which they originally descended.

Linguistic Research

What is wanted, or rather what will eventually be wanted (for the time is obviously not yet ripe) is not so much an English-speaking Academy as a Linguistic " Board of Invention and Research "—a Centre at which the fundamental relations of thought and speech may be studied systematically, more especially in relation to our own tongue—as for example on the lines suggested by Mr. C. K. Ogden, of Magdalene College, Cambridge, in connection with his researches on the Simplification of English.[1] At such a centre, the forms of English speech

[1] *Psyche*, April and July, 1928, developing an " orthological " programme based on *Op. cit. The Meaning of Meaning* and the linguistic theories of Jeremy Bentham. Cf. the Appendix to *Automaton* by Dr. H. Stafford Hatfield (London & New York, 1929), where a translation of a portion of the book is given in a vocabulary of a little over 500 words.

will be critically compared with those of other tongues, the anomalies of our own language laid bare and the remedies supplied.

The changes proposed will all be based on reason—not on personal preference or mere historical literary or archæological authority or analogy—they will be guided by the principles of science, of rational utility, and of the beauty which arises from perfection in performance.

It must be admitted, of course, that if and when we change our present language, our present books will to that extent become antiquated and obsolete. But if, as has been postulated, we make the study of English one of the subjects of all education, everyone will be able to read and enjoy the old books, just as a present-day reader may (with but little trouble and a short glossary) read and enjoy Chaucer.

It is with no bolshevist desire for radical change, that I have ventured to advocate these experiments—nor have I forgotten the proverb about those who rush in where angels keep outside. I believe firmly that the improvement of language is one of the great outstanding needs of the human mind—that it will give to human thought an increase of power such as the substitution of Arabic for Roman numerals gave to arithmetic, or the development of mathematics has given to science, and that we should not allow conservatism or indolent dislike of change to prejudice our minds against the trial, at least, of the experiments to which I have referred.

I am conscious that in this matter of language—its deficiencies and need of improvement—I speak as one with little knowledge and no authority. Yet, I am not alone in the opinion that our present language is imperfect, or that these imperfections are injurious to our welfare and in need of remedy. All that I plead guilty to, if anything, is an over-strong conviction of the need of active effort to formulate " that inductive, æsthetic theory of language which has still to be developed in a truly scientific spirit ",[1] and an over-confident belief in the benefits which a scientific improvement of our language would bring to the English-speaking peoples.

In conclusion, I would make one final quotation from Professor Jespersen,[2] to stand as the confession of my linguistic faith, and of my hope for the future of English speech :—

[1] Jespersen, p. 31.   [2] Ibid., p. 442.

"An ideal language would always express the same thing by the same, and similar things by similar means; any irregularity or ambiguity would be banished; sound and sense would be in perfect harmony; any number of delicate shades of meaning could be expressed with equal ease; poetry and prose, beauty and truth, thinking and feeling would be equally provided for: the human spirit would have found a garment combining freedom and gracefulness, fitting it closely, yet allowing full play to any movement."

If to all these virtues we add—as I believe we justly may—the advancement and clarifying of thought itself, and the extension, in power, of human reason, then surely we may claim that the active search for this ideal is a pursuit worthy to be undertaken by us, in our generation, and to be handed on, as a high ideal, to our children.

APPENDIX I

A Note on the Double-Resonator Theory of
Vowel Sounds

By
W. E. BENTON

APPENDIX I

1. The Double-resonator Theory

In Chapters I–V, it is shown that the essential character of a vowel is independent of the larynx note which may be used to amplify it. The vowel sound is due to the resonance frequencies excited in the cavities of the mouth. Further, each vowel is characterized, in general, by two principal resonance frequencies, which bear no simple harmonic relation one to another.

We have seen that in the production of vowel sounds the position of the tongue and the degree of opening of the mouth appear to be the deciding factors. The tongue apparently divides the whole space into two volumes, which we will speak of as the front and rear cavities, separated by a passage formed between the tongue and either the back of the throat, or the roof of the mouth. We also know that in uttering either a whispered or spoken vowel the opening of the mouth may be varied over a considerable range. We have therefore a form of double-resonator consisting of two cavities of variable size communicating one with another by a passage of unknown conductivity, with the external air by an opening capable of very large variation, and with the wind-pipe and lungs by means of a very small aperture, also of unknown conductivity.

We know, however (p. 228), that all the vowels can be articulated with one (suitably chosen) size of mouth opening. Where this condition holds we may also assume with some confidence that although the individual sizes of the two cavities vary with the position of the tongue, the total volume of the resonator remains constant. We will now try to use these data to explain the dual character of vowel sounds.

2. A First Approximation

Consider a model (Fig. 156) in which two volumes S and S' are contained in a rigid cylinder of total volume Δ, where $\Delta = S + S'$, and separated one from another by a movable diaphragm containing an aperture of fixed conductivity c_2. The volume S communicates with the atmosphere by means

THE DOUBLE-RESONATOR THEORY

of a very small opening of conductivity c_1, the volume S' by means of a larger aperture of conductivity c_3. It is our problem to determine how the natural modes of vibration of the air in the resonator vary as the diaphragm is moved along the cylinder.

There is a method, due to Lord Rayleigh, which under certain special limitations (which we will examine presently) can be applied to this vessel. Let n be one of the frequencies, and let p be a quantity related to n through the equation :—

$$n^2 = \frac{-p^2}{4\pi^2}$$

For real values of n, only real and negative values of p^2 will be considered. The physical meaning of p may be realized

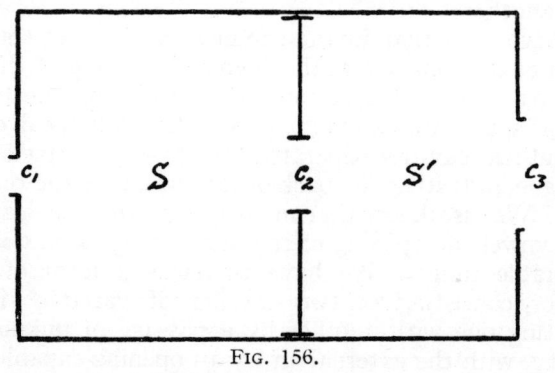

FIG. 156.

more clearly by remembering that n denotes the number of complete vibrations performed in unit time, and that if these vibrations are of simple harmonic character the rectilinear motion of any particle of air in the resonator may be considered as the projection on a diameter of an imaginary circular motion of constant angular velocity, the centre of the imaginary motion being the mean position of the real movement. ip would then represent the total angle swept out by the imaginary particle in unit time, where i has the usual meaning of $\sqrt{-1}$. If we use Lord Rayleigh's method, we arrive at the following equation for the natural modes of vibration :—

$$p^4 + p^2 a^2 \left\{ \frac{c_1 + c_2}{S} + \frac{c_3 + c_2}{S'} \right\} + \frac{a^4}{SS'} \left\{ c_1 c_3 + c_2(c_1 + c_3) \right\} = 0.$$

. . . Equation (1).

where a denotes the velocity of sound in air, i.e. :—

THE DOUBLE-RESONATOR THEORY 277

$$-p^2 = \frac{1}{2}\left[a^2\left\{\frac{c_1+c_2}{S}+\frac{c_3+c_2}{S'}\right\} \\ \pm\sqrt{a^4\left\{\frac{c_1+c_2}{S}+\frac{c_3+c_2}{S'}\right\}^2 - \frac{4a^2}{SS'}\left\{c_1c_3+c_2(c_1+c_3)\right\}}\right]$$

$$-p^2 = \frac{a^2}{2}\left[\frac{c_1+c_2}{S}+\frac{c_3+c_2}{S'} \\ \pm\sqrt{\left(\frac{c_1+c_2}{S}\right)^2+\left(\frac{c_3+c_2}{S'}\right)^2 - \frac{2}{SS'}\left\{\begin{matrix}c_1c_3+c_2c_3+c_1c_2\\-c_2^2\end{matrix}\right\} \\ +\frac{4c_2^2}{SS'}}\right]$$

In order to avoid the occurrence of the square root of a negative quantity we will assume that :—

$$\frac{c_2+c_3}{S'} > \frac{c_1+c_2}{S}$$

$$\therefore -p^2 = \frac{a^2}{2}\left[\left(\frac{c_1+c_2}{S}\right)+\left(\frac{c_2+c_3}{S'}\right) \\ \pm\sqrt{\left\{\left(\frac{c_2+c_3}{S'}\right)-\left(\frac{c_1+c_2}{S}\right)\right\}^2+\frac{4c_2^2}{SS'}}\right]$$

This transformation shows that the double resonator has in general two natural frequencies, and that these are related to those of the two simple resonators from which it has been formed. Substituting for p^2, we have :—

$$n^2 = \frac{a^2}{8\pi^2}\left[\left(\frac{c_1+c_2}{S}\right)+\left(\frac{c_2+c_3}{S'}\right) \\ \pm\sqrt{\left\{\left(\frac{c_2+c_3}{S'}\right)-\left(\frac{c_1+c_2}{S}\right)\right\}^2+\frac{4c_2^2}{SS'}}\right]$$

$$\ldots (2)$$

The whole effect due to joining the two cavities is therefore contained in the term $\frac{4c_2^2}{SS'}$, for if c_2^2 is made very small compared with SS', we have the approximate solutions :—

$$n^2 = \frac{a^2}{4\pi^2}\left(\frac{c_2+c_3}{S'}\right), \text{ or } \frac{a^2}{4\pi^2}\left(\frac{c_1+c_2}{S}\right)$$

That is, if n_1 denote the greater, and n_2 the smaller frequency, we have (approximately) :—

$$n_1 = \frac{a}{2\pi}\sqrt{\frac{c_2+c_3}{S'}}$$

$$n_2 = \frac{a}{2\pi}\sqrt{\frac{c_1+c_2}{S}}$$

and these are the natural frequencies of the two vessels which form the double-resonator, it being understood that in making or breaking the junction, the conductivity c_2 remains unaltered.

Returning to Equation (2) it will be observed that since $\frac{c_2^2}{SS'}$ is a real positive quantity, the effect of joining the two resonators is always to raise the greater frequency n_1 and depress the lower frequency n_2.

Let us now try the effect of moving the diaphragm. To do this we must introduce the condition that

$$S + S' = \Delta$$

Let $c_1 = c$, $c_3 = m_1 c$, $c_2 = m_2 c$.
Let $S' = aS$
$S + S' = (a + 1)S = \Delta$.

It will be seen that the position of the diaphragm in the cylinder is best defined by means of the quantity

$$\beta = \frac{1}{1+a}$$

i.e. the distance of c_2 from c_1, referred to the distance between c_3 and c_1 as unity. Substituting for c_1, c_2, c_3, S and S', Equation (1) becomes :—

$$n^2 = \frac{a^2 c(a+1)}{8\pi^2 \Delta}\left[\left\{(1+m_2) + \left(\frac{m_1+m_2}{a}\right)\right\} \pm \sqrt{\left\{(1+m_2)+\left(\frac{m_1+m_2}{a}\right)\right\}^2 - \frac{4}{a}\left\{m_1 + m_2(1+m_1)\right\}}\right]$$

$$\ldots (3)$$

THE DOUBLE-RESONATOR THEORY

From this equation the two values of n,——n_1 and n_2——may be calculated for any value of a, corresponding to a known position of the diaphragm. In Fig. 157 are shown the frequencies obtained in this way for a typical example:—

$$m_1 = 20, m_2 = 5.$$

If we compare this diagram with the chart of vowel resonances at Fig. 65 (p. 86) we notice a distinct resemblance. In each case the ordinates are frequencies, the only difference being that the former are shown in linear and the latter in logarithmic scale. In Fig. 157 the abscissae represent the positions of the diaphragm in the cylinder, whereas in Fig. 65, they are the full series of vowels. Since each vowel is characterized by a definite position of the tongue, one might also think of the abscissae of Fig. 65 as representing the successive positions of the tongue in the mouth. In both cases there appear to be in general for each position of the diaphragm or tongue two natural frequencies, related to each other in no simple harmonic manner. We have shown, too, in the case of the cylinder, that if the conductivity c_2 is small each of the two frequencies appears to associate itself with one of the two cavities, in much the same way as we speak of the front and back resonances of the human mouth. On the basis of these resemblances the human mouth has sometimes been compared to a resonator of this type (e.g. Irving B. Crandall's *Dynamical Study of the Vowel Sounds*, January, 1927). We can test this idea in a very simple way. We have already seen (p. 45) that the two frequencies in the vowel resonances can be brought very close to one another, and that possibly a single resonance can be heard if the attempt is made to bring them yet closer. For the same condition to be satisfied by our artificial resonator, equation (3) must have equal roots in n.

i.e. $\left\{(1+m_2) + \left(\dfrac{m_1+m_2}{a}\right)\right\}^2 = \dfrac{4}{a}\left\{m_1 + m_2(1+m_1)\right\}$

i.e. $a^2(1+m_2)^2 + 2a(m_2^2 - m_1 - m_2 - m_1m_2) + (m_1+m_2)^2 = 0.$

The condition that this shall have real roots is that:—

$$(m_2^2 - m_1 - m_2 - m_1m_2)^2 \geqslant (1+m_2)^2(m_1+m_2)^2$$

i.e. $(m_2^2 - m_1 - m_2 - m_1m_2) \geqslant \pm (1+m_2)(m_1+m_2),$

which is impossible, since m_1 and m_2 are always real and positive fractions, from which it follows that the two frequencies can

280   THE DOUBLE-RESONATOR THEORY

FIG. 157.

Resonance Frequency →

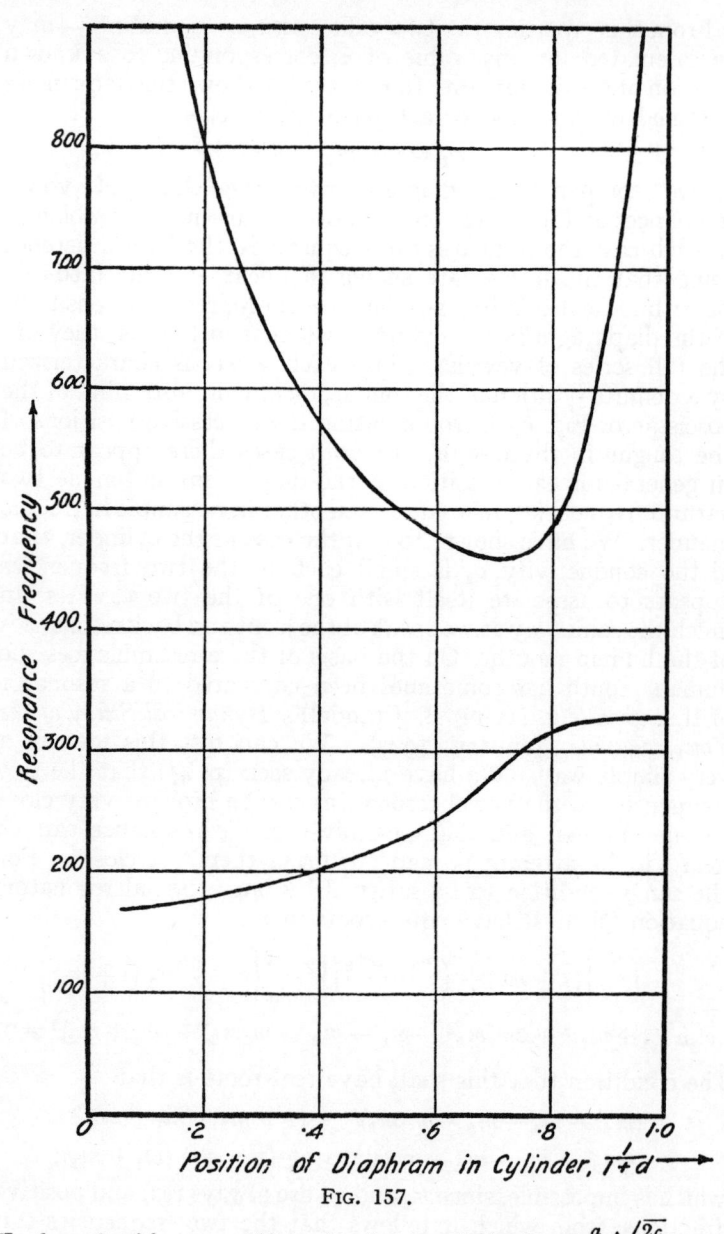

Position of Diaphram in Cylinder, $\frac{l}{l+d}$ →

[In the scale of frequency 100 denotes the numerical value of $\frac{a}{2\pi}\sqrt{\frac{2c}{\Delta}}$

THE DOUBLE-RESONATOR THEORY

never be equal. If the experimental result were equally definite, we would have here an interesting test of this theory. In the circumstances, however, we must go further and examine the reasoning leading up to the equation, and in particular the validity of the assumptions used.

3. THE BASIS OF THE RESONATOR THEORY

In the human mouth is contained a body of air capable of vibration. It is clear that the greater part of the movement occurs in the narrow parts, i.e. the mouth opening, the gap between tongue and roof, and the opening of the glottis.

Lord Rayleigh's first assumption in obtaining Equation (1) is that all the movement occurs in these passages. He pictures the two volumes of air in the two cavities acting as springs maintaining the motion of the air in the narrow parts. And again for simplification he assumes that no time is required for the pressure exerted at the neck to be transmitted to all parts of the cavity, an assumption which can alternatively

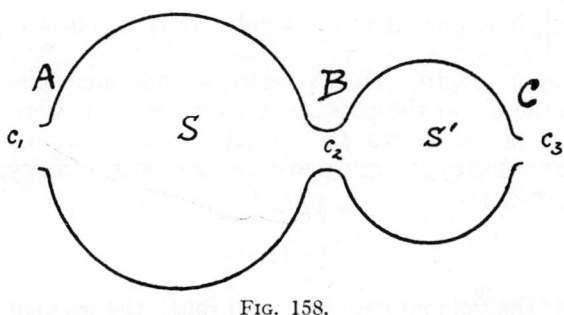

FIG. 158.

be expressed by saying that "the dimensions of the resonators are small compared with the quarter-wave-lengths of the resultant tones". This second assumption is also applied to the narrow parts, the air in each passage being considered as a rigid piston, maintained in motion by the air on either side.

In obtaining Equation (1) other simplifications are made, such as the neglect of friction and dissipation, but the two assumptions described above are the more important, and together define the limits of usefulness of the equation.

The general form of the kind of double resonator we have in mind (of which the apparatus shown in Fig. 156 is a particular case) is represented in section in Fig. 158, using the same symbols

THE DOUBLE-RESONATOR THEORY

for the volumes and conductivities. Suppose that at any instant the total amount of air which has crossed the central plane of the passage A in a given direction (e.g. towards the left) is X_1. The kinetic energy K, of the motion through A at this instant will be proportional to the square of the bulk velocity and to the density, ρ.

$$\text{i.e. } K \propto \rho \left(\frac{dX_1}{dt}\right)^2$$

$$\text{or } K = \tfrac{1}{2} \rho \frac{\left(\frac{dX_1}{dt}\right)^2}{c_1}$$

where c_1 is the quantity to which we have hitherto referred as the conductivity of the orifice A. Since kinetic energy is of dimensions $\left[\dfrac{M.L^2}{T^2}\right]$, and the expression $\rho\left(\dfrac{dX_1}{dt}\right)^2$ is of dimensions $\left[\dfrac{M.L^3}{T^2}\right]$, it follows that the conductivity c_1 must be of the nature of a length. This is perhaps made more clear if we imagine the air in the passage A to move, as it were, in the form of a piston of area f, of length l, and density ρ. If v be the linear velocity at a given instant, the kinetic energy, K,

$$= \tfrac{1}{2} \rho f l v^2$$
$$= \tfrac{1}{2} \rho (fv)^2 \frac{l}{f}$$

Now fv is the volume transference through the passage in unit time. Hence the conductivity of the passage, c_1,

$$= \frac{f}{l} = \left[\frac{\text{Area}}{\text{Length}}\right]$$

The motion in the passage A is maintained by the potential energy, P, of the air in the cavity S, and since we have assumed that there is no dissipation of the energy of the system, we have:—
$$K + P = \text{constant.}$$

Now consider the operation of producing the volume displacement, X, from the position of equilibrium. In sound vibrations the movements are very rapid. We will therefore assume that there is no escape or transference of heat during the motion,

THE DOUBLE-RESONATOR THEORY

i.e. the compression and expansion are adiabatic. Let us think for a moment of a simple case, a volume S communicating with the atmosphere by means of a single orifice of area f and conductivity c. Let each molecule of the air in the aperture be displaced from its mean position a distance x towards the interior of the resonator. The total volume-displacement will therefore be fx, and the difference of pressure produced will be numerically equal to $\gamma p f \dfrac{x}{S}$, where p is the atmospheric pressure.

During the compression the work done over any small element δx will be equal to the product of the mean opposing force, and the distance over which it is applied.

i.e. Work done $= \gamma \dfrac{pf}{S} \cdot fx \cdot \delta x$

Hence over the whole movement the work done

$$= \gamma \dfrac{pf^2}{S} \int_0^x x\, \delta x = \tfrac{1}{2}\gamma p \dfrac{f^2 x^2}{S}$$

$$= \tfrac{1}{2}\gamma p \dfrac{X^2}{S}$$

$$= \tfrac{1}{2} a^2 \rho \dfrac{X^2}{S}$$

where a denotes, as before, the velocity of sound in air, and ρ the density.

For the simple resonator in question, therefore, we have the equation of energy

$$\tfrac{1}{2}\rho \dfrac{2\dot{X}}{c} + \tfrac{1}{2}\rho a^2 \dfrac{X^2}{S} = \text{constant.}$$

Differentiating with respect to time the equation becomes:

$$\tfrac{1}{2}\rho \cdot \dfrac{2\dot{X}}{c}\ddot{X} + \tfrac{1}{2}\rho a^2 \dfrac{2X}{S}\dot{X} = 0.$$

i.e. $\ddot{X} + \dfrac{a^2 c}{S} X = 0.$

This clearly depicts a motion of simple harmonic character, with a natural frequency :—

$$n = \dfrac{a}{2\pi}\sqrt{\dfrac{c}{S}}$$

284   THE DOUBLE-RESONATOR THEORY

Applying this method in turn to each aperture in the double resonator, we observe that the motion in A is maintained by the excess pressure in S, which is proportional to the difference between the displacements X_2 and X_1. The equation of energy for the passage A is therefore :—

$$\tfrac{1}{2}\rho \frac{\dot{X}_1{}^2}{c_1} + \tfrac{1}{2}\rho a^2 \frac{(X_2 - X_1)^2}{S} = \text{constant,}$$

. . . (4)

and for the passage C.

$$\tfrac{1}{2}\rho \frac{\dot{X}_3{}^2}{c_3} + \tfrac{1}{2}\rho a^2 \frac{(X_3 - X_2)^2}{S'} = \text{constant.}$$

. . . (5)

The motion in the passage B is maintained by the potential energy of both cavities. The equation of energy is therefore :—

$$\tfrac{1}{2}\rho \frac{\dot{X}_2{}^2}{c_2} + \tfrac{1}{2}\rho a^2 \frac{(X_2 - X_1)^2}{S} + \tfrac{1}{2}\rho a^2 \frac{(X_3 - X_2)^2}{S'} = \text{constant.}$$

. . . (6)

Returning to Equation (4) we can describe the motion of the air in the passage A at the instant chosen if we consider the instantaneous rate of change of the kinetic and potential energies of the system. Regarding X_2 therefore as a constant and differentiating with respect to time, we obtain the equation

$$\tfrac{1}{2}\rho \frac{2\dot{X}_1}{c_1} \cdot \ddot{X}_1 + \tfrac{1}{2}\rho \frac{a^2}{S} \cdot 2(X_2 - X_1)(-\dot{X}_1) = 0$$

and hence the equation of motion :—

$$\frac{\ddot{X}_1}{c_1} + a^2 \cdot \frac{(X_1 - X_2)}{S} = 0 \qquad \ldots (7)$$

and similarly for the passages B and C.

$$\frac{\ddot{X}_2}{c_2} + a^2 \left\{ \frac{X_2 - X_1}{S} + \frac{X_2 - X_3}{S'} \right\} = 0 \quad \ldots (8)$$

$$\frac{\ddot{X}_3}{c_3} + a^2 \frac{(X_3 - X_2)}{S'} = 0 \qquad \ldots (9)$$

[This method of writing down the energy equations for the three different apertures is not strictly correct. Lord Rayleigh expresses the whole potential energy of the resonator as :—

$$\tfrac{1}{2}\rho a^2 \left\{ \left(\frac{X_2-X_1}{S}\right)^2 + \left(\frac{X_3-X_2}{S'}\right)^2 \right\}$$

and the whole kinetic energy as:—

$$\tfrac{1}{2}\rho \left\{ \frac{\dot{X}_1{}^2}{c_1} + \frac{\dot{X}_2{}^2}{c_2} + \frac{\dot{X}_3{}^2}{c_3} \right\}$$

and hence obtains the three equations of motion by three partial differentiations. On the other hand we think that the less exact method has, perhaps, the virtue of showing rather more clearly the physical meaning of the expressions.]

Adding these equations together, we obtain:—

$$\frac{\ddot{X}_1}{c_1} + \frac{\ddot{X}_2}{c_2} + \frac{\ddot{X}_3}{c_3} = 0.$$

and hence by integration, and the use of initial conditions

$$\frac{X_1}{c_1} + \frac{X_2}{c_2} + \frac{X_3}{c_3} = 0 \qquad \ldots (10)$$

On eliminating X_2, we obtain:—

$$\ddot{X}_1 + \frac{a^2}{S}\left\{ (c_1+c_2)X_1 + \frac{c_1 c_2}{c_3} X_3 \right\} = 0 \qquad \ldots (11)$$

$$\ddot{X}_3 + \frac{a^2}{S'}\left\{ (c_3+c_2) X_3 + \frac{c_3 c_2}{c_1} X_1 \right\} = 0 \qquad \ldots (12)$$

If the motion is of simple harmonic character we can make the assumptions that:—

$$X_1 = A e^{pt}$$
$$X_3 = B e^{pt}$$

where A and B are constants.

Hence on substitution for $X_1, X_3, \ddot{X}_1,$ and $\ddot{X}_3$ in (11) and (12) and elimination of A and B we obtain the final relation:—

$$p^4 + p^2 a^2 \left\{ \frac{c_1+c_2}{S} + \frac{c_3+c_2}{S'} \right\} + \frac{a^4}{SS'}\left\{ c_1 c_3 + c_2(c_1+c_3) \right\} = 0$$

which we have already used as Equation 1.

4. A Mechanical Analogy

There is another way of demonstrating the effect of coupling two simple vibrating systems which affords an interesting comparison with Lord Rayleigh's method. Consider a system in which a mass m_1 displaced a distance x_1 from its mean position

THE DOUBLE-RESONATOR THEORY

is subjected to a restoring force parallel to the direction of motion and of magnitude $k_1 x_1$. If no external forces act on the system, the equation determining its motion is:—

$$m_1 \frac{d^2 x_1}{dt^2} + k_1 x_1 = 0$$

i.e. $\quad \dfrac{d^2 x_1}{dt^2} + \dfrac{k_1}{m_1} x_1 = 0$

which represents simple harmonic motion of period $2\pi \sqrt{\dfrac{m_1}{k_1}}$

Similarly a second system of mass m_2, displacement x_2, and restoring force $k_2 x_2$, will have an equation of motion

$$\frac{d^2 x_2}{dt^2} + \frac{k_2}{m_2} x_2 = 0$$

representing simple harmonic motion of period $2\pi \sqrt{\dfrac{m_2}{k_2}}$

When these two systems are coupled together the motion of each is affected by that of the other. The manner in which the motion will be affected depends upon the physical conditions of the particular problem. In the case of two pendulums hanging from a common non-rigid support, the effect of each system on the motion of the other is partly of the form of an added acceleration, partly a periodic restoring force. When two resonators, however, are joined by means of a central conductivity the effect is to destroy the condition that each aperture shall communicate with air at atmospheric pressure. The restoring force in each system is altered, in a degree proportional to the finite pressure (above or below atmospheric) in the added resonator. We may therefore suggest that after coupling the resonators the equations of motion become:—

$$\begin{cases} m_1 \dfrac{d^2 x_1}{dt^2} + k_1 x_1 + g_1 x_2 = 0 & \quad \ldots \ (13) \\[1em] m_2 \dfrac{d^2 x_2}{dt^2} + k_2 x_2 + g_2 x_1 = 0 & \quad \ldots \ (14) \end{cases}$$

Differentiating (13) twice with respect to time, we have:—

$$m_1 \frac{d^4 x_1}{dt^4} + k_1 \frac{d^2 x_1}{dt^2} + g_1 \frac{d^2 x_2}{dt^2} = 0 \qquad \ldots \ (15)$$

and on substituting for $\dfrac{d^2 x_2}{dt^2}$ in (15) its value in (14), we have:—

$$m_1 \frac{d^4 x_1}{dt^4} + k_1 \frac{d^2 x_1}{dt^2} - \frac{g_1}{m_2} k_2 x_2 - \frac{g_1 g_2}{m_2} x_1 = 0 \qquad \ldots \ (16)$$

THE DOUBLE-RESONATOR THEORY

and again for x_2 its value in (13)

$$m_1 \frac{d^4 x_1}{dt^4} + k_1 \frac{d^2 x_1}{dt^2} - \frac{g_1 g_2}{m_2} x_1 + \frac{k_2 k_1}{m_2} x_1 + \frac{k_2}{m_2} m_1 \frac{d^2 x_1}{dt^2} = 0 \ldots (17)$$

i.e. $$\frac{d^4 x_1}{dt^4} + \frac{d^2 x_1}{dt^2}\left(\frac{k_1}{m_1} + \frac{k_2}{m_2}\right) + x_1 \left\{\frac{k_1 k_2 - g_1 g_2}{m_1 m_2}\right\} = 0 \ldots (18)$$

Let us again assume that the motion is of simple harmonic character, and that we can express the displacement in the form:—
$$x_1 = De^{qt}$$

Then by substitution in (18):—

$$q^4 + q^2\left(\frac{k_1}{m_1} + \frac{k_2}{m_2}\right) + \left(\frac{k_1 k_2 - q_1 q_2}{m_1 m_2}\right) = 0 \quad \ldots (19)$$

If we make the further substitutions:—

$$q^2 = -4\pi^2 n^2$$
$$\frac{k_1}{m_1} = 4\pi^2 n_1^2$$
$$\frac{k_2}{m_2} = 4\pi^2 n_2^2$$

we obtain the equation of frequencies:—

$$n^4 - n^2(n_1^2 + n_2^2) + n_1^2 n_2^2\left(1 - \frac{g_1 g_2}{k_1 k_2}\right) = 0 \quad \ldots (20)$$

Now the product of Lord Rayleigh's method, Equation (1), may also be converted into a frequency relation by means of similar substitutions:—

$$p^2 = -4\pi^2 N^2$$
$$\frac{a^2(c_1 + c_2)}{S} = 4\pi^2 N_1^2$$
$$\frac{a^2(c_2 + c_3)}{S'} = 4\pi^2 N_2^2$$

$$p^4 + p^2 a^2\left\{\frac{c_1 + c_2}{S} + \frac{c_3 + c_2}{S'}\right\} + \frac{a^4}{SS'}\left\{c_1 c_3 + c_2(c_1 + c_3)\right\} = 0$$

i.e. $$p^4 + p^2 a^2\left\{\frac{c_1 + c_2}{S} + \frac{c_3 + c_2}{S'}\right\} + a^4\left(\frac{c_1 + c_2}{S}\right)\left(\frac{c_3 + c_2}{S'}\right) - \frac{c_2^2 a^4}{SS'} = 0$$

i.e. $$N^4 - N^2(N_1^2 + N_2^2) + N_1^2 N_2^2\left(1 - \frac{c_2}{(c_1 + c_2)} \cdot \frac{c_2}{(c_2 + c_3)}\right) = 0$$

$$\ldots (21)$$

THE DOUBLE-RESONATOR THEORY

On comparing Equations (20) and (21) it will be seen that the two methods yield similar results, with the exception that Lord Rayleigh's gives a real physical value to the coupling terms :—

$$\frac{g_1}{k_1}, \frac{g_2}{k_2}$$

The limitations restricting the usefulness of Equation (1) are also represented in the method of obtaining Equation (19). It is assumed that there is no inertia in the mechanism producing the restoring force of the system, and that the latter instantly responds to the motion of the vibrating mass, conditions which are mathematically identical with those imposed by the first method.

TABLE I

n_1 = Frequency (No. per sec.) of Front Resonance.
n_2 = Frequency (No. per sec.) of Back Resonance.
λ_1 = Wave-length in cm. of Front Resonance.
λ_2 = Wave-length in cm. of Back Resonance.

Vowel.	n_1	$\dfrac{\lambda_1}{4}$	n_2	$\dfrac{\lambda_2}{4}$
i (eat)	2430	3.55 cm.	330	26 cm.
ɪ (it)	2300	3.72	360	23.8
ei (hay)	2170	3.95	470	18.25
e (men)	1930	4.44	525	16.3
æ (hat)	1820	4.7	700	12.25
ɜ (earth)	1530	5.6	470	18.25
ə (sofa)	1490	5.75	610	14.05
ʌ (up)	1490	5.75	765	11.2
ɑ (calm)	1255	6.82	790	10.85
ɒ (not)	1115	7.68	700	12.25
o (all)	885	9.68	555	15.4
ou (no)	790	10.85	430	19.9
u (who)	720	11.9	380	22.25
ʊ (put)	965	8.9	360	23.8

THE DOUBLE-RESONATOR THEORY

5. Dimensions of the Mouth-Resonator

We have already seen that Equation (1) would fail to explain the production of two equal frequencies, if that were ever shown to be experimentally possible in the human mouth. Let us now see how far the latter satisfies the important condition that the dimensions of the resonator cavities shall be small compared with the quarter-wave-lengths of the resultant tones. In Table I are shown the mean frequencies and quarter-wavelengths corresponding to the whole series of the English vowels. It will be observed that the vowels appear to be divisible into three natural groups, with the vowel " ɑ " as a solitary " boundary " state between the second and third groups.

Group I, or Front Vowels. i, ɪ, ei, e, æ

In this series $\frac{\lambda_1}{4}$ varies from 3·55 cm. to 4·7 cm., i.e. $\frac{\lambda_1}{4}$ is of the same order as the length of the front cavity. $\frac{\lambda_2}{4}$ varies from 26 cm. to 12·25 cm., dimensions very much greater than those of the back cavity. Hence we may assume that in resonance the back cavity acts as a spring, the condensation at any given moment being uniform throughout the space, whereas in the front cavity a system of stationary waves is formed.

Group II, or Middle Vowels. ʊ, ə, ʌ

These vowels are characterized by an approximately constant $\frac{\lambda_1}{4}$, of the same order as the length of the front cavity (about 7 cm.), indicating the probable existence of stationary waves. $\frac{\lambda_2}{4}$ decreases rapidly from ʊ to ʌ, but is large compared with the length of the cavity (about 10–6 cm.).

Boundary Vowel, ɑ

This vowel is exceptional in that $\frac{\lambda_1}{4}$ (6·8 cm.) is little more than half the length of the front cavity (10–12 cm.). $\frac{\lambda_2}{4}$

x

(10·85 cm.) is large compared with the length of the back cavity (about 4 cm.).

Group III, or Back Vowels. ɒ, ɔ, ou, u, ᴜ

$\frac{\lambda_1}{4}$ varies from 7·68 cm. to 11·9 cm. The series is characterized by the progressively decreasing mouth opening which is employed in voicing these vowels in turn from ɒ to ᴜ. It is probable that stationary vibration of a very modified form exists in the front cavity, and the high values of $\frac{\lambda_2}{4}$ indicate uniform condensation behind the tongue. These vowels alone approximate to the conditions required by Equations (1) and (19).

6. Stationary Vibration

So far the general name double-resonator has been used to embrace any vessel which exhibits two natural frequencies of vibration, but our equations have only applied to the ideal form (Fig. 158), known as the Helmholtz Double-Resonator, in which at any moment the condensation is uniform throughout either of the two cavities. When this condition is not satisfied, and the condensation varies from point to point, there exists in the resonator a form of stationary vibration. We have seen that by the exercise of great care it is possible to construct for any given vowel a double-resonator which will give a good imitation of the sound, and from the shapes of some of these models it is clear that stationary vibration must be taking place. Only the members of Group III approximate to the shape of the Helmholtz double-resonator. The vowels of Group II represent a " half-way stage " between the ideal Helmholtz vessel and the perfect pipe-resonator, in which the vibration is wholly of stationary form. We have very little knowledge of the conductivities belonging to these vowels, and therefore at present any equations representing them would contain a number of unknowns.

In Group I, however, we find a type of vibration which has a distinctive and peculiar character. There are five vowels, for each of which $\frac{\lambda_1}{4}$ is of the same order as the length of the front cavity, and $\frac{\lambda_2}{4}$ is great compared with the length of the back cavity. By observation it is easily seen that the general shape of the mouth is common to every member of the group. In breathing the vowel i the tip of the tongue rests closely behind the lower teeth, the tongue being arched to leave a broad but shallow passage between itself and the roof of the mouth. As one passes to the other members of the group, in order of frequency, the tongue falls and recedes, still, however, preserving the rough parallelism with the roof of the mouth. The front cavity is in every case a broad shallow curved funnel, and it will be observed that the lips and teeth form a natural continuation of the walls of the funnel at its outward end. These vowels may be uttered over a considerable range of mouth opening, but in every case the tongue adjusts itself to maintain the diverging tubular form of front cavity. The

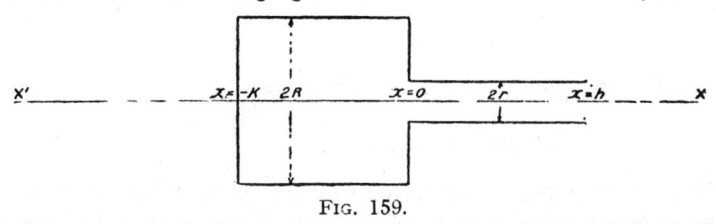

FIG. 159.

change from æ to ɐ is very marked, the tongue becoming concave, giving a cavity to which the teeth form the edges of a natural front orifice.

In order to introduce the conception of stationary vibration we must use a method which at first sight appears very different from that of our former examination. It will be shown, however, that the results are in accordance with and an extension of our former equations.

Let us consider a resonator of bottle form, consisting of a narrow parallel tube in communication with a coaxial tube closed at the further end (Fig. 159).

Let the wide tube be of length k and radius R; the narrow tube of equivalent length h and radius r. Let x and t denote distance along the axis, measured from the junction, and time respectively. For a condition of stationary vibration throughout the system we have :—

Displacement in Open Pipe :—
$$= y_1 = A \cos m (h - x) \cos 2\pi n t.$$

Displacement in Closed Pipe :—
$$= y_2 = B \sin m (k + x) \cos 2\pi nt$$
where $m = \dfrac{2\pi}{\lambda}$, λ being the wave-length of the vibration, and A and B the maximum displacements in the narrow and wide tubes respectively.

At the junction, $x = 0$, it is obvious that we must have :—

(1) Condition of Displacements of Equal Volumes :—
$$r^2 A \cos mh = R^2 B \sin mk \quad \ldots (22)$$

(2) Condition of Equal Excess Pressures :—
$$p_1 = -E \frac{dy_1}{dx} = -EmA \sin mh \cos 2\pi nt$$
$$= p_2 = -E \frac{dy_2}{dx} = -EmB \cos mk \cos 2\pi nt$$
i.e. $\qquad A \sin mh = B \cos mk \quad \ldots (23)$

Combining (22) and (23) we obtain :—
$$\tan mh . \tan mk = \frac{r^2}{R^2} \quad \ldots (24)$$

This is the general equation determining the modes of vibration of this kind of resonator. If both h and k are small compared with λ, we may substitute mh and mk for $\tan mh$ and $\tan mk$ respectively, by which we obtain :—
$$m^2 hk = \frac{r^2}{R^2}$$
$$\frac{2\pi}{\lambda} = \sqrt{\frac{\pi r^2/h}{\pi R^2 k}}$$
i.e. $n = \dfrac{a}{2\pi} \sqrt{\dfrac{c}{S}}$,

where c is the conductivity of the neck and S the volume of the reservoir. (This conclusion was first demonstrated by Dr. Paris in *Nature*, 27th September, 1924.) When the dimensions are small compared with the wave-length, the fundamental mode of vibration is that of a simple Helmholtz resonator, the whole of the narrow tube acting as the conductivity to the large reservoir.

In general, however, a correction must be applied for the

THE DOUBLE-RESONATOR THEORY

finite length of the neck. A better approximation will be given by the equation :—

$$\tan mh = \frac{r^2}{mkR^2} = \frac{\pi r^2}{mS} \qquad \ldots (25)$$

and when mh is small

$$\tan mh = mh + \tfrac{1}{3}(mh)^3 = \frac{\pi r^2}{mS}$$

Let $\pi r^2 h = S' = aS$, where a is a fraction. To a first approximation :—

$$mh = \frac{\pi r^2}{mS}$$

i.e. $(mh)^2 = \dfrac{\pi r^2 h}{S} = a$

i.e. $mh \left(1 + \dfrac{a}{3}\right) = \dfrac{\pi r^2}{mS}$

Then
$$n = \frac{a}{2\pi} \sqrt{\frac{c}{S(1 + a/3)}} \qquad \ldots (26)$$

This correction was first applied by Lord Rayleigh.

The effect of the finite length of the neck is to add one-third of the volume of the neck to that of the reservoir.

This solution is that of the fundamental tone of the resonator. The determination of the first over-tone from Equation (6) is much less satisfactory. As λ decreases, m increases, and $\dfrac{\pi r^2}{mS}$, already small, diminishes still further. As a rough approximation, therefore, we may write :—

$$\tan mh = 0$$
$$mh = \pi, 2\pi, 3\pi, \ldots$$
$$\lambda = 2h, h, \frac{2h}{3}, \ldots$$
$$n = \frac{a}{2h}, \frac{a}{h}, \frac{3a}{2h} \cdot \cdot \cdot$$

That is, the first over-tone is approximately equal to that due to a parallel pipe of equivalent length h, open at both ends.

A more accurate result will be obtained if we take account of the finite value of S.

$$\tan mh = \frac{\pi r^2}{mS}$$

$$mh = \pi + \frac{\pi r^2}{mS} \text{ approximately.}$$

$$= \pi + \frac{\pi r^2 h}{\pi S} \text{ by a second approximation.}$$

$$= \pi + \frac{a}{\pi}$$

$$\frac{1}{\lambda} = \frac{1}{2h}\left(1 + \frac{a}{\pi^2}\right)$$

$$n = \frac{a}{2h}\left(1 + \frac{a}{\pi^2}\right) \qquad \ldots (27)$$

This result, in a slightly different form, was also given by Lord Rayleigh.

Denoting the fundamental frequency by n_2, and that of the first over-tone by n_1, we obtain, firstly, by a very rough approximation :—

$$\frac{n_1}{n_2} = \frac{a/2h}{\frac{a}{2\pi}\sqrt{\frac{c}{S}}} = \sqrt{\frac{\pi^2 S}{ch^2}} = \frac{\pi}{\sqrt{a}} \qquad \ldots (28)$$

and secondly, and more accurately :—

$$\frac{n_1}{n_2} = \frac{\frac{a}{2h}\left(1 + \frac{a}{\pi^2}\right)}{\frac{a}{2\pi}\sqrt{\frac{c}{S\left(1 + \frac{a}{3}\right)}}}$$

$$= \left(\pi + \frac{a}{\pi}\right)\sqrt{\frac{1}{a} + \frac{1}{3}} \qquad \ldots (29)$$

In Fig. 160, the two relations (28) and (29) are shown graphically, by which means their divergence one from another, as a increases, is clearly demonstrated.

If in the production of a vowel of Group I, the mouth operates as a double resonator of this form, one should be able to predict the musical interval n_1/n_2 from the ratio of the volumes of the two cavities. The only difficulty which arises is in the estimation of the total end correction to be applied to the length of the front cavity. The dimension "h" in our equations is the

FIG. 160.

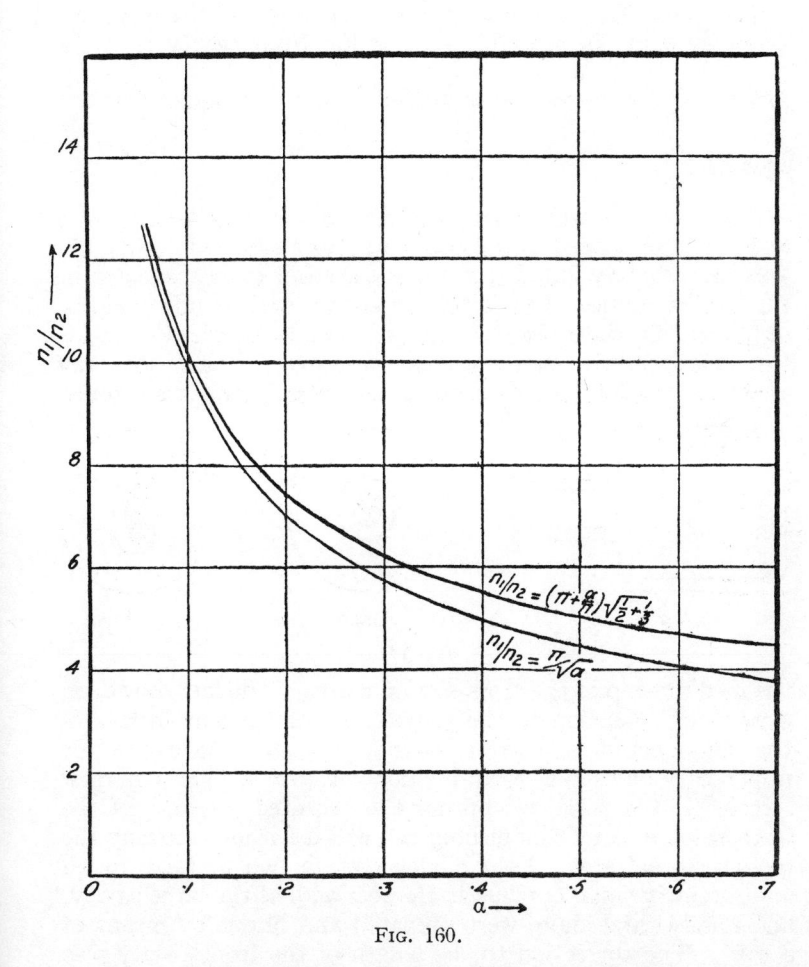

Note : The equation for the upper curve should read:

$$n_1/n_2 = \left(\pi + \frac{a}{\pi}\right)\sqrt{\frac{1}{a} + \frac{1}{3}}$$

THE DOUBLE-RESONATOR THEORY

equivalent length of the tube, and will include an addition at either end to the actual length.

The correction is considerable, and explains the apparent anomaly that the actual length of the front cavity is of the order of $\frac{\lambda_1}{4}$, whereas the equivalent length is approximately equal to $\frac{\lambda_1}{2}$.

A few models were made in plasticine, each consisting of a wide cylinder joined by a flange to a short tube (Fig. 161). It was immediately found that when the front cavity was a tube of circular section (Fig. 161b), no good vowel sounds could be obtained. On flattening the section into a rectangle (Fig. 161c), the characteristic vowel quality appeared. This does not affect the truth of our equations, since r^2 only appears through

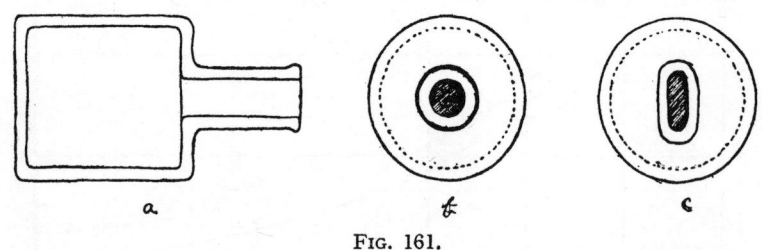

FIG. 161.

the mediumship of the cross-sectional area. The fact, however, draws our attention to the importance of the amplitudes of the components of a vowel sound. In order to excite the upper harmonics the organ-builder will give a pipe a narrow "scale". Similarly we obtain the required strength of the front resonance by diminishing the width without altering the cross-sectional area. Four models were blown by air through an extremely small opening in the rear wall of the large cavity, and finally three more were prepared and blown by means of a reed. The correction to the length of the front cavity was made by adding $\frac{1}{4}\pi d$ to each end, where d is the "equivalent diameter", i.e. the diameter of a circle of equal area. This embodies the assumptions that a complete open end correction is required to the inner end of the tube, and that the correction to a flattened tube is equal to that required by a circular tube of equal cross-sectional area. Experimental examination of these assumptions is needed, although the errors involved are certainly not very great. In the following table S' denotes the corrected volume of the front cavity, S the volume of the rear cavity, α the ratio $\dfrac{S'}{S}$.

Under the heading $\dfrac{n_1}{n_2}$ are given the mean experimental values of the musical interval between the components, and also the ratios obtained by substitution of α in Equations (28) and (29).

TABLE II.

Manner of Excitation.	Vowel.	S	S'	α	Ratio of Frequencies = N_1/N_2		
					From Eq. (28)	From Eq. (29)	By experiment.
By Air-jet	i	84 c.c.	12·3 c.c.	0·15	8·1	8·45	7·4
	ɪ	78·5	22·7	·29	5·8	6·2	6·4
	ei	78·5	45·5	·58	4·1	4·8	4·6
	ei	108	68	·63	4·0	4·6	4·6
By Reed	i	138 c.c.	29 c.c.	0·21	6·9	7·2	7·4
	ɪ	138	40	·29	5·8	6·2	6·4
	ei	138	86	·62	4·0	4·65	4·6

It will be seen from the table that Equation (29) provides a better agreement than Equation (28). Bearing in mind the tentative assumptions which have been used, and the limits of accuracy of the experiments (about 2 per cent), it would appear that the theory of the bottle-shaped resonator offers a fairly satisfactory explanation of the frequency-ratios found in the vowels of Group I.

In the human mouth there are departures from the ideal shape of the resonator which we have considered. The rear conductivity though very small, must be included in the calculations. More knowledge must be obtained concerning the end-corrections and the effect of slight expansions or restrictions. There is also the question of the constrictions produced in the human pharynx by the varying projection of the epiglottis. This projection tends more or less to produce a subsidiary neck between c_1 and c_2 of Figs. 156 and 158, and a corresponding small subsidiary volume immediately adjoining the reed (vocal cords) at c_1.

It has been found that even better models of the Front Vowels can be made with front cavities of expanding conical shape, instead of the parallel tube which we have considered. If the expansion is slight the effect on the frequencies will be inappreciable, but for a considerable divergence the theory of the conical pipe must be applied. For small changes in cross-section we have the general rule that at a node enlargement lowers, and contraction raises, the pitch—conversely at an anti-node.

An experimental fact of great interest is that the value of $\dfrac{n_1}{n_2}$ for a given vowel is capable of slight variation about a mean value without loss of quality. The ear judges a vowel by the form of the compound wave. The ratio of the amplitudes is possibly quite as important as the ratio of frequencies, and a resonator is only successful in imitating a vowel when both ratios can be reproduced. It is probable, too, that in the front vowels other over-tones of very high pitch help to give the distinctive character to the group.

7. Conclusion

It may be seen from this brief investigation that the use of mathematics in this study is subject solely to the value of the initial assumptions. The theory of the Helmholtz double resonator affords an interesting comparison with the results of experiment, but the assumptions on which it rests are too rigid for it to be of much use to us. The general theory of the coupling of two vibrating systems may be of use, however, in explaining the influence of the larynx note on the resonance tones of the mouth cavities. By introducing the conception of stationary vibration, a more general relation is obtained, which in a particular form appears to offer a satisfactory explanation of one group of the vowels. The characters of the other groups have only been indicated. The difficulties attending their investigation are much greater than those which we have experienced in examining Group I, but surely it is not too much to hope that in time they also will yield to analysis.

W. E. Benton.

APPENDIX II

TABLE OF FREQUENCIES, I.E. NUMBER OF COMPLETE VIBRATIONS PER SECOND, CORRESPONDING TO THE EQUAL TEMPERAMENT SCALE.

	$C_{,,}$	$C_{,}$	C	c	c'	c''	c'''	c''''
C	16	32	64	128	256	512	1024	2048
C♯	17	34	68	135	271	541	1084	2169
D	18	36	72	144	287	574	1149	2298
D♯	19	38	76	152	304	608	1217	2434
E	20	40	81	161	322	645	1290	2579
F	21	43	85	171	342	683	1366	2732
F♯	23	45	90	181	362	724	1448	2895
G	24	48	96	192	383	767	1534	3067
G♯	25	51	102	203	406	812	1625	3249
A	27	54	108	215	430	861	1722	3443
A♯	28	57	114	228	456	912	1824	3648
B	30	60	121	242	483	966	1932	3864

Fig. 162.

APPENDIX III

Audiogram of the Author's Hearing

The Chart on p. 301 indicates the author's hearing, as measured at the Bell Telephone Laboratory, New York, for notes of pitch varying between 64 vibrations per second (low C below the bass clef) and 8192 vibrations per second an octave above the top C on the piano. The Chart shows normal hearing up to 2048, followed by a comparatively deaf spot at 4096, and a return to about normal at 8192. Fortunately (for the author) the speech resonances at about 4096 are relatively unimportant—the vowel resonances are nearly all below that frequency while the high frequencies of S and Z are mostly above 5000.

THE DOUBLE-RESONATOR THEORY 301

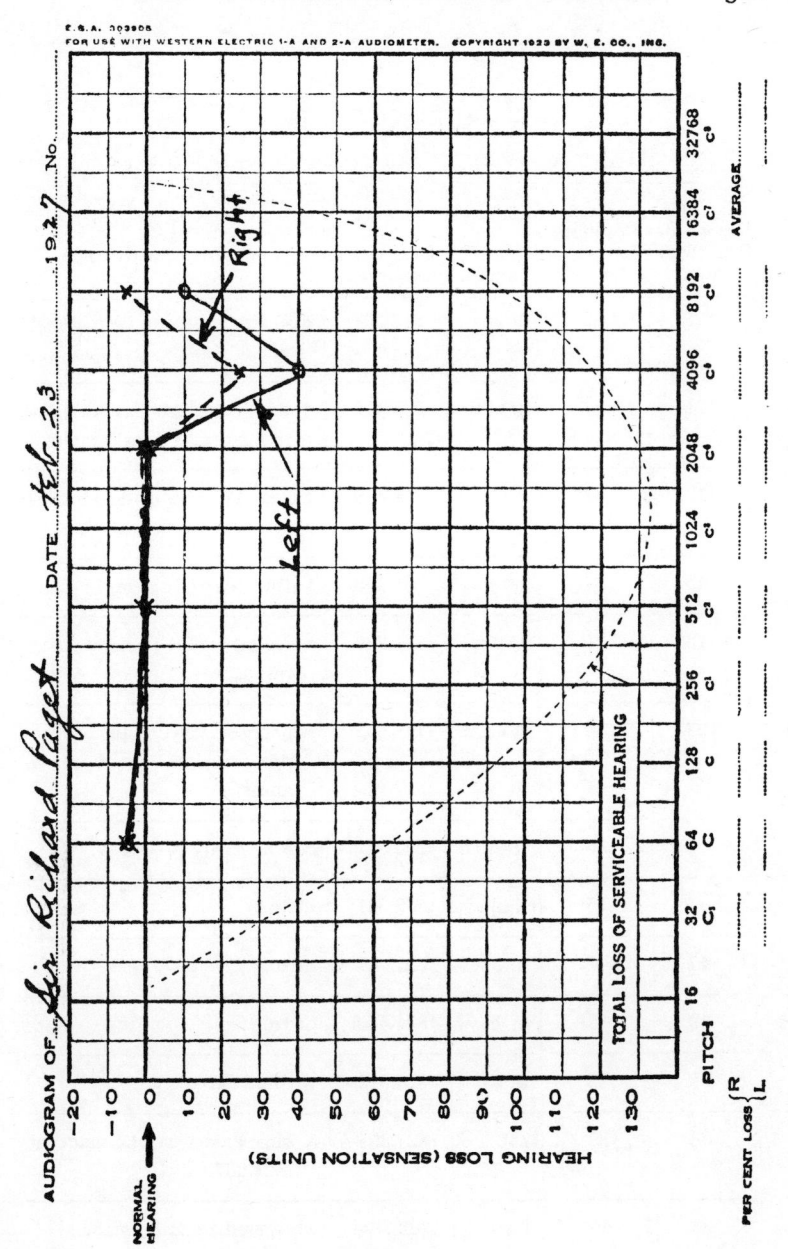

Fig. 163.

APPENDIX IV
Paget and Clay Variable Vowel Model

Front Resonator Length in mm.	Back Resonator Length in mm.	Vowel Sound.	Resonance Observed.	Comparison with voice Resonances.
125	83	u who	812.304	a whispered u can be made at 812.304.
121	27	ɒ not	966.512	a whispered vowel with these resonances is ɒ inclining to ɔ.
117	34	ɔ all	912.456	a clear ɔ can be made at these resonances.
113	47	ou no	861.406	within charted range.
113	71	ʊ put	861.287	voiced ʊ can be made at these resonances.
107	15	ɑ calm	1149.645	whispered vowel can be pro-produced at these resonances.
71	30	ɞ earth	1290.541	can be easily produced.
64	15	ʌ up	1366.861	ditto.
47	47	e men	1625.483	ditto.
43	56	ei hay	1824.430	ditto.
38	15	æ hat	1824.812	within charted range.
38	87	ɪ it	1824.304	a whispered ɪ can be made at 1824.287.
33	96	i eat	1932.304	whispered i can be made.

APPENDIX V
Some Experiments with Tubular Vowel Models

A number of tubes were cut in graduated lengths of 9·6 cm., 12·3 cm., 17·5 cm., 20·6 cm., and a corresponding number of cork stops, giving (with the wall of the tube) lenticular apertures of 27 mm. × 7 mm., 23 × 11, 24 × 13·5, and 26 × 18·5 respectively. See Fig. 164.

The stops were fitted as before with wire handles, by which to adjust them inside the tubes. Intermediate sizes of orifice we got by adding plasticine to the "cut-away" portion of the corks.

27 mm. × 7 mm.   23 mm. × 11 mm.   24 mm. × 13·5 mm.   26 mm. × 18·5 mm.

Fig. 164.

When the best position and size of stop-orifice and length of tube for a particular vowel had been determined, a new stop with central orifice of equivalent opening was substituted —the general arrangement being as shown in Fig. 165.

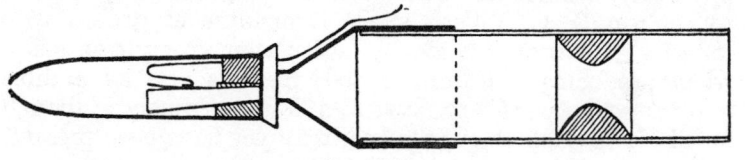

Fig. 165.

The orifice in the cork was cut so as to give a fairly streamlined passage between the front and the back resonators. The best length of tube, size of orifice, and position of the diaphragm were found by trial and error.

An isolated experiment, made with a long tube (61 cm. × 3·9 cm.) may deserve mention. With this tube, when fitted to the reed, the following resonances were observed—by tapping and blowing :—135 (which was heard on blowing, across the mouth of the tube but was also the reed note), and 203, 406, 683, 966, and 1217 heard on tapping the tube at different parts in its length. When the reed was blown, the vowel sound was found to vary with the pitch of the reed. Thus on changing the reed frequency from 406 to 228, the vowel was found to vary in the following way :—i →u → ɔ → e → i → u. This tube had no stop and was therefore comparable with Willis' early experiments. The reed and socket, when blown by themselves, also gave a vowel sound of a " thin " character, the vowel being ʌ to ɑ, with two resonances 1290 to 1217 and 767 ; it could be changed to ɒ (not), ɔ (all), ou (no), and u (who) by varying degrees of closure by hand. The explanation, no doubt, is that, with these particular dimensions, the two resonances were lowered equally as the front aperture was reduced, just as they are seen to be in the vowel resonance chart.

A short length—5·3 cm.—of tube was cut off and tested at various degrees of projection beyond the mouth of the socket. At 2·05 (corresponding to 6 cm.) from the mouth of tube to rear

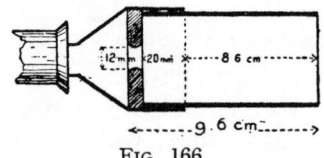

FIG. 166.

end of cylindrical socket) a good ɑ (calm) was found, with apparently a single resonance at 966. This, at first sight, seems to confirm D. C. Miller's single resonant ɑ at 910 to 1050 (*Science of Musical Sounds*, pp. 226-7), but in my own voice, when producing ɑ (calm) at 966, there is also an audible lower resonance of 812. Such a lower resonance, though inaudible through the upper one, may yet have been present.

The vowel was not altered in character by altering the resonance behind the reed.

With a 9·6 tube, projecting 8·6, and a stop consisting of a cork disc with 12 mm. diameter hole, pressed right back in the cylindrical socket, so that the face of the stop was 20 mm. from the mouth of the socket—see Fig. 166—a good ɑ was got with resonances 1084/683. But when a smaller aperture stop (10 mm.) was moved forward 8 mm. in the socket—so as to enlarge the back resonator and a projection of a 7·5 cm. tube was consequently increased from 5·2 to 6, the lower resonance fell from 767 to 724, while the upper resonance rose from 1217 to 1290.

TUBULAR VOWEL MODELS

A series of experiments was tried with different projections of the 7·5 cm. tube and different apertures and positions of the stop—the resonances being noted at each setting. With a 15 mm. aperture of stop, set 9 mm. from the mouth of the socket and the tube pressed back against the stop, a good ɑ 1217/633 was got—though the lower resonance was one semitone too low. This model also was considered too short for adoption.

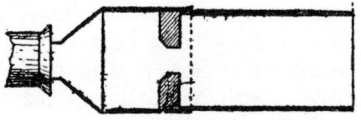

FIG. 167.

With a very similar setting (projection 6 cm., but stop set further back), it was found that partial closure of the stop aperture, by means of a conical plug on the end of a wire, varied the resonances of both cavities exactly equally.

In view of the difficulty of controlling the resonances independently, the experiment was tried of reducing the section of the back cavity by lining it with plasticine. It was found that by reducing the interior bore of the socket in this way to 20 mm., with a further constriction to 18 mm. at the mouth of the socket, to form the central orifice, a back resonator of 767 to 966 was obtained, which combined well with a tube extending about 9½ cm. from the central orifice. See Fig. 168.

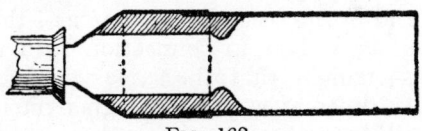

FIG. 168.

In this way a good broad ɑ (calm) was produced with resonances 1024/645—though, as will be seen, the resonances were actually within the range of ɒ (not), which, even in the chart, overlap those of ɑ.

It is certain that in ordinary speech we commonly use the same resonances to do duty for ɑ or ɒ, in which case we distinguish the two vowels only by their duration, ɒ (not) is (as is well known) always a very short-lived sound in English speech.

For the final model for ɑ (calm) the cardboard tube was made long enough to extend to the bottom of the cylindrical socket, and was lined with cork, so as to form a passage of 20 mm.

Y

diameter from the reed opening to the central orifice of 12 mm. diameter at 10·2 cm. from the open end of the tube. The total length, from mouth of tube to reed opening in the back resonator, was 15·5 cm. The resonances were now 1084/683 and produced a good ɑ.

It was found that the substitution of cork for plasticine reduced the resonant quality of the model and that the vowel sound was not so clear as with the plasticine construction. The lower resonance was difficult to hear. A denser lining material would doubtless give a better quality.

For a model to give u (who), it was realized that if it was to be of comparable length with the rest of the series it must be given a reduced mouth opening. It was found that with a tube of 12·3 cm. a good u was obtained with a central stop of 18·5 mm. aperture (circular), set at 80 mm. from the centre of stop to mouth of tube and a mouth stop of 17 mm. aperture. It was also found that, with a lenticular orifice 27 × 12 mm. and a plasticine cap, giving a 14 mm. front orifice, a 19·5 cm.

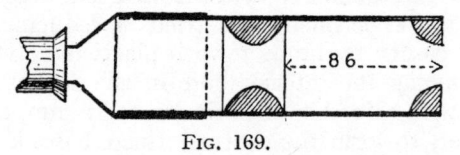

FIG. 169.

tube gave a good *u*, whether the stop was set at 6·4 cm. from the open end or at 12·5 cm. In the first case the resonances were 812/304 and in the second case 304/724—thus confirming the conclusions arrived at in connection with the plasticine ou (no) models—namely that the same vowel sound may be produced in two different ways—the higher pitched resonance being formed either in the front or the back cavity, while the lower resonance is formed in the opposite cavity.

A still better u was produced by increasing the space from stop to mouth of tube, and the final model was made as shown in Fig. 169, and gave a clear u with resonances 812/322.

e (men). A similar series of trials to those already described was made with a tube projecting 9·5 cm. from the socket, to find the best orifice and setting. Finally, a stop was made with central orifice of 20 mm. and this, at 4·8 cm. (from centre of stop to mouth of tube) the tube itself projecting 9·3 cm. from the socket, gave a good e of 1722/406, and was adopted as a model, as in Fig. 170.

TUBULAR VOWEL MODELS

i (eat). With a tube projecting 11·1 cm. and lenticular stop of 24× 13·5 mm. set at 1·3 cm. (from face of stop to mouth of tube) a good i of 2434/342 was got.

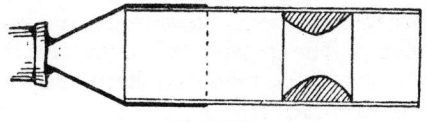

FIG 170.

For the model, a corresponding stop of 16 mm. circular aperture was made and when set at 3·1 cm. (from centre of stop to tube-mouth) gave a good i of 2298/342. This vowel was not quite so good as that with the tongue-shaped stop, but

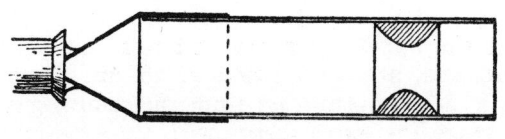

FIG. 171.

was apparently improved by increasing the slope of the front of the stop, so as to give a more rapid expansion at this point. The final form was as shown in Fig. 171.

ɔ (all). In order to get an idea as to the relative capacities

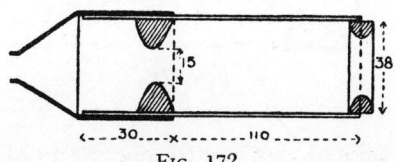

FIG. 172.

of the two resonators for this vowel, a preliminary model, giving ɔ 812/430, was built up in plasticine, and its capacity measured with water. A tubular model of similar capacity and orifices was built, as in Fig. 172. It had cork stops at centre and mouth of tube. This model was found to give 1024/406, instead of 812/430 ; the upper resonance being four semitones higher and the lower resonance one semitone lower than that of the plasticine model. This, though not recognized at the time, was probably due to the different transparency of the materials used—the cardboard front resonator being more transparent and the cardboard and metal back resonator less so than the original plasticine. The perforated stops too, being of cork, should probably have been made smaller to compensate for the transparency of the material.

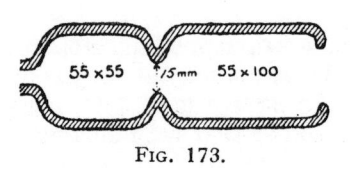

FIG. 173.

To lower the upper resonance, a longer tube (18 cm.) was substituted, and, at a projection of 16 cm. (beyond socket) with a 24 × 13·5 stop at 14·3 from the mouth gave a fair ɔ.

At this stage the experiments with the plasticene ɔ model were renewed, in order to obtain resonances of 912/541. This was done—by adjustment of front orifice and length of back resonator—the form of the model being then as shown in Fig. 173.

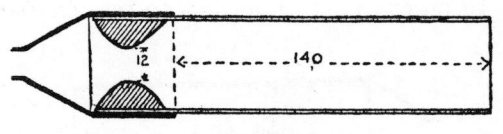

FIG. 174.

A cardboard tube of 17·5 cm. (projecting 14·0) with a 12 mm. cork stop set with its centre about 17 mm. from the back of the tube (see Fig. 174) gave resonances 812/406. The tube was then progressively shortened, with the object of raising both resonances, but though the first 10 mm. off raised 812 to 861, and 406 to 512, the next 4 mm. off are recorded as having lowered 512 to 483 ! The anomaly was noticed at the time, and can scarcely have been an observational error.

TUBULAR VOWEL MODELS

The central orifice was then enlarged from 12 to 13 mm.—which restored the 483 to 512—but with a further enlargement to 14 mm. brought back the anomalous 483. Finally, with a

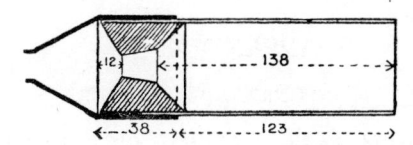

FIG. 175.

160 mm. tube, projecting 123 and a 12 mm. orifice, set as shown in Fig. 175, a good ɔ of 861/483 was obtained and this (though much lower in tone than the optimum) was adopted for the model.

APPENDIX VI
Consonant Resonances

In the following Table a comparison is made between the author's English consonant resonances (whispered) and the (American) English consonants recorded by purely instrumental means by the late Dr. Irving B. Crandall (*Bell System Tech. Journal*, October, 1925, pp. 614-20).

The present author's results have been re-investigated (by ear) and the figures represent the results of various consonant observations so far made—it being understood that single values given are typical, but not invariable.

It would appear that Crandall's method, while very reliable for analyzing sounds whose components maintain their pitch for an appreciable time, was less certain in the case of sounds of varying pitch.

For the analysis of transient sounds such as the characteristic resonance changes which produce such sounds as *la*, *li*, *ta*, *ti*, *ka*, *ki*, etc., it is suggested that the human ear is still the more sensitive and accurate analyser.

The author's consonants (except **m**, **n**, and **ng**) are now recorded as when produced without nasal resonance.

In comparing the results of the two series it must be borne in mind that there are many differences of pronunciation involved.

Thus, the American tendency to constrict the pharynx is calculated to raise the pitch of the lower resonances, and sometimes (as in the case of **th/dh**) that of a higher resonance also—namely by reducing the volume of the resonators.

The author has found that he can produce a resonance of 512 in the consonant **m**—which in his voice has no audible frequency between 215 and 1217—by constricting his pharynx as if to talk with a twang. The correspondence between the two series is the closest in the case of the continuing sounds.

As to the variation of the resonant pitch of certain consonants, according to that of the associated vowel there seems no room for doubt that, in the author's voice, such a change

CONSONANT RESONANCES

is invariably made in the case of t/d, k/g, l, m, n, f/v, θ/ð, ʃ/ʒ, s/z.

Crandall's resonances are recorded under three headings, viz. Near Start, High Frequency; Mid-portion to end, High Frequency; Transitional Characteristics, Low Frequency, High Frequency (possibly due in some cases to the a sound). These are here indicated by In. (initial), Mid. and Tr. respectively.

PA.BA

P.	pa. ba. Lower res. about 228 to 256, rising to that of associated vowel. (Not recorded in first expt.)	1084–1217 rising about 1 semitone to the upper vowel resonance.
		2800–3800 Mid.
C.	pa 900–1000. Tr.	3600 Tr.
	ba 700 Tr.	2700–3100 Tr.

DA

P.	406–430 at release ta/da rising to 724.	3249 (in front of tongue) falling to 1932–2048 at release and thence to upper vowel res.
C.	ta 900 Tr.	3600–4300 Mid. 3000–3200 Tr.
	da 500–600 Tr.	3600–3800 Mid. 2800–3200 Tr.
	Transients lower for ta than for da.	

FA.VA.

P.	fa/va 215–256 (unstable) (louder than in θ/ð)	1217–1824 (louder than in θ/ð)	5464 (weaker than in θ/ð)
C.	fa 500–600 Tr.	3100–3200 In. 3200–3500 Mid. 2800–3600 Tr.	6400 In. 6400–7000 Mid.
	va 600 Tr.	3000–3200 (trace) In. 2700–3400 Tr.	

CONSONANT RESONANCES

SA.ZA

P.	sa. za. 271	1625 falling to upper vowel resonance varies over 13s.t. according to assoc. vowel	5464–5780
C.	sa 500–650 Tr.	⎧ 4000–5600 In. ⎨ 4200–6000 Mid. ⎩ 2900 Tr.	⎧ 6400–8000 In. ⎩ 6600–7800 Mid.
	za 400–500 Tr.	⎧ 2200–2800 In. ⎨ 2800–5200 Mid. ⎩ 2800–3100 Tr.	⎧ 4400–5600 In. ⎩ 5600–7000 Mid.

In In. and Mid. the lower frequency appears in first part of fundamental cycle, higher frequency in latter part of cycle.

THA.DHA.

P.	th. dh. 256	1625 made behind tongue, i.e. not so loud as in f.v. Falling to upper res. of associated vowel.	2434 made between teeth and upper lip	5148 stronger than in f.v. (not observed in first expts.).
C.	tha 600 Tr. dtha		3200 ⎧ 2600–4000 In. ⎨ 2700–4200 Mid. ⎩ 2600–3000 Tr.	

SHA.ZHA.

P.	271	1824	2895 + faint hiss about 6000, varying over 8 s.t. with a.v.
C.	sha 450–500 Tr.	⎧ 2200–2800 In. ⎨ 2600–2800 Mid. ⎩ 2800–3200 Tr.	⎧ 3600–5000 In. ⎩ 4600–5000 Mid.
	zha 500 Tr.	⎧ 2600–3000 In. ⎨ 3000 Mid. ⎩ 2000 Tr.	⎧ 4000–4200 In. ⎨ 4000–4200 Mid. ⎩ 2900 Tr.

The In. and Mid. res. are alternating; lower frequency in first part of fundamental cycle higher frequency in latter part of cycle.

CONSONANT RESONANCES

LA

P.	256–304	362	625 variable over 16 s.t. with a.v.	2732 (faint)

On closure of lips with finger during phonation of la, the vowel sound is ɐ to ə as compared with a vowel soundlike i when li is phonated.

C.	110. 230	450	1200–1300	2700

RA

P.	304	1625	2048
C.	483–574	1218–1448	1933–2896

The higher pitch of C.'s lower resonance is probably due to pharyngeal constriction.

KA.GA

P.	304 rising to 406 at release and thence to lower vowel res. (812)	1625 (release in two stages) falling to 1366 and thence to upper vowel res. (1217) Res. varies over 26 s.t. with a.v.	2169
C.	ka ga 550–600 Tr.	{ 1500–1600 Mid. { 1200–1300 Tr. 1400–1600 Mid.	{ 4000–4200 Mid. { 3800–4000 Tr. { 2800–4000 Mid. { 3000–3600 Tr.

MA

P.		181–215 not recorded in 1st expts.	1217 (nasal)	1625 principal res.	2434
C.	115	240	668	1360	2400

NA

P.	203–228	—	683–812	1217–1366	1722–2048 (principal res.)
C.	270	430	570	1150	2400

NGA

P.	—	203–228	645–683	1366–1448	2579–2732
C.	130	250	540	1217	2500

APPENDIX VII
AMERICAN AND ENGLISH VOWELS
A

Comparison of the Vowel Resonances of American (male) Voices from Irving B. Crandall's " Sounds of Speech " (*Bell System Tech. Journ.*, October, 1925, vol. iv, No. 4, pp. 610–16), and the author's " Vowel Resonances ", *Proc. R.S.A.*, vol. 102, 1923, p. 753.

M.L.C. = Mean Low Characteristic Frequency.
S.L. = Scattered Low Frequency—recorded by Crandall only in the number of instances noted in brackets.
M.H. = Mean High Characteristic Frequency.
S.H. = Scattered High Frequency—recorded as for S.L.

(*Note.*—Crandall's S.L. Frequencies for " pool ", " put ", " tone ", " talk ", " ton ", and " father " compare with the upper resonances for the author's corresponding vowels. Crandall's S.H. Frequencies compare with the author's (additional) high resonances originally recorded for u and ʊ.

Similar additional resonances have since been recorded for the vowels ou, ɔ, ɒ, e ei, ɪ, and i—these are inserted (in brackets) in the column headed " Remarks ".

I.B.C. = I. B. Crandall, *Sounds of Speech*, Table IV, p. 611.
R.A.S.P. = R.A.S. Paget.

I.B.C.		R.A.S.P.	M.L.C.	S.L.	M.H.	S.H.	Remarks
oo	pool	—	411	750 (1)	—	3700 (4)	
—	who	u	362–406	—	608–861	2434	
u	put	—	457	988 (4)	—	3637 (4)	
	put	ʊ	322–406	—	861–1084	2434	
o	tone	—	520	830 (3)	—	3475 (4)	
	no	ou	383–483	—	683–912	—	(2895)
a	talk	—	722	950 (2)	—	3612 (4)	
	not		608–812	—	1024–1217	—	(3249)
	all	ɒ to ɔ	512–608	—	812–966	—	(3067)

AMERICAN AND ENGLISH VOWELS

I.B.C.		R.A.S.P.	M.L.C.	S.L.	M.H.	S.H.	Remarks.
o	ton not	— ɒ	654 608–812	1100 —	— 1084–1217	3212 (4) —	(3249)
a	father calm	— ɑ	955 724–861	1150 —	— 1149–1366	3683 (4) —	(high res. not heard.)
ar	part	—	630 483–574	917 1218–1448	1965 1933–2896	3800 (2) —	
	Wessex ŗ	ŗ	342	1534	1932	—	See RASP Consonants, 1924, p. 152.
a	tap hat	— æ	796 608–812	— —	1900 1722–1932	3150 (3) —	(high res. not heard.)
e	ten men	— e	612 483–574	— —	1800 [1] 1824–2048	2925 [1] (4) —	[1] the e frequencies are described as centred about 2400 (2732).
er	pert earth	— ɜ	570 406–541	— —	1688 1366–1722	3050 (2) —	(high res. not heard.)
a	tape hay	— ei	494 430–512	— —	3000 2048–2298	— —	(2732)
i	tip it	— ɪ	450 322–406	— —	2950 2169–2434	— —	(3067)
e	team eat	— i	296 304–362	— —	2987 2298–2579	— —	(3067)

B

Comparison of the Vowel Resonances of American voices and the author's voice. By Irving J. Crandall, "Dynamical Study of the Vowel Sounds," Part 2, *Bell System Tech. Journ.*, January, 1927, p. 106.

Table I
Natural or Characteristic Frequencies of the Vowel Sounds (Male Voices)

Sound	$\omega_1/2\pi$ Crandall & Sacia	Paget centred about	Mean	Equiv. pitch	$\omega_2/2\pi$ Crandall & Sacia	Paget centred about	Mean	Equiv. pitch
1 oo (pool)	431	383	407	$G_3\sharp$	861	724	793	$G_4\sharp$
2 u (put)	575	362	473	B_3 —	1149	966	1058	C_5 +
3 o (tone)	575	430	502	C_4 —	912	790	851	A_4
4 a (talk)	645	558	602	$D_4\sharp$	1024[1]	886	955	B_4
5 o (ton)	724	703[2]	713	$F_4\sharp$ —	1218	1116[2]	1167	D_5
6 a (father)	861	790	825	$G_4\sharp$ +	1149	1254	1202	$D_5\sharp$
7 ar (part)	861	767	814	$G_4\sharp$	1290	1491	1390	F_5 +
8 a (tap)	813	703	758	G_4 —	1825	1824	1825	$A_5\sharp$
9 e (ten)	609	527	568	D_4 —	1825	1932	1879	B_5 —
10 er (pert)	{ 542 / 700[3]	470	{ 506 / 700	C_4	1448	1534	1491	G_5 —
11 a (tape)	609	470	540	$C_4\sharp$	2048	2169	2108	C_6 +
12 i (tip)	512	362	437	A_3	2170	2298	2234	$C_5\sharp$ +
13 e (team)	431	332	381	G_3	2435	2434	2435	$D_6\sharp$ +

[1] Poorly resolved on our charts.
[2] In Paget's notation, for the sound o as in "not".
[3] Considering er to have triple resonance.

APPENDIX VIII
POLYNESIAN LANGUAGE [1]
By Dr. J. Rae

The following essay on the Polynesian language, was written by Dr. J. Rae, of Hana, Maui, author of *Political Principles*, etc., and addressed to His Excellency R. C. Wyllie, by whose permission we now publish it.—Ed. *Polynesian*.

HANA, MAUI, *March*, 1862.

To His Excellency R. C. Wyllie, Esq., etc., etc.

MY DEAR SIR,—I wish to give you a very brief sketch of what I have been doing about the Hawaiian, or, rather, the Polynesian language, in its connections with language in general, and with the Asio-European languages in particular.

My motive for this is two-fold : First I know the subject, as connected with our Insular Kingdom is of itself of interest to you, and also that the kindly feeling that you have for myself will make you anxious to know what I have accomplished already, and what I expect or hope to accomplish, in an inquiry, the importance of which cannot be doubted. The second is, that it has more than once already happened to me, to have reached important and brilliant discoveries, and that, while waiting to follow up their details, some blast of adverse fortune, hurrying me to other scenes, has prevented me attaining that fullness of proof I desired, and I have seen what I had treasured up taken, as it were piecemeal, out of my hands, by those who were more propitiously circumstanced than I.

The briefness to which I must necessarily confine myself must, I am aware, prevent you from seizing altogether my thoughts, but you will be able to gather something of what I believe I have attained to, and something of what I think it, to say the least, very probable, I may presently reach ; and

---

[1] A bound copy of *The Polynesian*, containing this essay, is in the British Museum Library under Pressmark, P. 1533.

should death or some other mischance overtake me, what I write to you may serve as a record of the things really done by me in this matter. Without further preface I commence.

There are two inquiries running parallel to each other, and having intimate relations, but which are capable of being separated.

The first of these is, from whence did the Polynesian race come, and at what period of the world's history did they take possession of these islands ? The second, what is the nature of their language ; what light does it throw on the original formation of language itself ; and what connections has it with other tongues ?

As to the first : Asia is the acknowledged great mother of Nations. Her vast dimensions, her generally warm, yet varied, climate, and the original fertility of her soil, even yet but partially exhausted, mark her out as such ; all recorded history assigns her this honour ; ethnological inquiries prove it. How many distinct civilizations may have arisen there, how many may have either partially or wholly dominated over, and nearly, or perhaps altogether, extinguished preceding civilizations, we know not, nor at present at least, have the means of knowing. There is every reason however to believe, that they have been numerous. Everywhere we see traces of various races. Many questions here arise. I will only notice two. First. What has given rise to the various races, and has successively enabled one to dominate over the other ? I answer, a main cause has been the progress of invention. We, for instance, the dominant civilization of the day, may be said to be a steam-using people. We have been so for only half a century, yet what superiority has it given, is it giving, and will it give us, and how much (if other and still more important inventions do not come into play) will it alone change us in two or three centuries ? I shall take another example. What steam is doing to and for us, the taming and domesticating of sheep, cattle, and horses, must have done for those who first subjugated them. We may see this in North America. The Indians who have troops of horses are essentially different, and altogether superior, to the Indians of two or three centuries since ; live in greater comfort, are gathered together in larger bodies, and are far more formidable. We see the same in Africa, where the black Caffres and other herding races rise greatly above the original Negro both bodily and mentally. There are very many facts going to prove that this was a cause which operated largely in Asia, in founding new races, and enabling them to subdue and extinguish others.

This succession of race to race seems to have been one of the main causes of the progress of mankind—the superior always overcoming the inferior, and either absorbing or exterminating it. It (the superior) has then gone on, by its own proper force, gathering new powers as it advanced, until some internal disease attacking it, it became either stationary or retrograded, and was in turn subjugated, and sank under the advance of some people having more of the elements of vigorous social life within them.[1]

It may be thought that Asia itself is opposed to this theory, showing in the main, with the exception of China, only as it were the *residua* of numerous peoples once powerful and prosperous, but now prostrate, imbecile, without the energy to advance a single step. In reality it is strikingly exemplative of its correctness. Look at the facts: Geographically as we look on the map, Europe seems, and really is, but a part, and a small part, of Asia—a little northern nook, outshotten from that great continent. Some three or four thousand years since, our ancestors Celts and Germans, pressed probably by the redundant population of their native Asiatic seats, begun to move into this Europe, and take possession of that hitherto neglected region. Necessity, that severe but excellent schoolmistress, taught them many things in their northern advance; for to encounter and overcome difficulties, gives strength to nations as to individuals. The sterner the trial the greater the vigor. Accordingly, the farther north the stronger men. The northmen, or Normans, have given Kings and Nobles to almost all Europe. That force and strength, and vigor of character, which we thus aquired, now renders us the dominant race of the whole globe, and as such we are spreading ourselves

---

[1] "As the race of trees so is that of men," The Analogy might be carried further than Old Homer thought of. Nature scatters widely the seeds of life, and each whether of plant or animal, has a struggle for existence. Those best adapted to their position—that is in our phraseology, the stronger crowd out the weaker. If particularly strong, the peculiarities which gave them their strength harden in them and their descendants into what we call first a variety, and then a species, which dominates over others and presses them out of being. Hence what have been termed centers of creation in the vegetable world, have, as it seems to me, their analogies in the world of man, and these make so many starting points for the true philosophic history of our race.

over all its more inviting parts, over Central Asia among the rest. There seems at present every probability that, in two or three centuries, all that region will be possessed by the Anglo-Saxon, and perhaps other European men, the pure blood occupying the higher, more cool, and healthy parts, a mixed race the lower and hotter portions; and that the English language, arts, and literature, will be things giving a new fashion to society and obliterating the ancient forms. But in doing all this, we shall only be returning to, and repossessing our ancient seats; we shall be but enacting on a grander scale, one scene of the great drama of human progress, of which many similar have preceded, and others may possibly follow.

Some such change was probably wrought on the aspect of society in Southern Asia by the domestication of cattle. When these began to multiply and be collected in herds, men would pass with them into the rich northern pastures, the abode before of the wandering hunter. At first they would exist as separate tribes, otherwise there would be strife between the herdsmen, to avoid which, as in the case of Abraham and Lot, one would say to the other: " Is not the whole land before us? If thou wilt go to the right, I will go to the left; and if thou prefer the left, I will go to the right. But in the course of years, cattle and men would multiply, tribes would become nations—nations battling with each other—for herdsmen are naturally, we may say necessarily, the fiercest of warriors. Ages of this sort of life would beget a numerous, vigorous, and warlike race in the north, requiring only to be united under some able and ambitious chief, to pour down on the South, and stamp it with a new impress. I think there is evidence of such a revolution, or perhaps of a series of such revolutions having had place there.

The other question is this: When one people or race is vanquished and overrun by another, or by its arts, where are we to expect to find traces or remnants of it? I answer, the new force always strikes at the rich central parts—at the heart of the Empire. The fragmentary outer parts often remain untouched. Thus, there is no doubt that the Laps are the remnants of a race once occupying at least the Northern parts of Europe. They now, therefore, exist only on the outskirts of their ancient domain. The Celts came next, and once occupied the larger part of that continent. The Germans, including in the term both the Teutonic and Gothic divisions,

z

came next, and, with the Romans subjugated the Celts. Where, nowadays do we find the Celts? In the uttermost borders, on the Westermost shores of Ireland and Scotland. Classic and French literature and science have operated as a foreign force over the Teutons and Goths, in all the richer parts of Northern Europe. Where do the learned, nowadays go for the pure idiom as it was probably spoken in the time of Christ? To remote, cold and barren Iceland.

If, then, as there is reason to believe, these Islands were peopled by a race once dominating over a small, or great part of Asia, all analogy would lead us to conclude, that, while that race must there have been overrun, and its original characteristics crushed out by foreign forces and arts, they remained in these Islands very much in their primeval form. They must, it is true, have undergone some modifications, either greater or less. Were these for the better or the worse?

When Cook and his companions gave to the world their account of the condition of this new people, the conclusion to which men came was, not that they were savages, not that they were barbarians, but that they had a civilization, though that civilization was rude.

Guizot defines civilization as advance. That cannot be accepted as a just definition, but we may with truth affirm that civilization, implying the practice of various arts, and these arts in their play on each other begetting new arts, and rudimentary sciences, there ought always in all civilizations, regarded only from this point of view, to be an onward progress. The want of it, therefore, marks a disease in the body politic, which must ultimately bring on decay and death. It is natural for a tree to grow, and some we know have been growing for thousands of years. If it does not grow, it is because there is disease in the trunk, or roots, and decay is at last certain. So it is with man in society. He either advances or recedes.

Had the movement here been forward or backward? I believe it had been retrograde, though slow, and spread over many, many centuries. Many facts with which you are no doubt acquainted demonstrate this. I will refer you to only one, viz. the decline of the art and practice of navigating long distances. It is quite clear from various circumstances and traditions, that, in the ancient times, the natives of these

Hawaiian Islands frequently sailed to all the kindred groups. When Captain Cook arrived they had no canoes fitted for such voyages.

If then the arts had been in a declining state, we may conclude with great probability, that such as were found existing here, had come to these Polynesian Islands with the original settlers, and hence we may draw some conclusions as to the time of the settlement, and the character of the people who formed it, and from that character as to their *habitat*. The arts in which these islanders excelled were fishing, navigation, irrigation. These would, I think, indicate that the parent stock had inhabited a warm climate, a country near the sea, and traversed by rivers. Again, there are some arts of which we find no trace here, which we can scarce suppose to have perished had they ever been introduced. First, written language. Had writing been known to the colonizing race, most assuredly that knowledge would have been kept up, if by none others, at least by the priests. Again cattle. Had these been largely domesticated among the parent people at the colonizing period, I can conceive no cause that could have prevented their, being brought here. The young could certainly have been transported.

It is, indeed, impossible from these circumstances, to fix the exact epoch of the emigration, but it certainly must have been at a very remote antiquity. It also must be allowed that the present Hindoostan has characters that would accord with the country indicated by the circumstances I have mentioned. There are many facts, which add to the probability of the supposition that I pass by.

It seems to me, therefore, that from the considerations alone which I have briefly stated, the following might be maintained as a probable hypothesis :—

At a period antecedent to the invention of letters, antecedent also to the full and general domestication of cattle, there was a great people inhabiting some part of Asia, very probably Hindoostan, who, for those remote ages, had carried navigation to a pitch of great excellence. That this people colonized the Polynesian groups. That they were subjugated, and their nationality, language, and institutions obliterated by some other race, probably by one of shepherd warriors. That this revolution caused a complete break to the intercourse of the islanders with their mother country, which, for purpose of trade and government had before been frequent, isolated them from the rest of the world, and gradually sank them lower in the scale of civilization. That this deterioration, somewhat retarded by the intercourse of group with group, became more rapid as that intercourse ceased, and was most marked in the smaller and more detached islands.

For the sake of brevity, I omit to notice the fact of the irruption of a black race from the West, and the support it gives my suppositions.

I propounded this hypothesis, not as of itself being a matter of great consequence. Without something of more certain import, it were only one of curious speculations, or perhaps of unprofitable disputation. But my investigations into the structure of the Polynesian language and its connection with the Indo-European tongues, have led me to two discoveries, which, if their truth be allowed, must be granted to be of very great and decided importance. One of these implies that the original seat of the Polynesian race was in Central or Western Asia. I believe it will be found that all those tongues which we designate as the Indo-European languages have their true root and origin in the Polynesian language. I am certain that this is the case as regards the Greek and Sanscrit ; I find reason to believe it to be so as to the Latin and other more modern tongues, in short, as to all European languages, old and young. The precise relation which these bear to it is not so easily traced, but it is that of filiation ; they are not cognate. The Polynesian is *parens*, whether *pater*, *avous*, *proavus*, *abavus* or *atavus*.

Now, this, you will allow, is one of those discoveries which startle, and which are altogether so contrary to previous conceptions, that they are apt to be thrown aside without looking at, as bearing on their very face the impress of ridiculous paradoxes. Had a race been found in Central Asia whose language was thought to have these pretensions, men would take up the inquiry as one connecting with their preconceptions. But to seek for a solution of the great problem in these, the uttermost parts of the earth, seems, at the first glance on it, to be an absurdity. The question is removed from the rank of absurd paradoxes, if it can be shown that altogether apart from the consideration of language, there are reasonable grounds to conclude that these people are the remnants of a race inhabiting, in ancient days, some central point in Asia, and subsequently blotted out from the light of day, by the irruptions of more warlike tribes.

The second discovery which I believe I have made, and with which the former is connected, is, that the study of the Polynesian language gives us the key to the original formation of language itself, and to its whole mechanism.

I commence with this latter. I can only give you the heads, mostly mere titles of what would require separate chapters.

(1) Man is an imitative animal, and all his arts have had their beginnings in this propensity.

(2) Language has its origin in the same source.

(3) We do not now make absolutely new words, but when we would express thoughts and feelings too deep for utterance by the common diction, we have recourse to poetry. The principles, therefore, guiding the creation of poesy, must have an analogy to those which guided the original inventors of language in creating names for things. These depend in part at least on the imitative propensity. Not to speak of its imagery, power by simile, etc., we have the precept, "the sound should seem an echo to the sense".

(4) But whatever be the principles on which poetry is based, it is not a knowledge of them that makes a poet. No one can be educated into a poet, as he can to be an engineer or surgeon. The delight of the poet is to have bodied forth his thoughts in such form that their full depth may be fathomed by other minds. Neither he, nor the men who listen to him, think of, or care for, the mechanism by which the feat has been accomplished. He and they feel that it has been done, and that is all. Hence the notion of poetic inspiration. To analyse poetry itself as an art, and endeavour to trace its principles, is a later business. Homer and Sophocles came before Aristotle.

(5) It is reasonable therefore, to conclude that, as in poetry, so with the first framers of speech at each separate invention, they only felt that through means of the breath and the organs called into action they had given utterance to something, that to themselves, and consequently to others, would serve to bring before the mind the object or event which it was wished to note. Neither the inventor, nor they who profited by the invention would at all attend to the mechanism by which this was brought about.

(6) It is reasonable, however, also to conclude that, as in poetry, so in the first sounds giving names to events or objects,

there was really something suggestive by analogy of the things they were intended to mark.

(7) Language is defined articulate sound. Its general progress therefore would be from the slightly articulated to the strongly articulated. That is to say, from being but little broken by what we term consonants, to being greatly broken by them; speaking in the general therefore, the fewer the consonants the older the language. This conclusion, however, is modified by the fact that the farther removed from the equator the greater seems to be the tendency to insert consonants.

(8) Men first discern in the concrete: the abstract, whether real or verbal, is later of being seized. Hence the conclusion may be drawn that, at first the distinctions we make between noun, adjective, verb, etc., would be little observed. (To make this clear, I should have to run into metaphysics.) The inflections also to which we give the name of declensions, and conjugations, not being essential to language, seem not likely to have had a place in the primitive tongues. And, as to the words we term verbs, as an action is not such till it is done, the primitive form would express simply the complete action, or would stand for what is termed the aorist tense. The present, the future, and the connections of the complete action with other events, would naturally be expressed by additions to that primitive form. In the first language, or languages, the aorist would thus be likely to be the simple form.

(9) Mere sound, by its very nature, is very confined in its capacity to suggest ideas of external objects, because it has no resemblance to them. It would seem almost limited to the representation of the cries of animals, and therefore also of the animals uttering them. (Other considerations which I omit go to prove this bounded capacity of sound considered apart.) But, when we utter an articulate sound, we call into play the breath, and all what are termed the organs of speech, the lips, the tongue, the cheeks, etc. Now, these being things, of which the nature and action are cognizable to the senses, they have resemblances, more or less near to the objects making up what we call the visible world. They may possibly therefore have analogies to many of these, sufficiently close to indicate or suggest them and to serve to recall them to the mind. They differ in this from any sound the voice can emit, for it obviously can have no resemblance to anything but some similar sound, and can only therefore suggest to the mind bodies

which give a sound. Of the organs of speech, the larynx is the chief, but its action lies concealed, and would not be known to rude uncultured men. They would know only what they felt, that something issued as a stream from the mouth, when they uttered a sound. Accordingly the more ancient Greeks whose language was comparatively little broken by consonants, conceived of the voice as a stream. Now a stream is capable of being variously modified, so as to have a resemblance to many things. It may be broad and shallow, or deep and narrow; it may flow slowly or swiftly, it may be made to pass rapidly through a contracted opening, or in a jet up or down; or sideways, or straight forward, etc. The lips, the tongue, the whole mouth, assume different forms in the utterance of different syllables, and all these forms may have resemblances to objects and actions external. It is to be observed, however, that this stream, its modifications and adjuncts, are only capable or representing force, form, and movement.

Three consequences follow :—

First. That the primitive significant sounds were all monosyllabic.

Second. That these primitive, articulate, and significant sounds only expressed force, form, and movement; on these, other significations were subsequently engrafted.

Third. That the nearer we come to original language the more scanty the nomenclature as to things remote from force, form, and movement as for instance, colours.

(10) Language either advances or recedes. Its natural tendency is to advance.

It has always been a great power, as well in what we call a savage life as in civilized. Hence men who from position or talent hold an eminent place as speakers or writers, seek for what seems to them the forms which are best suited to give the most powerful expression to their thoughts. Most men of mark have a style of their own. If the community be large, and there be many who have made language their study, it is only such innovations as have real merit that become permanent. If it be small, a single eminent man, especially where writing is unknown, may make great changes. There being no one to challenge the propriety of his innovations, they become first fashionable and then lasting. The old and better vocabulary drops. If, for instance, England had been a small country, and scarce a writer of distinction in it but Carlyle, he without doubt would have much altered the language. As it is, though he has his imitators, it is little probable that he will have a perceptible influence over the common diction. Hence, where writing is unknown, if the community be broken up into small tribes, the language very rapidly changes, and for the worse. An offset from an Indian tribe in a few generations has a language unintelligible to the parent stock. Hence the vast number of languages among the small hunting tribes of Indians in North and South America, which yet are all evidently of a common origin, for their principles are identical. The larger, therefore, the community, the more permanent the language; the smaller, the less it is permanent, and the greater the degeneracy. The smaller the community the more confined the range of ideas, consequently the smaller the vocabulary necessary, and the falling into abeyance of many words.

(11) When we have to compare two languages in which similar words with similar meanings occur, it may be a question which is the parent and which the offspring. Thus, if the times to come are to be like the times that have gone by, a period in the world's history may possibly arrive, when the annals of modern Europe may have been so obscured by antiquity that men shall not know whether what then may remain of the Latin and English languages were spoken by contemporaneous people, or whether by races existing at different epochs, and if the latter, which was antecedent to the other? The question, were it to arise, might be thus determined: See if there be any words common to both which are compound in the one, and not so in the other. The one in which they exist as compounds is the primary tongue. The reason is plain. The materials existed in it, out of which to form the word. They did not exist in the other. Thus omnipotent in English has the same signification as omnipotens in Latin, but the parts of which it is made up, *omnis* and *potens*, are significant words in the Roman tongue, but are not to be found in English, and so with hundreds of others. The Latin, therefore, might be confidently pronounced to have been the elder tongue.

The Polynesian language has every sign indicative of antiquity. It abounds in vowels, the proportion of these to consonants being twice or thrice that of the average of other languages (see above (7)). In it the same word may be verb, adjective, noun, or adverb, and the simple form of the verb is an aorist (8). It is monosyllabic, that is to say, every syllable has its own proper significance and force, even in the longest words. It is very scanty in its nomenclature as to things to which force, form, and movement cannot be attributed as characteristics. Thus in colours there are but five or six names. Black and blue, and dark green are not distinguished, nor bright yellow and white, nor brown and red, etc. This proceeds from no obtuseness of sense, for the slightest variation of tint is immediately detected by this people, and they have a very keen and just perception of what is called the harmony of colours. In the same way those affections of the mind which have no relation to external objects, and which do not manifest themselves by external signs, have a very scanty nomenclature. Thus for love, friendship, gratitude, benevolence, esteem, etc., they have but one term, *ulcha*. Those affections of the mind, on the contrary, which have relation to eternal objects or which exhibit outward tokens, are pretty fully represented; thus, *huhu*, anger—literally, swelled out; as we say, swollen by rage, etc. (9) Very many words which are compound in Polynesian, are held as primary roots in languages which we term ancient, as for instance, Sanscrit and Greek (11).

(Issue of 4th October, 1862.)

Its simplicity (the Hawaiian language) gives great facilities for analysing it. Every syllable is either a vowel, or a vowel preceded by a consonant. In no case does a consonant close a syllable. This distinctive peculiarity may partly have arisen from the greater difficulty of articulating a syllable closing with a consonant. Ask an adult Hawaiian, knowing no language save his own, to pronounce the syllable formed by the two first letters of our alphabet, and he will be sure to pronounce it as if written ab*a*. And, in reality, if we pronounce the same syllable slowly, and attend to our pronunciation of it, we shall be sensible that we ourselves have a slight tendency to add to it a feeble *a* sound. As the lips open, after being closed upon the *b*, there issues out a faint breathing like that vowel. It is quite a task for a native to avoid giving a distinct vowel sound, after any consonant. It would thus seem likely that this perfect cutting the current of the voice, this distinct *articulation* was a thing not existing in rudimentary speech, and which had not entered the conception of those who framed the Polynesian language.

There is, however, another possible explanation of the peculiarity. For the fancy to be able to form any image of things external, out of the current of the voice, it may be necessary that it should be felt as flowing (I omit details). However we account for it, the circumstances shows, or goes to show, that the Polynesian language ascends far up towards the times when human speech was in a rudimentary condition.

The Protestant missionaries to these islands, following the judicious advice of one skilled in these matters, made the Hawaiian alphabet as simple as possible. The letters as given by them are twelve. First come the five vowels, *a, e, i, o u,* pronounced after the manner of the Scotch, and of most European nations, and not after that of England. These, therefore, unconnected with consonants form five separate syllables. There remain seven consonants, and as each consonant can take any of the five vowels after it, and $7 \times 5 = 35$, there would be altogether only forty possible syllables in the Hawaiian dialect of the Polynesian. I believe, however, the matter is not quite so simple; some of the vowels have more than one sound, and the variation serves to mark distinct conceptions. Thus *a* in the first syllable of *Hana*, this place, and in that of *hana* to work, has different sounds; in the former, *ha* signifies a gap or opening, answering to the Greek χa, or *cha*, from whence our chaos, chasm, etc.; whereas in the latter it means personal, bodily effort. I shall not, however, pursue this part of the subject. I will only make one or two observations necessary to elucidate what follows.

In the first place, then, the Hawaiians often give a slight ruffling or roughening to their enunciation of vowels, which is in effect a nascent consonant. Thus in pronouncing the letter *a*, an *r* seems often to accompany it. That this is so appears by the fact that foreigners hear this faint *r* sound, and in consequence in their first attempts at pronunciation give it full force. Thus you will hear men who have picked up a little smattering of the tongue, pronouncing *aikane*, as if it were written high carney; and, indeed, I have seen it so written. I might give many other examples: it is probable, therefore, that in the progress of language, these nascent consonants would become more marked, and pass into written language. Thus, according to my interpretation, *ka* denotes a forcible action proceeding from a definite point. Add to this another *a*, which marks continued action, and you have a forcible and continued movement, commencing at a definite point. Now the only movement of this sort familiar to rude men, would be a rolling movement. Accordingly, a stone or a tree on rolling down a hill, is said to " kaa ", so a horse when he rolls on his back, so a man when rolling from his sleeping place, etc. When the Hawaiians saw a wheel carriage, they naturally called it a " kaa "—a thing that rolls—thus " pipi " being ox, a " kaa pipi " is an ox cart. This root " kaa " passing into the Sanscrit became " char ", which, in that language, means a movement onward from a definite point ; hence probably " caravan ", a word of Persic origin. Passing into the German it became " karre " into the Celtic, *karr*. Cæsar Romanized this by adding an " us " (carrus), but in French it is still " char ". We write it " car " ; and yet, though they have come down to us by a very long detour, were a stranger to these islands— say a Hungarian—to hear first one of us pronounce the two words " a car ", and then a Hawaiian " he kaa ", he would probably discern no difference, but that the latter were uttered after a more raucous fashion, like Hawaiian speech in general.

As there seem nascent consonants on many of the vowels, so great part of the consonants themselves may be said to be only incipient. Hence the diversities in writing ; the Protestant missionaries printing with a *k*, the French with a *t*. It takes months of patient labour to teach a Hawaiian youth to know the difference between *d*, *g*, *k*, and *t* ; *l* and *r* also are not to be distinguished. All this may be referred to in the same general principle, the further up you trace language the less articulate it is. That is to say, the less seldom, and less completely, is the current of the voice broken. The Hawaiian pours out a stream of sound, in which to the unpractical ear, vowels and consonants seem blended together. Hence the strange mistakes the first voyagers made, writing the same proper name in half a dozen different manners.

From a consideration of this circumstance, we may draw the conclusion that the different dialects of the Polynesian language are not really so far apart as they seem from printed books, because in writing, some have put down very lightly pronounced consonants as if distinctly uttered, and some have chosen one letter, others another, to represent sounds nearly or quite identical. Add to this that with us perfectly articulating Europeans, the consonants are esteemed the fixed points, the vowels the easily interchangeable, whereas the contrary is the case with the Polynesian, and you have a cause for the misapprehension. European philologists of eminence, their view obscured by this erroneous apprehension, and giving the subject probably only a cursory examination, have authoritatively, but very falsely, pronounced the different dialects of the Polynesian to have but little affinity to each other. A European in seeing in one written dialect " koki " and in another " hoi ", in one " kela " and in another " tea ", would not think they were the same words, only probably slightly different in their pronunciation. In effect if you show the New Zealand Testament to a Hawaiian he will say it is a book written in a foreign language, but if you take it up, give a slight turn to the pronunciation of the words, and here and there substitute others, you will find that there are many passages quite intelligible to him.

In the same way, as there are many words in the Polynesian which require only a very slight turn in the pronunciation to become Sanscrit, Greek, Latin, etc., I think it is a conclusion authorized by analogy to the above, and by the practice of philologists in general, to affirm that they are either cognate or that one has sprung from the other.

To have recourse again to the syllable " ka ". I have said that it denotes a forcible action proceeding from a definite point, a repetition of it has much the force of what is termed the frequentative in grammar, denoting a recurring action, and according to the nature of that action, either intensifying it or diminishing its force. Thus " ka ka " denotes any quick repeated movement proceeding from a definite point, say from the hand, as for instance in extinguishing a fire in grass by striking repeatedly with a branch is " kaka wela ", or splitting firewood is " kaka wahie "! When reference is made to the action itself, the place being indefinite, a " la " is added as denoting place generally, something like a French " la ", there. Hence " kakala " comes to signify the breaking of the surf, the striking of a cock with his spurs, and hence again the spur itself. Now compare " kakala " with the Latin calcar or kalkar, which is also a cock's spur, and you perceive it requires but a very small twist of the voice in the pronunciation to convert the one into the other. So it is with very many Polynesian words in Greek, Latin, and all other languages with which I am acquainted.

There are then some forty or fifty possible syllables in the

POLYNESIAN LANGUAGE

Hawaiian language. Is it possible to conceive that these are all, as it were, random sounds, having no connection with the nature of the things which singly, or in combination, they serve to denote ? I think not. Everything as it seems to me, must proceed from some cause, and therefore everything, even the slightest breeze that blows, has a cause, could we only find it out. Take, for instance, a parcel of these syllables, say *ma, mi, no, ke, hi*. Why should the one be used instead of the other ? What is there in " no ", why should it be employed in any other word rather than " ma " ? Or, let us take a collection of words in which any syllable, say " mi " occurs, and see if we can discover anything in them which makes it appropriate, and which would render any other, say " la ", " li ", " ha ", etc., unfit for the purpose. Here is a short list. " Umi " or " mi ", a rat-trap ; " umi," infanticide ; " umi," the number ten ; " emi," to lessen ; " emiemi," in the New Zealand dialect, to assemble ; " umiki," to wrinkle ; " umiumi," the beard ; " mimilo," a whirlpool ; " omimi," to wither ; " milo," to spin ; " mio," to flow, as water through a narrow passage ; " mihi," to sigh, New Zealand " mihi ", to repent ; " mimi," to make water ; " amiomio," to be giddy, New Zealand, " amiomio," unsettled, Tahiti dialect ; " romiromi," to hide from approaching visitors, T.D. ; " lomilomi," to chafe the limbs ; " minomino," rumpled ; " milomilo," to regard with curiosity ; " minamina," to pity ; " umiumihahehahe," the white billows of the sea, T.D. ; " umiumihahehahe," an undaunted warrior, T.D.

Now in reading over this list it is impossible to doubt, that there must be some cause for the syllable " mi " entering into all these words. It is impossible to conceive that it is mere accident which has brought it there. It must, so to say, have some inherent *force* of its own which renders it appropriate, and would render other syllables less appropriate for the place. Yet, utter it as often as I will, and give it any inflection I can, I find nothing in its mere sound, indicative of any suitableness it has for giving the meaning of any one of the things or actions which we know these several words represent. Furthermore, the matter acquires additional difficulty from the consideration that whatever this appropriateness of the syllable " mi " for filling the place it holds in any one of these words may consist in, it must be a something adapting it to them all ; and yet the several things and actions represented by the words I have written down would seem to have nothing in common. What, for instance, can have less apparent connection than rat-trap, infanticide, and the number ten ?

This is the problem which my theory, or system, or what you like to call it, proposes to attack and solve. I repeat the main points in it :—

(1) When the syllable " mi " was first uttered as a name for any thing or action, Society was in a very rude and elementary condition ; the perceptions of men were formed from their immediate sensations, and language was in its infancy.

(2) The voice was conceived of as a current, flowing from the mouth, and capable of being bodied forth by the sensible organs of speech into this or that form

(3) These organs themselves being material, and flexed into different shapes in uttering, or attempting to utter, different sounds, might have analogies as thus modified, this way, or that, to material things and actions.

Now place yourself in this condition. Suppose your language is syllabic and very meager and scanty ; that you hear someone utter the syllable " mi ", and, never having heard this exact sound before, that you endeavour to give utterance to it yourself. We may separate the two letters and consider them apart : *i* that is the English *e* (as in " bee ") takes for its utterance the smallest opening of the mouth of any of the vowels. The stream of the voice is therefore confined. To give the modification to this stream implied by the letter *m*, the lips are first compressed through their whole extent, and then slightly opened through that extent, to allow the *i* to escape. You have thus a broad, but thin stream flowing through a wide orifice whose sides approach. There is, therefore, nothing impossible in the supposition that the effort to pronounce the sound in question might be suggestive of that idea.

It is likely that the natural evacuations would be among the first things to which men would give names. I shall, therefore, take the Polynesian word used to express the voiding of urine as the first example. Suppose then, that in the rudimentary state of things we are considering, someone, imagining he has found a proper term for the act, calls the attention of another to it, uttering at the same time the two syllables " mi mi ", and that this other individual attempts to reproduce, and succeeds in reproducing, the sound. Would not the two actions, the one which he was performing by means of the organs of speech, the other at which he was looking, have a certain resemblance to each other ? Would they, in effect, have any essential difference, but that in the one there was an aerial, in the other a liquid stream ? Is there anything, therefore, impossible in the supposition that he might instinctively feel that the utterance of the sound mi mi had in it some certain appropriateness to the act of urinating ? That the uttering it had some connection or other, unknown probably to him, and which he would not think of tracing out, with the thing, was, in short, a fitting name for it, as serving, on again hearing it, to recall the act to his memory ? Is not this supposition much strengthened by the fact that this double syllable has, in truth, become the name for the thing in question over "islands", scattered for many thousands of miles over this ocean ; that the same syllable is found in other languages for that evacuation, as in Sanscrit, " mih " ; in Greek, " omicho," in Latin, " mingo," and that we shall in vain search for any other syllable, the utterance of which produces in the organs a movement having any, or equal, analogy to the thing ? I proceed to the other words. In these I shall simply point out the analogy. They are mostly compounded with other syllables ; these I will translate, not with critical accuracy, but shortly, by the English word coming near the idea.

First is " mio ", in which *o* may be rendered on. The lips here are represented by two rocks nearly meeting, and, pressing through them the stream flows *on*. A correct enough representation this for a mountain torrent confined by rocks, for which the word " mio " stands.

(2) " Amio "—is applied to denote a current of air passing through a door, or between rocks, with force. This force is indicated by the *a* prefixed, and the whole word may be translated—a gust of wind.

(3) " Amiomio "—Subject to sudden *gusts* of passion—Tahitan.

(4) " Amiomio "—Nearly the same in N.Z. dialect. These two may be from *ami* " a hinge " ; in this case they may be translated easily—moved hither and thither. " Ami " and its cognates I have not put down.

(5) " Milo "—To spin. In this case the fingers take the place of lips, and the thread that of the slender current. " Lo " is for long. If I might coin a word, one might say it " mees "

long—it is spun out long. This action gives a whirling movement to the thread, hence the next.

(6) " Mimilo "—To whirl, and—

(7) " Mimilo "—a whirlpool. Here the meaning of the opposing currents takes the place of the lips or fingers, and the whirl that of the stream or thread.

(8) " Umi " or " mi "—a rat-trap. Look at it! Have not its firmly closed serrated lips, which, however, may be opened some analogy to the compressed human lips as they prepare themselves to utter the " mi " ? The *u*, strictly, a jutting out, when prefixed, stands for the other part of the trap.

(9) " Umi "—ten. Think of the mode in which men, who have no other mode of reckoning but their fingers, denote this number. With extended arms they first stretch out all their digits, and then suddenly close them on the palms. The former action is the *u*, the latter the " mi ".

(10) " Umi "—Infanticide. This was generally done by compressing the windpipe with the fingers.

(11) " Umiumi "—the beard. The Polnesians plucked it out by means of two pieces of shell, used in the way of pincers. These shells represent the " mi ", viz. the compressed lips; the *u* the action of applying them. From this daily pluck, pluck, plucking the thing plucked, the beard, doubtless received the name.

(12) " Umiki "—To pinch, to stretch out the arm and press the thumb and fingers forcibly together. The *ki* denotes the forcibly.

(13) " Lomilomi "—To chafe the limbs; a pressing of the thumbs and fingers together here and there—" lo-lo ".

(14) " Romiromi " (the same word, with the Tahitian *r* in the place of *l*)—To hide suddenly. This is done by placing the things to be concealed, here and there (lo-lo) under the mats, and *pressing* these down on them.

(15) " Minomino "—Wrinkled; as cloth pinched by the fingers or something else into wrinkles. The *no* is passive; the cloth or paper having been operated on, not itself operating. I may remark that our word crumpled seems to me to have had a similar origin in a verb in the ancient German, signifying to compress with thumb and finger, of which we have a trace in our word *crumb*, a morsel broken off by thumb and finger.

(16) " Umiki "—To wrinkle; pinch.

(17) "Omimi"—Withered; as leaves corrugated into wrinkles.

(18) "Emi"—To lessen. Here the "mi" is to squeeze, and the *e* out. Now to squeeze out implies a lessening of the thing squeezed.

(19) "Emiemi"—To assemble. We speak of an assembled multitude as a press. Thus, in the New Testament "he could not come to him for the press". Now, emiemi may here be translated a pressing together from all quarters, which is a sufficiently just conception of the idea implied in the word assemble.

(20) "Umiumihahehahe"—The white billows of the sea. In a storm when the waves of the sea are large, we see here and there their crests or projecting lips elevating themselves on high. Sometimes this movement goes so far that some of these overshoot themselves, go beyond the perpendicular, break, and fall down on the body of the billow, making what we call a breaker. The *u* the projecting of the lips or crest; the "mi" the closing down of it upon the body of the wave. "Hahehahe" may, I think, be shortly translated tumultuous. Thus we should have the phrase—" The waves tossed into breakers over the tumultuous sea."

(21) "Umiumihahehahe"—An undaunted warrior. We speak of the *press* of the battle—mi. The *u* pushing broadly, that is boldly, forward. Thus we have "pushing boldly forward through the tumultuous press of the battle".

Matter and movement being all that the organs of the voice can be moulded to represent, it may be said to have been impossible for the Polynesian race to form words to express those emotions which give no external signs. All those emotions, however, which give manifestations of their existence by visible signs, however slight, have a place in the language. The eye, as changing its appearance under the influence of shame, rage, etc., has furnished names to several of these. We must seek elsewhere, however, for the three following:—

(22) "Mihi"—Repent. If you hear one Kanaka ask another what he should do concerning his wife, who has been guilty of a grave fault, the question will probably be put. "Ua mihi anei ia?" "Has she repented?" Now what is the thing implied in the *mihi*? it is this: she has fallen down before her husband, moaning out the "uwe!" her visage contracted into wrinkles, down which, if she can force them out the tears

roll. The *mi* has reference to the wrinkles, the *hi* to the flow of tears. This is the full " mihi ", but the term is used more frequently as a simple acknowledgment that wrong has been done.

(23) " Minamina "—to pity. Strong pity of compassion, such for instance, as felt when looking at a ghastly wound inflicted on the person of a friend, produces a deep furrow in the middle of the forehead and draws back the mouth so as to cause a fold at the corners. So at least the emotion is depicted in plates of the passions. This is, I think, a probable derivation of the term for the emotion in its stronger form. It is used, however, generally for much more trivial matters in the sense of to spare, and may then be nearly equivalent to giving out a thing in mere pinches, *mi*. It is opposed to " minomino ", the *na* being active and implying that the *mi* is produced by the act of the person spoken of.

(24) " Milimili "—a curiosity, or to regard with curiosity. Observe how a native acts when something curious, and which he has never before seen, is presented to him. He takes it up grasping it with his fingers, and turning it from hand to hand. The repeated *mi* is the grasping ; the *li* is the passing from hand to hand. Or if you ask a native what is the meaning of " milimili ", the chances are he will endeavour to explain it to you by putting his hands through these movements.

I think you will admit that our problem has been solved—that we have found a reason why *mi* in the several words is more appropriate than any other syllable would be in the place it occupies. That we have also discovered a certain bond connecting these several names of things, seemly so altogether unlike, this same *mi* indicating forms or movements, or both, existing in all these things, and through which each has certain analogies to the others.

I could easily more than quadruple the list, giving you after the same fashion, a true, or at least a probable explanation of the sources of the forces which the same syllable *mi* has in all the terms.

I could in a similar manner take up one by one, all the syllables of which the Polynesian language is composed, dissecting each, and showing how its force depends on the configuration of the organs at the moment of pronouncing it, and that thus we have a clue to unravel the most intricate mysteries of the language, and to guide us to a point of view whence the sources of its very considerable powers and beauties are disclosed to us. That moreover we are thus furnished with a sufficient cause for the phenomenon, otherwise inexplicable, that words identical, or nearly identical in form, are used as the names of things seemly utterly different in nature. In any such attempts to display its whole mechanism, no doubt one more thoroughly versed in its use, and better acquainted with the feelings, habits, and customs of the race than I am, or can be supposed to be, would detect many inaccuracies, but he would also, I am convinced, see under them a solid substratum of truth.

You are probably inclined to ask me if I can thus decipher all the words in all the dialects. No. About two-thirds or three-fourths of those in the Hawaiian Bible and one-third in the other dialects. But you will best understand what I can do by my telling you the difficulties yet before me.

When chance threw me on these shores I could not forget that, many years before, when engaged in collecting materials for a rather ambitious work I then meditated on what I may call the history of civilization, I had come to the conclusion that the Polynesian race were a remnant of some very ancient Asiatic civilization. Arrived here, therefore, I had a great desire to make myself acquainted with the language of these islands. Two obstacles met me—my innate inaptitude for acquiring any language, for, though I have attained some knowledge of several, it has been at the expense of three-fold the labour most other men require and then I had arrived at an age when the sounds of new languages strike dully on the ear. By plunging directly into the midst of Kanakanism, the flood of strange sounds in which I became immersed found gradually a passage into that organ; but yet, when spoken rapidly or by a stranger, I often miss great part, or all that is said. I am thus far from that mastery of the tongue which I might have acquired had I come here at an earlier period of my life. With books it is different. We have the Bible, on the whole, in so far as I am capable of judging, well translated. But then, there are many Hawaiian words not there, and such as are, not readily come-at-able. This requires a dictionary, and we have no good one. About three years since I got from Judge Andrews a pretty copious manuscript of Kamakau's, but presently afterwards, on coming here himself, he told me it was of little value, having been written when he was very young, and advised me to see and get one which he had made afterwards. About the same time I saw notice of appropriation to aid Judge Andrews in publishing his dictionary, and concluding it would soon appear, and thinking he must have had all the aids which Kamakau and others could furnish, I have been waiting for it, and have not made that use of the manuscript I otherwise might.

As for the other dialects, although from your kindness and that of others I have Bibles, New Testaments and Prayer Books, in several of them, and two dictionaries, one a New Zealand, and the other a Tahitian, I am sorry to say they have very grave defects. It would seem as if the writers had not themselves well known the languages into which they were translating. I cannot otherwise account for the very great number of English, Latin, Greek, and Hebrew words which are introduced. Thus you have tavana, governor; tavani, servant; anatole (Greek), east; orebi (Hebrew), a fly; paleke (Greek), a concubine; osa (Hebrew), a moth, etc. It is impossible that such things as these have no names in Tahiti.

The most scanty languages have some word to denote the most of them. The veriest savage has always a name for the sun, and for the quarter in which he rises. In the Tahitian dictionary there is a list of 400 foreign words, and these are not all. There are, I am certain, a great many more introduced into the Bible, and which are not to be found in the dictionary. For as there is at least a third of the apparently native words used in the Bible not be to found in the dictionary, we may conclude that this is also the case as to the foreign. Indeed, I am certain of the fact, though to what extent this foreign invasion goes I am unable to say. Now this is very puzzling to the etymologist. Take any word, say orama, it has a Tahitian look about it, and even a good Greek scholar might not think of its being Greek, for it is of rare occurrence in that language. About the same may be said of the New Zealand Bible and dictionary. One is tempted to think that the translators knew but imperfectly the language, and when their memory failed them, turned over their Hebrew, Greek, and Latin dictionaries till they found a word easily pronounced by natives, and so clapped that down. What makes the matter worse for me is that Hebrew seems to have been the great resource, possibly because, as I have been told by those I have met with here having some knowledge of that language, there are striking analogies between it and the Polynesian. Now I know nothing of Hebrew. All this renders these books of far less value to me, than they otherwise would be, for it is only such words as being connected with the Hawaiian dialect, and therefore evidently Polynesian, that I dare venture to use.

(Issue of 11th October, 1862.)

I have, however, been enabled to make a sufficient study of many different dialects, to arrive at the conclusion that they all most certainly took their rise from one great mother tongue, and that they have all more or less degenerated from it. Thus you will find words used in one dialect in some secondary and accidental sense, you find the primary sense in another. Now it is plain that the word in its primary sense, must at one period have existed in that dialect in which its secondary signification now alone remains. It being then a fact that the use of some words in their more extended sense has been lost in certain islands, it seems to follow that others are likely to have altogether died out, and that probably the majority of words found now in only one or two groups, have belonged to the original language, which therefore must have been far more copious than any remaining dialect. I say nothing of what may be termed corruptions, the changed pronunciations, the contractions, the coining of new words, or the more extended and strained use of others, though all these would naturally take place and have seemingly done so. Viewed merely on the side of copiousness, and judging from the printed language, I should say that, of the various dialects, the Hawaiian is the most copious, and therefore most probably the nearest the original. This no doubt may be partly owing to the different ability or care of translators. Nevertheless, these islands, as having had the largest population, ought to have had the dialect least degenerated.

This great mother language must have been an original one, It is impossible to conceive it to be the corruption of any other tongue. Its structure forbids this supposition.

It is eminently a natural language. It may be said to be natural, because every sound, in every word, has significance, and denotes something having a real connection with the thing or things denoted. The pronunciation of each separate syllable induces a certain configuration of the organs, and that particular configuration has positive analogies, direct or indirect, with the actions or objects indicated. There is thus a real connection between the sign and the thing signified.

Again, it is natural, because, if we view speech as an invention of man, it must have commenced like other inventions from the simplest beginnings. Now, we can conceive this language existing in its rudimentary state in two, or three, or four syllables, and out of these growing by the laws regulating the progress of other inventions into its perfect form. No change would have been required in its original elements. The process would have been one of simple, though very skilful, agglutination.

If again, without yielding ourselves to the interpretation of the phenomena before us, by the established laws of the inductive philosophy, we rest on a literal following out of the history of the affair as given in Genesis ; then considered in itself, as it existed at one time somewhere on the great Asiatic continent, it has, I think, a better claim than any other of which I know to be held as the original universal language of the earth, before men attempted to construct the Tower of Babel. For

    . . . " The great first cause
    Acts not by partial, but by general laws."

And this language being the most natural, is consequently most in accordance with the great plan of the God of Nature.

Such being its innate claims to our attention, another would seem to arise out of its very structure and constitution. For, its being a natural language, ought to have given it a tenacity of life superior to that of others. Do, then, any traces of its existence remain in the great Asiatic-European continent, in some part of which it once had its seat ? This is a question to be determined by those learned in the languages ancient and modern, that flourish, or once flourished, in these vast regions. I myself am but poorly fitted for the inquiry, for I am no great linguist. Latin I have studied and read pretty largely. But the original Roman tongue seems to have grown out of the coalescent speech of various races, and that ancient tongue was unintelligible to Cicero. Few words therefore retaining much of their original form, can be supposed to have come down to us. Yet in the Latin tongue, as we have it, there are a very considerable number of words seemingly of Polynesian descent In Greek I am but moderately skilled ; that is to say, I read Homer and the more easy prose writers with tolerable facility, yet not without occasional difficulty. I, however, found in that language, a great mass of words amounting probably to hundreds, which are, I conceive, of undoubted Polynesian origin, and had I the Odyssey (I have only the Iliad by me) could considerably augment the number. Of Sanscrit I never had but a smattering, and I have not seen a Sanscrit book for more than twenty years, yet from my recollections, and from occasional Sanscrit words picked up in dictionaries, etc., I can trace out a Polynesian origin, for so many, that I have no doubt, had I the books by me, I might make out a long list. Once I knew a little Gaelic or Celtic. Of the very few words that remain to me, a considerable portion are identical with the Polynesian. Of German I know next to nothing, yet there too there are many Polynesian-looking roots. I am a tolerable Frenchman, but though in that language there is much that smacks of Polynesian yet, as it is mainly compounded of Celtic, Latin and German, and I have no French dictionary with the supposed derivations, I cannot put anything French to account.

Yet notwithstanding the scantiness of my resources, my researches warrant me in saying that the Polynesian has been the prototype of some of the Asio-European tongues, and that therefore, to say the least, it is not impossible it may have been that of all, for there is an appearance of consanguinity in them all that seems to mark their having had a common parent.

That you may see I have good grounds for so affirming, I subjoin a list of words expressing ideas the most frequently recurring in all languages, and which, while they are likely to be most permanent, afford also the surest proof of identity of speech. The name of a particular thing—tobacco, for instance—may easily spread with the thing itself over many distant countries, but general names are very different.

I have therefore made choice of the four following classes of words, as being most general, and affording therefore the fairest criterion for you to arrive at some judgment on the matter :

(1) The sexes—man and woman.
(2) The elements—fire, air, earth, and water.
(3) Those affections of the mind which seem primarily at least to have regarded material objects—as to see, to know, etc.

(4) Words relating to speech itself. I put them down in two columns—the Polynesian to the left, the Indo-European on the right.

As I am not sure if you are familiar with the Greek characters, I put down the corresponding letters in English, but suppose them to be read with the broad sound. I use the letter *h* for the asperate ('), but would remark that this seems too strong for it. Its exact force, like other questions of the exact pronunciation of extinct languages, is a matter difficult to decide, but it seems to me to have been generally much slighter than that indicated by the letter *h*.

I take some liberty with words, that is, in some cases I assume a likeness to exist where perhaps that likeness may not be very apparent to you. But I go not half so far as most etymologists. The just principle seems to be this: When we see a series of words evidently passing from one language into another, or into a set of kindred languages, we are warranted in assigning a similar origin to others, though their likeness be not so apparent, provided there be no other source for them known to us.

Thus when we see that No. 2 has passed into general European speech, we may be allowed to assign a probable, though only a probable, passage of No. 1. And though the resemblance of "karl" to "kane" be far from close, yet as the ancient Germans and Greeks were seemingly of one parent stock, we have a right to expect that the words in both languages expressive of masculine vigor, would show tokens of affinity or that if they were different words, that we should be able to trace their origin into some other language, or into some two or more of the words of these respective tongues compounded into one. But "aner" in Greek and "karl" in German are both esteemed primitives, nor can we find any father for either but "kane", which they both more resemble than they do each other. I may illustrate this by the analogy of the features of the face.

If curious in genealogies, you may have observed, in a long gallery of family pictures, that often brothers, first cousins, second cousins, etc., struck you at first as having little or no resemblance to each other, but, on looking at father and mother, grandfather and grandmother, or perhaps much farther back, you would be able to trace a certain cast of countenance, or perhaps some particular feature, appearing now distinctly,

POLYNESIAN LANGUAGE

and now but just perceptible, but still running through the whole, and marking them as one race. You may perhaps have heard the late Dr. Gregory, of Edinburgh, in his lectures expatiating on this subject. He was accustomed to do so. So it is with languages, and the proofs of their relationship by their likeness to a common parent.

Class I—Male and Female
Man as a Male

No. 1—A.
Kane, the male   *Aner* (Greek).
                                Karl (German), a man, *vir*.

In Greek, "aner" plural "aneres", is a man by excellence, as in the often repeated phrase in Homer, "Oh my friends, be *men*"—"*aneres*." In German "karl" seems to have marked a man by excellence—thus, "Karl magnus," the great karl, Charlemagne. In broad Scotch there is much old Saxon and Danish or Gothic. Carl is not only an old man, but also a male, as "carl cat", and *manly* energy, as when Burns speaks of resolution as the stalk of carl hemp in man.

B.
Wi (Hawaiian).   *Vis*.
Vi (Tahitian).   *Vi* (Latin) force, strength.
Viri and *viri alo* (Tahitian), *Vir*, a man.
   the front rank in battle,   *Viri*, the men.
Iwi (New Zealand), the men
   of a tribe.

In my interpretation, "wi" or "vi" in the Polynesian language, in one of its senses, denotes a strait, a difficulty, and consequently the force necessary to overcome it. Thus, "wi," scarcity of food, famine. Therefore "wi" or "vi" is nearly equivalent to the Latin "vis", "vi", and "viri", as also "viri alo" Tahitian (*alo* or *ano* front) to "viri" (Latin) the men. "Vir," in Latin being a man in the sense of "aner" and "karl", hence "virtus", manliness, and our "virtue".

No. 2.
Wahine (Hawaiian).   *Favini* (Sanscrit), woman.
Vahine (Tahitian), woman.   Femina (Latin), female woman.
Vaine
Fifine other dialects.

BB

From " Favini " (Sanscrit), Latin etymologists derive, and that without any hesitation, the Latin " femina ", a woman or an animal of the female sex—hence our " female " and " feminine ". I may remark that as " wahine " is undoubtedly a compound word in Polynesian, denoting the physical characteristics of the sex ; if what I have advanced be admitted as correct, this single word would be alone sufficient to prove the priority of the Polynesian to the Sanscrit.

CLASS II—THE ELEMENTS : FIRE, AIR, EARTH, WATER

FIRE

No. 3—A.

Kapura (New Zealand), fire.

Mapura (New Zealand), fire.
Pura (Tahitian), to blaze as a a fire.

Pur, genitive *puros*, plural fire, or fires.

Pura (singular), a fire, a funeral fire : hence *pyra* (Latin) a funeral fire, and hence our *pyre*.
Fur (Ger.), fire : hence probable the French *feu*, fire ; *foyer*, a place for fire, a hearth, and hence probbably our *fire*.

B.

A, action ; hence the most powerful of agents in early stages of society—fire.
Aa, to burn on.
Ahi, a fire, the flame bursting forth.
Ai, the same in some dialects.

Daiō and *kāio*, to burn. Etymologists derive *kaio* from the Sanscrit *cush*. I think it more reasonable to consider the *d* in *daio* and the *k* in *kaio* as mere strengthening additions to the root : and thus as ō is merely terminal, there remains *ai* or *ahi* for the root.
Agni (Sanscrit), fire : hence Latin *ignis* is said to be derived, and hence again our *ignite, igneous*, etc.

C.
La (Polynesian), sun.

La (Celtic), sun.
Alea, ele, elios (Greek), sun.

D.
Ao (Poly.), sunrise or dawn.

Aŏs, eŏs, auos (Greek), dawn: hence aurora, etc.

E.
Lama (Poly.), fire in motion, a torch.
Lama

Lampas, a torch, a lamp, Latin *lampas*, lamp.
Flamma (Latin), flame; Spanish *Lluma*.

AIR

No. 4—A.
Ea (Poly.), breath.

Ear, aer (Celtic), air.
Aar (Syriac), air.
Ayer (Arabic), air.
Aer (Greek), air.
Aer (Latin), air.

I think it doubtful if the Polynesian had any definite idea of air when at rest. Kamakau, however, thus defines *ea-*, " He makani ku malie, oia ka makani e hanu nei kakou, e puka ana iwaho, e komo ana iloko." " Wind at rest, which we breathe, which issues out from us and comes within us."

B.
Puhi (Poly.), the breath.

Psyche (Greek), breath, life; the soul: hence many Greek words and some English derived from them, as psychology, etc.

C.
Puhi (Poly.), to blow.
Akapuhi (Poly.), blow gently.

Psychein (Greek), to blow.
Eka psychein or *aka psychein* (Greek), to blow gently as did Minerva when she blew aside the spear of Hector.

EARTH

No. 5—A.
Aina (Poly.), the earth as furnishing food, *ai* being food.

Aia, gaia, gē (Gk.), earth, land, *soil*.

B.

Honua, the earth as extended.

Chthon, accusative: *chthōna*, the earth as extended.

C.

Kainga, aina, in New Zealand means a place or a time of eating, and hence an abode.

Ngai in Rorotonga, a place of abode, a place.

Naio (Greek), to inhabit.

D.

Mauna (Hawaiian), a mountain.

Mount, mountain.

Maunga (New Zealand), a mountain.

Saxon *mount*.

Moua (Tahitian), a mountain.

Latin *mons*.

Mouna (Tahitian), a mounttain.

E.

Pii ana (Hawaiian), ascending.

Ben (Celtic), a mountain. I do not know how the Celts write *ben*, but in the deep and long pronunciation of the Scotch Highlanders, they bring the *ben* to have a near resemblance to *pii ana* in all but the final *a*.

F.

Awaawa (Hawaiian), valley.

Awn, is, I think, valley in Gaelic.

G.

Avaava (Tahitian), valley.

Valla (Gothic), valley, as *thing valla*, in Norway and Shetland, the valley where popular assemblies were anciently held, *Valles* Latin.

WATER

No. 6.

Wai (Hawaiian) water.

Aqua (Latin), water.
Vari (Sanscrit), water.

A. Water having no constant form, the organs cannot assume a form having any analogy to it. In the Polynesian language its name was necessarily derivative. It is generally seen as a body moving or flowing. This property seems to have furnished one name for it. In Polynesian, " wa " is a space, or what fills a space, as " wa-onahale ", the space where trees grow wild, wilderness : " wa-nanalua, " the space that looks both ways, the easternmost point of this island, whence you look north and south over the ocean ; " waa," a space to which action is an attribute, a canoe. The notion is analagous to Byron's " She walks the waters like a thing of life." So " i " being here like the Latin " i " in " *eo* "—to go—" wa i " may be translated, the space, or the body that goes or flows — water.

An interrogation is put, partly by the accent of the voice and partly by some conventional arrangement of the words. Should a person put his head into the door of a house, and cry out, " Any body here ? " he would be understood to be asking a question. In the Polynesian idiom it is not " any body here ", " but, any body goes," *wa* being space, or what fills space, as matter or body, and seeming at the early stages of the Polynesian language to have been used as we use " body " for person. " Wai," therefore, is equivalent to " any person goes ", the form being, however, " *o wai*," and thus, as it seems to me, it is that water and the interrogative pronoun have, in Polynesian, the same form. Now, not having the authorities by me, I cannot speak with certainty, but through many, and I believe through most of the Indo-European languages, the two words expressing *who* ? and *water* run with all the look of being first, second, or third cousins. Thus we have in Latin, " quis," " quae," and " qua "—who, or *owai*, and " aqua "—wai, water : in Scotch, " wha " and " whae " —owai—(" water " equal to wai) ; in Danish, wie—owai ; and Saxon, " waes—wai ; etc. Now whence shall we take a common progenitor, for them, if not in the Polynesian ? I believe no other can be found.

B. Another word to express a fluid, and so to denote water, was found in the connection between milk and the female breast ; and hence a set of correlative terms running through various languages.

U—the projecting nipple of
   the female breast ; hence
U—Milk ; and hence

U—to be damp or wet and moisture.

Ulu—wetted (Hawaiian).

Ua—the action of wetting—rain. From *u*, the nipple comes *Uma* (N. Zealand)—the female breast—that is both the *u* and the broad seated gland or organ which supplies the secretion.

Umauma (Polynesian)—the two breasts—that is the whole front of the chest in man and woman.

Uda—Sanscrit wet; Latin udus—wet; uveo, old verb —I am wet, uvedus, etc.

Uo ue uei, I rain, he rains, it rains. That *a* was in the original root, appears probably from the compounds "ualos"—glass, from its transparency, and "uades"— the watery stars Hyades.

"Huetos"—wet, "Hudor" —water.

"Hydra"—water-serpent.

"Hygros"—wet, etc. Latin *udus uridus*, etc.

The Greeks and Romans rejecting the *u*, took *mamma* for the fleshy substance, and *mazos* for the breast in woman, the *u* remained for the inferior animals. Sanscrit *udara*, German *uder*, English *udder*, Latin *uber*, Greek *onthar*, etc.

N.B.—I find that this analysing of each word is more tedious than I thought it would be: I shall therefore confine myself to putting down the words with only a few notes.

CLASS III.—WORDS RELATING TO THE AFFECTIONS OF THE MIND CONNECTED PRIMARILY WITH EXTERNAL OBJECTS.

A.

Ike, he saw, or he knew.

Ide (Gr.), he saw, or he knew.
Vidit (Lat.), he saw.

B.

Manao, I think.

Mnao (Gr., obsolete form), I think.

C.

Noo, I perceive at a distance, or I endeavour to see at a distance.

Sanscrit *Man*, I think.
Mnaomai (Gr.), I think.

Noonoo, the habit of reaching far in thought; wise, prudent. As a verb and a noun, the signification is similar.
Noonoo ole, without sense.
D.
Oiaio, truth.

Noos (Gr.), judgment, discretion, sense.
Gnoeo (Gr.), participle *gnous*, the Latin *nosco*, the French *connoitre*, and Eng. *know* seem all to come from this root.

Parek noon (Gr.), without sense.
Oiomai
Oio (Gr.), I believe it true.

Class IV—Words Relating to Speech

A.
Leo or *reo*, the sound of the voice.

Reo (Gr.), old form I speak, changed afterwards to *ero*, I speak, hence "rhetoric", etc.

B.
O, a single utterance of sound by the voice, a shout, as at night, on hearing this shout one might say, "Oh, that is a Kanaka passing, I know his "*O*".

Os (Latin), genitive, *oris*, the mouth.

C.
Orero or *olelo*, a continuous speech or to speak continuously.

Oratio (Lat.), a speech, *oro*, I speak continuously, I entreat.

D.
Kala, I strain my voice that the will of the chief may be known—I proclaim.

Kala Kalare (Old Latin), hence the "Kalendae", calling out by the priests of feast days.
Kaleo (Gr.), I call: Sanscrit *Kal*, Swedish *Kalla*, Dutch *kallen*, etc.

E.
Kalanga or *karanga* is used in N.Z. and Rorotonga for "olelo", a continual speech.

English *harangue*, Spanish and Portuguese *arenga*, Celtic *harencg*.

F.

Kani and *kakani* to make a sharp sound, to play on a musical instrument, to sing.	Latin *cano, cecini*, to make a loud noise, to play on a musical instrument : hence " canto " to sing frequently and our *cant*.

G.

Mele, a chaunted poem.	*Ta mele* (Gr.), lyric, poetry, especially choral songs.

I said I would attempt no further analysis of these words, but leave them to speak for themselves. I must, however, make a partial exception as to one of them, *oiaio*, as I see it will enable me to illustrate two or three points. The first of these is, that no syllable in the Polynesian language is superfluous, but that each by its peculiar force, contributes to give its proper significance to the term. In fact, if we consult the real genius of the language, what we call a word ought rather to be considered as a short sentence descriptive of the idea which it is desired to indicate. Hence natives, even those who have been carefully instructed to model their writing after our system, seldom write a page without grouping some syllables after a fashion, that we think faulty ; and those who have not been so taught, seem to have no other rule as to the syllables that should be united to make a word, than the idea uppermost in their minds at the time of writing.

My analysis of the word must be partial—even that I fear will be tedious. If we can make a verb of it, it appears under the form *hooiaioai*, to testify. Now a European on looking at it, would be apt to think it altogether barbarous, and that such an assemblage of vowels can have been only put together to make a sort of cry that might give strength to the affirmation by sheer noise. On the contrary, each of the eight vowel syllables has its own force, and helps to point out the full image. To see this we must begin at the middle, at the second *i*. I must therefore give you some such partial explanation of its force and of that of the accompanying *o*, as may lead you to apprehend the part they play here.

In uttering the *i* (the same sound as *ee* in *bee*) the breath is compressed into the smallest and seemingly swiftest current possible. It represents therefore a swift and what we may call a sharp movement.

Of all the vowels *o* is that of which the sound goes farthest. We have it therefore in most words relating to distance, as in *holo, lo, long*, etc.

In joining the two, the sense is modified by their position. If we write *oi* it is an *o* going on with an *i*. This is exemplified in *oi*, " lame." Observe how a lame man advances. Standing on the sound limb, he puts the lame one leisurely out and sets it to the ground ; this is the *o*. But no sooner does it get there, and the weight of the body begin to rest on it, than, hasting to relieve it of the burden, he moves the other leg rapidly forward, lessening the pressure at the same time by relaxing every joint he can bend, as thus letting his body sink as far as possible : this rapid sinking movement is the *i*.

Again, *oi* a passing in advance, excellency. Here *o* is the general advance, *i* is the going ahead of some particular one.

If, again, we write *io*, it is an *i* going on with an *o*. That is to say, it is a rapid, penetrating movement—*i* and that movement long continued. Thus we have in Hawaiian *io*, a chief's forerunner. He would be a man rapid in his course—*i*, and of good bottom—*o*. In Greek, *ios* an arrow, and *Io*, the goddess who went so far and fast. Hence *io* is anything that goes quite through; that is *thorough*, complete, real, true. Like Burn's " facts are chields that winna ding ", that is, cannot be forced out of their course. Hence *io*, flesh, real food, in distinction to bone, etc., and reality or fact, or truth generally.

Ia is the pronoun that, analogous to Latin *is, ea id*. Putting together these we have *o, ia, io*—Oh, That is fact. Prefixing the causative *hoo*, we have " make that to be fact ", affix *ai*, completion of the action, and we have, " make that completely out to be a fact," that is testify to its truth.

It is to be remarked that the stress of the voice is loud on the second *i*, the *oia* being pronounced very lightly, and that in Greek the *i* is always strongly accented, a mark of the contraction the word has suffered.

INDEX

ɑ, vowel sound, production by rubber tube, 112
Abnormal speech, 224
Accentuation, English, 261-2
Adam's Apple, 31
Adjustable vowel model, 241; consonant model, 116
Advancement of language and its notation, 249
Affections of the mind, words for, 350-1
Aikin, Dr. W. A., Resonator scale, 26, 47; theory, 221-2
American and British vowel sounds compared, 315-17
Animal gestures, 126
Apes, 130
Arabic numerals, 263-5
Arawak, mouth gesture, 171
Articulation, changes, 198; consonant postures, 136; deaf persons, 199; importance of technique, 259-60; vowel postures, 134-5
Artificial languages, 250
Artificial speech, first experiment, 231; and song, 230-48
Aryan roots, pantomimic symbolism, 148-53; proportion of pantomimic words, 153, 156; tongue tracks, 152
Asquith, Lord, 256
Audibility, limits, 2
Audiogram of Author's hearing, 300-1
Away! Signal horn, 232-3

Barker, Miss G. M., Audible range of consonants, 123
B.B.C. recommendations, 261
b, d, g, differentiated from p, t, k, 34
Beckoning gesture words, 138
Bees, honey and pollen dances, 127
Bell, A. Graham, double resonance observations, 22, 47
Bell, Alexander Melville, visible speech, 253-4
Bell-mouth, 81

Bell-whistle, 8
Benton, W. E., double resonance theory, 20; mathematical note, 275-98
Biting, gesture words, 146
Bragg, Sir William, 41
Brewster, Sir David, 12
British Association, Committee on International language, 250

Chancellor, Mrs. C., analogy of binocular vision, 98; audible range of vowels, 37
Cheatle, Sir Lenthal, 227
Cheirophone, 123, 241; plosive consonants, 226, 241; sounds produced, 242-6
Chest resonances, fallacy, 31
Children's invented words, 138, 148
Chimpanzees, gestures, 128-9; he, hæ, sound, 129
Chinese, archaic, mouth gesture, 165; Canton dialect, 165; homophones, 166-8; tone, 161-2; word order, 258-9
Cistercian monks, sign language, 131
Clapping to emphasize vowel resonance, 44, 45; musical notes produced, 8, 9
Clayton, Rev. H. E., 40
Cleft palate speech, 226
Closed-ended tube, resonance, 10
Consonants, classification, 114, 115; effect of convergent or divergent mouths, 100-1; experiments to produce, 100-6; fricatives, 99; musical effects, 102-3; nasal—m, n, ŋ—resonances, 116; nature, 124-5; observations and experiments, 99-125; plosives, 99; positions, diagram, 136; production of n, ð, and k, 104; t, d, 105; k, z, 106; n, 106, 107; production by manipulation of vowel models, 100; p, b, m, w, 100; by manipulation of ʊ model, 101;

INDEX

g, k, l, v, ð, 102 ; k (abnormal) by tongue tip, 226 ; n (abnormal) without tongue, 227 ; s (abnormal) without tongue, 227 ; t (abnormal) without tongue, 227 ; nasal consonants, m, n, ŋ, by models, 117 ; r inverted cerebral, 103 ; resonance of, 103 ; experimental production, 104 ; resonances—author's and I. B. Crandall's compared, 311–14 ; variations in *it*, Δ*t*, and *ut* 107'; variations in *l*, 125 ; explanation, 108 ; semi-vowels, 99 ; monkey's, 128–9 ; voiced and unvoiced, 36, 37, 117 ; effect on range, 123, 124 ; voiced ʃ, 117 ; pharyngeal action 117, 122 ; experiments, 117, 118

Copenhagen Conference, 1925, 134, 255
Coustenoble, Mlle H., vowel resonances, 90–3
Cracking of boys' voices, 34
Crandall, I. B., double resonator theory, 279 ; observations on consonants, 123, 315
Cratylus of Plato, origin of names, 134
Cross, Dr., 129
Cylindrical resonator, effects of back orifice, 65, 66 ; resonances, 64, 65

Darwin, Charles, 133
Deaf, speech for, 199
Delitzsch, F., 164
Dictaphone, transformation of vowels, 78
Diphthongs, 36
Dog's gestures, 128
Donders, F. C., vowel postures, 20
Double resonator, diagrammatic model, 275–6 ; effect of dimensions, 289 ; mechanical analogy, 285 ; stationary vibrations, 290 ; mathematical theory, 275
Dutch vowel sounds, 94

Eating, drinking and smoking words, 145
Eccles, Dr. W. H., 75–6
Echo, interference, 198

Eijkman, L.'P. H., glottal aperture, 33
Electrical resonators producing vowel sounds, 73–5 ; Eccles, 75–6 ; Stewart, 74
Ellis, Alexander, J., 254
Emotions and laryngeal sound, 132
Empis fly, courtship, 126
English, development, 258–60 ; education, 269 ; improvement, 194–5, 268–71 ; simplified, 269
Eology, dawn language, 108–1
Epiglottis, 35
Esperanto, 250

False vocal cords, consonants, 123 ; function, 33, 34 ; phonation, 34
Fire, air, earth, water, words, 346–50
Forchhammer, Professor J. G., 200
French vowel sounds, analysis, 90–2
Frequencies of equal temperament scale, 299
Frisch, Professor Dr. K. von, 126
Furness, Dr. W. H., 129

Gault, Professor R. H., 201
Gesture language, 130 ; theory, 132 ; prior statements, 156 ; Rae, 157, 318–53 ; summary, 174 ; Wundt, 156–7 ; words, reinvention, 148 ; outline, 146–8 ; summary, 174 ; supplementary or alternative, 195–6
Gilbert, Grenville, 148
Goeje, C. H. de, 171
Grasshopper Warbler, courtship, 127
Gray, Professor L. H., 156 ; test of models, 83
Gregory, Dr., 132
Gulliver's Travels, 248

Hall, Miss, 148
Hardy, Sir W. B., 250
Hatfield, Dr. H. S., 269
Headnote as standard of pitch, 41
Hearing, author's audiogram, 300–1
Helmholtz, resonator, 8, 20 ; single and double resonance theory, 20 ; vowel resonances, 47–8 ; vowel synthesis by piano, 27
Hilger, Adam, 201
Hoka languages, 162–4
Homophones, 166–8, 257
Hrdlička, Professor, 162
Hurd, Dr. Lee M., 224
Huxley, Professor J., 126, 127

Ideographs, 262–6
Ido, 250

INDEX

Improvement of languages, 251, 256
Indonesian (*see* Malayo-Polynesian Languages), 162–4
Intelligibility in speech, 197–9
International Phonetic Association, 14, 15, 266
International Research Council, 250
International words, 180

Japanese ape, nasal sounds, 129
Jespersen, Professor Otto, 137–8, 257, 258, 260, 270
Johnson's Dictionary, 265
Jones, Professor Daniel, 41, 103
Jones, R. L., The nature of language, 2
Jousse, M., 159

ka, denoting "cutting", 180; denoting "forcible action", 330–2
Karlgren, Professor B., 164; tone in Chinese, 161–2, 258, 260
Keller, Miss Helen, 174; phonation experiment, 200
Kempelen, de, talking machine, 13, 14
Kratzenstein, Professor, vowel-sounding pipes, 12, 13

Language, artificial—Wilkins, 12; differences, 176; imperfections, 12; poverty, 256–7; primitive, 326
Laryngeal cavity, vowel-production, 33
Larynx, rubber strip, 54–5
Legg, J. W., 201
Linguistic change, 189–92; gestural reasons, 190
Lips, 36
Liscovius, 10
Lisp, 225
Lloyd, Dr. R. J., Fourier analysis, 79; genesis of vowels, 22, 24; vowel resonances, 22–3
Lloyd James, A., 134
Louisiana heron, courtship, 127
"Love Whose Month was ever May," 186–7
Lowell, J. R., 258
Lungs, cellular structure, 29; function in voice production, 203; inflation and deflation, 30; sound absorption, 31

m-sound Siamese monkey, 129
Mackay, S., double phonation, 34

McAllister, Miss A. H., 83
McMordie, J. A., 132
Malayo-Polynesian languages, mouth gesture, 162–4
Male and female, words, 345
Mandrill, gesture, 128
mi, in Polynesian, 333–8
Micronesian (*see* Malayo-Polynesian languages), 162–4
Miller, Professor D. C., consonant noises, 99; organ pipes, 101; single resonances tested, 77, 79, 80; single resonator theory, 304; vowel analysis and synthesis, 27
Miniature models, 247–8
" Minny " model, 116
Mobility of tongue and lips, 213–14
Möller, Professor H., 164
Monkey, consonants, 128; gestures, 128; language—H. N. Ridley, 132; song, 129; vowel-sounds, 128; welcome-sound, 129
Monosyllables, 257–8
Mosolova, Miss T., vowel resonances, 94
Mouth gesture, acoustic limitations (*see also* Tongue gesture), 160; Arawak, 171; classification, 171–4; M. Jousse, 159; Plato's Cratylus, 134; Rae's theory, 157–8, 325–39; Sumerian, 170–1; theory tested, 159; unconscious, 325; Wallace's theory, 158–9
Mouth pantomime, 136–8
Mouth stopper, 118
Müller, Professor Max, references to Dr. J. Rae, 157; *Science of language*, 249
Musical pitch, nature, 2
Myers, Dr. C. S., test of models, 83–4

Nasal cavity, Crandall and Sacia, 94; resonances, 93; stethoscope test, 36; vowel-sounding organ pipes, 237–8; resonance, consonant production, 217–18; test, 214–15; vowel production, 214, 216; Weston's theory, 215; quality, Eijkman, 96; experimental production, 96; model, 211; vowel sounds, 95; vowels, French, 93
National Research Council, Washington, 250
Neck of a cavity, resonance, 6, 7, 292

INDEX

Negus, Dr. V. E., 204
ŋ (*ng*) production, 218
Notation of speech, 261–7
Numerals, symbols, 263–5

Ocarina, acoustic principles, 7, 8; experiments, 97
Ogden, C. K., orthological research, 269
Ogden and Richards, 256
Onomatopœia, 175; limitations, 326
Open-ended tube, resonance, 11
Orang-outan, speech, 129
Organ pipes, vowel-sounding, 233–8; adjustable, 236; coned gamba, 234–5; dimensions, 237; free reed, 238; nasal cavity, 237–8; pierced diaphragm, 234; whistle, 238–9
Orifice of a cavity, 6, 7, 10
Oscilloscope, 201
Osiso, 201

p, t, k, differentiated from b, d, g, 34
Palate, artificial, 227
Palatopharyngeal folds, 96
Paris, Dr., 292
Parrot, foot gesture, 127–8
Patents, author's British, 230, 242
Perrett, Dr. W., 103
Pharynx, 35; compression, 122; models, 119, 121; production of p, b, and f, v, 119–20; s, z; θ, ð; t, d, 121
Phonetic alphabet, 266; symbols, 14, 15
Phonation, action, 97; for the deaf, 199–201; effect on range, 37–8; emotional significance, 182; excessive, 197; function, 37–9; inconsistent, 182; by lip action, 246
Phonoscope, 200–1
Pig-tailed monkey, 128
Pitch, musical standard, 24; scientific, 24; vocal resonances and laryngeal sounds, 25
Plasticine, 105; models, 52–68, 100–7
Podiceps cristatus, courtship, 127
Polynesia, language—analogy with Greek and Latin, 343–52; antiquity, 328–9; derived from mouth gesture, 325–39; gesture theory, 341–2; gesture words, 339; monosyllabic, 329; parent of Indo-European, 324
Polynesian, The, Dr. J. Rae's articles, 157–8, 318–53
Potter, vowel-sounding models, 21

Queen's Dolls' House, 247

Radio Rex, 79–80, 211
Rae, Dr. J., gesture theory, 157–8, 164, 318–53
Range of voiced sounds, 208
Rayleigh, 3rd Baron, 9; double resonator theory, 276, 281, 293, 294
Recognition tests of models, 81–4
Reconstruction of tongue-tracks, 168–9
Red Indians, sign language, 130–1
Registers of human voice, 26
Resonance, auditoriums, 199; cavities, 4, 5, 6; double, 19, 275–98; energized, 9; mouth and laryngeal pitch, 213; optimum conditions, 219–20; selective, 9; tube closed at one end, 10; tube open at both ends, 11; of speech, musically transcribed, 184–8
Resonators, bottle-necked, 296; conical front cavity, 298; effect of material, 69; in parallel, 66, 67, 68
Ridley, H. N., on monkey sounds, 132
Rivet, P., *Les Malayo-Polynésiens en Amérique*, 162–4
Roots, Aryan, pantomimic symbolism, 148–53
Royal Society, Committee for improving English (1664), 251
Rubber tube, resonances, 108–14; tabulated, 110; production of ch, 114; f, 109, 112, 113–14; k, 109, 114; p, 109, 112; r, 114; s, 109, 112, 113–14; ʃ, 109, 111, 112, 113–14; t, 109, 113–14; ð, 113; θ, 113; v, 112; w, 112; z, 113–14; ʒ, 113–14; whistled note, 111
Rushworth and Dreaper, models made by, 241
Russell, Dr. G. O., 32, 33, 208;

INDEX

pharyngeal periscope, 122–3; X-ray photographs of tongue postures, 220–1
Russian Imperial Academy (1791), prize essay, 12
Russian vowel sounds, analysis, 94

Savi's Warbler, courtship, 127
Scale, Equal temperament, 299
Scientific improvement of language, 256
Scott, General (U.S.A.), 131
Semon, Sir Felix, 208, 209
Shelley, *Prometheus Unbound*, 249
Siamang monkey, m-sound, 129
Sign language, apes, 129–30; Cistercian monks, 131; deaf mutes, 129–34; Red Indians, 130–1
Signal horns, 231–3
Similar words, archaic Chinese and English, 179; Aryan and archaic Chinese, 179–80; Polynesian, Greek and Latin, 343–52; Sumerian and archaic Chinese, 177; unrelated languages, 176–81
Soft palate, 214, 216, 218
Somerville, Miss M., vowel resonances, 85, 87
Sondhaus, 10
Song, 39, 181–2; relation to speech, 202; voice production, 201; current theories, 203
Sonometer, optical, 201
Sound absorption by lungs, 31
Sound, characteristic frequency, 2; sensation, 1; sensitiveness of the ear, 2; wavelengths, 3, 4; waves, 2
Soundboard action, Fallacy, 211–12
Speech abnormal, 224–8; audible range, 38; intelligibility, 198; notation, 14, 15, 255–6; Wilkins', 12; of orang-outan, 129; origin and development, 126–53; Polynesian and Aryan, 351–2; without larynx, 224
Spelling reform, 266–8
Stationary air-waves, 10
Stewart, J. Q., electrical resonators, 74
Stumpf, C., vowel and consonant resonances, 27
Sumerian, Waddell's Dictionary, 164; mouth gesture, 170–1
Sutty Mangaby, consonant sounds, 129

Swannee whistle, 239–46
Syllables, 184, 261
Symbolism, vowel and consonant, 154–6
Synthetic words, 138–48; biting, tasting, 146; confirmation, 139; eating, drinking, smoking, 145; trees, plants, shoots, 146–8

Talking machines, de Kempelen, 13 14; Wheatstone, 18
Tasting, gesture words, 146
Technique of Speech, Chinese, 194; deterioration, 192, 193; importance, 194
Teeth, 36
Temple, Sir William, 11
Tone languages, 161–2, 188–9
Tone quality, 209–11
Tongue, 36; excision, 227; protrusion, 144; volume, 134–5
Tongue gestures, 133; audibility, 134; Plato, 134; recognized by resonance, 98; sympathy with hands, 133; two-dimensional, 134
Tongue postures and laryngeal pitch, 221; X-ray photographs, 220–1
Tongue track, 134; reconstruction, 168–9
Torquemada, 131
Trachea (windpipe), 31
Transparency to sound, cheeks and throat, 219
Trees, plants, shoots, gesture words, 146–8
Trevelyan, G. M., 258
Tubular vowel models, 303; a, 305, 306; e, 306; i, 307; o, 307–9; u, 306
Tuning resonators, parallel, 104; series, 103–4
Tylor, Sir E. B., 130; mouth gestures, 156

Unvoiced speech sounds, 182–3; vowel sounds, 41

Variable vowel model (Paget and Clay), 302
Ventriloquism, 227–8; labial consonants, 228, 275
Verbal inflexion, 258
Visible speech (Melville Bell), 253–5
Vocal cords, 31, 32; attitudes, 32, 33; dimensions, 34; effect on

INDEX

vowel sounds, 207–8; experimental phonation, 204–5; imitation by lips, 246; model, 206–7; photographs, Dr. French, 209; Dr. G. O. Russell, 32, figs. 18–20; tongue and throat substitute, 224
Vocal inflexion, 188–9, 261; systematic, 189
Vocal organs, 29
Voice, orchestral analogy, 97
Voice production, 197; range, 208–9; song, 201–2
Voiced speech, 181–2
Voiced and unvoiced consonants, 160; symbolism, 161
Volapuk, 250
Völkerpsychologie (W. Wundt), 156
Volume of a cavity, 6, 7
Vowel and consonant symbolism, 154–6
Vowel postures, diagram, 135
Vowel production, constant aperture, 228
Vowel-sounding models, a model with larynx, 58; a model, 62; added capacity, 58; adjustable capacity, 71, 241; resonances, 302; Benton's mathematical investigations, 63, 275; cylindrical, 64, 65, 69, 70, 73; ei model, 60, 61; ʊ model, 62 ʊ (original), 53; ʊ with larynx 56; i model, 60, 67; (original) 55, 56; location of resonances, 59; Jones, Professor D., 17; on Lord Rayleigh's organ, 61; material, 69; methods of tuning, 56, 57; miniature, 246–7; ou model, 62; ɔ model, 68; parallel coupled, 66–8; plasticine, 52, 53; reaction of resonators, 61, 62; recognition tests, 81–4; series coupled, 63; u model, 59; ʌ model, 64, 66; Willis' model, 15–17
Vowel symbolism, 137
Vowel resonances, additional components, 85; Aikin, Dr. W. A., 26, 47; artificial modification, 52; author's first experiments, 40; chart, 42; author's and I. B. Crandalls, compared, 315–17; Bell, Graham, 22; dependence on larynx note, 50, 51; dictaphone experiment, 78; discordant values, 47; Dutch, 94; emphasizing devices, 44; English (Miss M. Somerville), 85, 87; French (Mlle Coustenoble), 90–3; Helmholtz, 20; imperfect spacing, 72; independence of phonation, 47; Lloyd, 22; musical notation, 46; pharyngeal, 85; Russian (Miss Mosolova), 94; similar in different vowels, 45; single or double, 77–80; upper and lower series, 43; independence, 45; variation range, 84–5; voiced sounds, 47–51
Vowel sounds, 12; and laryngeal pitch, 222–3; glottal aperture, 33; laryngeal cavity, 33; limitation, 223; monkey's, 128; recognition, 97; single resonators, 97; symbolism, 137; wave form, 98

Waddell, Dr. L. A., 164
Wallace, Dr. A. R., 158–9
Wavelengths, human song, 4; sound waves, 3, 4; tubes, 10, 11
Wessex dialect, 183
Wheatstone, Professor, 19; talking machine, 18
Whispered speech, 37–9; blowing into the mouth, 39; Chinese, 189; invariable tone, 38
Whistle, actuating vowel resonator, 239; human, 111; muting device, 239; pitch identification, 48
Whymant, Dr. N., 139
Wilkins, John, 11, 12, 251; lesser figures, 252
Willis, Robert, 15–17
Word order, 258
Wow-wow mute, 240

Yerkes, Professor R. M., 129
" You weigh our air," 46

Zwaardemaker and Eijkman, on vowel resonances, 94

The
International Library
OF
PSYCHOLOGY, PHILOSOPHY
AND SCIENTIFIC METHOD

Edited by
C. K. OGDEN, M.A.
Late Fellow of Magdalene College, Cambridge

The International Library, of which over one hundred and fifty volumes have been published, is both in quality and quantity a unique achievement in this department of publishing. Its purpose is to give expression, in a convenient form, to the remarkable developments which have recently occurred in Psychology and its allied sciences. The older philosophers were preoccupied by metaphysical interests which for the most part have ceased to attract the younger investigators, and their forbidding terminology too often acted as a deterrent for the general reader. The attempt to deal in clear language with current tendencies whether in England and America or on the Continent has met with a very encouraging reception, and not only have accepted authorities been invited to explain the newer theories, but it has been found possible to include a number of original contributions of high merit.

Published by
ROUTLEDGE & KEGAN PAUL LTD
BROADWAY HOUSE: 68-74 CARTER LANE, LONDON, E.C.4.
1963

INTERNATIONAL LIBRARY OF PSYCHOLOGY, PHILOSOPHY AND SCIENTIFIC METHOD

All prices are net

A. PSYCHOLOGY

GENERAL AND DESCRIPTIVE

The Mind and its Place in Nature. By C. D. Broad. £2 15s.

Thought and the Brain. By Henri Piéron. Trans. by C. K. Ogden. £1.

The Nature of Laughter. By J. C. Gregory. 18s.

The Gestalt Theory and the Problem of Configuration. By Bruno Petermann. Illustrated. £1 5s.

Principles of Gestalt Psychology. By K. Koffka. £3.

Analysis of Perception. By J. R. Smythies. £1 1s.

The Psychology of Character: with a Survey of Personality in General. By A. A. Roback. *Revised Edition.* £2 10s.

ANALYSIS

The Practice and Theory of Individual Psychology. By Alfred Adler £1 5s.

Psychological Types. By C. G. Jung. Translated with a Foreword by H. Godwin Baynes. £2.

Character and the Unconscious: a Critical Exposition of the Psychology of Freud and Jung. By J. H. van der Hoop. £1.

LANGUAGE AND SYMBOLISM

The Symbolic Process, and Its Integration in Children. By J. F. Markey. 14s.

The Meaning of Meaning: a Study of the Influence of Language upon Thought and of the Science of Symbolism. By C. K. Ogden and I. A. Richards. £1 8s.

Principles of Literary Criticism. By I. A. Richards. £1 5s.

The Spirit of Language in Civilization. By K. Vossler. £1.

CHILD PSYCHOLOGY, EDUCATION, ETC.

The Growth of the Mind: an Introduction to Child Psychology. By K. Koffka. Translated by R. M. Ogden. £2.

The Language and Thought of the Child. By Jean Piaget. Preface by E. Claparéde. *Third Edition (revised and enlarged).* £1 5s.

Moral Judgment of the Child. By Jean Piaget. £1 12s.

The Child's Conception of the World. By Jean Piaget. £1 10s.

The Child's Conception of Number. By Jean Piaget. £1 5s.

Judgment and Reasoning in the Child. By Jean Piaget. £1 5s.

The Origin of Intelligence in the Child. By Jean Piaget. £1 12s.

The Child's Conception of Space. By Jean Piaget. £2 2s.

The Child's Conception of Geometry. By Jean Piaget, Bärbel Inhelder and Alina Szeminska. £2 5s.

The Mental Development of the Child. By Karl Bühler. 15s.

The Psychology of Intelligence. By Jean Piaget. 18s.

The Psychology of Children's Drawings: From the First Stroke to the Coloured Drawing. By Helga Eng. *Second Edition.* £1 5s.

ANIMAL PSYCHOLOGY, BIOLOGY, ETC.

The Mentality of Apes, with an Appendix on the Psychology of Chimpanzees. By W. Koehler. With 9 plates and 19 figures. £1 5s.

Theoretical Biology. By J. von Uexkuell. £1 4s.

ANTHROPOLOGY, SOCIOLOGY, RELIGION, ETC.

Crime and Custom in Savage Society. By B. Malinowski. With six plates. 18s.

Sex and Repression in Savage Society. By B. Malinowski. £1 1s.

B. PHILOSOPHY

Philosophical Studies. By G. E. Moore. £1 10s.

The Philosophy of "As If": a System of the Theoretical, Practical, and Religious Fictions of Mankind. By H. Vaihinger. Translated by C. K. Ogden. £1 10s.

Five Types of Ethical Theory. By C. D. Broad. £1 10s.

Speculations: Essays on Humanism and the Philosophy of Art. By T. E. Hulme. Edited by Herbert Read. With a frontispiece and Foreword by Jacob Epstein. £1 1s.

The Metaphysical Foundations of Modern Physical Science, with special reference to Man's Relation to Nature. By E. A. Burtt. £1 8s.

Bentham's Theory of Fictions. Edited with an Introduction and Notes by C. K. Ogden. £1 10s.

Ideology and Utopia: an Introduction to the Sociology of Knowledge. By Karl Mannheim. £1 8s.

The Philosophy of Peirce. Selected Writings. Edited by Justus Büchler. £1 15s.

Ethics and the History of Philosophy: Selected Essays. By C. D. Broad. £1 3s.

Sense-Perception and Matter : A Critical Analysis of C. D. Broad's Theory of Perception. By Martin E. Lean. £1 5s.

The Structure of Metaphysics. By Morris Lazerowitz. £1 5s.

Methods and Criteria of Reasoning. An inquiry into the structure of controversy. By Rupert Crawshay-Williams. £1 12s.

Reasons and Faiths. By Ninian Smart. £1 5s.

LOGIC

Tractatus Logico-Philosophicus. By L. Wittgenstein. German text, with an English Translation en regard, and an Introduction by Bertrand Russell, F.R.S. £1 1s.

The Foundations of Mathematics, and other Logical Essays. By F. P. Ramsey. £1 3s.

The Nature of Mathematics: a Critical Survey. By Max Black. £1 4s.

Logical Syntax of Language. By Rudolf Carnap. £1 10s.

Bertrand Russell's Construction of the External World. By Charles A. Fritz, Junr. £1 3s.

Logical Studies. By G. H. von Wright. £1 8s.

C. SCIENTIFIC METHOD

Scientific Thought: a Philosophical Analysis of some of its Fundamental Concepts in the light of Recent Physical Developments. By C. D. Broad. £2.

The Limits of Science: Outline of Logic and of the Methodology of the Exact Sciences. By Leon Chwistek. Introduction and Appendix by H. C. Brodie. £1 12s.

HISTORY, ETC.

An Historical Introduction to Modern Psychology. By Gardner Murphy. With a Supplement by H. Kluver. £2.

The History of Materialism and Criticism of its Present Importance. By F. A. Lange. Introduction by Bertrand Russell. £3.

Outlines of the History of Greek Philosophy. By E. Zeller. £1 8s.

Psyche: the Cult of Souls and the Belief in Immortality among the Greeks. By Erwin Rohde. £2 5s.

Plato's Theory of Art. By R. C. Lodge. £1 5s.

The Philosophy of Plato. By R. C. Lodge. £1 8s.

Plato's Phaedo. A translation with an Introduction, Notes and Appendices, by R. S. Bluck. £1 1s.

Plato's Theory of Knowledge. The Theaetetus and the Sophist of Plato. Translated, with a Running Commentary, by F. M. Cornford. £1 8s.

Plato's Cosmology: The Timaeus of Plato. Translated, with a Running Commentary, by F. M. Cornford. £1 12s.

Plato and Parmenides. Parmenides' "Way of Truth" and Plato's "Parmenides". Translated with an Introduction and Running Commentary, by F. M. Cornford. £1 4s.

Aristotle's Theory of Contrariety. By John P. Anton. £1 5s.

A LIST OF BOOKS PUBLISHED IN THE LIBRARY BUT AT PRESENT OUT OF PRINT

Analysis of Matter. By B. Russell.
Art of Interrogation. By E. R. Hamilton.
Biological Memory. By Eugenio Rignano.
Biological Principles. By J. H. Woodger.
Chance Love and Logic. By C. S. Peirce.
Charles Peirce's Empiricism. By Justus Büchler.
Child's Conception of Physical Causality. By Jean Piaget.
Child's Discovery of Death. By Sylvia Anthony.
Colour Blindness. By Mary Collins.
Colour and Colour Theories. By Christine Ladd-Franklin.
Communication. By K. Britton.
Comparative Philosophy. By P. Masson-Oursel.
Concentric Method. By M. Laignel-Lavastine.
Conditions of Knowing. By Angus Sinclair.
Conflict and Dream. By W. H. R. Rivers.
Conscious Orientation. By J. H. Van der Hoop.
Constitution-Types in Delinquency. By W. A. Willemse.
Contributions to Analytical Psychology. By C. G. Jung.
Creative Imagination. By June E. Downey.
Crime, Law and Social Science. By J. Michael and M. J. Adler.
Development of the Sexual Impulses. By R. E. Money Kyrle.
Dialectic. By M. J. Adler.
Doctrine of Signatures. By Scott Buchanan.

Dynamics of Education. By Hilda Taba.
Dynamic Social Research. By J. T. Hader and E. C. Lindeman.
Education Psychology. By C. Fox.
Effects of Music. By M. Schoen.
Eidetic Imagery. By E. R. Jaensch.
Emotion and Insanity. By S. Thalbitzer.
Emotions of Normal People. By W. M. Marston.
Ethical Relativity. By E. Westermarck.
Examination of Logical Positivism. By Julius Weinberg.
Foundations of Geometry. By Jean Nicod.
Growth of Reason. By F. Lorimer.
History of Chinese Political Thought. By Liang Chi-Chao.
How Animals Find their Way About. By E. Rabaud.
Human Speech. By Sir Richard Paget.
Individual and the Community. By Wen Kwei Liao.
Infant Speech. By M. M. Lewis.
Integrative Psychology. By W. M. Marston *et al.*
Invention and the Unconscious. By J. M. Montmasson.
Law and the Social Sciences. By H. Cairns.
Laws of Feeling. By F. Paulhan.
Measurement of Emotion. By W. Whately Smith.
Medicine, Magic and Religion. By W. H. Rivers.
Mencius on the Mind. By I. A. Richards.
Mind and its Body. By Charles Fox.
Misuse of Mind. By K. Stephen.
Nature of Intelligence. By L. L. Thurstone.
Nature of Learning. By G. Humphrey.
Nature of Life. By E. Rignano.
Neural Basis of Thought. By G. G. Campion and Sir G. E. Smith.
Neurotic Personality. By R. G. Gordon.
Philosophy of Music. By W. Pole.
Philosophy of the Unconscious. By E. von Hartmann.
Physique and Character. By E. Kretschmer.
Personality. By R. B. Gordon.
Plato's Theory of Education. By R. C. Lodge.
Plato's Theory of Ethics. By R. C. Lodge.
Pleasure and Instinct. By A. H. B. Allen.
Political Pluralism. By Kung Chuan Hsiao.

Possibity. By Scott Buchanan.
Primitive Mind and Modern Civilization. By C. R. Aldrich.
Principles of Experimental Psychology. By H. Pieron.
Problems of Personality. Edited by A. A. Roback.
Problems in Psychopathology. By T. W. Mitchell.
Psychology and Ethnology. By W. H. R. Rivers.
Psychology and Politics. By W. H. R. Rivers.
Psychology of Animals. By F. Alverdes.
Psychology of Emotion. By J. T. MacCurdy.
Psychology of Intelligence and Will. By H. G. Wyatt.
Psychology of Men of Genius. By E. Kretschmer.
Psychology of a Musical Prodigy. By G. Revesz.
Psychology of Philosophers. By Alexander Herzberg.
Psychology of Reasoning. By E. Rignano.
Psychology of Religious Mysticism. By J. H. Leuba.
Psychology of Time. By Mary Sturt.
Religion, Philosophy and Psychical Research. By C. D. Broad.
Religious Conversion. By Sante de Sanctis.
Sciences of Man in the Making. By E. A. Kirkpatrick.
Scientific Method. By A. D. Ritchie.
Social Basis of Consciousness. By T. Burrow.
Social Insects By W. M. Wheeler.
Social Life in the Animal World. By F. Alverdes.
Social Life of Monkeys and Apes. By S. Zuckerman.
Speech Disorders. By S. M. Stinchfield.
Statistical Method in Economics and Political Science. By P. Sargant Florence.
Technique of Controversy. By B. B. Bogoslovsky.
Telepathy and Clairvoyance. By R. Tischner.
Theory of Legislation. By Jeremy Bentham.
Trauma of Birth. By O. Rank.
Treatise on Induction and Probability. By G. H. von Wright.
What is Value? By Everett M. Hall.